RESEARCH AS MORE THAN EXTRACTION

Studies in Conflict, Justice, and Social Change

Series Editors: Susan F. Hirsch and Agnieszka Paczyńska

This series is funded in part through the generous support of the Jimmy and Rosalynn Carter School for Peace and Conflict Resolution at George Mason University.

Susan F. Hirsch and E. Franklin Dukes, *Mountaintop Mining in Appalachia: Understanding Stakeholders and Change in Environmental Conflict*

David Rawson, *Prelude to Genocide: Arusha, Rwanda, and the Failure of Diplomacy*

Agnieszka Paczyńska and Susan F. Hirsch, eds., *Conflict Zone, Comfort Zone: Ethics, Pedagogy, and Effecting Change in Field-Based Courses*

Annie Bunting, Allen Kiconco, and Joel Quirk, eds., *Research as More Than Extraction: Knowledge Production and Gender-Based Violence in African Societies*

RESEARCH AS MORE THAN EXTRACTION

Knowledge Production and
Gender-Based Violence
in African Societies

EDITED BY ANNIE BUNTING,
ALLEN KICONCO, AND JOEL QUIRK

Ohio University Press
Athens

Ohio University Press, Athens, Ohio 45701
ohioswallow.com
© 2023 by Ohio University Press
All rights reserved

To obtain permission to quote, reprint, or otherwise reproduce or distribute material from Ohio University Press publications, please contact our rights and permissions department at (740) 593-1154 or (740) 593-4536 (fax).

Printed in the United States of America
Ohio University Press books are printed on acid-free paper ∞ ™

Library of Congress Cataloging-in-Publication Data
Names: Bunting, Annie, 1964– editor, author. | Kiconco, Allen, editor, author. | Quirk, Joel, editor, author.
Title: Research as more than extraction : knowledge production and gender-based violence in African societies / edited by Annie Bunting, Allen Kiconco, and Joel Quirk.
Other titles: Studies in conflict, justice, and social change.
Description: Athens : Ohio University Press, 2023. | Series: Studies in conflict, justice, and social change | Includes bibliographical references and index.
Identifiers: LCCN 2022054529 (print) | LCCN 2022054530 (ebook) | ISBN 9780821425251 (paperback) | ISBN 9780821425244 (hardcover) | ISBN 9780821447987 (pdf)
Subjects: LCSH: Women—Violence against—Research—Africa, Sub-Saharan. | Sexual abuse victims—Research—Africa, Sub-Saharan. | Research—Moral and ethical aspects.
Classification: LCC HV6250.4.W65 R45885 2023 (print) | LCC HV6250.4.W65 (ebook) | DDC 362.880820967—dc23/eng/20221109
LC record available at https://lccn.loc.gov/2022054529
LC ebook record available at https://lccn.loc.gov/2022054530

CONTENTS

List of Illustrations	vii
Acknowledgments	ix
Introduction	
Research as More Than Extraction? Sexual Violence, Fieldwork, and Knowledge Production	
Joel Quirk, Annie Bunting, and Allen Kiconco	1

PART ONE: ETHICAL AND METHODOLOGICAL DILEMMAS

one The Ethical Dilemmas and Realities of Doing Research in Conflict and Postconflict Settings	
Teddy Atim	39
two Reflections on a Collaboration between a European Doctoral Student and a Congolese Assistant Interpreter	
Sylvie Bodineau and Appolinaire Lipandasi	68
three Research with Children Born of War A Sensitive and Ethical Methodology	
Beth W. Stewart	90
four Sheltering Survivors and Localizing Research Ethics in Northeast Nigeria	
Lawan Balami and Umar Ahmad Umar	117
five Research with Formerly Abducted Mothers and Fathers in Postconflict Northern Uganda A Plea for Transparency	
Leen De Nutte	134

Contents

six Slavery and Its Meanings in the British World
Historiography, Knowledge Production, and Research Ethics
Ana Stevenson and Rebecca Swartz   155

PART TWO: ORGANIZATIONS, INSTITUTIONS, AND KNOWLEDGE PRODUCTION

seven Conducting Participatory Research with Male Survivors of Wartime Rape in Northern Uganda
Philipp Schulz   179

eight Research Ethics Governance and Epistemic Violence
The Case for a Decolonized Approach
Samuel Okyere   199

nine Research Ethics in Complex Humanitarian Settings
The Case of USAID/Nigeria's Evaluation of Its Northeast Nigeria Portfolio
Judith-Ann Walker   215

ten Video Documentation and Video Advocacy
The Story of the Documentary *Bringing Up Our Enemies' Child*
Otim Patrick Ongwech   232

eleven Resolving Justice
Frictions between Community-Based Organizations and the United Nations Women, Peace and Security Agenda
Heather Tasker   248

Afterword
From Extraction to Equity? Pathways to Better Practice
Allen Kiconco, Annie Bunting, and Joel Quirk   273

Contributors   297

Index   303

ILLUSTRATIONS

Figures

2.1.	Appolinaire Lipandasi and Sylvie Bodineau, a research team	78
3.1.	Drawing by Junior	99
3.2.	Drawing by Junior	99
3.3.	Drawing by Idro	102
3.4.	Journal entry by Idro	103
10.1.	Otim Patrick Ongwech with pastor	242
10.2.	Otim Patrick Ongwech with pastor	242
10.3.	Otim Patrick Ongwech with pastor	242

Table

9.1.	Research ethics in DevTech concept notes	226

ACKNOWLEDGMENTS

This collection has two main goals. We have attempted, first, to bring together a series of applied examples and experiences that speak to the practical methodological and ethical challenges associated with researching gender-based violence and other related questions in Africa. It is our hope that these reflections will contribute to ongoing conversations regarding better practices when it comes to both methods and ethics, and will consequentially prove to be of use for future researchers who end up grappling with similar kinds of challenges. We have attempted, second, to reflect upon the larger political, economic, and ideological factors that shape how and why knowledge on Africa and its peoples gets produced and consumed. Our primary goal in this context is to identify and analyze the layered effects of entrenched knowledge economies, to reflect upon the effects of different kinds of positions within these economies, and to explore strategies for mitigating some of their impact. Research plans are directly affected by these knowledge economies in all kinds of ways, so we have tried our best to present an integrated approach that captures how these two intersect.

Most of the contributions to the collection originated from a conference held at the University of the Witwatersrand, Johannesburg, focusing upon methods, ethics, and knowledge production. This event brought together an expert group of researchers, academics, activists, and civil society representatives to share their experiences. Many people contributed to the success of this conference. We would especially like to thank Véronique Bourget, Joshua Walker, and Sarah Delius for their work putting things together. Thank you, all.

Some papers from the conference made their way into an e-book focusing upon similar themes that was published by openDemocracy in 2020 under the title of *Research as More Than Extraction? Knowledge Production and Gender-Based Violence in African Conflicts*. This collection features some of the same contributors as the earlier e-book but also brings new voices into the conversation. The e-book benefited hugely from the work of Cameron Thibos, whose careful editing of all the draft papers greatly improved the final product. Cameron also did some additional editing work on some of the chapters in this collection. Thank you.

This project is closely connected to the Conjugal Slavery in War project (CSiW), an international partnership focusing on enslavement, marriage, and masculinities. This project was directed by Annie Bunting, with Joel Quirk and Allen Kiconco as collaborators. The CSiW project was housed at York University, Canada, and primarily took place in six African countries: Sierra Leone, Liberia, Uganda, Rwanda, the Democratic Republic of the Congo, and Nigeria. We are deeply grateful to everyone associated with the CSiW project whose ideas, experience, and expertise influenced and shaped this project in countless ways. We also further acknowledge the Social Sciences and Humanities Research Council of Canada for its financial contribution to this project. Thank you.

The majority of the work for this collection was completed during the pandemic, when working conditions were less than favorable for most people. As a result, we would like to express our gratitude to our contributors, who persevered with this project despite these adverse circumstances. We hope the final product rewards your faith and investment. Thank you.

It took longer than expected to finalize the manuscript and prepare for publication. We really appreciate the professionalism and editorial input of Ricky Huard at Ohio University Press, and of the Studies in Conflict, Justice, and Social Change series editors, Susan Hirsch and Agnieszka Paczyńska. Thank you.

Finally, Annie would like to acknowledge and thank Michele Johnson and Bruce Ryder, Allen would like to thank her family for their support over the life of this project, and Joel would like to acknowledge and thank Stacey, Kyle, and Leif Sommerdyk.

Introduction

Research as More Than Extraction? Sexual Violence, Fieldwork, and Knowledge Production

JOEL QUIRK, ANNIE BUNTING, AND ALLEN KICONCO

In late 2020 the Nigerian insurgent group Boko Haram once again made front page news. Over three hundred students from a secondary school in the northwestern state of Katsina had been violently abducted by armed men on motorcycles. An audio recording attributed to Abubakar Shekau, the then leader of the insurgency movement, explained that this action was "done to promote Islam and discourage un-Islamic practices as Western education is not the type of education permitted by Allah and his holy prophet" (Abrak and McKenzie 2020). The raid was distressingly similar to Boko Haram's most notorious exploit, the 2014 raid on Chibok that featured the violent abduction of 276 schoolgirls, many of whom were later forced to marry Boko Haram fighters. There were, however, two important differences: the 2020 mass abduction in Katsina featured boys rather than girls. And after a week of captivity the boys were handed over to security forces.

Much of what most outsiders know—or think they know—about Boko Haram remains heavily colored by the focal point created by the 2014 raid on Chibok and, more specifically, the impact of the #bringbackourgirls hashtag that went viral on social media in its aftermath. This was not the first time that Boko Haram had targeted children in mass kidnappings or sexual violence (Matfess 2017; Onapajo 2020). However, news of this specific event traveled well beyond Nigeria's borders, with voices from all over the world expressing their outrage at the brutality and demanding the swift return of the abducted girls to their families. It should come as no surprise, therefore, that the 2020 abductions in Katsina were framed in terms of #bringbackourboys, with coverage of the incident linked to Chibok. However, the media spotlight also proved to be short lived. Once the "Katsina boys" had been released, interest in the incident faded.

In January 2021, young people in Katsina blocked a major highway to protest against the continuing failure of the Nigerian government to provide security against bandits. Over fifty people were reported to have been kidnapped from their communities and held by gunmen within a week (Ibrahim 2021). In February 2021 over three hundred girls were abducted from a school in neighboring Zamfara state, only to be released again shortly thereafter. Only some of the violence that occurs in northern Nigeria can be traced back to Boko Haram. These later abductions appear to have been chiefly motivated by ransom payments rather than political agendas (Sanni and Sotunde 2021). It is clear, furthermore, that the Nigerian state and its agents have a long history of indiscriminate violence, as the recent #EndSARS campaign against police brutality has highlighted. Some acts of violence become political focal points. Most remain in the background.

There is no question that the international expressions of solidarity and support channeled through #bringbackourgirls/boys reflect genuine concerns. It is equally clear, however, that these local complexities are regularly lost upon outside audiences, who frequently gravitate toward familiar narratives regarding violence, vulnerability, and suffering in Africa. Following the Chibok abductions, Boko Haram was portrayed as the latest exemplar of the "coming anarchy" (Kaplan 1994), the "hopeless continent" (*The Economist* 2000), and the "clash of civilizations," with enduring colonial images of "savagery" and "darkness" resurfacing in new guises. This is reflected in the widespread portrayal of Boko Haram as irrational and primordial rather than political, with Islamic extremism yet again offering a shorthand explanation for their violent behavior (religious extremists do extreme things). Events at Chibok also attracted international attention thanks to the gender and young age of the abductees, which activated deeply rooted notions of innocence and vulnerability (Carpenter 2006). Once political violence and terrorism in Nigeria has been defined in terms of protecting innocence and punishing evil, then certain kinds of solutions take center stage: militarization, external interventions, and carceral "solutions."

None of these themes are new. Two years prior to the violent abductions at Chibok, there was a similar outpouring around the actions of Joseph Kony, the leader of the Ugandan Lord's Resistance Army (LRA), when a short video by Invisible Children, a US nongovernmental organization, also unexpectedly went viral with over one hundred million views. This 2012 video was designed to draw attention to abuses instigated by Kony and to support military efforts to bring about his capture. Much of the case against the LRA was similarly based on their use of abductions and sexual violence, with women and girls once again being forced to marry their captors. The plight of the "Chibok girls" itself harkened back to the earlier 1996 abduction of 139 girls from St. Mary's College, a boarding school in Aboke, which similarly garnered international attention.

This is yet another telling example of how acts of violence perpetuated by enemies of the state tend to be viewed differently to acts of violence perpetrated by agents of the state. Members of the Ugandan military are also responsible for sexual violence, yet their actions have not generated the same kind of salience or audience, despite being a recurring issue (e.g., HRW 2017). In February 2022 the International Court of Justice ruled that the Ugandan government was liable for $225 million (from an overall total of $325 million) USD in damages to the Congolese government for "damage to persons . . . loss of life, rape, recruitment of child soldiers and displacement of civilians" arising out of its military activities in eastern Congo (United Nations News 2022). The Ugandan government immediately rejected this ruling. Impunity for state crime remains the norm.

As this example demonstrates, some forms of violence and abuse come to be prioritized and thus acquire certain forms of "visibility" and "legibility" (Hesford 2011). Others fall outside dominant representations and consequently remain at the margins (Ba 2020). International perspectives and priorities interact with local experiences in complex ways (Gray, Stern, and Dolan 2020). As Marsha Henry (2013) argues, it can be challenging to write about and conduct research into patterns of sexual violence during conflict without reproducing—or at least being strongly influenced by—any number of simplistic and voyeuristic scripts. Anyone who wants to better understand the underlying issues at stake must wade through the many layers of interpretation and representation that mark conversations about violence, conflict, and gender.

Violence against women and girls in Africa has been a major international focal point since the end of the Cold War. This has included a sustained focus on "rape as a weapon of war," investigations into sexual abuses perpetrated by peacekeepers, a significant investment in codifying and prosecuting specific acts of gender-based violence, and numerous projects focusing on the gendered dimensions of postconflict reconstruction (e.g., Baaz and Stern 2013; Crawford 2017; Ní Aoláin et al. 2018; Wibben 2016). It is hard to evaluate the practical effects of these activities. It is widely believed that the political focus on sexual violence and conflict has had beneficial effects, but it has also indirectly helped to underscore the tremendous scale of the central challenge, as researchers and campaigners have also called attention to many different issues that go well beyond "rape as a weapon of war," such as the relationship between wartime abuses and peacetime practices, or sexual violence against men (Schulz, this volume). Although it may be trite to suggest that "more needs to be done," it is also the truth. Around a third of the girls abducted at Chibok remain with Boko Haram. While the conflict within Uganda has abated, Joseph Kony remains at large. Wartime atrocities and gender-based harms remain common, as recent events in Mozambique (Cabo Delgado) and Ethiopia (Tigray) have highlighted. Multiple problems persist in the aftermath of conflict despite efforts to target and address them.

Research as More Than Extraction?

All the issues identified above feature prominently in the pages that follow, but they are not our main focus. We are instead interested in the different ways in which both information and experiences associated with gender-based violence and other related issues have been—and should be—generated and disseminated. Put more directly: we want to understand where new information comes from, what happens after it has been secured, and what steps and strategies need to be taken to improve current practices. Our core concerns are research methods, research ethics, and the politics of knowledge production.

Lived experiences of violence and trauma invariably present many serious methodological and ethical challenges. They also directly implicate any number of different actors and institutions, including policymakers and researchers. How and why do you ask someone to talk about the worst experiences of their lives? What—if anything—do they get in return? What happens when people participate in research hoping to improve their fortunes but then hear nothing further? How do the backgrounds of the individuals who are asking and answering questions end up affecting outcomes? What steps are required to ensure personal safety? What roles do intermediaries such as interpreters, brokers and assistants play in shaping how information gets generated? What kinds of effects do institutions and gatekeepers have on the actions of individuals? How are various activities funded and by whom? What ends up happening after experiences have been shared?

Most researchers who undertake fieldwork spend years grappling with these and other related questions. However, they do not necessarily make their own experiences and dilemmas a primary focal point when it comes to writing up their findings. In most cases, the final product overshadows the behind-the-scenes (field)work that went into its development. Questions of ethics and methods tend to be addressed in relatively brief and frequently perfunctory terms. In most cases, they are treated as (at best) the prelude rather than the main event. It is also important to keep in mind, moreover, that there are certain experiences and questions that people rarely want to talk about. Academics undertaking fieldwork regularly mention having secured ethics approval from their institutional review board, but they are unlikely to publicly discuss their frustrations with the process or their assessment of its limitations (Okyere, this volume).

Questions relating to race, privilege, and positionality are also routinely avoided, which means that the cumulative effects of hierarchies and power relations are only rarely acknowledged or analyzed. Funders will be ritually acknowledged and thanked, yet much less will be said regarding the effects of funding streams and donor expectations on the kinds of knowledge that get produced. It is very hard to publicly declare that the preferences of your funders are counterproductive or ill-suited to local circumstances when you are obliged to tailor your work to their preferences in order to get funding. The established convention is to present the data collection process as a neutral and technically proficient process, yet anyone who has done fieldwork knows that it is frequently anything but. It can be hard to admit to any uncertainties or difficulties or to various compromises made to secure access or information. There are strong incentives to pretend that ethical and methodological issues have been definitively "solved."

This book is concerned with these behind-the-scenes dynamics. This overall brief brings together both practical and political considerations. From a practical standpoint, we are chiefly concerned with the nuts-and-bolts challenges associated with undertaking research and fieldwork focusing on experiences of sexual violence in Africa and other related matters. This includes reflections and practical guidance when it comes to issues such as designing and undertaking fieldwork, asking sensitive questions, negotiating access, collecting and evaluating information, and validating results. Drawing on years of experience, our contributors both describe and analyze their experiences with survivors of sexual violence, other vulnerable populations, their partners and brokers, community representatives, and/or governments and other actors.

As this introductory chapter makes clear, these kinds of practical matters cannot be disentangled from larger political and ideological considerations. In the case of the latter, we are chiefly concerned with questions of power, positionality, institutional hierarchies, and knowledge economies. All of these questions can be traced back to a central preoccupation with the ways in which knowledge gets produced and consumed, which we frame in terms of the politics of extraction. As historians of colonialism and imperialism have demonstrated, Europeans have been extracting valuable resources from the African continent for centuries. These extractive tendencies are usually understood in terms of commodification and unjust enrichment (mining, cash crops, land appropriation, enslaved Africans), but they also have further applications when it comes to knowledge production, where lived experiences and expertise can once again be commodified and consumed by outsiders. This politics of extraction cannot be ignored. The underlying dynamics and interests involved are too deeply embedded to be definitively resolved. We instead seek to contribute to larger efforts to expose how and why extraction takes place and to identify and develop pathways for mitigating its effects.

It is important to be cautious. There are many ways of revealing, resisting, and (at least hopefully) reconfiguring the politics of extraction, but it is also essential to keep in mind that individual actions tend to be constrained by the effects of larger institutions and interests. It is also clear, moreover, that even projects motivated by a sincere desire to improve the world can nonetheless end up being counterproductive or compromised. Take, for example, recent reports by the New Humanitarian on institutional racism within Médecins Sans Frontières / Doctors without Borders, with its international president stating that the organization had "failed people of colour, both staff and patients," "failed to tackle institutional racism," and is part of "white privileged culture" (Parker 2020; Majumdar 2020). Other high-profile examples include recent investigations into sexual abuse by humanitarian aid workers in the Democratic Republic of Congo during the Ebola crisis between 2018 and 2020 (Flummerfelt and Peyton 2020) and the case of Renee Bach, a US missionary in Uganda with no medical training, who settled a civil suit claiming that her amateur care resulted in the deaths of 105 children (Mwesigwa and Beaumont 2019). Most cases of malpractice and abuse don't make headlines but are no less consequential for the people involved. From the sensational to the quotidian, research on gender violence in various parts of Africa must reckon with a political economy of knowledge production and humanitarianism marked by colonialism, racism, and exploitation (Crane 2013). It is entirely possible to start with good intentions yet still end up doing tremendous harm.

These examples help to bring the political and ideological side of the equation into focus. Political considerations have an impact on all forms of knowledge production, but there are additional layers here owing to the cumulative effects of European intrusions on the African continent. This does not mean, however, that developments and dynamics within Africa are only relevant to Africa. It is a mistake to treat African politics and history as an (exotic) case that "stands apart" from a (Eurocentric) "norm." The underlying knowledge economies, institutional hierarchies, and power relations that operate within Africa also have similar kinds of effects elsewhere. Developments within Africa help to explain larger dynamics globally.

Any attempt to grapple with these issues must confront uncomfortable and challenging questions regarding how and why knowledge gets produced, by whom, for what types of audiences, and in the service of which interests. It also means taking a hard look at processes of collaboration with specific focus on the "dehumanisation and erasure faced by researchers from the Global South which often occurs when collaborating with researchers from the Global North" (Bahati 2020; see also Bouka 2018; Nyenyezi et al. 2020). As this quote helps to illustrate, there are many scenarios in which research functions as yet another extractive industry, with European outsiders traveling to "exotic" locations, accumulating knowledge with the help of local assistants, and then returning home to process their findings and advance their careers. Key aspects of the process of knowledge production are too often rendered invisible.

These dynamics have received increased attention in recent times, contributing to a renewed emphasis on the moral and political urgency of decolonization. Like all fundamental concepts, decolonization can mean different things at different times (Mbembe 2021, 75–151). For our purposes, it can be broadly understood to refer to cumulative efforts to overcome European systems of material dependency and ideological hegemony and to help bring about a less extractive and more egalitarian future. Exactly what this future might look like remains contested. Decolonization has also been both complicated and expanded by African feminists, who have argued that efforts to challenge structures of racial oppression have often ignored "institutions of gendered oppression and, in some cases, even reinforced them" (Tamale 2020, 62). It has also become apparent that decolonization is much easier to talk about than to realize in substantive terms. Countless researchers have eagerly taken up the banner of decolonization in recent times, but this new popularity has also led to growing concerns that its radical potential is increasingly at risk of being eroded or co-opted. In their call for an "ethic of incommensurability" Tuck and Yang (2012, 3) argue that "decolonization is not a metaphor." Rather, "when metaphor invades decolonization, it kills the very possibility of decolonization; it re-centers whiteness, it resettles theory, it extends innocence to the settler, it entertains a settler future." There is also a further issue here regarding the degree to which conversations about decolonization have been dominated by abstract and highly specialized theoretical exchanges and can thus end up displacing or diluting the more practical politics of resource exploitation, land expropriation, and struggles for sovereignty.

Our goal in this collection is to make these underlying tensions and systems visible without pretending that they can be resolved or transcended. A project such as ours must be recognized as arising out of—rather than standing apart from—broader extractive tendencies regarding knowledge production in Africa. We hope that it will eventually contribute to ongoing efforts to change the overall terms of engagement, but the effects of "colonial knowledge chain(s)" still mark this project as they mark others (Mbembe 2021, 98).

The rest of this introduction develops these core themes in greater depth. There are three substantive sections. In the first section, we dive into the politics of knowledge production and the dimensions and challenges of collaboration. From here, we look in more detail at the political and practical challenges associated with undertaking fieldwork in Africa. In the third section, we specifically concentrate on the multiple challenges presented by sexual and gender-based violence. This sequence may seem counterintuitive, at least at first glance, but we have made a conscious decision to start with the larger political picture and then move on to more specific challenges, since the politics of fieldwork can be fully understood only within this larger context. We conclude by both contextualizing and introducing the key contributions of the chapters that follow.

The Political Economy of Knowledge Production

The image of the "ivory tower" evokes many different responses. For some people it is a symbol of intellectual excellence and aspiration where academics strive to advance the frontiers of knowledge. For others it is a symbol of disconnection in which academics who have little understanding of practical concerns pursue esoteric projects of limited social value. Neither of these popular responses adequately captures the effects of market forces and market incentives on modern academic institutions. Universities are compelled to compete with each other for rankings, resources, and student registrations, while academics are similarly compelled to compete with their peers for positions, prestige, and publications. This academic marketplace has powerful effects on knowledge production. Instead of being valuable for its own sake, or for its social value, knowledge is now increasingly understood in terms of commodified value, with numerical performance metrics increasingly determining relative market position (Smyth 2017).

International partnerships and collaborations have been increasingly prioritized and incentivized within this marketplace. As a rule, partnerships are organized along two main axes: (1) partnerships between academics in different corners of the globe, and (2) partnerships that reach beyond the ivory tower to include business, civil society, government, and/or international organizations. While these partnerships sometimes emerge organically, their overall design and operation tends to be strongly affected by both funding streams and institutional hierarchies and positionality (Halvorsen and Nossum 2017). Several recurring issues can be highlighted. First, there is the power of the purse. Securing funding means speaking in ways which funders expect, using concepts and criteria that funders favor, and making the case for projects which align with their priorities and ideologies. Anything too "radical" or "unconventional" is unlikely to find favor. Technocratic languages and institutional logics play an important behind-the-scenes role in constraining possibilities for political engagement and social mobilization (Fassin 2012).

Many organizations have become adept at leveraging funding streams on adjacent topics to keep their core operations going, but there are limits to how far funding calls can be stretched. A good example of this larger dynamic is the way in which funding streams relating to Women, Peace and Security (WPS) have increasingly been tied to countering violent extremism (CVE), resulting in situations where organizations working on gender-based violence have been forced "to shift or adapt their priorities to those that funding agencies care about." This includes an example from Kenya that featured "groups trying to frame their work on water shortages, teenage pregnancy and gang violence in the coastal regions as countering terrorism." Tying gender activism to counter-terrorism can put activists at risk by aligning them with governments, yet this is the kind of price that frequently needs to be paid to secure funding (ICG 2020).

The vast majority of funding for international partnerships comes from the Global North. These means that they also tend to be administered and audited by Northern institutions, whether private or public. As Loren Landau has argued, this tends to create incentives for research partners based in Africa to gravitate toward short-term "piece work" for which researchers are commissioned or subcontracted to execute a small piece of a larger project, yet have little or no capacity to influence the design of the whole. This can in turn indirectly contribute to "a global division of labour where southerners become data collectors while northerners produce knowledge and offer scholarly and policy critiques" (Landau 2012, 563). And since this "piece work" is frequently short term, there are also further incentives to produce results that align with expectations since this is the most likely route to future commissions. "Once you are inside a frame—that you may not have created or labelled—your main task is to oil it and keep it alive" (Pattanaik 2020).

This global division of labor is especially pronounced when it comes to agenda setting. Institutions and academics based in the Global North consistently have the loudest voices when it comes to determining which issues get prioritized, how they get talked about, the activities that take place, and the kinds of criteria used to evaluate "deliverables." Take, for example, the dominant role of university-based academics in North America and Europe in adjudicating committees for allocating funding. Similar North–South hierarchies have been identified in numerous fields, including development (Andrews and Bawa 2019), health (Mama 2011), gender (Briggs and Weathers 2016), conflict (de Guevara and Kostić 2017), migration (Landau 2012), and science (Macamo 2016). This also extends to the process of being credentialed as an "expert" and to the kinds of knowledge and status recognized as authoritative (Sending 2015). As Grace Musila observes, there has been a long-standing tendency to dismiss work by researchers in Africa as being "dated or poor, because it 'fails' to engage with the latest theories on the subjects or frame itself in the legitimised registers as prescribed by the Northern academy" (Musila 2019, 288).

As this quotation highlights once again, knowledge production is not based on straightforward meritocracy, where the most compelling ideas rise to the top, but needs to be approached in sociological terms. This is partly a question of the politics of publication and prestige, which contribute to academic hierarchies that typically favor the Global North; but this is also a question of the relationship between academics and nonacademics (as well as between government officials and civil society organizations), where the former tend to be regarded as the holders of superior forms of expertise, while other kinds of expertise are not valued in the same way. One further layer here is the connective tissue that weaves together localized developments and more general processes. While researchers and practitioners in the South tend to be valued for their "on the ground" experience, their counterparts in the North tend to exercise primary responsibility for interpreting what these local experiences mean. This means that academics and institutions in the Global North tend to enjoy further advantages due to their capacity to speak authoritatively about general patterns and processes and to thereby command the "big picture."

The practical effects of academic work should not be overstated. It remains an open question how much impact different types of research and knowledge production actually have on either public policy or institutional behavior. One of the most significant issues for our purposes is the extent to which key decision makers gravitate toward findings that align with their own preferences and interests (Drezner 2017, 35). This is sometimes described in terms of "motivated reasoning," which refers to scenarios where information gets selected and interpreted to justify an already-established position (Kraft, Lodge, and Taber 2015). These and other related considerations bring into focus the tremendous challenges associated with doing "research that matters," since most knowledge that gets produced has little effect. Increasingly sophisticated techniques have been developed in response to these challenges, with modern communication strategies and lobbying techniques being marshaled to support "theories of change" designed to maximize the chances of specific forms of knowledge impacting on policy and behavior (Stachowiak 2013).

Maximizing your chances of success means carefully tailoring your message to your target audience. A familiar example here is the now ubiquitous "executive summary," which is designed to capture key findings and recommendations in a short and simplified format for readers who may not have the time or inclination to delve deeper. Making knowledge more accessible is by no means a bad thing, but there is usually much more going on here. Many theories of change attach a great deal of importance to the connection between message and target audience, which means that both the format *and content* of the message ends up being strongly tailored toward the preferences of the audience. Positions regarded as "radical" or "unrealistic" will be routinely discarded in the early stages in favor of "safer" alternatives that are more likely to be favorably received. When billionaires become philanthropists they are unlikely to support projects that challenge the foundations of the systems that helped them become fabulously wealthy (Giridharadas 2018).

Further issues arise when it comes to the choice of language used to communicate, which is frequently not a choice but an imperative, given the global dominance of English (and, to a lesser extent, other languages of empire such as French). Not being able to write and speak preferred modes of English can be a significant constraint, which means that the task of communicating often goes to people who can convey messages in ways that are more easily digestible for audiences in the Global North. There are many different audiences, both local and global, but not all audiences carry the same weight. As Talal Asad argued nearly forty years ago in his chapter "The Concept of Cultural Translation in British Social Anthropology":

> "Cultural translation" must accommodate itself to a different language not only in the sense of English as opposed to Dinka or English as opposed to Kabbashi Arabic, but also in the sense of a British, middle class, academic game as opposed to modes of life of the "tribal" Sudan. The stiffness of a powerful established structure of life, with its own discursive games, and "strong languages" is what among other things finally determines the effectiveness of the translation. The translation is addressed to a very specific audience. (1986, 159)

This politics of cultural translation is further compounded by highly selective restrictions on travel, where both the financial costs and institutional labor demanded of researchers with African/Southern passports, stand in stark contrast to the relative ease and visa-free travel typically enjoyed by holders of European/Northern passports (Albayrak-Aydemir 2020).

These and other related themes are especially acute in the case of sub-Saharan Africa. Researchers in Africa tend to be outnumbered by researchers elsewhere, and the cumulative legacies of European imperialism also continue to have far-reaching effects. In 2013 UNESCO estimated that the Big Five—China, the European Union, Japan, the Russian Federation, and the United States—accounted for 72 percent of researchers globally. Europe comprises roughly 11.4 percent of the global population yet hosts around 31 percent of researchers. By contrast, Latin America and South Asia host 3.6 percent and 3.1 percent of researchers against 8 percent and 23.3 percent of the global population. Only 1.1 percent of researchers are found in sub-Saharan Africa, with around a quarter (0.3) of this overall total coming from one state: South Africa. This translates into 91.3 researchers per million inhabitants, compared with Europe at 2,941.9 (calculated as full-time equivalents, see Soete et al. 2015). This is a ratio of more than thirty to one. Not all numerical estimates regarding Africa are especially reliable or useful, but on this occasion the key indicators are particularly stark. These differences have important effects when it comes to the capacity of African researchers to (1) play a major role in both interpreting and shaping knowledge regarding the "big picture" (both governance and theory), and (2) play a key role in knowledge production in relation to specific developments within Africa.

This second point raises many challenging questions. As a now extensive literature demonstrates, much of what is "known" about the history and politics of Africa has been written by Europeans in European languages for European audiences and, in many cases, to advance European interests (Ndlovu-Gatsheni 2013; Wai 2018). This dynamic was especially pronounced under European colonial rule in Africa but has continued to have major effects in the postcolonial period. Several key themes can be highlighted. First, we have a long-standing tendency to define experiences and institutions in Africa in terms of perceived absences or deficiencies, on the basis of self-serving comparisons with idealized European norms. As Mahmood Mamdani famously observed, this has frequently taken the form of history by analogy, which revolves around sharp distinctions "between experiences considered universal and normal and those seen as residual or pathological," which has the effect of seeking to understand Africa "not in terms of what it was, but with reference to what it was not" (Mamdani 1996, 9). This dynamic is most powerfully associated with the history of European efforts to define and classify both Africa and Africans in terms of binary oppositions, such as enlightenment/darkness, civilized/savage, Christian/pagan, White/Black, modern/primitive, and advanced/backward. Within each of these binaries, the African side of the ledger is structured in terms of qualities which Africans are said to lack in comparison to Europeans (Mudimbe 1988; Quirk 2021).

Contemporary relationships between Europeans and Africans are invariably colored by these histories and categories. Even peoples from other parts of the world, such as the increasingly prominent Chinese, also tend to be similarly evaluated in terms of their proximity to—or distance from—the mostly negative precedents set by Europeans in Africa (i.e., are the Chinese as bad as the Europeans?). This intellectual and ideological scaffolding continues to have all kinds of effects. Former colonial rulers, such as the French, Portuguese, and British, continue to play major roles in producing knowledge about their former colonies, contributing to a larger pattern in which extremely privileged outsiders parachute into "exotic" locations for short "fact-finding" expeditions. Postcolonial states in Africa continue to be classified as "failed" on the basis of Eurocentric criteria (Grovogui 2001). Simplistic, sensational, and misleading images continue to resonate (Wainaina 2005). Models of gender imported under European colonialism remain central to law and practice (Oyěwùmí 1997). Educational models established under colonial rule continue to have profound effects on contemporary teaching practices, despite growing calls to decolonize the curriculum (Mupotsa 2020). Efforts to redeem or reclaim African perspectives and experiences sometimes end up juxtaposing a singular "African" essence against a singular "European" one and can thereby end up tacitly reinforcing, rather than contesting, the centrality of the original binaries (Appiah 1993, 60). As this final point helps to illustrate, speaking about a single African experience does not necessarily do justice to variations in history and experience. There are some experiences with common features. Others are more distinct. Both need to be taken into account.

This is a daunting list of issues. When it comes to knowledge production, our primary focus here, it is necessary to think in terms of long-term collective efforts to overhaul the key terms of engagement. This is the overall approach we favor here, which starts with the premise that the politics of knowledge production must be an integral component of any conversation about ethics and methods. Building upon the analysis above, we would suggest that the following questions must be considered when thinking about how knowledge gets produced and consumed:

- Who gets to speak, and on what kinds of terms?
- How are the benefits associated with the production of knowledge distributed?
- Who holds the purse strings, and how are resources distributed? What kinds of effects did funding streams have upon core priorities, conceptual categories, and project activities?
- Who has final authority when it comes to making key decisions?
- Who is regarded as an "expert"? What kinds of credentials are used to determine expertise?

- How much value is attached to theory? What criteria are used to determine what a valuable theoretical contribution might look like?
- Who holds primary responsibility for making sense of the "big picture"?
- Who are the intended audiences? How do their expectations shape outcomes?
- What are the primary languages and formats used for communication?
- How is labor renumerated? Who holds positions with long-term contracts and good salaries and benefits? Who holds positions with short-term contracts and limited benefits?
- Who gets to travel, and how easy is it for them to cross international borders?
- What are the effects of historical legacies, hierarchies, and patterns of privilege?

This list is by no means exhaustive, but it does capture a number of core issues which should ideally be part of the larger story when it comes to the core relationship between ethics, methods, and knowledge production. Most importantly, these are not questions which can be definitively resolved and thereby put aside, but instead demand careful and constant attention and reflection.

It is important to keep in mind that there is much more going on here than a singular relationship between a homogenous Global North and a homogenous Global South. One of the most significant challenges is the degree of internal variation *within* categories. Take, for example, the question of "Who holds the purse strings?" While senior researchers and officials routinely leverage their financial position in all kinds of ways, their power is not limited to the South but also applies to junior researchers within the North. Similarly, there are important variations in experience within the South. Researchers undertaking piece work on projects funded from the North may be placed in subordinate positions in these projects, but they can also experience elevated standing in their own communities, especially if they went to well-known national universities (e.g., Makerere, Lagos, Cheikh Anta Diop, or Cape Town) or were able to study abroad. Most researchers, officials, and other elites in the Global South come from privileged classes within their own societies, so there are further layers to their positionality that are not easily reducible to North versus South. Numerous social and institutional layers can separate researchers from respondents even if they share a common African identity and/or ethnicity (Bodineau and Lipandasi, this volume; Mwangi 2019; Mwambari 2019; Bouka 2015; Ojok 2013; Mandiyanike 2009; Keikelame 2018; Davenport 2013; Henderson 2009; Munthali 2001). In keeping with larger trends, inequality has also been increasing within African states (Seery, Okanda, and Lawson 2019). There are many facets to positionality.

As volume editors we are similarly embedded in these hierarchical knowledge economies—we are two women and one man: a Canadian, a Ugandan, and an Australian; two full professors (the Australian man and the Canadian woman), and one postdoctoral fellow (the Ugandan woman supervised by the Australian man and paid through a Social Sciences and Humanities Research Council of Canada [SSHRC] grant the Canadian woman directs). While we worked together well as an editorial team for over four years, we cannot wish away the hierarchies of power and privilege within our team. We divided up the writing, editorial, and communication tasks equally between us, but our relationships to institutions, individuals, publishers, and fieldwork all differ as a result of our positions.

Africa as a Field Site for Research

These interlocking systems associated with the political economy of knowledge production also define the context within which "on the ground" research takes place. As the term itself implies, fieldwork was initially conceived as a journey to the "field," which was typically a small, rural community inhabited by "natives" who were assumed to be very different from persons at "home" (Schumaker 2001). Within Africa, this image of the field is inextricably linked to the larger history of colonial anthropology, which has seen "adventurers," missionaries, and other European agents attempt to both understand and define the peoples they encountered/conquered. Their cumulative efforts played both a direct role in colonial state-building and an indirect and longer-term role by establishing templates and pathways that researchers continue to grapple with today.

For most researchers, the colonial period now represents a negative example of "what not to do" (contemporary anthropology being strongly defined in opposition to colonial anthropology), yet enduring hierarchies and patterns of interactions established in the past still shape the present. While African researchers tend to conduct research into their own communities, and/or neighboring communities, their more privileged European counterparts routinely travel to distant parts of the globe in order to ask people questions about their opinions/experiences and to observe how and why they live differently (Nhemachena, Mlambo, and Kaundjua 2016; Mitchell 2013). As Cronin-Furman and Lake (2018, 607) observe, undertaking research in Africa can also be attractive to Europeans from a practical standpoint, owing to "the diversity of political spaces, availability of cheap labor, ease of access to powerful figures, and safety net of a foreign passport." As cultural outsiders, the presence of Europeans in the field will always be mediated by the cumulative effects of their forebears' incursions into the African continent—irrespective of their individual intentions—and by the cultural, financial, and political expectations that these bring.

Cultural outsiders also tend to be reliant on assistants, brokers, translators, and intermediaries. In some circles, this topic brings to mind the infamous figure of the "native informant," who most commonly functions as descriptive shorthand for a scenario where unnamed and largely unacknowledged African assistants end up playing an indispensable role collecting "raw data," which then ends up benefiting European researchers and European audiences. One of the main reasons this kind of scenario comes to mind is that many experienced researchers in Africa have direct knowledge of similar cases (see Mitchell 2013; Coetzee 2019; Cramer et al. 2015; Lewis et al. 2019; Marchais, Bazuzi, and Lameke 2020). As Cronin-Furman and Lake also observe (2018, 607), "Environments of extreme state weakness and ongoing conflict permit research behavior that would be frowned on in the global north." It is also important to recognize, however, that not all forms of collaboration are the same and that there are any number of less overt yet still problematic cases that may not look like the most egregious "native informant" scenario. Crucially, terms like "raw data" and "data collection" do not necessarily capture the kinds of expertise and experience that are frequently required to conduct fieldwork, especially when the research involves sensitive and challenging topics or vulnerable respondents (see especially Atim; De Nutte; Stewart; Schulz, all this volume). Fieldwork collaborations are more likely to be coproductions, rather than emerging out of sharp divisions of labor between data collectors/assistants and data interpreters (Bodineau and Lipandasi, this volume). African research assistants may occupy subordinate positions, but this does not also imply a lack of agency or expertise. The most significant issue in this context is whether and on what terms this agency is recognized and renumerated. Many factors become relevant here, including conditions of employment, visibility and erasure, and pathways to future positions.

This underscores a simple yet still important point. While all fieldwork collaborations are invariably shaped by power relations and hierarchies, not all fieldwork collaborations are organized along the same lines. Some researchers will be more attuned to dynamics of positionality and privilege than others. Some make conscious efforts to establish more collaborative relationships, ensure that their collaborators are appropriately recognized and renumerated, and take steps to ensure that any knowledge that gets produced reaches local audiences and has local applications. Other researchers have little to say about any of these concerns. There are definitely models of both worse and better practices available, and in this volume we hope to offer some applied examples of the latter. It is also important to keep in mind, however, that the dominant partners in fieldwork collaborations invariably retain a great deal of individual discretion, so their efforts to make collaborations more equitable and less extractive usually stem from individual action and introspection rather than reforms to the sector as a whole. Individual researchers sometimes make concerted efforts to make things at least slightly more equitable, yet their peers remain under no obligation to do the same. Individual actions do not necessarily alter larger systems.

Undertaking fieldwork usually requires successful negotiations with a series of gatekeepers, including securing permission from both central governments and local authorities (De Nutte, this volume; Parashar 2019). In these kinds of scenarios researchers are obliged to respectfully request, since they cannot obtain access without first securing approval. Careful diplomacy and negotiation are also required to secure support from civil society organizations and other institutional actors, such as the administrators of refugee camps, shelters, and government offices. As Balami and Umar demonstrate in this volume, refugee camps can be a valuable site for undertaking research, but they also present a number of distinctive challenges. Many researchers establish connections with civil society organizations because they regard this as the best (and sometimes only) way of identifying and accessing their target populations. This is often because local people can be reluctant to share information with outsiders, especially when they are "embedded in uncertain and highly threatening social and political contexts" (Chakravarty 2012, 251).

Using organizations to facilitate introductions can undoubtedly be effective but also raises further methodological and ethical challenges. As Dodsworth and Cheeseman observe (2018, 130), "Sub-Saharan Africa is the region of the world in which these new approaches [research collaborations] are particularly prevalent, and one where the challenges created by those approaches tend to manifest in distinct or acute ways." When researchers engage only (or at least predominantly) with respondents who are already known to specific organizations, it can push their analyses in particular directions. Different researchers can also end up asking the same kinds of questions to the same group of respondents, since they have all been referred by the same organization or drawn from the same brokers and networks. And once people have already been interviewed multiple times they may end up "tailoring" their stories to what they think interviewers want to hear. Identifying people who have not previously shared their experiences may be challenging if researchers follow already-established channels, but without local institutional assistance they may not be able to identify enough suitable respondents.

Researchers and civil society organizations can also have important goals in common. Many researchers gravitate to topics that align with their political and personal interests, such as gender equality, human rights, or rehabilitation, and they consequentially end up entering into collaborations/arrangements with civil society organizations with similar normative and political concerns. This can result in mutually beneficial arrangements in which researchers make contributions to organizations and organizations make contributions to research (Schulz, this volume). In an ideal world, both parties end up benefiting while advancing a shared set of goals, such as ensuring that survivors of sexual violence receive more targeted support. In this context, researchers frequently support organizations by securing access to different audiences and funding streams, sharing their expertise, leveraging the "expert" status associated with their academic affiliations, and ensuring that organizational members share input into outputs. It is important to recognize, however, that external researchers are by no means the only "experts." Civil society organizations frequently have many years of applied experience with both methods and ethics, and typically have much stronger community ties (Ongwech, this volume). This expertise and experience can make civil society organizations attractive interlocutors for external researchers in their own right, especially when it comes to policy (Tasker, this volume).

There can also be tension and trade-offs associated with these kinds of collaborative arrangements. In their seminal article on "the dual mandate" in refugee studies, Jacobsen and Landau (2003, 187) demonstrate that an understandable desire to be "policy relevant" and make a "real world" difference can sometimes end up compromising methodological rigor, since researchers "already know what they want to see and say and come away from the research having 'proved' it." This means that there is frequently little appetite for publicly grappling with trade-offs between methods/ethics and policy/practice; yet there will invariably be occasions when collaborations will make it challenging for external researchers to be overly critical of their organizational partners, and vice versa. This is especially true when funding streams are involved.

The widespread use of brokers, organizational intermediaries, and chain referrals can also contribute to financial incentives and expectations. As part of her research into ex-combatants in Sierra Leone, Sayra Van Den Berg (2020, 40) points to the "commercialisation of conflict identities," where previous external researchers have created a market for "selling stories." The existence of this market goes against the grain of established injunctions against paying research subjects, but Van Den Berg recognizes that it comes with both opportunities and complications. Humanities researchers conducting fieldwork in Africa and elsewhere have sometimes embraced a model of compensation for respondents' time and experience, either in cash or kind. This practice stems from a recognition that many respondents have limited time and resources and that some form of (usually modest) compensation is appropriate given the value of the information they share. Some researchers raise the issue of compensation only after people have consented to sharing their experiences to try and limit the role of payment in compelling participation. However, the prospect of payment can still shape decision-making even if nothing is promised upfront (De Nutte, this volume). When international development agencies and NGOs play major local roles, researchers can find it challenging to separate themselves from the institutions with which local populations are accustomed to interact and from which they expect assistance (Wood 2006; Lake 2018).

It is by no means clear, however, that modest gifts/cash to individuals is sufficient compensation. In their research on refugees, Mackenzie, McDowell, and Pittaway (2007, 229) assert that "researchers should seek ways to move beyond harm minimisation as a standard for ethical research and recognise an obligation to design and conduct research projects that aim to bring about reciprocal benefits for refugee participants and/or communities." However, this can also be a challenge if they lack cultural competence (Thomson, Ansoms, and Murison 2013). There is a strong case for some kind of compensation given the value of the information that gets shared, but the more significant challenge remains how to effectively translate principle into practice (Molyneux et al. 2012). These kinds of ethical challenges only rarely come up when academic researchers seek approval from their institutional review boards. Questions of legal liability are increasingly the decisive factor in ethics approval processes, contributing to an often inflexible insistence on adhering to specific protocols irrespective of context, such as written consent forms (Wynn and Israel 2018). While there have been some moves toward embracing oral forms of consent in some contexts, such as the United States, this trend is by no means universal; review boards remain notorious for being inflexibly concerned with liability. As anyone who has undertaken fieldwork in Africa will tell you, the kinds of procedural criteria typically associated with ethics approval processes offer limited and frequently unhelpful guidance when it comes to actually conducting research. While familiar axioms such as "do no harm" and "informed consent" can undoubtedly be useful in establishing minimum thresholds, it would be a grievous mistake to confuse ethical certification with ethical obligation (Okyere, this volume; Basini 2016; Cramer, Hammond, and Pottier 2011; Huysamen and Sanders 2021). As Campbell (2017, 89) observes, this is especially true of conflict and postconflict settings, where "basic ethical principles established to guide research on human subjects are necessary but insufficient." This effectively shifts the task of ethical reflection from the institutional to the personal. Moving beyond negative injunctions against harm means entering into complex and frequently ambiguous terrain where it is not always clear what the "right" course of action looks like.

This in turn brings into focus larger questions regarding positionality—identity, race, position, class—which are foundational to lived experiences in the field (Porter et al. 2005; Keikelame 2018; Yacob-Haliso 2018; Johnstone 2019; LaRocco et al. 2019; Wibben 2016). Positionality plays a central role in all aspects of the research process but is especially consequential when it comes to ethical questions. As our contributors to this volume demonstrate further, there is no way to separate ethics from positionality. African researchers have different experiences in the field than their European counterparts. Men experience things differently to women, yet not all women have the same experiences or positionality either (Strathern 1986). Differences of institutional status, background, age, and wealth create further layers. The ethical challenges associated with fieldwork take different forms for different kinds of people.

Researching Sexual and Gender-Based Violence in Africa

Further challenges come into focus once sexual and gender-based violence becomes the primary focus of inquiry. Gender-based violence in Africa is *not* a topic that should be easy to research or write about, yet many people continue to jump in without fully considering the sensitivity and complexity of the issues involved. Highly stylized and simplistic narratives tend to be deployed whenever sexual violence becomes a topic of conversation, especially in relation to wartime violence in Africa, where rape and other related abuses are routinely portrayed as elemental forces that almost inevitably arise whenever social and political order has irreparably broken down. This has in turn provided fuel for now well-documented forms of sensationalism, voyeurism, and exoticism, with similar stories regarding sexual violence repeated time and again (Engle 2020).

For our purposes, there are three overlapping issues that need to be considered here. First, we have issues associated with researching the dimensions and effects of gender-based violence in conflict settings within Africa. This raises both ethical and methodological challenges since it usually means asking intimate and confronting questions regarding highly traumatic experiences while also navigating the social and familial stigma that survivors and their children continue to endure. There is an acute risk of doing further damage, so applied examples of better practice are crucial (see especially Atim; Balami and Umar; De Nutte; Schulz; Stewart, all this volume). Moreover, it is also essential to grapple with forms of gender-based violence that go beyond "rape as a weapon of war" archetypes, such as forced marriage and sexual violence against men. Second, we witness complex relationships between wartime violence and peacetime practices, which require careful attention to larger social practices in shaping the context, characteristics, and long-term social effects of wartime violence (Kiconco 2021). This in turn means expanding our gaze to grapple with the "raced, classed and heteronormative dimensions of sexual violence, [and] their logics and manifestations" (Drumond, Mesok, and Zalewski 2020, 1147). Treating gender-based violence as a violation of established social norms runs the risk of overlooking the extent to which violence takes place because patriarchal norms regarding sexuality and gender have been upheld.

Finally, we have issues associated with policy and advocacy, which means focusing on the logic and effects of political interventions and campaigns centered on gender-based violence. It is necessary to take into account both ideologies and institutions here. As Pamela Scully (2009) observes, the contemporary politics of humanitarianism shares key features in common with earlier interventions in the name of saving women and girls. Interventions which are primarily justified in humanitarian and paternalistic terms cannot be taken at face value but instead need to be scrutinized for their tensions, exclusions, and violence (Asad 2015; Quirk 2023; Cole 2012). There is no question that (at least some cases of) gender-based violence can generate strong emotions, but these emotions have not always been channeled in productive directions. This is why researching gender-based violence also means focusing on how and why different institutions respond, whether their actions have the intended effects, and how advocacy might improve policy.

This book project approaches these overlapping issues from a distinctive vantage point: it emerges from a longer-term collaborative project focusing on gender-based violence in African conflicts. The formal title of the project is "Conjugal Slavery in War (CSiW): Partnerships for the Study of Enslavement, Marriage and Masculinities," funded by the SSHRC. Many of our contributors have been involved in this project in one way or another, and for this reason many chapters in this collection primarily focus on wartime abductions which feature women and girls who are forced to marry their captors. This distinctive combination of violent abduction and marriage has been documented in a series of armed conflicts in different parts of Africa, including Liberia, Sierra Leone, Nigeria, Congo, Rwanda, and Uganda (Coulter 2009; Bunting 2012; Baines 2017). While the "marriages" begin with violent capture, some persist years after the war has ended and can sometimes be regarded as legitimate by family members and society. Adding marriage to the equation both complicates and deepens the familiar narratives around gender-based violence in wartime. Claiming captive women and girls as "wives" changes experiences of captivity by introducing models of sexual exclusivity and domesticity. It also creates additional complications once conflicts come to an end since both parties to the "marriage" retain at least some connection to the other, greatly affecting long-term relationships with family, children, communities, and future marriage partners/experiences.

Marriage also opens the door to other challenging questions (Quirk and Rossi 2022). As Ferme (2016, 231) has demonstrated in her work in the Special Court of Sierra Leone, all kinds of problems arise in efforts to sharply distinguish "forced marriage in war" from "arranged marriage" in peacetime, since this risks creating a "benign construction of 'community'" which erases forms of abuse that are routinely associated with marriage in Sierra Leone. Treating marriage as an ideal(ized) type of institution risks reinforcing conventionally gendered and heteronormative views of relationships and roles while superimposing a misleading image of "real marriage" upon complex gradations in lived experiences (Baumeister 2020). Wartime and peacetime experiences should not be regarded as clearly demarcated categories where entirely different rules apply. What happens in peacetime has complex and variegated effects upon conflict, and vice versa. In some cases it is not even clear which category should apply, such as "post-conflict" Congo. The crude imposition of ideal type categories on complex local practices also has historical roots in the colonial period, including the regulation of child marriages by missionary and colonial administrators (Shadle 2006), "marriage by capture" (Thornberry 2016), and female genital cutting as a "harmful traditional practice" (Hodzic 2017). It is therefore a mistake to assume, following many colonial administrators, that cultural forms in Africa are "static" and unchanging since this quickly results in over-simplifications of both marriage and gender (Dery and Bawa 2019).

It is also important not to conflate gender and sexuality with vulnerable "womenandchildren" (Enloe 2014). As a growing literature has demonstrated (Kirby and Henry 2012; Schulz and Touquet 2020), there is an urgent need to pay much closer attention to men and boys as both perpetrators and/or victims of sexual violence and to connect these specific experiences to larger models of masculinity, patriarchy, and gender justice. Important examples include recent studies into "why men rape" (Baaz and Stern 2009; Kelly et al. 2012), male victims of sexual violence (Dolan 2014; Gray, Stern, and Dolan 2020; Sivakumaran 2007; Solangon and Patel 2012; Schulz 2018; Schulz and Touquet 2020; Zarkov 2001), and fatherhoods in conflict situations (Aijazi,

Amony, and Baines 2019; Bunting 2018). In the specific case of forced marriage, the study of masculinities extends to lived experiences of being "given a wife," forced to "take a wife," or having a "wife taken away" as punishment by a more senior commander. It also connects to postconflict experiences such as the role of fathers concerning "children born of war" (Baines and Oliveira 2020). Focusing on men and boys should not mean studying "gender and masculinities without women and without feminist inspiration" (Henry 2017, 195) but ideally involves a deeper analysis of how different identities and statuses intersect. However, it is hard to capture these complexities due to the weight of simplistic "narratives about hypermasculinized (or sometimes feminized) racialized men who need to be 'civilized' by white men, and sometimes women" (Wright 2020, 664).

This focus on masculinity has begun to feed into policy languages and responses. Within the WPS agenda, several key themes can be highlighted:

> (1) "men as allies" arguments, which emphasize the need to leverage men's power in order to achieve gender equality; (2) "male vulnerabilities" arguments, which highlight how patriarchal gender norms harm men and boys in conflict; (3) strategic arguments, which promote relational approaches as a means to move WPS up the international policy agenda; and (4) antimilitarist arguments, which promote the transformation of masculinities as a means to prevent violent conflict. (Wright 2020, 657)

These arguments help to bring into focus some of the tensions and complications which arise once the conversation shifts from research to policy and advocacy. One of the main goals of recent studies of masculinities has been to capture the complexities of lived experiences through careful fieldwork, but it can be difficult to keep the nuances within the frame once policy becomes the primary focal point, since many interventions continue to be organized around the foundational assumption that men are perpetrators, and women and children are their victims.

Efforts are being made to destabilize this assumption. Both the 2017 *International Protocol on the Documentation and Investigation of Sexual Violence in Conflict* (Ribeiro and van der Straten Ponthoz) and UNSC Resolution 2467 (UNSC 2019) explicitly recognize men and boys as potential victims of conflict-related sexual and gender violence. The 2017 *International Protocol* reports that "men form a significant percentage of victims of sexual violence. Although data is limited, recent findings indicate that there is less of a disparity between male victims and female victims than has historically been acknowledged" (2017, 21). While this statement is evidence of some shift, individuals who have worked with male victims for a sustained period, including the Refugee Law Project in Uganda (Schulz; Ongwech, both this volume), recognize that the stigma associated with this issue still presents major challenges.

The limitations of both government and international policy responses focusing on sexual and gender-based violence are well known to experts in this field. Legal instruments and legal remedies have been a major focal point in the now extensive body of literature concerned with the ethics and mechanics of international criminal justice, especially the International Criminal Court and predecessor courts for Rwanda and Sierra Leone. Rulings by these courts have played a major role in shaping debates over how a range of criminal offenses should be defined and operationalized, including forced marriage and enslavement. They have also resulted in high-profile offenders, such as Charles Taylor, being prosecuted and convicted. Despite these advances, these international courts remain deeply flawed. There is currently rich critical scholarship from Third World Approaches to International Law (TWAIL) scholars as well as feminist and critical race scholars pointing to the ways in which international law constructs particular victims and particular perpetrators. Models of individual criminal responsibility are ill-suited to understanding systemic harms and thus struggle to make sense of cases such as Dominic Ongwen, who was abducted as a child and climbed the ranks of the Lord's Resistance Army by committing numerous crimes, including sexual violence and forced marriage (Bunting 2018).

There is also an argument to be made that too much energy has been directed toward international criminal prosecutions, which only affect a very small proportion of relevant cases. While national prosecutions are not unheard of in some jurisdictions, varying combinations of amnesty and impunity remain the dominant model, creating a situation where countless perpetrators of gender-based violence face few if any consequences for their actions. Trading justice for peace via amnesty and power sharing remains common (Koko 2019), contributing to a situation where large numbers of survivors of grievous abuses are routinely obliged to rebuild their lives knowing that many perpetrators of past abuses remain at large. In this environment, policy and advocacy tend to splinter into a range of frequently lower-profile issues: having access to reparation and other sources of state financial support, improving government programs, securing funding support from donors, or supporting affected communities.

Political advocacy can sometimes have a beneficial effect on policy, but there will also be many occasions when campaigners find it hard to break through. This presents additional challenges from a research standpoint, since different causes and campaigns can also be treated as methodological objects of inquiry in their own right (Quirk 2018). It is also clear, however, that campaigners regularly seek inspiration and instruction from earlier historical experiences and parallel contemporary causes, thereby attempting to leverage past experiences in order to maximize future political prospects (Stevenson and Swartz, this volume). This can sometimes make it difficult to disentangle one campaign from another; key concepts are routinely redeployed—or stretched—to help make larger political arguments. While this is entirely understandable from a strategic political standpoint, it presents further ethical and methodological challenges since there are likely to be trade-offs associated with forcing lived experiences into the conceptual boxes favored by governments and donors. The political economy of knowledge production can be very hard to disentangle from the political economy of political advocacy, especially when it comes to "hot button" issues such as gender-based violence.

Introducing the Chapters

The chapters that follow are divided into two distinct sections. The first section, "Ethical and Methodological Dilemmas," provides a series of applied examples and reflections when it comes to researching gender-based violence and related challenges. The contributors to this section describe how and why they conducted their research, the effects of knowledge economies and hierarchies, and the effects of positionality and history. It begins with Teddy Atim, who draws upon her decades of experience as a researcher in Uganda. Atim observes that "research is largely framed and seen as something Northern researchers do better than locals," despite the fact that the latter usually enjoy key advantages relative to outsiders, such as language(s) and lived experience (this volume, 51). Much of her chapter focuses on the tensions and complications associated with projects which have their origins in the Global North, but she also pays careful attention to the practical context and consequences of the research process itself. "Individual good intentions can be limited by institutional and structural conditions built on colonial legacies and White privilege," yet there remain ways of making research more sensitive and equitable (this volume, 52).

This is followed by a unique chapter by Sylvie Bodineau and Appolinaire Lipandasi, who collaborated on a doctoral research project undertaken by Bodineau focusing on child soldiers in the Democratic Republic of the Congo. Each author describes their relationship in their own words, creating a narrative that captures their different perspectives and interests. It also reveals how even the best collaborations remain embedded within knowledge economies. The challenges associated with doing research with children are also the primary focus of Beth Stewart's contribution. Like Bodineau, Stewart established local collaborations in order to explore the lives of children born to mothers abducted by the Lord's Resistance Army in northern Uganda. Over the course of many years, Stewart used a carefully considered combination of play, journals, group discussions, and home visits to understand how children narrated their lives and experiences. One crucial theme to emerge here is the degree to which her life became entangled with the lives of the children, their families, and others in challenging ways, making it necessary to engage in constant reflection regarding the most appropriate and ethical course of action.

The next chapter, by Lawan Balami and Umar Ahmad Umar, considers the challenge of doing research in internally displaced persons' camps in northeastern Nigeria established in response to the Boko Haram insurgency. Camps providing refuge can be valuable sites for conducting research with displaced and traumatized populations, but they also come with significant challenges. As Balami and Umar observe, both household heads and camp officials tend to have a great deal of power over potential respondents, who may therefore feel compelled to participate in research projects. Further complications arise when certain categories of survivors are singled out for attention, creating an impression they may secure resources not available to others. Compensating respondents for their participation is rarely straightforward. As Leen De Nutte argues, many of these issues can be at least partly addressed through a commitment to transparency, fully informing all parties involved in the research what the research process does—and does not—involve. Her chapter reflects upon her research into the experiences of mothers and fathers who had previously been abducted by the Lord's Resistance Army. One key theme that emerges from her analysis is the degree to which new research projects follow in the wake created by precedents established by earlier research projects. References were repeatedly made to "previous examples of researchers and organizations who had come in, collected data, and disappeared without properly informing participants about the objectives of the research, what data was collected, or what would happen with the information" (this volume, 144).

Our first section concludes with a chapter from Ana Stevenson and Rebecca Swartz, who place recent debates over methods, ethics, and representation within their larger historical and ideological context. Building upon a historical case study of Sara Baartman, a key figure within the larger history of European enslavement and colonialism in Africa, Stevenson and Swartz explore how and why European historical paradigms and colonial terminologies continue to "stay with us," creating layers of meaning in relation to colonialism, race, enslavement, and gender that shape the language of contemporary political struggles in Africa and elsewhere.

The second half of the book focuses on "Organizations, Institutions and Knowledge Production." Our chief focus here is the relationship between researchers and institutional actors—civil society organizations, universities, funders, governments—and the effects these institutional actors can have upon different stages of the research process and associated political and policy goals. This section begins with a chapter by Philipp Schulz, whose research into male survivors of wartime rape in Uganda was conducted in conjunction with Refugee Law Project (RLP). Working closely with RLP, Schulz structured his research around a series of workshops and related engagements with members of a male survivor group, the Men of Courage. Instead of coming with a fixed agenda, Schulz carefully designed a more open-ended and participatory framework, with the primary goal being to "carry out research *with* local communities, rather than *on* them" (this volume, 194). This research could not have been undertaken without contributions from RLP, whom Schulz continues to work with to this day, with the goal of creating knowledge and engagement which is directly beneficial to male survivors.

Relationships between researchers and institutions are not always positive. This theme is taken up in Samuel Okyere's chapter, which focuses upon the role of university ethics approval processes. His primary goal is to call attention to "the subtle and overt ways in which the criteria for evaluating ethical considerations, such as consent and risk, can be laced with ethnocentrism and 'othering'" (this volume, 200). Especially important are the perverse effects of an institutional insistence that parental consent be secured before talking to children, which appeared as either "offensive" or "astonishing" to Okyere's teenage respondents in Ghana and Nigeria. This line of argument is further complicated by Judith-Ann Walker's contribution, which focuses upon USAID/Nigeria's humanitarian-assistance interventions. It is frequently assumed that institutional actors in the Global North have superior ethical standards to their counterparts in the Global South. Walker complicates this narrative by highlighting how USAID ends up placing technical principles and methodologies ahead of research ethics.

Ethical principles also have important applications when it comes to policy and advocacy. This is reflected in the work of Otim Patrick Ongwech, who captures the behind-the-scenes work undertaken by RLP to produce documentary films designed to effect social and political change. The chief focus is a documentary entitled *Bringing Up Our Enemies' Child*, which explores the experiences of men raising children conceived via the wartime rape of their partners. He describes the numerous ethical steps required to get people to participate in making a film on such a sensitive subject, including procedures for ensuring informed consent and confirming that participants are comfortable with how they have been represented. As this chapter demonstrates, RLP is one of many African organizations with tremendous expertise regarding sexual violence and its effects. This theme is further developed in Heather Tasker's chapter, which revolves around a six-country survey focusing upon African community organizations working on gender justice. Tasker is especially concerned with points of friction that emerge between the technocratic languages of global governance and local experiences and interests. She underscores the importance of having a "research methodology that values the expertise of frontline workers" and thereby focuses attention on their strategic priorities and perspectives (this volume, 253).

One of the key themes which ties together these different contributions is the difficulty associated with conducting research into gender-based violence and related issues. As this introduction has helped make clear, this can be tremendously demanding work. Simplistic and misleading narratives continue to color how key issues are represented. Colonial hierarchies and classifications continue to have lasting effects. Getting people to talk to you about sensitive topics can be exceptionally challenging on its own, and there are major challenges to be addressed when it comes to what can and should be offered in return for their stories. Organizations and intermediaries can provide invaluable help, but they also bring additional obstacles. Complex considerations associated with positionality and privilege mark every step of the process, compounded by the effects of funding streams, hierarchies, and audience expectations.

This does not mean, however, that nothing ever changes. Some of the ideas behind this book were initially conceived well over a decade ago, and the conference where many of these chapters were originally presented as papers took place in 2018. Conversations about knowledge economies and the politics of extraction have changed tremendously over this period. Many constructive proposals have emerged regarding how to bring about change. The complex effects of power relations within partnerships are now much better understood. There has been a major investment in the project of decolonization, which is hugely important despite its flaws and limitations. In our afterword we reflect upon these recent developments, grapple with the backlash they have provoked, and identify models that might lead to something better.

References

Abrak, I., and D. McKenzie. 2020. "Boko Haram Claims to Have Kidnapped Nigerian Schoolboys, in Unverified Audio Message." CNN, December 15. https://edition.cnn.com/2020/12/15/africa/boko-haram-nigerian-schoolboys-intl/index.html.

Aijazi, O., E. Amony, and E. Baines. 2019. "'We Were Controlled, We Were Not Allowed to Express Our Sexuality, Our Intimacy Was Suppressed': Sexual Violence Experienced by Boys." In *Research Handbook on Child Soldiers*, edited by M. Drumbl and J. Barrett, 95–109. Cheltenham, UK: Edward Elgar.

Albayrak-Aydemir, N. 2020. "The Hidden Costs of Being a Scholar from the Global South." London School of Economics, February 20. https://blogs.lse.ac.uk/highereducation/2020/02/20/the-hidden-costs-of-being-a-scholar-from-the-global-south/.

Andrews, N., and S. Bawa. 2019. "People Come and Go but We Don't See Anything: How Might Social Research Contribute to Social Change?" *Qualitative Report* 24 (11): 2874–90.

Appiah, K. A. 1993. *In My Father's House: Africa in the Philosophy of Culture*. Oxford: Oxford University Press.

Asad, T. 1986. "The Concept of Cultural Translation in British Social Anthropology." In *Writing Culture*, edited by J. Clifford and G. E. Marcus, 141–64. Berkeley: University of California Press.

———. 2015. "Reflections on Violence, Law, and Humanitarianism." *Critical Inquiry* 41 (2): 390–427. https://doi.org/10.1086/679081.

Ba, O. 2020. *States of Justice: The Politics of the International Criminal Court*. Cambridge: Cambridge University Press.

Baaz, M., and M. Stern. 2009. "Why Do Soldiers Rape? Masculinity, Violence, and Sexuality in the Armed Forces in the Congo (DRC)." *International Studies Quarterly* 53 (2): 495–518.

———. 2013. *Sexual Violence as a Weapon of War? Perceptions, Prescriptions, Problems in the Congo and Beyond*. London: Zed.

Bahati, I. 2020. "Challenges Facing Female Researchers in Conflict Settings." *LSE Bukavu Series*, March 6. https://blogs.lse.ac.uk/africaatlse/2020/03/06/challenges-facing-female-researchers-in-conflict-settings-bukavu-series/.

Baines, E. 2017. *Buried in the Heart: Women, Complex Victimhood and the War in Northern Uganda*. Cambridge: Cambridge University Press.

Baines, E., and C. Oliveira. 2020. "Securing the Future: Transformative Justice and Children 'Born of War.'" *Social & Legal Studies* 30 (3): 1–21.

Basini, H. 2016. "'Doing No Harm': Methodological and Ethical Challenges of Working with Women Associated with Fighting Forces / Ex-combatants in Liberia." In Wibben, *Researching War*, 163–84.

Baumeister, H. 2020. "Forced Marriage Real Simple." *Journal of Human Trafficking, Enslavement and Conflict-Related Sexual Violence* 1 (1): 25–47.

Bouka, Y. 2015. "Researching Violence in Africa as a Black Woman: Notes from Rwanda." Working paper, Conflict Field Research. http://conflictfieldresearch.colgate.edu/wp-content/uploads/2015/05/Bouka_WorkingPaper-May2015.pdf.

———. 2018. "Collaborative Research as Structural Violence." Political Violence at a Glance, July 12. http://politicalviolenceataglance.org/2018/07/12/collaborative-research-as-structural-violence/.

Briggs, R. C., and S. Weathers. 2016. "Gender and Location in African Politics Scholarship: The Other White Man's Burden?" *African Affairs* 115 (460): 466–89. https://doi.org/10.1093/afraf/adw009.

Bunting, A. 2012. "'Forced Marriage' in Conflict Situations: Researching and Prosecuting Old Harms and New Crimes." *Canadian Journal of Human Rights* 1: 165–85.

———. 2018. "Gender Politics and Geopolitics of International Criminal Law in Uganda." *Global Discourse* 8 (3): 422–37.

Campbell, S. P. 2017. "Ethics of Research in Conflict Environments." *Journal of Global Security Studies* 2 (1): 89–101. https://doi.org/10.1093/jogss/ogw024.

Carpenter, C. 2006. *Innocent Women and Children: Gender, Norms and the Protection of Civilians*. Burlington, VT: Ashgate.

Chakravarty, A. 2012. "'Partially Trusting' Field Relationships Opportunities and Constraints of Fieldwork in Rwanda's Postconflict Setting." *Field Methods* 24 (3): 251–71.

Coetzee, C. 2019. "Ethical?! Collaboration?! Keywords for Our Contradictory Times." *Journal of African Cultural Studies* 31 (3): 257–64. https://doi.org/10.1080/13696815.2019.1635437.

Cole, T. 2012. "The White-Savior Industrial Complex." *The Atlantic*, March 21, 2012. https://www.theatlantic.com/international/archive/2012/03/the-white-savior-industrial-complex/254843/.

Coulter, C. 2009. *Bush Wives and Girl Soldiers: Women's Lives through War and Peace in Sierra Leone*. Ithaca, NY: Cornell University Press.

Cramer, C., L. Hammond, and J. Pottier, eds. 2011. *Researching Violence in Africa: Ethical and Methodological Challenges*. Vol. 6. Leiden: Brill.

Cramer, C., D. Johnston, C. Oya, and J. Sender. 2015. "Mistakes, Crises, and Research Independence: The Perils of Fieldwork as a Form of Evidence." *African Affairs* 115 (458): 145–60. https://doi.org/10.1093/afraf/adv067.

Crane, J. 2013. *Scrambling for Africa: AIDS, Expertise, and the Rise of American Global Health Science*. Ithaca, NY: Cornell University Press.

Crawford, K. 2017. *Wartime Sexual Violence: From Silence to Condemnation of a Weapon of War*. Washington, DC: Georgetown University Press.

Cronin-Furman, K., and M. Lake. 2018. "Ethics Abroad: Fieldwork in Fragile and Violent Contexts." *Political Science and Politics* 51 (3): 607–14. https://doi.org/10.1017/S1049096518000379.

Davenport, C. 2013. "Researching While Black: Why Conflict Research Needs More African Americans (Maybe)." *Political Violence @ a Glance* (blog), April 10. https://politicalviolenceataglance.org/2013/04/10/researching-while-black-why-conflict-research-needs-more-african-americans-maybe/.

de Guevara, B. B., and R. Kostić. 2017. "Knowledge Production in/about Conflict and Intervention: Finding 'Facts,' Telling 'Truth.'" *Journal of Intervention and Statebuilding* 11 (1): 1–20. https://doi.org/10.1080/17502977.2017.1287635.

Dery, I., and S. Bawa. 2019. "Agency, Social Status and Performing Marriage in Postcolonial Societies." *Journal of Asian and African Studies* 54 (7): 980–94. https://doi.org/10.1177/0021909619851148.

Dodsworth, S., and N. Cheeseman. 2018. "The Potential and Pitfalls of Collaborating with Development Organizations and Policy Makers in Africa." *African Affairs* 117 (466): 130–45. https://doi.org/10.1093/afraf/adx041.

Dolan, C. 2014. "Letting Go of the Gender Binary: Charting New Pathways for Humanitarian Interventions on Gender-Based Violence." *International Review of the Red Cross* 96 (894): 485–501. https://doi.org/10.1017/S1816383115000120.

Drezner, D. 2017. *The Ideas Industry: How Pessimists, Partisans, and Plutocrats Are Transforming the Marketplace of Ideas*. Oxford: Oxford University Press.

Drumond, P., E. Mesok, and M. Zalewski. 2020. "Sexual Violence in the Wrong(ed) Bodies: Moving beyond the Gender Binary in International Relations." *International Affairs* 96 (5): 1145–49. https://doi.org/10.1093/ia/iiaa144.

The Economist. 2000. "The Hopeless Continent." *The Economist*, May 13. https://www.economist.com/weeklyedition/2000-05-13.

Engle, K. 2020. *The Grip of Sexual Violence in Conflict: Feminist Interventions in International Law*. Stanford, CA: Stanford University Press.

Enloe, C. 2014. *Bananas, Beaches and Bases: Making Feminist Sense of International Politics*. 2nd ed. Berkeley: University of California Press.

Fassin, D. 2012. *Humanitarian Reason: A Moral History of the Present*. Berkeley: University of California Press.

Ferme, M. C. 2016. "Consent, Custom, and the Law in Debates around Forced Marriage at the Special Court for Sierra Leone." In *Marriage by Force? Contestation over Consent and Coercion in Africa*, edited by A. Bunting, B. N. Lawrance, and R. L. Roberts, 227–46. Athens: Ohio University Press.

Flummerfelt, R., and N. Peyton. 2020. "More Than 50 Women Accuse Aid Workers of Sex Abuse in Congo Ebola Crisis." *New Humanitarianism*, September 29. https://www.thenewhumanitarian.org/2020/09/29/exclusive-more-50-women-accuse-aid-workers-sex-abuse-congo-ebola-crisis.

Gerber, R., and G. K. Chuan. 2000. "The Power of Fieldwork." In *Fieldwork in Geography: Reflections, Perspectives and Actions*, edited by R. Gerber and G. K. Chuan, 3–12. Dordrecht, Netherlands: Springer.

Giridharadas, A. 2018. *Winners Take All: The Elite Charade of Changing the World*. New York: Knopf.

Gray, H., M. Stern, and C. Dolan. 2020. "Torture and Sexual Violence in War and Conflict: The Unmaking and Remaking of Subjects of Violence." *Review of International Studies* 46 (2): 197–216. https://doi.org/10.1017/S0260210519000391.

Grovogui, S. N. 2001. "Sovereignty in Africa: Quasi-statehood and Other Myths in International Theory." In *Africa's Challenge to International Relations Theory*, edited by Kevin C. Dunn and Timothy M. Shaw, 29–45. London: Palgrave Macmillan.

Halvorsen, T., and J. Nossum, eds. 2017. *North–South Knowledge Networks: Towards Equitable Collaboration between Academics, Donors and Universities*. Cape Town: African Minds.

Henderson, F. B. 2009. "'We Thought You Would Be White': Race and Gender in Fieldwork." *Political Science & Politics* 42 (2): 291–94.

Henry, M. 2013. "Ten Reasons Not to Write Your Master's Dissertation on Sexual Violence in War." *Disorder of Things*, June 4. https://thedisorderofthings.com/2013/06/04/ten-reasons-not-to-write-your-masters-dissertation-on-sexual-violence-in-war/.

———. 2017. "Problematizing Military Masculinity, Intersectionality and Male Vulnerability in Feminist Critical Military Studies." *Critical Military Studies* 3 (2): 182–99. https://doi.org/10.1080/23337486.2017.1325140.

Hesford, W. 2011. *Spectacular Rhetorics: Human Rights Visions, Recognitions, Feminisms*. Durham, NC: Duke University Press.

Hodzic, S. 2017. *The Twilight of Cutting: African Activism and Life after NGOs.* Oakland: University of California Press.

HRW (Human Rights Watch). 2017. "Central African Republic: Ugandan Troops Harm Women, Girls Repeated Sexual Exploitation and Abuse." Human Rights Watch, May 15. https://www.hrw.org/news/2017/05/15/central-african-republic-ugandan-troops-harm-women-girls.

Huysamen, M., and T. Sanders. 2021. "Institutional Ethics Challenges to Sex Work Researchers: Committees, Communities, and Collaboration." *Sociological Research Online* 26 (4): 942–58. https://doi.org/10.1177/13607804211002847.

Ibrahim, T. 2021. "Insecurity: Youths Protest in Katsina, Block Road." *Daily Trust,* January 3. https://dailytrust.com/insecurity-youths-protest-in-katsina-block-road.

ICG (International Crisis Group). 2020. "A Course Correction for the Women, Peace and Security Agenda." *Crisis Group Special Briefing* N°5, December 9. https://www.jstor.org/stable/resrep31554.

Jacobsen, K., and L. Landau. 2003. "The Dual Imperative in Refugee Research: Some Methodological and Ethical Considerations in Social Science Research on Forced Migration." *Disasters* 27 (3): 185–206. https://doi.org/10.1111/1467-7717.00228.

Johnstone, L., ed. 2019. *The Politics of Conducting Research in Africa: Ethical and Emotional Challenges in the Field.* London: Palgrave.

Kaplan, R. D. 1994. "The Coming Anarchy." *The Atlantic,* February. https://www.theatlantic.com/magazine/archive/1994/02/the-coming-anarchy/304670/.

Keikelame, M. J. 2018. "'The Tortoise under the Couch': An African Woman's Reflections on Negotiating Insider-Outsider Positionalities and Issues of Serendipity on Conducting a Qualitative Research Project in Cape Town, South Africa." *International Journal of Social Research Methodology* 21: 219–30.

Kelly, J., J. Kabanga, W. Cragin, L. Alcayna-Stevens, S. Haider, and M. Vanrooyen. 2012. "'If Your Husband Doesn't Humiliate You, Other People Won't': Gendered Attitudes towards Sexual Violence in Eastern Democratic Republic of Congo." *Global Public Health* 7 (3): 285–98. https://doi.org/10.1080/17441692.2011.585344.

Kiconco, A. 2021. *Gender, Conflict and Reintegration in Uganda: Abducted Girls, Returning Women.* Abingdon, UK: Routledge.

Kirby, P., and M. Henry. 2012. "Rethinking Masculinity and Practices of Violence in Conflict Settings." *International Feminist Journal of Politics* 14 (4): 445–49. https://10.1080/14616742.2012.726091.

Koko, S. 2019. "The Challenges of Power-Sharing and Transitional Justice in Post–Civil War African Countries: Comparing Burundi, Mozambique and Sierra Leone." *African Journal of Conflict Resolution* 19 (1): 81–108.

Kraft, P. W., M. Lodge, and C. S. Taber. 2015. "Why People 'Don't Trust the Evidence': Motivated Reasoning and Scientific Beliefs." *The ANNALS of the American Academy of Political and Social Science* 658 (1): 121–33.

Lake, M. 2018. *Strong NGOs and Weak States: Gender Justice and Human Rights Advocacy in the Democratic Republic of Congo and South Africa.* Cambridge: Cambridge University Press.

Landau, L. B. 2012. "Communities of Knowledge or Tyrannies of Partnership: Reflections on North–South Research Networks and the Dual Imperative." *Journal of Refugee Studies* 25: 555–70. https://doi.org/10.1093/jrs/fes005.

LaRocco, A., S. Alfina, E. Jamie, and K. Madise. 2019. "Reflections on Positionalities in Social Science Fieldwork in Northern Botswana: A Call for Decolonizing Research." *Politics and Gender* 16 (3). Published ahead of print, July 2. https://doi.org/10.1017/S1743923X19000059.

Lewis, C., A. Banga, G. Cimanuka, J. D. D. Hategekimana, M. Lake, and R. Pierotti. 2019. "Walking the Line: Brokering Humanitarian Identities in Conflict Research." *Civil Wars* 21 (2): 200–227. https://doi.org/10.1080/13698249.2019.1619154.

Macamo, E. 2016. "'Before We Start': Science and Power in the Constitution of Africa." In *The Politics of Nature and Science in Southern Africa*, edited by M. Ramutsindela, G. Miescher, and M. Boehi, 323–34. Basel, Switzerland: Basler Afrika Bibliographien.

Mackenzie, C., C. McDowell, and E. Pittaway. 2007. "Beyond 'Do No Harm': The Challenge of Constructing Ethical Relationships in Refugee Research." *Journal of Refugee Studies* 20 (2): 299–319. https://doi.org/10.1093/jrs/fem008.

Majumdar, A. 2020. "Bearing Witness inside MSF." *New Humanitarianism*, August 18. https://www.thenewhumanitarian.org/opinion/first-person/2020/08/18/MSF-Amsterdam-aid-institutional-racism.

Mama, A. 2011. "What Does It Mean to Do Feminist Research in African Contexts?" *Feminist Review* 98 (S1): e4–e20. https://doi.org/10.1057/fr.2011.22.

Mamdani, M. 1996. *Citizen and Subject: Contemporary Africa and the Legacy of Late Colonialism*. Princeton, NJ: Princeton University Press.

Mandiyanike, D. 2009. "The Dilemma of Conducting Research Back in Your Own Country as a Returning Student: Reflections of Research Fieldwork in Zimbabwe." *Area* 41:64–71. https://doi.org/10.1111/j.1475-4762.2008.00843.x.

Marchais, G., P. Bazuzi, and A. Amani Lameke. 2020. "'The Data Is Gold, and We Are the Gold-Diggers': Whiteness, Race and Contemporary Academic Research in Eastern DRC." *Critical African Studies* 12 (3): 372–94. https://doi.org/10.1080/21681392.2020.1724806.

Matfess, H. 2017. *Women and the War on Boko Haram: Wives, Weapons, Witnesses*. London: Zed Books.

Mbembe, A. 2021. *Out of the Dark Night: Essays on Decolonization*. New York: Columbia University Press.

Mitchell, A. 2013. "Escaping the 'Field Trap': Exploitation and the Global Politics of Educational Fieldwork in 'Conflict Zones.'" *Third World Quarterly* 34 (7): 1247–64.

Molyneux, S., S. Mulupi, L. Mbaabu, and V. Marsh. 2012. "Benefits and Payments for Research Participants: Experiences and Views from a Research Centre on the Kenyan Coast." *BMC Med Ethics* 13, article 13. https://doi.org/10.1186/1472-6939-13-13.

Mudimbe, V. A. 1988. *The Invention of Africa: Gnosis, Philosophy, and the Order of Knowledge*. Bloomington: Indiana University Press.

Munthali, A. 2001. "Doing Fieldwork at Home: Some Personal Experiences among the Tumbuka of Northern Malawi." *African Anthropologist* 8 (2): 114–36.

Mupotsa, D. S. 2020. "Knowing from Loss." *Sociological Review* 68 (3): 524–39. https://doi.org/10.1177/0038026119892403.

Musila, G. A. 2019. "Against Collaboration—or the Native Who Wanders Off." *Journal of African Cultural Studies* 31 (3): 286–93. https://doi.org/10.1080/13696815.2019.1633283.

Mwambari, D. 2019. "Local Positionality in the Production of Knowledge in Northern Uganda." *International Journal of Qualitative Methods* 18 (July). https://doi.org/10.1177/1609406919864845.

Mwangi, N. 2019. "'Good That You Are One of Us': Positionality and Reciprocity in Conducting Fieldwork in Kenya's Flower Industry." In *The Politics of Conducting Research in Africa: Ethical and Emotional Challenges in the Field*, edited by Lyn Johnstone, 13–34. London: Palgrave.

Mwesigwa, A., and P. Beaumont. 2019. "Did Children Die Because of 'White Saviour' Renee Bach?" *The Guardian*, October 17. https://www.theguardian.com/global-development/2019/oct/17/did-a-white-saviours-evangelical-zeal-turn-deadly-uganda-renee-bach-serving-his-children.

Ndlovu-Gatsheni, S. 2013. *Empire, Global Coloniality and African Subjectivity*. New York: Berghahn Books.

Nhemachena, A., N. Mlambo, and M. Kaundjua. 2016. "The Notion of the 'Field' and the Practices of Researching and Writing Africa: Towards Decolonial Praxis." *Africology: The Journal of Pan African Studies* 9 (7): 15–36.

Ní Aoláin, F., N. Cahn, D. F. Haynes, and N. Valji, eds. 2018. *The Oxford Handbook of Gender and Conflict*. Oxford: Oxford University Press.

Nyenyezi, A., A. Ansoms, K. Vlassenroot, E. Mudinga, and G. Muzalia, eds. 2020. *Bukavu Series: Toward a Decolonising Research*. Leuven, Belgium: PUL Presses.

Ojok, M. J. 2013. "Power Dynamics and the Politics of Fieldwork under Sudan's Prolonged Conflict." In *Research Methods in Conflict Settings: A View from Below*, edited by D. Mazurana, K. Jacobsen, and L. A. Gale, 149–65. New York: Cambridge University Press.

Onapajo, H. 2020. "Children in Boko Haram Conflict: The Neglected Facet of a Decade of Terror in Nigeria." *African Security* 13 (2): 195–211. https://doi.org/10.1080/19392206.2020.1770919.

Oyěwùmí, O. 1997. *The Invention of Women: Making an African Sense of Western Gender Discourses*. Minneapolis: University of Minnesota Press.

Parashar, S. 2019. "Research Brokers, Researcher Identities and Affective Performances: The Insider/Outsider Conundrum." *Civil Wars* 21 (2): 249–70. https://doi.org/10.1080/13698249.2019.1634304.

Parker, B. 2020. "Médecins Sans Frontières Needs 'Radical Change' on Racism: MSF President." *New Humanitarianism*, June 24. https://www.thenewhumanitarian.org/news/2020/06/24/MSF-racism-black-lives-matter-debate.

Pattanaik, B. 2020. "It Isn't Just Anti-trafficking: We Must Always Ask Whose Interests We Really Serve." *openDemocracy*, December 16. https://www.opendemocracy.net/en/beyond-trafficking-and-slavery/it-isnt-just-anti-trafficking-we-must-always-ask-whose-interests-we-really-serve.

Porter, E., G. Robinson, M. Smyth, S. Marie, E. Albrecht Osaghae, eds. 2005. "Conclusion: Reflections on Contemporary Research in Africa." *Researching Conflict in Africa: Insights and Experiences*. New York: United Nations University Press.

Introduction

Quirk, J. 2018. "Evaluating the Political Effects of Anti-slavery and Anti-trafficking Activism." In *Researching Forced Labour in the Global Economy: Methodological Challenges and Advances*, edited by G. LeBaron, 60–78. Oxford: Oxford University Press.

———. 2021. "Africa and International History." In *The Routledge Handbook of Historical International Relations*, edited by B. de Carvalho, J. Costa Lopez, and H. Leira, 441–53. Abingdon, UK: Routledge.

———. 2023. "Political Cultures." In *A Cultural History of Slavery and Human Trafficking in the Age of Global Conflict*, edited by Henrice Altink. London: Bloomsbury.

Quirk, J., and B. Rossi. 2022. "Slavery and Marriage in African Societies." *Slavery & Abolition* 43 (2): 245–84. https://doi.org/10.1080/0144039X.2022.2063231.

Ribeiro, S. F., and D. van der Straten Ponthoz. 2017. *International Protocol on the Documentation and Investigation of Sexual Violence in Conflict*. 2nd edition. London: Foreign and Commonwealth Office.

Sanni, S., and A. Sotunde. 2021. "Nigerian Schoolboys Freed as Forces Search for 300 Abducted Girls." Reuters, February 28. https://www.reuters.com/article/uk-nigeria-security-idUSKCN2AS064.

Schulz, P. 2018. "The 'Ethical Loneliness' of Male Sexual Violence Survivors in Northern Uganda: Gendered Reflections on Silencing." *International Feminist Journal of Politics* 20 (4): 583–601. https://doi.org/10.1080/14616742.2018.1489732.

Schulz, P., and H. Touquet. 2020. "Queering Explanatory Frameworks for Wartime Sexual Violence against Men." *International Affairs* 96, no. 5 (September): 1169–87. https://doi.org/10.1093/ia/iiaa062.

Schumaker, L. 2001. *Africanizing Anthropology: Fieldwork, Networks and the Making of Cultural Knowledge in Central Africa*. London: Duke University Press.

Scully, P. 2009. "Vulnerable Women: A Critical Reflection on Human Rights Discourse and Sexual Violence." *Emory International Law Review* 23 (1): 113–23.

Seery, E., J. Okanda, and M. Lawson. 2019. "A Tale of Two Continents: Fighting Inequality in Africa." Oxfam Briefing Paper. Oxford: Oxfam.

Sending, O. J. 2015. *The Politics of Expertise: Competing for Authority in Global Governance*. Ann Arbor: University of Michigan Press.

Shadle, B. 2006. *"Girl Cases": Marriage and Colonialism in Gusiiland, Kenya, 1890–1970*. Portsmouth, NH: Heinemann.

Sivakumaran, S. 2007. "Sexual Violence against Men in Armed Conflict." *European Journal of International Law* 18, no. 2 (April): 253–76. https://doi.org/10.1093/ejil/chm013.

Smyth, J. 2017. *The Toxic University: Zombie Leadership, Academic Rock Stars and Neoliberal Ideology*. London: Palgrave Macmillan.

Soete, L., S. Schneegans, D. Eröcal, B. Angathevar, and R. Rasiah. 2015. "A World in Search of an Effective Growth Strategy." In *UNESCO World Science Report*, 21–55. Paris: UNESCO.

Solangon, S., and P. Patel. 2012. "Sexual Violence against Men in Countries Affected by Armed Conflict." *Conflict, Security & Development* 12 (4): 417–42. https://doi.org/10.1080/14678802.2012.724794.

Stachowiak, S. 2013. *Pathways for Change: 10 Theories to Inform Advocacy and Policy Change Efforts*. N.p.: ORS Impact. https://www.orsimpact.com/DirectoryAttachments/132018_13248_359_Center_Pathways_FINAL.pdf.

Strathern, M. 1986. *The Gender of the Gift: Problems with Women and Problems with Society in Melanesia*. Berkeley: University of California Press.

Tamale, S. 2020. *Decolonization and Afro-Feminism*. Ottawa: Daraja Press.

Thomson, S., A. Ansoms, and J. Murison, eds. 2013. *Emotional and Ethical Challenges for Field Research in Africa: The Story behind the Findings*. Basingstoke, UK: Palgrave Macmillan.

Thornberry, E. 2016. "*Ukuthwala*, Forced Marriage, and the Idea of Custom in South Africa's Eastern Cape." In *Marriage by Force? Contestation over Consent and Coercion in Africa*, edited by A. Bunting, B. N. Lawrance, and R. L. Roberts, 137–58. Athens: Ohio University Press.

Tuck, E., and K. W. Yang. 2012. "Decolonization Is Not a Metaphor." *Decolonization: Indigeneity, Education & Society* 1 (1): 1–40.

United Nations News. 2022. "UN's Top Court Orders Uganda to Pay $325 Million to DR Congo." United Nations News, February 9. https://news.un.org/en/story/2022/02/1111612.

UNSC (United Nations Security Council). 2019. Resolution 2467 (2019), S/RES/2467.

Van Den Berg, S. 2020. "Selling Stories of War in Sierra Leone." In *Research as More Than Extraction? Knowledge Production and Sexual Violence in Post-conflict African Societies*, edited by A. Bunting, A. Kiconco, and J. Quirk, 40–42. London: openDemocracy.

Wai, Z. 2018. "Africa in/and International Relations: An Introduction." In *Recentering Africa in International Relations: Beyond Lack, Peripherality, and Failure*, edited by M. Iñiguez de Heredia and Z. Wai, 1–30. London: Palgrave.

Wainaina, B. 2005. "How to Write about Africa." *Granta* 92 (Winter). https://granta.com/how-to-write-about-africa/.

Wibben, A. T. R., ed. 2016. *Researching War: Feminist Methods, Ethics and Politics*. New York: Routledge.

Wood, E. 2006. "The Ethical Challenges of Field Research in Conflict Zones." *Qualitative Sociology* 29 (3): 373–86.

Wright, H. 2020. "'Masculinities Perspectives': Advancing a Radical Women, Peace and Security Agenda?" *International Feminist Journal of Politics* 22 (5): 652–74. https://doi.org/10.1080/14616742.2019.1667849.

Wynn, L. L., and M. Israel. 2018. "The Fetishes of Consent: Signatures, Paper, and Writing in Research Ethics Review." *American Anthropologist* 120 (December): 795–806. https://doi.org/10.1111/aman.13148.

Yacob-Haliso, O. 2018. "Intersectionalities and Access in Fieldwork in Postconflict Liberia: Motherland, Motherhood, and Minefields." *African Affairs* 118 (470): 168–81. https://doi.org/10.1093/afraf/ady046.

Zarkov, D. 2001. "The Body of the Other Man: Sexual Violence and the Construction of Masculinity, Sexuality and Ethnicity in Croatian Media." In *Victims, Perpetrators, or Actors? Gender, Armed Conflict, and Political Violence*, edited by Caroline Moser and Fiona Clark, 69–82. London: Zed.

ONE

Ethical and Methodological Dilemmas

ONE

The Ethical Dilemmas and Realities of Doing Research in Conflict and Postconflict Settings

TEDDY ATIM

Northern Uganda experienced protracted conflict between the government of Uganda and the Lord's Resistance Army (LRA) rebels that lasted over two decades, from 1986 to 2006 (although the government of Uganda continued its war against the LRA until 2018 in the Democratic Republic of Congo [DRC], the Central African Republic [CAR], and South Sudan). In the LRA's brutal war campaign on the population of northern Uganda, the entire Acholi subregion, large parts of the Lango subregion, and parts of the Teso subregion were affected (Apio 2016). During the conflict, the population suffered multiple forms of war crimes and violations, including forced displacement, pillaging, looting and destruction of property, abduction, forced recruitment, the disappearance of family members, slavery, forced marriage, sexual violence, psychological harms, mutilation, killings, torture, and inhumane and degrading treatment overall (UHRC and UN OHCHR 2011). The impact of these crimes is debilitating, with lifelong and intergenerational impacts on the survivors, their families, and communities.

The horrors experienced in this war in Uganda have led researchers to focus on the experiences of the population most affected by them. Research in similar contexts has increased over the years to improve humanitarian interventions needed by conflict-affected populations and provide evidence for advocacy and policy formulation. For example, wartime rape and other forms of gender-based violence continue to dominate the narratives of scholars and policymakers reflecting on girls' and women's suffering in conflict and postconflict contexts (Hilhorst and Douma 2018). Conducting research in these contexts has become fraught with ethical dilemmas pertaining to the safety and protection of research participants and ensuring that the processes follow high ethical standards. In particular, the heightened level of vulnerability and instability complicates research approaches in these contexts (Ford et al. 2009; Mazurana, Gale, and Jacobsen 2013).

Whereas research processes may be regarded as straightforward, the complexities of conflict and postconflict environments require the adaptation of research methodologies to suit the context and to "do no harm" (Ford et al. 2009; Wessells 2013). In the absence of careful considerations of research approaches, researchers and research projects can unknowingly harm study participants. How the research is framed, what questions are asked, and which processes are engaged to conduct the research—such as obtaining informed consent—are all vital steps. For example, researchers may sometimes have to reformulate their study questions once in the field or spend time building relationships with study participants before commencing the research to better understand events and processes that cannot be learned through traditional research approaches (Shaw 2007). For instance, the spaces people choose for the interviews can reveal their sense of safety and the need for confidentiality and privacy. The choice of spaces is dedicated by gender norms in some societies, which sanctions are considered appropriate for men and women in their culture. However, people's experiences and sense of safety may also influence their choice of a place to hold the interview (Mazurana, Gale, and Jacobsen 2013).

Similarly, signing informed consent in contexts of high illiteracy and mistrust of researchers or others may be risky and meaningless. While obtaining informed consent in informal interactions, such as those in people's homes, or casual places may be complex (Ford et al. 2009; Shaw 2007), some of these concerns are especially critical in contexts where the line between researchers, humanitarian actors, private contractors, and other actors are blurred and where research activities may raise suspicions (Mazurana, Gale, and Jacobsen 2013).

Therefore, careful consideration and some degree of sensitivity in research approaches and methodologies are needed to gain legitimacy. It is important to pay attention to research approaches and styles, including what questions to ask, who to speak with, how and where to minimize risks, and to reflect different voices and experiences. An important step is to undertake sound and rigorous research methodologies to understand the implication of the conflict on people's lives and larger social changes (Mazurana, Gale, and Jacobsen 2013). Some of these may, for example, require a reevaluation or reformulation of research questions and approaches to ensure confidentiality and anonymity of responses to protect respondents where the risk of participation is assessed to be high (Shaw 2007).

It is important that researchers carefully consider who collects the information and how it is collected to ensure reliability of the finding. Also, the challenges related to access due to insecurity, language, and other trying factors, such as the impact of trauma from the conflict on people's everyday lives, require adaptable research methodologies and approaches (see Mazurana, Gale, and Jacobsen 2013). To address some of these ethical and methodological challenges, there is increased collaboration between local or South-based researchers or organizations and international or North-based researchers and institutions. Collaborative research ensures that research processes and methodologies incorporate local perspectives and insights into the study context, grant access where international researchers would otherwise be limited, and contribute to building local expertise and skills in research. Yet, these collaborations are not without challenges, including the lack of resources and capacity (perceived) in research methods on the part of the South-based researchers and institutions, as well as the inherent power imbalance and inequality between the North- and South-based researchers and institutions (Mazurana, Gale, and Jacobsen 2013; Bouka 2018; Adriansen 2017). Notably, some of these collaborations foster knowledge hierarchies in ways that do not respect the capacity or intellectual advancement of researchers from the Global South (Bouka 2018; Adriansen 2017).

Even when collaborative research is framed as an important approach to building local capacity and enlisting local perspectives as part of the research, it can also be a site of structural violence in knowledge production for scholars from the Global South. There is a call to consider the nature of research collaborations between Global North and South researchers to ensure equity in knowledge production that augments the capacity and growth of South-based researchers (Bouka 2018). Research can be an extractive and exploitative process that needs to be recognized for what it is: it is extractive when data is appropriated from countries of the Global South without direct benefit to the respondents or the countries under study (Wessells 2013).

In this chapter I reflect on the realities and dilemmas of conducting research with conflict-affected populations in northern Uganda, particularly with victims of highly stigmatized crimes such as women survivors of wartime sexual violence and their children born of war, young women engaged in transactional sex in the postconflict period, as well as other victims of the conflict, the missing and formerly abducted persons and street children in the same period. I reflect on what it takes methodologically to research these highly sensitive groups, the dilemmas I encountered, and the strategies that were helpful to deal with some of the challenges. I also reflect on my positionality as a native woman and researcher conducting research in her own community and a highly internationalized research environment. I reflect on how my position influenced my research endeavors and my experiences working and collaborating on research projects with Western-based researchers and institutions. I engage in deep reflections on the ethics of these collaborations from the perspective of a Global South researcher.

The Journey from Practitioner to Researcher

I worked as a practitioner and researcher with children, women, and communities affected by armed conflict in northern Uganda, and my involvement in humanitarian work was partly shaped by my childhood experiences. From the age of eight, I witnessed and experienced the chaos that ravaged northern Uganda, beginning with the 1985 overthrow of the Obote II government, then the Karamojong cattle rustling, the Holy Spirit Movement of Alice Lakwena, the government of Uganda, and the Lord's Resistance Army (LRA) conflict. A big part of my life was lived through periods of conflict and instability; in fact, my entire life has been marked by instability.

I completed a hard-won bachelor of arts in social sciences at the Makerere University in Kampala, Uganda. Upon completion in early 2000, when the war intensified, I returned to northern Uganda to support humanitarian assistance to the conflict-affected community. I joined the Concerned Parents Association Uganda, an NGO that employed me to help reunite families and reintegrate children who had been abducted and forcibly recruited into the LRA.[1] In this role, I helped run some of the first education and vocational training support programs for war-affected children and youth. I also managed the first program to support girls and young women who returned from captivity with children born of war in the Lango subregion. In this role, I collaborated with the Uganda military to release children held in the army's barracks after encounters with the LRA and trace the families of these returning children in preparation for reintegration. I also worked with parent networks to prepare them to receive returning children and youth.

At the height of the war in 2004–5, I worked with Save the Children in Uganda as a child protection officer, coordinating initiatives to support children affected by armed conflict.[2] At Save the Children, I ran the first study and a program in Lira town with street children, whose numbers had greatly increased as a result of internal displacement. I also collaborated closely with both the Concerned Parents Association and Save the Children and other like-minded organizations throughout the war-affected subregions of Acholi and Teso to refer cases of children and youth across the region. I maintained contact with some of the women survivors, youth, and children whom I met in the course of my work. Years later, some survivors helped shape my research role and work.

In 2008 I graduated with a master's degree in humanitarian assistance from Tufts University, in America. I completed coursework on gender, complex emergencies, transitional justice, human rights, forced migration and refugee studies, and research methods. Upon completion, a professor asked me to join a research project in northern Uganda. I gladly accepted, based on what I had learned from the literature about northern Uganda for the completion of my thesis, namely that most existing research and studies were largely authored by Global North researchers, with limited studies by those native to northern Uganda. Reading and watching documentaries on northern Uganda's conflict left me with many questions about some of the reports, their intentions, and whose interests they served. I was convinced that a stronger insider focus would add value and lead to a better understanding and analysis of the local context and dynamics in the region. Existing studies on the region were also not representative of the conflict-affected communities in the whole of northern Uganda but were focused on one subregion (most severely affected by the conflict), even though other subregions were also affected. Yet, the outcomes of these studies largely shaped global humanitarian responses and interventions.

Based on these facts, an offer to engage in a research process in northern Uganda was thus a timely invitation to contribute to the discourse on the conflict and its impact from an insider perspective and in ways that reflect both diversity and commonalities. I was hired as a researcher by the Feinstein International Center, Tufts University, to support and coordinate research roles in Uganda. My brief was to conduct research reflecting on the diverse ways the conflict was fought and experienced and its continuing impact on the population—men, women, boys, and girls. I worked with Western colleagues and other South-based researchers and organizations to design and lead research on a range of themes, including ones that documented and analyzed serious crimes and violations and the needs and priorities of victims with a focus on remedy and reparation for justice and accountability. I also coordinated research efforts with other Western-based think tanks and South-based organizations in Africa, especially in other conflict-affected countries.

A Native Researcher in the Study Context

The position of a "local researcher" conducting research in their own locality calls for critical reflection because of such an endeavor's deeply embodied and complex nature (Jerven 2016). Conducting research in my native community since 2008, I have learned to remain aware of my position and how it matters throughout the entire research process—from design to analysis. The position calls for both rigor and a critical and reflective lens to limit possible bias and tensions (Punch 2012). In my different research roles and processes, I have kept these in the forefront of my mind to balance my delicate position as a native living and working in the context of an outsider study to avoid pitfalls and ethical dilemmas.

The term "local" in research provides the benefit of extensive knowledge of the local language and social dynamics important to generate an in-depth understanding of cultural perspectives that add value to research processes and analyses. However, being local also involves ethical dilemmas. While it can shape a researcher's work and influence their position during research on the ground, it can also make objectivity difficult, with little room for analytical distance (Taylor 2011). Localness is also contested and varies across context. While it may present some advantages for "local" researchers, it also comes with some challenges. A researcher who is not from the same region or ethnicity, does not speak the same language, or possesses a different level of education, social status, or even gender may be seen as other and not local by the local community. Some of the researchers, even though local, are educated in the capital city or Western universities and may not experience the same challenges as the rest of their community. Thus, a researcher's social as well as geographic distance matter in determining their localness among the study community.[3]

Reflecting on my role as a "Luo" woman from northern Uganda conducting research in her native setting first created a sense of belonging and connection with the study participants through shared cultural knowledge, language skills, and gender. Second, being local meant I deeply understood the language and the power dynamics inherent in local communities. I also did not have to rely on translation to carry out my work (Apio 2016). Being a native who lived and experienced the context of my study and having lived through the war in northern Uganda also helped me to better navigate my place and position as a researcher with the respondents in terms of what questions to ask, who to interview, where, when, and how to interview. It also meant I better understood and appreciated the participants' narratives and experiences. These identities were very important to my own research.

Yet, even though I had personally experienced the conflict, which gave me a good understanding of the context I studied, I did not assume that I knew everything. I paid attention to every detail of the participants' narratives of their experiences and stuck to the script in my analysis. I also worked with some survivors of the conflict on the study team to navigate the challenge of gaining trust among the respondents I didn't have a close relationship with. Further, I appreciated the diversity of people's experiences. I crosschecked my findings with secondary literature sources and conversations with other researchers to ensure I had not overlooked important points or normalized my experience as someone native to the region. Indeed, I often called respondents or elders several times to seek clarification or to revisit participants to flesh out specific findings.

My background provided me with ready contacts of some potential research participants who became important sources over the years. To illustrate, I often started research with women survivors of wartime sexual violence through contacts I established in my years as a practitioner to avoid the stigma and challenges of discussing tabooed and sensitive subjects with unfamiliar people. Yet, I was still aware of the challenges the work presented. Some of these acquaintances felt obligated to speak to me, yet with the expectation that I would help them access some assistance. These challenges made it hard to maintain objectivity and analytical distance. To counter this, I sometimes asked previous contacts to introduce me to unknown participants. I also worked with some women survivors who had been educated as research assistants to reach out to other women and members of their communities. These strategies provided an opportunity to hold in-depth discussions on the subject and to gain extensive knowledge, understanding, and analysis of the cultural context while limiting possible biases.

However, my education, socioeconomic status, and researcher position situated me as an outsider and rendered me different from the research participants (Ganga and Scott 2006). I was also aware that my researcher position produced power relations and hierarchies between the participants and myself. Some research participants saw me as carrying certain privileges and access to opportunities unavailable to them. I therefore had to apply due measures to secure access. Some participants believed that because I held more privileges than they did, I could assist with demands for support—toward schooling their children and medical needs or small inputs to boost their businesses. Some women, especially those without an education, also occasionally reached out to seek my advice on making decisions and other personal matters, as well as gaining support from local offices and officials. I still sometimes receive phone calls from participants in the midst of my own challenges, making it hard to meet their expectations and demands. Wherever I can, I provide connections to officials or organizations who can offer assistance or simply listen, which is also very therapeutic. In other cases, I had to constantly negotiate my position to not be seen as different and more powerful—an impression that would, in turn, affect the quality of the data.

I spent long periods in the field getting to know the study participants and erasing any doubts and suspicions. To ease the pressure on study participants, I also ensured that interviews were conducted in the participants' locations of choice and, at times, in places that were convenient for them. Throughout the interviews, I remained aware that the participants had other commitments and could leave whenever they wished since I could always go back to them, considering I was locally based. I also try as much as possible to keep my identities of researcher and educated woman away from my interactions with respondents, both in my appearance and behavior, to make them feel at ease as much as possible. It is a delicate balance to strike, as it depends on the participants' perceptions and not so much on what I think or do.

Internationalized Research Environment

Whereas, in theory, the importance of Global North–Global South collaboration in research is highly acknowledged, this is still a challenge in practice. In most postconflict settings, such as northern Uganda, research remains heavily internationalized, limiting the extent of local participation. The nature of research in these settings is extremely competitive because researchers from the Global North, often with more connections and resources, have the advantage over their local counterparts. In this section, I reflect on my experiences in different research projects beginning in 2008. It is of course impossible to account for so many years of research in one chapter, but I reflect on what I have learned over the years of collaboration with Global North researchers and institutions.

Projects I have been involved with include the Secure Livelihoods Research Consortium (SLRC), a multicountry and multiyear research project funded by the British government,[4] One Nutrition in Complex Emergency,[5] a USAID-funded research project in northern Uganda, and the Conjugal Slavery in War,[6] which covers several African countries. In the SLRC project, I was a key member of the Ugandan research team and part of the global gender task team that supported efforts to ensure gender mainstreaming in the research process.

My participation in different research projects varied depending on whom I was working with, my relationships with them (how long I had known them or not), and their own orientation in conducting research. My relations and positions with international researchers provided different ways to engage in the projects as a locally based researcher. Sometimes I formed only part of the overall process in which grant applications plus knowledge production were Westernized. I also formed part of design, fieldwork, analysis, writing, and dissemination at local, national, regional, and international levels—often working alongside colleagues from the Global North, who were invariably principal investigators and lead researchers.

FUNDING

Accessing research funding is always challenging for local researchers. The research-funding landscape (Western based) is structured to benefit Global North researchers who have the right connections, know the funding-application processes, and can meet the donor requirements. In most cases, these researchers are also based at institutions (universities or organizations) with the research infrastructure to support the success of their research applications and projects.[7] Conversely, local researchers suffer from the inability to obtain similar research grants. Their opportunities to access this funding are possible only through their collaboration with Global North–based researchers and institutions. They are always brought on board after successful grant applications or in response to an apparent need, expressed by potential funders, to include local researchers. The structure of research funding results in a hierarchical relationship between local and international researchers or institutions.

This dependency leads to an imposing view and projectized approach to research that does not boost the continuous professional growth and institutional development of local researchers. In most cases, local researchers are crowded out by their Global North counterparts. They do not get to take research-leadership and decision-making roles, a preserve for Global North–based researchers, who are also always the study leads or principal investigators. Instead, local researchers and institutions are drawn into Northern partners and funders' timelines and logical frameworks, while local research priorities and interest often get lost in the research process.

RESEARCH DESIGN

Ethically, research should be contextually appropriate and relevant, which calls for the consultations and the involvement of local researchers or institutions as part of the research design. The design should also incorporate local conceptual frameworks and literatures. Yet from experience, most studies are designed by Northern researchers or institutions without the involvement of local researchers or inclusion of local perspectives from the start. Even the conceptual frameworks and literatures used are those most familiar and readily available to the West or Global North. This means that local researchers cannot influence and shape the focus of the research, questions, processes, and eventual outcome of the research. This results in a lack of inclusion of local contextual knowledge and the absence of a culture of mutual learning as part of the research. Here, a real opportunity to incorporate local perspectives and views is often missed, as it comes only after several steps have already been concluded or checked off a list. Even where local contexts and realities are acknowledged by international researchers in the application, they are often not meaningfully adopted, which means the research becomes politically irrelevant to the local context.

Studies designed without a consideration of the local context deprioritize local needs and perspectives. The outcome may also not be readily accessible to the study participants or inform local policies and practices. In one of the multiyear and multicountry research projects I was involved in, a decision was made to conduct data analysis at the global level as opposed to different country levels, as had been the case in past years. A related decision was made to compile a synthesis report for the donor only. This absence of a country-specific analysis and report left local researchers without any access to either the data or final report of the study.

Decisions such as these reinforce the extractive nature of research; data is appropriated from countries of the Global South without direct benefit to local researchers and participants.

INEQUALITY IN COLLABORATIVE RESEARCH ENVIRONMENTS

Research designed and conducted to serve donor or Western priorities limits the roles of local researchers. It also increases the vulnerability and exploitation of local researchers in contexts where the stability of local researchers or institutions is dependent on foreign funds. In this situation, local researchers and institutions may agree to limit their role to gathering data as "research assistants" or "interpreters" for nonnative speakers while conceptual thinking is left to international or Western-based researchers and never challenged.

It is thus not uncommon for North-based researchers to take the lead in conceptualization and research design. Local researchers, on the other end, are left to execute field research, gather and translate the data as research assistants, or provide logistical support to the Global North researchers and organize the data into a coding scheme designed by North-based researchers. In this process, the analysis is also conducted by North-based researchers. Local researchers also face logistical constraints: poor transportation, low-cost lodging that may be unsafe, or lack of travel insurance or evacuation plans, even when going to dangerous locations. These may put them at increased risk when conducting the study, but they cannot object since they need the income.

Their engagement in research collaboration is always devalued to junior and less professional roles. To illustrate, in one research project, the local researcher (highly qualified, with a doctorate) who took part in the entire study process, from design to fieldwork and write-up, was relegated to receive and register participants at the research-dissemination event. At the same time, the Western-based colleagues were flown in to present the study findings. Under these circumstances, local researchers are left invisible, affecting their professional growth. These examples illustrate how hierarchies, partly shaped by identities, operate in internationalized research environments to the disadvantage of local researchers.

Some of these challenges are also reinforced in South-based institutions and organizations. Junior researchers are limited from exercising intellectual capability and creativity by their seniors. In the interest of delivering what is required by a North-based partner in a timely manner, senior researchers who have experience working with North-based institutions tend to discourage younger research staff from articulating new ideas or interpreting findings in ways that interrogate the conceptual framework of the study. Such hierarchies in research practice engender a postcolonial orientation to research that privileges North-based researchers and institutional setup.

The inequality and exploitation of local researchers is ethically problematic. First, relatively devalued work in research labor is conducted by local researchers with low financial and intellectual returns. By contrast, North-based researchers conduct value-added labor, yielding higher financial and intellectual returns. If researchers are not part of the writing process, they are rarely listed as authors or as last authors, and the failure to list those who gather data as authors reinforces the devalued nature of their research labor. The fact that journals do not come from the Global South and that academic writing skills and the language used (mainly English) are not as entrenched in places like Uganda as they are in the Global North adds to the challenge. It is more difficult for local researchers to meet high publication standards and gain the recognition that comes with it. Second, it leads to the exploitation and abuse of local researchers in a context where there is very limited opportunities to engage in research. Last, it results in research outcomes that do not benefit local researchers and the study population.

At the very least, local researchers and participants of any research deserve access to the information generated by and from them for their own work and advocacy (Wessells 2013). The focus on research to serve Western or donor needs is unethical and disempowers and even mutes the "voice" of local researchers and participants.

MUTUAL LEARNING AND CAPACITY BUILDING

Research processes based on participatory approaches and co-creation have the potential to contribute better quality outcomes and mutual learning.

Yet, in reality, most Western researchers tend to prioritize the timely delivery of research outputs over procedural aspects that would ideally offer the most benefit and best outcomes to local researchers. Specifically, emphasis on a technocratic approach limits consultation with local researchers. This, together with applying a supervisory model and attitude and often micromanaging the entire process, undermines trust and capacity building.

Local researchers are perceived to lack the capacity to undertake independent research, let alone the ability to publish good reports or articles in high-end journals. On many occasions, young and less experienced researchers from North-based institutions are sent in as representatives of the senior Western-based researcher. At times, they act as agents or spies on the local research teams and provide alternative reports to the senior Western-based researcher, even in the presence of the local research leads. They are positioned as more senior than the local researchers. Unfortunately, this power differential undermines the ability of these young researchers to draw from the experiences of South-based researchers when they come into the country. While reasons for this may vary, it is a missed opportunity for learning exchange and research co-creation, much to the detriment of the quality of the research.

A truly collaborative research process should seek to build trust and confidence with local researchers. It should also be carried out to create and ensure an inclusive, safe, and participatory space to harness local contextual knowledge and expertise to inform the research.

BEING LOCAL WITHIN AN INTERNATIONALIZED RESEARCH ENVIRONMENT

Whereas being "local" means a better appreciation of the local context and better access to research participants and audiences, on some occasions it posed a challenge to researchers. I have witnessed situations where some research participants were reluctant to engage with local researchers, while Global North researchers were often granted an immediate audience by officials who would not afford local researchers the same courtesy. Making appointments with officials also had this outcome. I was thus sometimes dependent on a Global North academic research institution to help me navigate the internationalized environment.

Respondents, especially government officials or those from international organizations, often took my requests for interviews seriously only once the identities of Western colleagues or institutions were revealed. On one occasion, the head of a Western aid organization (a White man) lashed out at me when I tried to follow up on an interview appointment he had gladly agreed to at the request of a Western colleague. In fact, some research participants (as in the above example) are more likely to give Global North researchers more attention and information than they would to a local researcher.

Even when I was granted audience, some research participants still viewed local researchers like myself as lacking the requisite skills and capacity to conduct research. The perception that local-based researchers lack capacity, but also have fewer resources and connections, partly influences the shoddy, unequal treatment they receive, as well as the lack of interest shown in their work. In general, research is largely framed and seen as something Northern researchers do better than locals; as a result, local researchers remain in an inferior position to their Global North counterparts.

Moreover, local researchers affiliated with international institutions, like myself, carry other identities that may cause some contestations locally. The education, social class, income, gender, and other identities some local researchers hold may increase expectations from the study participants. Their inability to fulfill these expectations may lead to mistrust among study participants, who believe they are being "used by the local researchers for their own benefits," especially when working alongside Northern researchers. This mistrust—usually reserved for Northern researchers because of their perceived privilege and the expectation to provide material assistance—could lead to the withholding of vital information even during interviews conducted by local researchers.

The experiences of local researchers elaborated here demystify the idea that a local researcher has better access to the study participants and information than a Northern researcher. Being local carries some positives for the research; it also presents some risks to local researchers, especially when researching sensitive subjects under authoritarian regimes. Whereas Northern researchers can return to the comfort and safety of their countries, local researchers and their families may be exposed to ongoing risk from the research. These experiences challenge the North versus South and the local versus international binaries and the ideas that being a "local" is dependent on one's country of origin or makes a researcher safer in the study context. In some contexts, local researchers may benefit from their association with Northern-based researchers, especially when publishing sensitive research reports.[8]

WHAT HAS CHANGED SO FAR?

There have been some changes in the research environment following global movements such as Black Lives Matter and the #MeToo campaigns, with more awareness and consciousness to changing practices in academia and research that recognizes local skills and expertise. It is now considered important to incorporate local researchers or research institutions as part of any research process. However, these efforts are still more about ticking boxes than real engagement and collaboration or partnerships. Additionally, some Western-based institutions are increasingly taking steps to localize their institutions and bring on board non-Western professionals. However, the structures of most of these institutions are not designed to make this possible, and where changes are attempted, there are still marked differences and inequality in terms of engagement between Western and non-Western colleagues. Local staff have different terms and treatment compared to their international or Western-based colleagues in terms of pay and other benefits and opportunities.

For as long as global research-funding systems are still Western-dominated or Western-based, it will be difficult to realize real change that recognizes local perspectives. Global South researchers will remain on the short end of research projects and grants generated from the Global North. Without careful attention and thought about what it means, there is a risk of objectifying the local and reinforcing local narratives that are based on Western/colonial understandings, undermining the intellectual capacity of researchers in the Global South (Bouka 2018).

In my case, my ability to navigate the internationalized research environment was due to the personal commitment of a few trusted colleagues to develop my skills and capacity and created opportunities for me to navigate the research environment. I have benefited from over a decade of committed mentorship and the support of a trusted Western colleague who walked the journey with me wholeheartedly. This colleague shared a strong desire to develop local expertise and committed to realizing it in its entirety: she has been a constant guide and fallback, support, and safeguard who facilitated access to opportunities for my professional growth. This experience taught me that it takes dedication and commitment over a long period of time to build the required skills in addition to building the necessary social connections in the field of research and, broadly, in academia. Importantly, when people feel recognized and are treated with respect as colleagues, as opposed to subordinates and juniors, it builds their trust and confidence to engage as part of a team. Of course, it is important to note that individual good intentions can be limited by institutional and structural conditions built on colonial legacies and White privilege.

MOVING FORWARD

Local researchers still face many challenges to gain stability in research or in an academic setting. The majority simply engage in research for survival. Moreover, the project-based nature of most research studies means that as soon as a project ends, their roles cease, and they may take on other research projects outside their expertise or move on to NGOs or the UN. Yet it is important that people who have experienced conflict in the Global South bring their perspectives to projects that scholars from the Global North cannot bring. However, scholars like myself find it hard to gain recognition because the challenges many Global South countries grapple with cause research funding to fall as a priority.

While correctives are also needed on the part of local researchers and institutions, the responsibility of coordinating and leading research studies often lies with international researchers and institutions. It is important to be aware of and to take measures not to reinforce these hierarchies based on researcher identities, roles, and positions. This can be achieved by following a consultative process in designing and implementing research, discussing in detail the role of each researcher, encouraging researchers who gather data in the country to get involved in data analysis and writing, being sensitive to language difficulties (especially writing in English), allowing more time for nonnative English speakers/writers to be part of the writing process, practicing fair budgeting (both in terms of the number of days and financial resources) by allocating sufficient days and resources for South-based researchers to deliver written outputs, practicing transparency in budgets by openly sharing with South-based researchers and accommodating space for discussing budget matters, setting realistic goals in terms of deliverables when planning research with tight timelines, leaving space for South-based researchers to be fully integrated into the research process, and placing value on all aspects of the research process by extending final authorship to those who gather data for the study—even if they had not been part of the writing process. Upholding ethical standards in research should not only protect research participants but also offer the same measure of protection to local researchers.

Ethical Dilemmas in Conducting Research in Conflict and Postconflict Contexts

In the following sections, I recount some of the dilemmas encountered in the course of doing research in a conflict-affected community. I refer to the challenges, especially with victims or survivors of highly stigmatizing crimes, such as women survivors of wartime sexual violence, children born of war, and other marginalized groups.

RESEARCH DESIGN AND FRAMING

Research in conflict and postconflict contexts sometimes is aligned with existing global standards or requirements of the funding country or institutions. Yet, some of these standards are not attainable in some local contexts or are not universally applicable (see Balami and Umar, this volume; Okyere, this volume; Ford et al. 2009). It is thus important that research framing is grounded in lived experiences and reality as opposed to a preconceived hypothesis or orientation and beliefs.

The paucity of information about the diverse ways conflict is experienced in different contexts is real. At times, some research projects impose a generalized view and way of studying the impact of conflict in ways that are insensitive to local reality. In one of the multiple-year and multiple-country research projects, we had to reformulate the Uganda component of the study to suit the local context by building questions about people's experiences of serious crimes into the research. Adding this nuance to the Uganda component of the study addressed the specific country context and made the study more relevant.[9] The study outcome was able to inform some of the donors to prioritize their funding to address war injuries among conflict-affected populations—one of the critical findings of the Uganda findings.

Some of the research I have been part of has also evolved from the exchanges and interactions with survivors or victims of the conflict to reflect the different voices and views. For example, some of the ideas for research emerged after listening to survivors share their experiences in a workshop or after in-depth discussions with organizations that work with victims of the conflict. For example, little was known about the fate of the missing and disappeared in northern Uganda. At the same time, most victims were more interested in discussing their postconflict reintegration challenges as opposed to emphasizing their wartime experiences. Some of the women in my study described the hardships they endured in the postconflict society to meet daily needs of food, shelter, their children's education, and access to medical support for injuries sustained in captivity that affected their abilities to do daily tasks. Yet research projects are often framed as if people are still in the conflict periods or primarily focused on wartime experiences. Moreover, retelling past experiences involved re-presentation and re-interpretation, which can present ethical dilemmas (Coulter 2009).

To this end, my research has shifted over time to give voice and relate to the daily experiences of victims of the conflict. Most of the studies I have been part of examine the enduring impact of the conflict on people's lives in the postconflict society. As conflicts end and normalcy returns, people's expectations, views, and perceptions change with time. To illustrate, survivors in northern Uganda no longer want to be simply seen as victims but as citizens with equal rights and status in their communities. In particular, women survivors of wartime sexual violence in Acholi preferred to be known by their present lives as survivors as opposed to their wartime experiences and identity as victims. Some of them were now grandparents and mothers-in-law, while some had children at higher institutions of learning, giving them a new way of presenting themselves in the postconflict community.

Research approaches that exclusively focus on wartime experiences risk eclipsing people's agency and their new identities as survivors. These insights require reframing research design and approaches in ways that address the complexities of people's postconflict realities to "do no harm" and foster "agency and dignity" among survivors of the conflict. In this context, how can research identify or interview potential respondents without disclosing their wartime identities or heightening the stigma they already suffer in their communities? These are important ethical considerations before commencing the study.

To address these challenges related to survivors to research design and framing, I (a) developed and adapted the study to the local context, usually by piloting it to give room for adjustments before commencing the study; (b) used open-ended questions that allowed for a deeper examination of research participants' experiences in the postconflict periods; (c) acknowledged that lived experiences of people are "expressed and are also fleeting" depending on the situation and moment in time (Coulter 2009, 20); (d) interpreted the participants' narratives in view of specifics and general themes without necessarily emphasizing any particular narrative over others; (e) considered the participants' stories in light of information from other sources—including local and cultural leaders, government officials, and the work of others—to refine my analysis (Coulter 2009; Apio 2016).

GAINING AND NEGOTIATING ACCESS WITH RESEARCH PARTICIPANTS

In conflict and postconflict contexts, exposure to violence often results in physical and psychological distress that heightens the vulnerability of conflict-affected populations. Some of these harms may lead to further violence in the postconflict period, which may become less manageable or worse than the original violations. Examples of such individuals may include victims of wartime sexual violence, children born of war, and formerly abducted persons, among others.

I have found that building trust and gaining some respondents' confidence has been challenging, affecting the research project's success. Specifically, what happens to people in times of conflict may affect the possibility of gaining their trust and confidence in the postconflict period, especially when it comes to sensitive, frightening, or humiliating experiences. Interviewing such people may require sensitivity to issues such as gender and sociocultural norms, values, and taboos; religious beliefs; and the existing legal framework.

These factors may mean some questions or research approaches are not suitable to the context or require more sensitivity and a reformulation of the research and ethical requirements.

The numerous assessments and the research in northern Uganda have created an environment of suspicion and mistrust in the conflict-affected population, especially in situations where the benefits of the research are not evident or mutual—which is the majority of cases. In particular, research fatigue has caused hesitation among some locals to participate in research. At times, some people speak of making calculated choices of whether or not to participate in research, especially on what information to provide to whom. Some people noted that they provide information based on what the researcher wants and their personal relationship or trust in the researcher. During one of the field visits in Gulu, a town in northern Uganda, some of the young women survivors told me they give information based on what someone wants to hear and not necessarily on what they know can be trusted.

This experience taught me the importance of adopting different research approaches and styles (depending on the topic and context of the research) to gain the trust and confidence of the prospective research participants. Earning the trust of study participants also requires a good understanding of the events and processes on the ground, which my local researcher position and knowledge accorded me (Shaw 2007). In one of the studies with young people who were engaged in what would be considered socially deviant activities—sex work, drugs, theft—around Lira town, we started by establishing where these activities were taking place and identified who was involved and how to access them without raising concerns with the local authorities. We learned that because of the nature of their activities, most of these youths were paranoid about the police and local authorities, who had raided their base several times. Several of them had been arrested, causing suspicion to be directed at people they did not know who could potentially be affiliated with the police or be local authority informants disguised as researchers.

Starting research in these contexts may require building relationships through ordinary conversations and interactions to enable participants to feel comfortable enough with researchers. At times, it means engaging in participant observation or hanging out with would-be respondents over long periods. In fact, I had known some of the women since 2002, when they returned from captivity; this was when I still worked as a practitioner, which helped to broker my role as a researcher, gain entry to potential participants, and build trust. Those who knew me understood that I had a long history of work on sensitive issues in northern Uganda. And with new contacts, I took small steps to gain their support before initiating any research, which included prior visits and interactions.

To deepen my relationships with some of them, I hung out at their restaurants/work and homes, which provided great opportunities to learn about their lives outside the research project. I paid them random visits—even on holidays such as Christmas, and we enjoyed spending time with them and my children. Over time, they started to feel comfortable in my presence and developed trust in me. Some women phoned me for advice on various issues, such as children, health, family matters, and relationships. Some of them would take me to a friend's house and introduce me to women I didn't know and facilitate the conversation. I gained much more knowledge about people through informal interactions than through traditional interviews. I also worked with other women survivors as a research assistant. These long-term relationships enabled me to delve deeper into sensitive gendered and intimate subjects of sexual violence.

Contacting young women in transactional sex in one of the postconflict towns in northern Uganda took several days. I casually or informally met them at their hotel to talk about the issues I was interested in studying to elicit feedback from them and support for the study. We spent long hours chatting at the hotel where most of them stayed. After some trust building, it was easy to introduce the idea of speaking to them and agreeing on a convenient venue and time to talk about their lives without interference or compromising confidentiality. The women preferred to meet for the interviews at a public hotel garden where they could be more anonymous, which guaranteed their safety than if they were interviewed from their hotel rooms.

This initial mapping/scouting helped me to gain trust, generate feedback on the proposed study, and negotiate access with the would-be respondents of a highly stigmatized and hard-to-reach group. They became comfortable speaking about their lives and getting to where they were—engaged in sex work. Some of the young women later introduced me to a few of their colleagues in other hotels or rented houses. The initial contacts helped me to determine how the research could move forward and ensured that the young women felt they could trust me and accept being involved in the research.

I always started interviews with those young women I had known before or with whom I had established enough rapport to speak in depth about stigmatized topics. Second, I only interviewed the young women who felt comfortable talking about intimate matters. The importance of long-term relationships allows access to safe spaces, especially intimate, gendered safe spaces to discuss delicate subjects. While the above strategies helped to influence my work positively, there was still the dilemma of maintaining objectivity and ensuring that the women did not feel obligated to speak to me on account of my past relationship with them. The challenge of managing and ensuring informed consent exists during informal interactions in private spaces such as people's homes, work, and family gatherings. At the same time, some personal conversations can be met with suspicion, especially in communities with strict gender norms. Researchers should always be aware of the delicate balance required to gain access and the importance of meeting spaces when conducting interviews. While some people may prefer private spaces, in some context or with some groups of victims, such as women engaged in sex work, public spaces are preferable because of the anonymity and safety it offers them.

OBTAINING INFORMED CONSENT

Informed consent acknowledges the importance of protecting and safeguarding research participants where there are unequal power relationships between the researcher and the researched. It is also about taking the necessary steps to ensure the confidentiality and the privacy of research participants are respected and upheld. Obtaining informed consent must be cognizant of the local sociocultural norms and environment and the associated sensitivities or taboos that may affect the research process. Any research process should be mindful of the multiple languages, low literacy rates, and other social barriers that may affect the process. Informed consent should be simplified on the understanding that many research participants in conflict and postconflict contexts may not possess the necessary literacy level to comprehend or even sign it.

In northern Uganda, over two decades of armed conflict left a considerable portion of the population in the region without any education. Yet, the research ethics requirement prefers written informed consent, which is impossible in this context. Research respondents, especially in rural locations, do not know how to read and write and thus cannot append their signatures to forms. In particular, the demand for informed consent for all interviews, where participants either sign or thumbprint, formalizes the processes and raises expectations. People signing their names in most settings expect some benefit in return. It also causes mistrust of the research process, especially when people consider the research meaningless if it lacks any link to humanitarian assistance or could expose them to grave dangers.

Whereas ethical practice requires that the researcher read out the informed consent to research participants, detailing voluntary participation without benefits, the high levels of vulnerability create some expectations of benefits from the research. My dual role in the research community—I was once a practitioner responsible for the provision of humanitarian assistance and now a researcher—at times caused a clash. Some participants mistook my researcher role as linked to the provision of assistance, which could have compromised their decision to participate in the research.

Moreover, the informed consent process in research sometimes clashes with local culture in northern Uganda, requiring people to be hospitable and receptive to visitors (Wessells 2013). Sociocultural norms and values in northern Uganda consider it unkind to decline speaking to a visitor, in this case, a researcher. Sometimes, people are bound by these cultural expectations and will accept participation even though it is against their interests. This raises concerns about whether informed consent meets its intended purpose. On a few occasions when some people declined to take part in research, they were demonized by other community members for their actions, even though this is acceptable in research.

My position as a local-based researcher with education and perceived higher social status, including some privileges and access to opportunities, comes with some expectations and creates an unequal power relationship with the research participants. As already mentioned, on many occasions, I have been asked to support the schooling of research participants' children or to provide some assistance to the family. Where there are unequal power relations, it is impossible to obtain informed consent in the true sense of the word. People may agree to speak out of respect or courtesy to a visitor even when they do not fully understand or agree to it, expecting that it might yield some benefits or help solve some of their problems. I have also been asked for assistance by participants while in the company of my colleagues from the Global North. Even after reading the informed consent to the study participants in detail, some ask me to tell my Global North colleagues about their problems, hoping *they* might assist them. These expectations are reinforced by the participants' vulnerability and unequal power relationship with the researcher, creating false hope for some benefits of participating in research. Aware of the low literacy rates among the study population, I chose not to have potential respondents sign forms but obtained oral consent from them. This approach limits any risk to participants and lowers any unnecessary expectations resulting from signing the informed consent forms.

MANAGING HIGH EXPECTATIONS

Ensuring the benefits of research to study participants is a constant struggle for researchers. Even though it is not always possible, at times, this may require taking the necessary steps to address the emerging concerns from research participation in the study design, such as putting in place referral pathways or safety measures for participants who may require it after the study. This requires a clear understanding of the study context in terms of the existing humanitarian assistance and services that the research participants might require. There must be clear modalities for study participants to access these services when needed or deemed important.

However, the reality is that most conflict and postconflict countries are poorly resourced with limited infrastructures or services required by the affected population, putting high expectations on research projects. This challenges researchers who manage expectations caused by an increased vulnerability related to the conflict. For example, sometimes there is a need to put in place referral measures for trauma counseling and other psychosocial support services such as medical referrals for war injuries when working with victims of conflict. Yet, as researchers, we have minimal control over these services or the organizations providing them, or these services may be nonexistent in some communities.

Moreover, it is also hard to draw a clear link between research and programs in conflict and postconflict contexts, especially for research participants to understand the linkages. How research projects inform and feed into programs and policies that could benefit conflict-affected populations remains unclear. Researchers have no control over using the research outputs to inform policies and programs or who benefits. The lack of clarity makes it hard to explain to research participants the distinction between research and programs or policies in a context of high needs or vulnerability. It is especially challenging, considering that much past research has not yielded any benefits to the participants.

To make matters worse, some research processes are highly extractive without any mechanisms to take back the results to the study population to aid their work and advocacy with their leaders. Even when the study reports are shared, they are not packaged in accessible forms to most people who cannot read and write, rendering the reports meaningless. Efforts to share the study results usually target local, regional, and national leaders, at best, on the assumption that they represent their communities or would pass the information downward. This is never the case; most research participants never get to know anything about the study after it is published.

The inability to meet the expectations of research participants or share research results with them may breed frustrations and resentment. Researchers must know this and devise measures to manage these challenges from the onset. In recognition of high expectations and material deprivations in the research community, we nevertheless sometimes offered small tokens of appreciation to research participants, especially where research fatigue was apparent. For example, in some longitudinal studies, we go back to the same respondents and households over a specific period. In other small qualitative studies, we provided culturally appropriate tokens to show appreciation for the participants' time. The tokens are one-offs and based on local customs of reciprocity during which a visitor would take a gift to the host. The gifts were not declared at the start of the interviews but only provided at the end in order not to influence the participants' responses. The gifts were very modest and acceptable by local standards, comprising, for example, a bar of soap and a kilogram of salt—the most basic needs in rural households. Again, the gifts were not standard but given when possible depending on research budgets; we were careful not to set a bad example for future research. Additionally, the Uganda national ethics authority, the Uganda National Council of Science and Technology (UNCST), requires that all research provide direct benefit to potential participants.

ETHICS REVIEW AND APPROVALS

In Uganda, the UNCST is the official body responsible for coordinating and guiding national research and development, including research ethics approval. Part of its mandate is to ensure research quality assurance and application systematically. It oversees twenty-six accredited Review Ethics Committees (RECs) based at different institutions. The REC accreditation is valid for three years. It is subject to continuing compliance with all applicable national standards and guidelines for RECs in Uganda and any additional stipulations or guidelines that the UNCST may provide (Ainembabazi et al. 2021).

To gain ethics approval in Uganda, one must apply to an accredited REC through the UNCST.[10] After approval from the REC, the study is submitted to the UNCST for final approval, done by the office of the president. At present, the ethics approval in the country is still highly centralized, with almost all the RECs based in Kampala, the capital. Only one is regionally based in northern Uganda—at Gulu University. Ethics approval is not localized; it is based on established Western models of research, which often neglect local realities and contexts.

Compounding the challenge of ethics approval in the country is the fact that some members of the RECs were observed in a study to lack the competence to review research protocols to protect the safety, rights, and welfare of research participants, especially those who worked outside their areas of expertise (Ainembabazi et al. 2021). This contributes to delays in research approval processes.

The entire ethics-review process is costly and cumbersome: it is long, tedious, and expensive—and paid in US dollars. Due to bureaucratic complications, ethics approval can take from three up to six months, which frustrates research initiatives, especially when working against tight deadlines. The process is centralized and only available in the capital city, away from the research sites or conflict-affected communities. In most cases, research studies are conducted under temporary approval from the UNCST, while final approval from the president's office normally takes a long time. Most of the research projects I have been part of concluded before the final letter of approval was received. The delays in country approvals frustrate efforts to meet research timelines, which means that researchers have to include enough time to go through research approval before the commencement of research.

It is important to note that incorporating research ethics approval into political processes or as a political tool further undermines the relevance and purpose of research ethics to safeguard research participants and ensure high-quality, ethical review standards (see also Okyere, in this volume). In the context of northern Uganda, where the armed conflict was highly politicized, it was sometimes difficult to gain approval for studies deemed politically sensitive. Researchers may, sometimes, have to compromise to gain approval or go forward with the study.

It also appears that a few of the ethical review processes required in some Global South countries are based on Global North principles and procedures, which may be rigid and unadaptable to the local context. For example, the UNCST has introduced an online application system for all ethics review and approval, but the system is very complex and difficult to navigate, especially in areas with very limited internet connectivity and access. The online platform has, in my view, increased the bureaucracy and delays related to obtaining ethics-review approval in the country. Strictly adhering to ethical research requirements (most often based on Global North experiences and norms) may violate local norms and may not be on par with the local context. The strict procedures could also create the opposite of the intended purpose of protecting respondents. Nonetheless, it is still important to consider the practicality of attaining ethics approval in different contexts because it is an important step in safeguarding the rights and safety of research subjects and local researchers.[11]

RESEARCH "TARGETING"

Research targeting some groups of victims in times of conflict or the post-conflict period requires some degree of sensitivity and paying serious attention to their vulnerability. In some cases, the research could lead to increased or deliberate targeting of the study participants. Under this circumstance, it is not advisable to include some highly sensitive cases in the research if the risks outweigh the benefits for the study participants. Alternatively, the study could be undertaken by highly trained researchers under a clear methodological approach that guarantees the research subject's safety.

In the context of northern Uganda, where the armed conflict disproportionately affected some groups of people in the community more than others also led to the disproportionate targeting of some victims by research. For instance, the LRA primarily targeted boys and girls between ten and eighteen years of age. Girls as young as twelve years old were given out as forced wives to rebel commanders who repeatedly raped and sexually violated them (UHRC and UN OHCHR 2011). Studies report that one-quarter of all the girls and women abducted by the LRA in northern Uganda and kept in captivity for more than two weeks were given to commanders and other fighters as forced wives; half of these girls and women gave birth to children. The associated stigma and ostracization from experiencing sexual violence and returning with children born of war complicate the lives of female survivors and their children in their families and communities (Annan et al. 2008).

These experiences have led researchers in northern Uganda to "overtarget" and focus research projects on the populations affected by armed conflict: formerly abducted persons, women survivors of wartime sexual violence, and children born of war. For instance, many studies focus on young women returning from the LRA with children—not on men and other victims. This specific emphasis on categories of vulnerable children and women results from donor priorities and researchers' theoretical preconceptions. Notably, other categories of victims of the conflict, such as *the missing* (those who were abducted but never returned or are still unaccounted for), are often left out by research projects because their plight is not as apparent. Yet, in reality, the neglected categories often experience more or even tougher challenges in postconflict communities since they cannot find closure.

A mother whose three children went missing during the war and never returned tells how the experience changed her social status in the community; she spoke of the impact of not attending marriage ceremonies and other key social events since she will never be able to hold such ceremonies in her home. Other households who had lost children or loved ones during the armed conflict also explained their losses in terms of ongoing challenges in the postconflict period. Families who lost breadwinners are unable to send children to school or are forced off their land in traditional settings where land ownership is largely negotiated by the male head of the household.

The complex ways the conflict is experienced point to the fact that vulnerability is highly contextual and different for different people. As researchers, we ought to learn from conflict-affected people about the different causes of their vulnerabilities—and those who are the most desperate—to avoid assumptions. We should challenge our epistemologies to explore the difficult subjects and themes surrounding people's lives in conflict and postconflict periods.

RETRAUMATIZATION OF RESEARCH PARTICIPANTS

Having conflict-affected people talk about their frightening, humiliating, or degrading experiences with violence can result in increased trauma (Ford et al. 2009). In particular, experiences of some crimes, such as wartime sexual violence and rape, can lead to increased stigma and trauma for survivors in some communities.

The sensitivity related to cultural taboos around sex and the associated stigma makes it hard to approach the subject with ease, causing issues of trust and suspicion among the victims (Coulter 2009; Apio 2016). Most women survivors of wartime sexual violence have never openly identified or discussed their experiences of violation in depth. This could be because they question the relevance of the information and the confidentiality of the responses. When research questions, processes, and outcomes are disconnected from local reality, they may only add unnecessary stress to the study community, leading them to view the research as meaningless.

Working in the context of armed conflict for years made me aware of the emotional trauma and toll involved in having participants recount their histories of violence and the fact that it may not be meaningful to them. I was also aware of the associated taboo and stigma and designed the studies in ways that limited or avoided it altogether. I therefore chose to focus my central research on the impact of the conflict on people's lives *today*—with the understanding that it has an enduring impact. By doing this, the research participants did not have to actually describe their violent experiences but rather how their conflict experiences continue to influence their present-day lives and relations in their families and communities. I chose this path because I understand that recalling these violent episodes in their lives would cause additional pain for them.

All my in-depth qualitative interviews were conducted without voice recordings to avoid contributing to the participants' anxiety. I handwrote my notes with care to protect their anonymity and confidentiality. I carried out multiple conversations and followed up with each respondent to capture the diverse realities that were impossible to capture in one interview. I worked with local researchers, including research community members, to overcome trust issues and difficulties that could have arisen from the study. In some cases, I did not need to ask in-depth questions but could combine the interviews with observations, occasional chats, and secondary information from other studies. These multiple approaches enabled me to cross-check contradictions and seek clarifications from individual participants, which enriched the narratives without causing the participants distress or trauma.

Discussions and Conclusion

Research in conflict and postconflict contexts provides an important service to ensure that people's lived experiences are understood and addressed by programs and policies. However, due to the nature of armed conflict and the resultant danger to populations, unique ethical dilemmas are present in conducting research in these environments. Researchers must carefully consider their research designs and methods in order not to cause additional unintended harm to study participants.

Notably, a critical review of research methods in conflict and postconflict contexts provides an opportunity to improve research methodologies used in these settings to align them with international human rights standards and research ethical guidelines. The way the research unfolds also determines the validity and reliability of the study outputs, which means that research outputs are assessed on the strength of the methods applied and, in this case, whether the safety and rights of study participants were an important consideration. However, care must be taken to ensure that the ethical processes in these volatile contexts are appropriate and made less cumbersome—in consideration of the difficulties in these settings. Often conflict and postconflict contexts lack the necessary infrastructure to facilitate research, especially at the local level. At the same time, the exposure to violence in the population may also heighten their vulnerability and distress.

Embedding the research in the study context is an important first step to ensuring that research projects are ethically sound. This may entail a Global North–Global South research collaboration, either through a partnership with Global South research institutions or by working with researchers from the Global South as part of the research process. While this is laudable, the model has nevertheless presented challenges insofar as it neglects the actual contributions of Global South researchers. The latter are rarely meaningfully engaged as equal collaborators and partners from the start of the project. Beyond ensuring ethical standards, there is a call to ensure that research collaborations between the Global North and Global South are not exploitative and not harmful to the process of knowledge production and the professional growth of South-based researchers. Without acknowledgment of their contribution and work, they risk remaining on the periphery of research initiatives and academia at large.

Notes

1. Concerned Parents Association is a local grassroots organization created by the parents of abducted children in northern Uganda to advocate for the unconditional release of all children held by the LRA rebels and the army and to support

the return and reintegration of these children. See "Concerned Parents Association Uganda (CPA-Uganda)," Peace Insight, last updated August 2015, https://www.peaceinsight.org/en/organisations/cpa-uganda/?location=uganda&theme.
2. A consolidation of Save the Children Denmark, Norway, UK, Sweden; with Save the Children Norway as the lead organization.
3. See Fitzpatrick et al. (2023).
4. The Secure Livelihoods Research Consortium (SLRC) a global research program exploring livelihoods, basic services, and social protection in conflict-affected situations. SLRC was established in 2011 with the aim of strengthening the evidence base and informing policy and practice around livelihoods and services in conflict. Secure Livelihoods Research Consortium, accessed January 11, 2023, https://securelivelihoods.org/.
5. See "Feed the Future Uganda One Nutrition in Complex Environments," Research, Feinstein International Center, Tufts University, accessed January 1, 2023, https://fic.tufts.edu/research-item/one-nutrition-in-complex-environments/.
6. See "Home," Conjugal Slavery in War, accessed January 1, 2023, https://csiw-ectg.org/.
7. See Fitzpatrick et al. (2023).
8. See Fitzpatrick et al. (2023).
9. See the Secure Livelihoods Research Consortium, accessed January 11, 2023, https://securelivelihoods.org/.
10. Uganda has twenty-six RECs accredited by the UNCST. The REC accreditation is valid for three years and is subject to continuing compliance with all applicable national standards and guidelines for RECs in Uganda and to any additional stipulations or guidelines provided by the UNCST. See Ainembabazi et al. 2021.
11. See Fitzpatrick et al. (2023).

References

Adriansen, H. K. 2017. "The Power and Politics of Knowledge: What African Universities Need to Do." The Conversation. September 28. https://theconversation.com/the-power-and-politics-of-knowledge-what-african-universities-need-to-do-84233.
Ainembabazi, P., B. Castelnuovo, S. Okoboi, W. Joseph Arinaitwe, R. Parkes-Ratanshi, and P. Byakika-Kibwika. 2021. "A Situation Analysis of Competences of Research Ethics Committee Members regarding Review of Research Protocols with Complex and Emerging Study Designs in Uganda." *BMC Medical Ethics* 22: 1–7. https://doi.org/10.1186/s12910-021-00692-6.
Annan, J., C. Blattman, K. Carlson, and D. Mazurana. 2008. *The State of Female Youth in Northern Uganda: Findings from the Survey of War-Affected Youth (SWAY) Phase II*. Medford, MA: Tufts University, Feinstein International Center.
Apio, E. O. 2016. "Children Born of War in Northern Uganda: Kinship, Marriage, and the Politics of Post-conflict Reintegration in Lango Society." PhD diss., University of Birmingham.
Bouka, Y. 2018. "Collaborative Research as Structural Violence." Political Violence at a Glance, July 12. https://politicalviolenceataglance.org/2018/07/12/collaborative-research-as-structural-violence/.

Coulter, C. 2009. *Bush Wives and Girl Soldiers: Women's Lives through War and Peace in Sierra Leone*. Ithaca, NY: Cornell University Press.

Fitzpatrick, M., I. Cordua, T. Atim, A. Kattakuzhy, and K. Conciatori. 2023. "Co-investigators but with Different Power": Local Voices on the Localization of Humanitarian Research. Boston: Feinstein International Center, Friedman School of Nutrition Science and Policy at Tufts University, and Network for Empowered Aid Response.

Ford, N., E. J. Mills, R. Zachariah, and R. Upshur. 2009. "Ethics of Conducting Research in Conflict Settings." *Conflict and Health* 3 (1): 1–9.

Ganga, D., and S. Scott. 2006. "Cultural 'Insiders' and the Issue of Positionality in Qualitative Migration Research: Moving 'Across' and Moving 'Along' Researcher-Participant Divides." *Forum Qualitative Sozialforschung/Forum: Qualitative Social Research* 7, no. 3 (May). https://doi.org/10.17169/fqs-7.3.134.

Hilhorst, D., and N. Douma. 2018. "Beyond the Hype? The Response to Sexual Violence in the Democratic Republic of the Congo in 2011 and 2014." *Disasters* 42: S79–S98.

Jerven, M. 2016. "Research Note: Africa by Numbers; Reviewing the Database Approach to Studying African Economies." *African Affairs* 115 (459): 342–58.

Mazurana, D., L. Gale, and K. Jacobsen. 2013. "A View from Below: Conducting Research in Conflict Zones." In *Research Methods in Conflict Settings: A View from Below*, edited by D. Mazurana, K. Jacobsen, and L. A. Gale, 3–24. Cambridge: Cambridge University Press. https://doi.org/10.1017/CBO9781139811910.003.

Punch, S. 2012. "Hidden Struggles of Fieldwork: Exploring the Role and Use of Field Diaries." *Emotion, Space and Society* 5 (2): 86–93.

Shaw, R. 2007. *Rethinking Truth and Reconciliation Commissions: Lessons from Sierra Leone*. Vol. 130. Washington, DC: United States Institute for Peace.

Taylor, J. 2011. "The Intimate Insider: Negotiating the Ethics of Friendship When Doing Insider Research." *Qualitative Research* 11 (1): 3–22.

UHRC (Ugandan Human Rights Commission) and UN OHCHR (United Nations Office of the High Commissioner for Human Rights). 2011. *The Dust Has Not Yet Settled: Victims' Views on Remedy and Reparation in the Greater North, Uganda*. Kampala: UN OHCHR; Kampala: UHRC.

Wessells, M. 2013. "Reflections on Ethical and Practical Challenges of Conducting Research with Children in War Zones: Toward a Grounded Approach." In *Research Methods in Conflict Settings: A View from Below*, edited by D. Mazurana, K. Jacobsen, and L. Andrews Gale, 81–105. Cambridge: Cambridge University Press. https://doi.org/10.1017/CBO9781139811910.008.

TWO

Reflections on a Collaboration between a European Doctoral Student and a Congolese Assistant Interpreter

SYLVIE BODINEAU AND APPOLINAIRE LIPANDASI

The concept of *situated knowledge* developed by postmodern feminist scholars argues that all forms of knowledge reflect the particular conditions in which they are produced and are influenced by the (situated) points of view linked to the social positions (e.g., race, gender) of knowledge producers, as well as the power relations between researchers and their subjects. This perspective exposes the illusion of transparency of the scientist as a "modest witness" (Haraway 1988) who is supposed to guarantee an objective approach. It also challenges the classic subject/object of study binarism that puts researchers in a dominant position vis-à-vis the subjects of their research and the knowledge produced—a dynamic that is particularly operational (and common) in the context of research carried out in the Global South by researchers from the Global North. It calls for researchers to take a more accountable approach in recognizing the influence of affiliations and representations that come into play in the intersubjective relationships established by and during research, which in turn, influence the knowledge produced.

The setting up of any system of knowledge production, in particular by researchers from the Global North in the Global South, therefore requires reflexive effort by the researchers to identify the characteristics of their positionality in order to recognize—and mitigate—the influences it has on their data collection and analysis processes. The approach is progressively acknowledged in academe—particularly in anthropology and feminist studies—and required for all ethnographic process, even if it is still unevenly practiced. This reflexive approach is, however, far less often applied than desirable to collaborative relationships, which are nevertheless common, especially when researchers from the Global North "land" in the Global South. Indeed, as some authors have pointed out (e.g., Musila 2019; Bouka 2018), collaboration in its many different forms (Muzalia 2020) encapsulates unequal relations of domination and invisibilizing researchers from the Global South in multiple ways. It is in this context that in October 2018, researchers from Ghent University convened a two-day workshop entitled "(Silent) Voices from the Field: Exploring New Avenues for Collaborative Research" to reflect "on the challenges and dynamics of doing research together 'in (and beyond) the field.'" During this workshop, a manifesto[1] was published engaging researchers in an approach toward integrating transparency, equitability in diversity, modesty, creativity, and unsettling minds to transform the status quo. In the wake of this reflection, *(Silent) Voices* and the *Bukavu Series*[2] blogs emerged in 2019—a series focused on research in post-conflict environments or "under uncertain, unstable and insecure conditions" (GIC Network 2019) that "seeks to give space to those (Silent) Voices that often remain invisible in the production of knowledge" (Ansoms et al. 2019).

This chapter is our contribution to the effort of reflection for change in order to decolonize research. It provides an account of the collaboration between us (a European doctoral researcher and a Congolese assistant interpreter in the field of the study) in research on humanitarian interventions to protect child soldiers in Gemena, Democratic Republic of Congo (DRC). Rather than developing a common narrative that would run the risk of reiterating the domination of one voice over the other, we have chosen to present our individual points of view to offer readers our different perspectives on the research and our collaboration. The text, presented using our alternating perspectives, addresses the following: the research methods, our mutual interactions and interactions with the participants, our positionalities, and their implications. We underline the importance and sensitivity of mediation to establish a bond of trust with participants, to show how expectations and mistrust toward a White researcher in postcolonial Congo have been managed, to discuss the relationships and mutual interests of collaborators, and to attempt to identify the implications for the research results.

Sylvie

The objective of my doctoral project was to undertake an anthropological analysis of a humanitarian intervention aiming at protecting child soldiers known as *kadogos* ("small ones" in Swahili) in the DRC, where, since the "Liberation war" in 1996, child recruitment by armed forces and groups had become common practice. Drawing on Merry's concept of the vernacularization of rights (1996; 2007), I examined how the child rights regime that supports these interventions had been implemented, put into practice, and articulated—in particular, how the global ideal of childhood conveyed by the rights of the child had been circulated, put into action, and locally negotiated within the program. One of the most salient findings of this exploration was how former child soldiers, as a way of preserving their dignity, turned away from the victim position offered by the programs meant to protect them and refused to be caught in a humanitarian narrative that erased their voices. Instead, they used the encounter to claim—sometimes through violent means—what they considered to be "their due" as ex-combatants.

These findings emerged from a critical analysis of practices in the program. I focused on the discourses and practices of the protagonists (interveners and beneficiaries), considering that they were at the center of the humanitarian transactions, and where the "monolithic block" that the intervention represented confronted its field of application and crumbled, diluted, diversified, and/or deviated. Following a specific approach for an "ecumenical" (i.e., both critical and ethically committed) anthropology of human rights (Goodale 2006), my research scheme included a number of orientations.

In the first place, I adopted an interpretative approach integrated into a constructivist perspective which assumes that social phenomena and facts looked at in a "narrowed and specialized" way (Geertz 1973) are understandable in the context of those who use them, live them, and refer to them. My intention was to capture a collective experience of the intervention, and more particularly to understand it from the points of view of those involved in it: in particular, the stakeholders and beneficiaries. Because these are past events, the raw material of the research would consist of accounts of the protagonists' experiences.

Second, a certain amount of rigor was required to drive my entire approach. Following the proposal of Sardan for a "rigueur du qualitatif" (2008), I wanted to account for the phenomena on which my research was focused to do justice to the participants and "to recognize [my] subject as human as [me]" (Riles and Jean-Klein 2005, 190), while taking responsibility for the interpretation of their stories. My intention to think of a humanitarian practice with an aspiration to renewing the children's rights regime involved a search for a fair position between observation, mediation, and support for my interlocutors with the aim of understanding their aspirations and/or claims.

In the ideal setting, the tradition in and requirements by anthropology as a discipline, affirmed by many authors (Saillant, Kilani, and Bideau 2011;

Leservoisier and Vidal 2007), would be a stay in Gemena for a few months, or even a few years, in order to interact with the environment, to understand its history and language and how it shapes encounters, conversations, and interlocutions, and to grasp as closely as possible the meaning of my interlocutors' stories. As I did not have the time and resources for such a learning experience, I recruited a research assistant who could interpret and carry out logistical tasks and, as a consequence, accept what I considered at first to be an interpretation bias between the participants and myself. I asked the coordinator of the NGO working with child soldiers to recommend someone who was not directly involved in the program but who knew the relevant environment and spoke fluent French. This is how I met Appolinaire Lipandasi, who was the perfect candidate: a man of discreet, patient, and generous character, who demonstrated seriousness and competence and became a central pillar of the project.

Appolinaire

It all started when the executive secretary of the NGO, who was hosting a researcher, told me they were recruiting a research assistant, and that after consultation with their staff, the choice fell on my modest person, based on my background and experience in the local associative sector. I was immediately taken to the NGO office where Sylvie was; a smiling White woman who, getting up from her chair, greeted me as if we already knew each other from before—even calling me by my first name, "Appolinaire." This very first gesture of warm contact was enough to reassure me about what would happen next and put me at ease in the research process. In the room there were two tables with two chairs. Sylvie showed me the second one saying, "Here is your work table," and I occupied it immediately before starting the dialogue.

Our first discussions revolved around my background—who I was, and what I did—before getting to the heart of the matter. I told myself that I did not have much to tell her about myself: "I am Congolese, originally from the territory of Gemena, married, living with my small family in Gemena city. I am currently executive secretary for the Sud-Ubangi Red Cross, but before that I was a teacher and for years a manager of a private trading company based in Gemena. I am also a treasurer of the Bureau de Coordination des ONGD du Sud-Ubangi, an active member of the Coordination de la Société Civile, and initiator of a development NGO for environmental management and other community activities in the field of health and agriculture."

This was followed by Sylvie giving me a detailed presentation of the constituent elements of the research, its objectives, the interlocutors, the geographical area to be explored, the working methods, the advantages, the risks, and the potential disadvantages linked to participation in this research—with particular emphasis on the confidentiality of both data and the identities of the participants.

Feeling sufficiently informed about the ins and outs of the work, I agreed in principle to contribute to its implementation. I signed a written confidentiality agreement form that was to be our behavioral guide throughout the research and a contract stating the terms of payment and working conditions, including provisions ensuring that the process ran smoothly and would protect all stakeholders from any potential harm during research. These protective measures were a safeguard against any eventuality, and in fact, no problem was reported.

Sylvie

Taking into account the context, in consultation with Appolinaire and the coordinator of the NGO partner of the research, I decided on a data collection system whose modalities would evolve following a continuous back-and-forth movement between field and analysis, including a series of interviews and workshops/focus groups in four stages: three phases of data collection and a fourth phase of presentation of the main ideas emerging from a first data analysis followed by discussions and comments. The recruitment of the participants was carried out with the help of the NGO, starting with identifying the interveners (social educators, volunteers, psychologists, artisan trainers, transitional host families) who referred us to beneficiaries of the program (ex–child soldiers and demobilized young adults) whose number was increased by snowball sampling. After adding family and community members, the total number of participants was about sixty.

Much of my research relied on storytelling. Based on a biographical approach and in particular on the work of Ricoeur (1983) on the topic of narrative identity, I considered the personal stories told by my interlocutors as revealing their social universes. Working on stories with an interpretative approach invites us to question the nature of the distance between the actions as they were experienced and the story that is made of them because we have to deal with a sort of "mise en abyme,"[3] for example, in the specific case of my research: between the memory the narrator has of a (past) experience and the story he or she chooses to make of it in the (present) space of the interlocution. This space is itself influenced by the intersubjectivity between researcher, participant, and translator and made even more complex by the very nature of the experience, which is linked to violence. So I tried to frame the collection of stories in several ways. First, I limited them to the experience of the intervention (as opposed to life stories), while asking my interlocutors to go back to when the war broke out, wartime being both the origin and the framework of the child soldiers' recruitment. Furthermore, interested in the subjectivity of the participants, I asked them to tell me in their own way, taking as much time as they wanted, about their experiences directly or indirectly related to the humanitarian program before, during, and after the conflict.

Appolinaire's place in this arrangement was central: primarily to interpret our words but also and, importantly, to establish a bond of trust with the participants. Of course, the addition of a third party to the interviews added to the "thickness" of the ethnographic process (Marcus 1998). And there was of course a risk that the presence of someone from the community would result in our interlocutors holding back on certain aspects, or even adopting a performative position (speaking to the community through us). But by shifting the relationship, his presence elicited a more "local" form of discourse and counterbalanced the risk of the participants claiming, complaining, or repeating "official" narratives.

Appolinaire

The first task I was assigned was the translation of different consent forms from French into Lingala, which is the local language. It was my "baptism by fire" because after having finished the translations, Sylvie submitted the forms to be read and reviewed by the staff of the NGO to be sure it conformed with the French version (because, as the old Italian saying goes, *Traduttore, traditore* [To translate is to betray]). The feedback was positive, so I felt confident in my capacity to undertake the work.

Regarding the organization of the encounters (interviews and meetings), I was in charge of personally contacting the participants by phone, or at home the day before (especially young people, artisans, foster families), to confirm that everyone would be present. Every day I took Sylvie on my work motorcycle to our interlocutors' meeting places, which generally were their homes and sometimes their offices. A planning briefing would take place on the previous day and a debriefing at the end of the day before we separated. This gave us the opportunity to discuss the adventures of the day as well as the points of view of the interlocutors, not to modify them but to capture them better and agree on our understanding of them.

During the interviews or organized meetings, I bridged the gap between Sylvie and the research participants, translating her words to the participants and vice versa in order to allow everyone to fully understand the normal course of the discussions. My work, my past, and my personal relationships were an asset for connecting and initiating discussions with the various participants. Everywhere we went, it was rare for me not to recognize someone in the family, the office, or the environment where we were welcomed because my activities had allowed me to make contacts and have very good relations with the inhabitants of the town of Gemena and its surroundings.

Given that the city of Gemena is a cosmopolitan environment, my knowledge of the various local cultures was used implicitly (and explicitly) for the success of the interactions with the various interlocutors of the research. For example, I was in a position to facilitate situations in which research subjects experienced the following: reserve toward a foreigner with whom they had no affinity; wariness of a person who did not speak their language or dialect; desire to not give many details to NGO members and staff who come to the community with questions about their experiences, because when funding comes in, NGO staff do not or rarely want to include the people who participated in the initial assessment; hesitancy to speak, especially by women, who are expected to speak less when in front of a man or a group of men; and so on. My knowledge was expressed through the way we entered households, approached families, and held discussions, maintaining a climate of conviviality so that the interviews could be successful. This is also why it was rare for us to confront categorical opposition from our interlocutors identified by the staff of the NGO who had led the aid program for young people.

Sylvie

When we were in homes, our interviews took place in the shade of a wall, a tree, or a hut near the house; Appolinaire and I would sit on the seats that were offered to us—generally the most comfortable—at a sufficient distance so that passersby and neighbors would not be able to understand what we were saying.

It was an opportunity to travel around the city of Gemena, to understand its layout, the distances, peculiarities, dysfunctions, rhythms, and particular events—and to locate each of the participants in places that were, most of the time, familiar to them, which allowed them to feel more comfortable. It was also an opportunity to be seen everywhere on the back of a Red Cross motorcycle driven by a respected member of the community (constantly greeted by passersby), greeted by the children with cries of *mundele*—meaning "White" in Lingala—which was the subject of a joke with Appolinaire when I pointed out to him that his popularity was reinforced by my presence at his side.

After consulting with our interlocutors about the language in which they wished to be interviewed, each meeting commenced with reading the consent form—in Lingala by Appolinaire or in French by myself—followed by additional discussions on the subject of the research, its repercussions and its progress, in response to questions asked by our hosts. Before giving their consent, a few interlocutors discussed with us the risks involved in participating (fearing in particular re-recruitment or military retaliation), and one of them challenged the way we proposed to proceed, asking for remuneration. And even if they were not expressed at the time, concerns about risks or what we would do with the collected data appeared later and were often mentioned to Appolinaire outside of our interview times.

Once the consent formalities were completed, we began the interviews with "free" accounts from our interlocutors. We regulated the form of our communication based on the tone, emotion, and intensity evoked in them during this first story, according to their rhythms and to the degree of precision that they offered, not insisting on the subjects they wanted to keep quiet about. Our language evolved, incorporating the expressions most commonly used to talk about war, activities within armed forces and groups, within the program, or to express emotions and feelings.

In terms of translation, Appolinaire often interpreted my ideas rather than my sentences, giving, as Sardan describes, a "semiological translation, that is to say to the passage between the local system of meaning and the researcher's system of meaning" (2008, 85; my translation). This required not only a phenomenal memory to grasp long uninterrupted monologues but also a capacity to empathize with our two worlds whose different meanings he articulated. The particular nature of semidirective interviews following the same pattern allowed him to refine his interpretations upon requests for clarification or explanations. In fact, our interlocutors understood French most of the time but would ask for help to check their understanding and to feel more comfortable with their use of vocabulary.

During our meetings a triangular relationship was established. My interlocutors and I took turns to address Appolinaire, which allowed each of us (the participants and I) to address someone familiar and to observe the other while they were paying attention to the interpreter. I noticed how much this situation facilitated communication in comparison with the interviews carried out in French with participants who did not speak it fluently. When we conducted interviews only in French, the direct questions required increased attention and resulted in poorer content due to the lack of a common vocabulary rich enough to hold a conversation.

Appolinaire

At first glance I wondered if these young people would easily let themselves be convinced to conduct exchanges and/or discussions with us about their past, which for some were not good memories to recall. In the community these young people had a reputation for being capricious, not having sufficient regard for the elderly, and always ready to attack anyone who dared reveal their secrets (especially military ones) that would expose them.

It is in this context that many interview subjects asked questions in Lingala (either in private when we met or even before the start of the interviews with Sylvie) to establish if the research in question was not a veiled investigation in relation to the trial of Jean Pierre Bemba, who was then at the International Criminal Court, and especially those who had been part of the Mouvement de Libération du Congo (MLC) armed group. They sometimes expressed concerns about this, and some even thought that the Congolese government was considering reconscripting them into military service, which is why it used this strategy to identify them. Since I was sufficiently informed about the research, I always reassured them that I could not, as a son of the land, join a conspiracy that would likely harm them over time. The consent form with Sylvie's contact details and those of Professor Dibwe (from the University of Lubumbashi)[4] that they signed before the start of the interviews (and of which they kept a copy) was also reassuring for them.

I still remember the words of many who expressed their confidence in me about doubts that troubled them and made them wonder if they might not be threatened after the interviews: "Appolinaire, you are our old man. We know you very well in the arena. We know who you are, what you do, and you will not be able to betray us or hurt us. We trust you." As the days passed, the research process continued with meetings presenting the first results of the data collection, and they really understood that our exchanges fell exclusively within the framework of scientific research.

This trust from young people who had never participated in such research opened up new horizons for me; I became a reference person and/or adviser for some, and we still see each other from time to time. Not long ago, I ran into one of my former research subjects at his place of work (a private initiative) with his wife and who, seeing me, immediately warmly introduced me, saying: "Here is my old man I was telling you about." The woman greeted me with a welcoming smile, saying, "Thank you very much, *Papa*. I'm happy to meet you because my husband told me about you and I really wanted to meet you and say hello."

Sylvie

The position in which I was immediately placed vis-à-vis all my interlocutors, characterized by the recurring call mundele, was essentially linked to my gender and my "Whiteness" in contrast to their "Blackness." This positionality, induced by the weight of the history of Western intervention in the DRC (Koddenbrock 2013), placed us in a situation of social and economic inequality and introduced a presumption of superiority on many levels, influencing my relationships with Appolinaire and the participants.

Born in West Africa and having worked more than half of my life on the continent, I have long been fully aware of the unequal relations of power between Whites and Blacks that cause tension and also lead to certain expectations of each other. It is by identifying and acknowledging the manifestations of this injustice daily that we (Blacks and Whites) can mitigate any adverse effects as much as possible. I consider my scientific engagement fully included in this perspective, both in its ethical aspects and in the form of an epistemological approach committed to the full respect of human rights. During my research, I therefore strove to establish egalitarian interpersonal relationships in terms of work but also by sharing, when relevant, information about myself, my feelings, and my family. Because, as Rességuier very elegantly says about "small things" in the case of humanitarian workers,

> they may be a particular look or smile, a cigarette shared with a beneficiary, a brief chat with a refugee child, or a sense of shared commitment across one's team or organization.... These experiences are not the "cherry on the cake," they are the cake itself: the main chunk of what makes our lives meaningful and worth living.... Small can also be intense and beautiful when it comes to touch us from within. It is what connects us to the real matter, to what really matters. In that sense, it is the heart of the ethical experience. (Rességuier 2015)

Adding to the significance of this supposed superiority, the power relations between Appolinaire and me were characterized by our contractual relationship.[5] I was both initiator and head of research and indirectly the employer of Appolinaire, who acted as an assistant. It was therefore my responsibility to make and assume the epistemological and methodological decisions related to the research and lead the way as it unfolded. However, I systematically asked Appolinaire for his opinion on the method, the comments exchanged with the participants, and their interpretations. In the course of our encounters and meetings, we thus engaged in constant reflection on the modalities of the research methodology, which was evolving. We also held frequent exchanges on what was entrusted to us, as well as on sharing the various emotions evoked by our immersion in the memories and the present world of the participants.

With respect to the participants, my position was replayed at each new meeting. But by collaborating with Appolinaire, I no longer faced this alone. There was no longer a *researcher* but a *research team*. This contractual operation, which responded first to a linguistic necessity, undeniably transformed the positionality of the research as a whole. For several participants (in particular the former child soldiers), Appolinaire was the reference point of the research. I determined the central questions and led the epistemological approach (discussed with him outside the interviews), and Appolinaire played a mediating role between us (the participants and me) translating beyond simple interpretations. His role as a facilitator went in both directions. This played a considerable part in the degree of trust placed in me by the participants.

FIGURE 2.1. Appolinaire and Sylvie, a research team in the field.

Appolinaire

Since colonial times, the DRC has seen massive influxes of White people on its soil to live alongside the Black people there. Generally, the Whites led easy and comfortable lives: electrified houses, good food, quality clothes and shoes, convenient transportation, the best-equipped hospitals, access to drinking water, and so on. The Blacks lived miserably: in slums, scantily dressed in either animal skins or tree bark, walking barefoot, curing themselves with traditional medicine, living on the products of harvests and hunting, and so on. This lifestyle gap was even more noticeable between the natives and the White missionaries who came in the name of Black evangelization. They lived in parishes or missions built of durable materials and equipped with the necessary comforts for healthy and comfortable lives. The highest administrative functions in the country were occupied by the Whites who lived in obvious luxury while the Blacks had to be satisfied with hard manual labor inflicted on them by the settlers (in the plantations or mining deposits) sometimes without any compensation or remuneration, with the exception of a few rare Blacks emancipated by White settlers and selected from the families of customary chiefs of the host country.

The first traders who arrived were Whites from Europe, bringing manufactured goods with them to sell to Blacks who barely had any money. My grandmother, who had just reached ninety-eight years of age when I visited the other day, told me:

> My father exchanged his big rooster for a few cigarettes with the missionaries, and a basket of chicken eggs for a glass of salt or sugar. There was no standard of measurement. Banknotes and coins were more visible and in large quantities in White hands and rarely in Black hands. The schools where White children studied were well equipped compared to those of Black children, and no Blacks except those who worked as domestic workers were allowed to attend the White quarters, under pain of facing forced labour, lashes or imprisonment, etc.

Nowadays, even with independence, a semblance of democracy, and universities putting intellectuals in the job market, the country still has such an outward-looking economy that all the big funding that comes into the country comes from outside (from the northern hemisphere) in the form of development aid or public debt. Technology being more advanced in the Global

North than in the Global South, most products used in the countries of the South come from the North.

My work in the humanitarian world for over fifteen years has allowed me to observe many social and professional inequalities between Blacks and Whites. NGO funding for development projects in under-equipped countries comes from countries and international organizations with headquarters in the North (among Whites). And if an agreement is signed for financial support, we observe it is led by a team of Whites who arrive with working conditions totally different from those of the Blacks who are engaged or involved in the same project or program (office, salary, accommodation, means of transport, means of communication). When it is necessary to meet and have discussions with local communities and collect data on the ground, local project staff are put in the foreground until the preparation of reports, which are then cleaned up by White teams and finally bear their signatures. As the same causes produce the same effects, the situation is reflected in the production and dissemination of knowledge where collaborators from the Global South are used for data collection but are ignored during its dissemination for the benefit of researchers from the Global North.

This set of elements being visible and observed for decades by the Black population have been imprinted on their minds and has led them to believe that all that is good (represented by the color white) belongs to the Whites, while ailments (represented by the color black) constitute the lot of the Black man. This is how White skin has generally come to be considered as synonymous with wealth—and the presence of the White man in an environment is believed to augur the presence of money or wealth. So because I was very visible in the city in the almost permanent company of a foreigner (and moreover a White one), many people thought I was engaged in a new aid program brought into the community. And during that period, because I was keeping company with Sylvie, I was seen as someone who could not run out of money.

It is for this reason that many requests for help (financial or material) were addressed to me directly, or indirectly to my wife, by neighbors or friends in the neighborhood. There were times when friends would come to me and ask me for a position in the program they felt was run by the visitor and in which I held a high position. Others, like some Red Cross volunteers, were curious and thought that the provincial committee had received a visit from a partner of the International Red Cross and Red Crescent Movement (International Committee of the Red Cross and the Red Crescent, International Federation of Red Cross and Red Crescent Societies or Participating National Societies) to support community activities in favor of the population and especially the most vulnerable category, as they had seen them queuing in the province after the hostilities in the Dongo sector.

From personal conviction, I have always raised the awareness of my Congolese brothers (during our conversations, meetings in groups) and told them that the policy of begging from foreigners reduces our values and our dignity and that we must work courageously to earn our living. It is even for this reason (and to avoid encouraging this practice) that we made the choice not to pay the participants. In all cases, I was careful to explain to everyone that my work was simply done for the research. Some understood and believed me, while others were a little skeptical, thinking that I was refusing them the favor of including them in the program that would enable them to have a job and support their families. They eventually understood that my statements were not intended to deceive them.

My own family readily understood my participation in the research because I had explained the work that I had to do as a research assistant from the first day of my contact with the researcher, while refraining from giving them details about the interviews we had with the different target groups. I remember the words of my wife, who encouraged me by asking me to invest myself in the success of the work because I was going to be paid for it and that the result would count for the person who believed in me by collaborating with me.

Sylvie

What are the elements that may have gradually led our interlocutors to join this research initiative? And what are the indicators that permit me to consider that, in a way, my thesis is the result of collaboration?

Pragmatically, we can think that the participants who agreed to share part of their histories with us may have found an interest in the enterprise that was not only material or financial in nature. Participation in the first phase of the research was certainly granted out of respect and politeness to our intermediaries, mixed with curiosity and a few questions. But respect and curiosity are not enough to explain why some of the participants covered miles on motorcycles or bicycles and took two to three days of their time to join the workshops and meetings that followed the interviews. When questioned about their motivations, they said they appreciated the fact that our encounters allowed them to remember personal stories—buried or put aside—that they never had the opportunity to share in this way. They also expressed their interest in continuing the conversation, believing their experiences were worth sharing to improve similar programs in the future. For the former child soldiers, in particular, it was about being heard by the decision makers in national and global spheres. This also confirms the spirit of protest that emerged from their testimonies and shows how they intended to use my positionality—my belonging to the global world and my connections to the national space—to carry their message.

Many elements characterized our relationships and influenced the research. I identify three types here: mutual terms of address, emotion sharing, and the aid relationship. In Gemena, as in other parts of the Congo, one is addressed either by a term that qualifies the relationship, sometimes placed before our most familiar name (*mon petit, mon vieux, mon ami*); or by one's qualification or status (*coordo, chief, engineer, doctor, prefect, dean*); or by a generic title (*monsieur, madame*) which evolves, when familiarity and respect appear, into *papa, maman,* or *tantie*, intimating a bond and a certain tenderness. These names or terms of address mark the degree of distance or proximity between people but also the rights and duties that accompany it and the reciprocity that they imply. When French is used, we use the formal term *vous* to address a person, except with children and young people and people we are familiar with when we use the informal *tu*. At the beginning of my stay, people who knew me a little called me *madame Sylvie* and used *vous* with me; the members of the NGO were the only ones who simply called me *Sylvie* and used the informal *tu*.

Following the example of Appolinaire, I was formal with adults and informal with younger people. The use of *vous* or of *tu* did not change much over time between us. But the terms of address did. And this change—which saw young people, supervisors, and members of the NGO call me *maman Sylvie* rather than *madame Sylvie*, and call Appolinaire *vieux* or *papa Appolinaire*, rather than *secretary* (his function at the Red Cross), and saw Appolinaire and I calling participants *papa, maman, mon ami, mon cher,* or *mon petit*—testified to a greater proximity and mutual trust, allowing more in-depth exchanges and implying a reciprocity which committed me to a higher degree to account for their stories. The relationship between Appolinaire and myself also evolved. While I was familiar with him, using *tu* from the beginning, he addressed me with *vous* for a long time, before occasionally using the familiar *tu* (which is how he addresses me today), which perhaps testifies to a progressively more egalitarian collaboration, even if I remain his elder both in research and age (as he is a little younger than me, I often joke by reminding him that he is *mon petit*).

Emotions were another of the ingredients of our connections and emerged during our conversations and informal exchanges. During this research, they undeniably colored our understanding, appearing in a manner neither linear nor predictable but not unexpected as we, Appolinaire and I, were aware of their part in the conversation. I mentioned the care we took to match the tone of our remarks to that of our interlocutors. In the same spirit, before the meetings, we did our best to let go of our own concerns and to be fully available to follow their mood as closely as possible. We let this approach guide our relationship, allowing us to be attentive—in addition to their way of living in present events—to their recall of the past that we evoked together. Our interactions were diverse, made up of bitter discussions, provocations, jousting, teasing, jokes, and enthusiastic spikes but also moments of silence and intense listening, marked by crossed looks and smiles, tears, bursts of laughter, pride, annoyance, sadness, depression, avoidance, jaded airs, sharing, and recognition. There were moments of appreciation during the interviews or workshops, striving together in a joint endeavor to articulate their experience (them to explain as best as possible, me to question as accurately as possible, and Appolinaire to translate these two dynamics).

Finally, as already mentioned, in research with the most vulnerable, requests for aid are a regular recurring element. While we are aware of the inequalities and were tempted to help the research participants, professional ethics require a certain degree of caution in this area. We have to place our relationship in a framework that limits interference with data collection. During this research, requests most often manifested themselves in a very humble manner at the end of the interview, and once in a more aggressive form before I even started (a young man wanted me to offer him my recorder). Passersby also waited until the end of our interviews to call us out and ask if they could be enrolled in the aid program that they thought I represented. In close consultation with Appolinaire, who faced even more requests, I made sure not to establish any dependence on potential help from the beginning of our relationship with the participants. But we do not deny that help was provided to some individuals, following requests made at the end of my first stay (and at the beginning of the second), when our relationships became closer, and my data collection almost complete. All of this support was ad hoc, provided in an official manner (for example, aid from the Red Cross), and did not engage us in a relationship of interdependence that would have been complicated to manage in my absence, but nevertheless reaffirmed in a certain way the quality and humanity of our relationships.

Appolinaire

The research allowed me to acquire a sum of information that I had no access to and to understand what drove the people who designed the program to protect and assist former child soldiers at the global level, as well as the constraints confronted by humanitarian workers at both intermediate and local levels.

It was an opportunity for me to discover certain facts and realities of the environment relating to the social, economic, and psychological conditions of life of young people who have left or been demobilized from armed forces and groups in the DRC. Although I lived in Gemena and in the region, I was completely unaware of the realities and motivations of young people who joined armed groups, and behaved the way they did vis-à-vis civilians, members of their own families, and state and nonstate leaders. For example, it is generally known and widespread that children ended up in armed forces and groups by forced recruitment and that the programs were implemented to assist them as victims of circumstances although, according to some young people we met, they had voluntarily joined armed groups to defend their homeland, or to avenge a family member who had been tortured or murdered by other armed combatants.

The statements of some young people made a strong impression on me because, like most people of the province, I could not have imagined such reflections on their part. I realized that they had the skills to analyze situations and were able to understand the society in which they live. Some of them said they had joined, willingly or by force, either the MLC rebellion or the armed forces of the DRC: the former to defend Sud-Ubangi against the soldiers of the Congolese government with their allies who had mistreated the population, the latter to defend the homeland, which had been invaded by foreign forces. But ultimately, they saw themselves being abandoned without any program meeting their expectations and denounced the difference between the program for demobilized adults and the ones for children released from armed forces and groups, even though they had served the Congolese nation in the same way as adults. They stated that in the army there is no difference between child and adult with regard to the activities or tasks to be carried out (alluding to the guard service, participation in combat, border protection, and more). They considered this an injustice planned by the program designers in complicity with the implementing NGOs.

Sylvie

It is generally understood that completing a thesis is a rather solitary exercise, although not necessarily so, intended to assess a student's ability to carry out research from start to finish. In the process, those associated with the effort, as well as the consequences for both participants and collaborators, are often disregarded. My case was no exception. I was alone in initiating the research and defending my thesis before the jury. But I was definitely not alone in undertaking it. The result, my thesis finally written and defended, would have been quite different—or would not have existed at all—without my collaboration with Appolinaire. I should also acknowledge all the research participants, particularly the former child soldiers and social workers who were the focus of our attention.

The collective story told to us by the protagonists of the intervention demonstrates that the children who enlisted in the armed forces and groups during the conflict and who then became beneficiaries of the protection program aimed at reintegrating them into civilian life had many choices to make, motivated and constrained by circumstances. In fact, the question of their agency is central since, characteristic of their approach following their enlistment and in opposition to the humanitarian portrait of them as innocent victims, it places them as actors responsible for their own fate and articulates the tensions and the transactions that took place within the program. I would not have been able to perceive that with such richness without my collaboration with Appolinaire, who facilitated and enriched the participation of our interlocutors.

Therefore, when the moment came to design a postdoctorate project to continue my/our investigations into the situation of former child soldiers fifteen years after their demobilization in the same region, I wanted to undertake it with a more engaged and participatory approach. The group of young participants from my doctoral research who wished (to our great happiness) to be associated with it (thus becoming coresearchers) unanimously agreed that Appolinaire should be the local coordinator of the research and asked that the NGO overseeing this collaboration be the Red Cross, of which he was executive secretary.

We are therefore moving toward more collaborative research, which continues our triangular relationship. While within the framework of my thesis I was the only one making epistemological choices, together we will now have to think about and elaborate on the research questions, the methodology, and the interpretation and dissemination of the results but also conceive of the best way to manage both our diversity and the stark inequalities that characterize us. This effort will, I hope, contribute in a modest way to a meaningful reflection on the decolonization of research.

Appolinaire

Each time we ended a phase and Sylvie had to leave again, I was responsible for transcribing the various discussions that had taken place (interviews or meetings) while maintaining contact with the NGO, the participants, and Sylvie. The transcription work was an opportunity for me to recall the different stories told by each of them. It was also the first time I had given myself to such an exercise, which at first seemed a little difficult; however, since practice makes perfect, I ended up familiarizing myself with the work.

The methods of data collection—the way people were approached combined with a presentation of the results to the participants—constituted an apprenticeship for the young, ambitious future researcher I had been back then. I had unconsciously developed a desire to conduct research that could lead to the publication of an article or scientific work.

It is undeniable that apart from the scientific aspects one of my interests in the research was the financial aspect—that is to say, it boosted my household income in an environment which had recently emerged from various wars, each of which had a negative impact on the daily life of every citizen. The economic fabric of our lives had been completely destroyed, and recovery was still slow in coming. Bilateral discussions (between researcher and research assistant) or in groups with other people have greatly opened my mind to grasp and understand certain socioeconomic aspects of the daily life of the people of our province.

In short, I came to understand that the methods used for the collection of research data were appropriate for those involved in the research. By methods I mean field trips to meet the interlocutors at home instead of inviting them to our office. Or in other cases it was explaining the objectives pursued by the research, signing research participation consent forms with copies reserved for the participants, asking for their opinions before recording the interviews, or allowing the participants to tell their stories freely instead of simply using a questionnaire. The participants were even allowed to tackle topics that seemed outside the scope of the research so that they felt comfortable expressing themselves and asking questions on certain aspects that might have been touched on superficially. If I had been asked to do this job in my own way, I would have limited myself to using a simple questionnaire with a semistructured interview, which would not have given me enough information to analyze the situation. In addition, in most cases accountability in terms of feedback to people who participated in the research or to institutions that collaborated in carrying out the work is not considered systematically, as it was in this research.

In Europe and elsewhere, funds from public or private institutions support research studies around the world, and one can become eligible according to preestablished criteria. However, in our country, with its outward-looking economy, researchers are required to battle on alone (like a castaway without help on a desolate sea) with their own means, which, moreover, are paltry, or perhaps with the help of family members who occupy high positions in the country's political regime. In my opinion, this element constitutes a bottleneck for researchers from the Third World in general and from my country (the DRC) in particular, where even access to scholarships is a headache if one does not have a support in the upper echelons of the country's management.

Southern researchers' lack of information about funding mechanisms and the difficult process of accessing funding granted by countries of the North intended to support research throughout the world increase their vulnerability. As the research is done with a view to producing public knowledge (construction of knowledge), and keeping in mind that this is a long-term job, a certain number of elements are required: time, materials, methods, and techniques to be used for data collection and analysis, finances, relationships that must be maintained with all stakeholders and exchanges of experiences with other perspectives around the subject to be examined.

Another not-insignificant aspect is the southern researchers' knowledge of the study environment (security environment, population lifestyle, schedules, culture, and social relationships between men and women, between young and old, between able-bodied persons and persons living with disabilities, between civilian and military populations, between young girls and young boys, and between literate and nonliterate persons), which captures not only the visible but also the subtle elements expressed during encounters with participants, because in any community there are always things left unsaid and only understood by informed people. A researcher from the South has this knowledge of the field but for lack of the necessary means is confronted with constraints of a logistical, material, and financial nature and problems of identity (sometimes a simple student in search of data to supplement end-of-studies work is considered someone who seeks to earn a living at the expense of poor populations through the data collected—the inference applied to NGOs). A researcher from the North enjoys certain considerations from authorities and local populations and has easy access to the resources necessary for work—but sometimes comes up against difficulties of a cultural, linguistic, and security nature and problems of identity (as a result of being considered the bearer of wealth and thus creating expectations).

What We've Learned

Based on this experience, it is our view that when deciding to carry out research in a postcolonial country such as the DRC, a person coming from Europe or the northern hemisphere should take the realities of the countries and the factors mentioned above into account in order to integrate harmoniously into the geographical area to be explored. To achieve this, it is wise to consider frank collaborations based on a balance between researchers from the Global North and those from the Global South. This would be a key to success and an opportunity for fruitful exchanges between associates, which could be capitalized on by both sides for future situations or events. Considering decolonization of research as a dynamic rather than a "state," we hope that such collaboration will help to gradually and significantly reduce the gap between the Global North and the Global South in the field of scientific research; in short, a harmonious, equitable, and balanced combination of resources (material, human, financial, even temporal) needs to be mobilized for this purpose, hence the need to involve the local researcher upstream as a partner in the research project: not only for methodological reasons but also for the construction and analysis of the data resulting in publications of results that make the latter visible as well.

Notes

1. "Manifesto: New Avenues for Collaborative Research" (GIC Network 2019).
2. "The 'Bukavu Series' is the result of a collaboration between the Land Rush Programme, spearheaded by the Institut Supérieur de Développement Rural de Bukavu, and three partners of the Governance in Conflict network: the Université Catholique de Louvain, the Groupe d'études sur les conflits-Sécurité Humanitaire, and Ghent University" (Ansoms et al. 2019).
3. "Mise en abyme" is a process of telling a story within a story within a story in order to create perspective. It comes from the principle of fractal geometric figures or the mathematical principle of recursion.
4. Professor Donatien Dibwe dia Mwembu was the local academic referent in case of complaints or criticism about the research, which he was in charge of forwarding to the Office of the Ombudsman at Laval University. Consent forms mentioned this fact and provided Professor Dibwe's phone number.
5. Appolinaire had signed a formal employment contract with the NGO that I was partnering with. The partnership and cooperation between the NGO and myself was formalized by an agreement defining the conditions of research and the expenses that I would be funding. Appolinaire's salary, discussed between him and me beforehand, was part of these expenses.

References

Ansoms, A., E. Mudinga, K. Vlassenroot, A. Nyenyezi, and G. Muzalia. 2019. "Invisible Voices in the Production of Knowledge: Introduction to the (Silent) Voices *Bukavu Series*." *Bukavu Series* (blog), Governance in Conflict Network, June 3. https://www.gicnetwork.be/introducing-the-bukavu-series-invisible-voices-in-the-production-of-knowledge/.
Bouka, Y. 2018. "Collaborative Research as Structural Violence." Political Violence at a Glance, July 12. https://politicalviolenceataglance.org/2018/07/12/collaborative-research-as-structural-violence/.
Geertz, C. 1973. *The Interpretation of Cultures: Selected Essays*. Vol. 5019. New York: Basic Books.

GIC Network. 2019. "Manifesto: New Avenues for Collaborative Research." Accessed February 2023. https://www.gicnetwork.be/silent-voices-manifesto/.

Goodale, M. 2006. "Introduction to 'Anthropology and Human Rights in a New Key.'" *American Anthropologist* 108 (1): 1–8.

Haraway, D. 1988. "Situated Knowledges: The Science Question in Feminism and the Privilege of Partial Perspective." *Feminist Studies* 14 (3): 575–99.

Koddenbrock, K. 2013. "The Ambiguous Practice of Intervention: A Critique of the Self-Evidence of Humanitarianism and Peacekeeping in the Congo." PhD diss., Universität Bremen, Bonn.

Leservoisier, O., and L. Vidal. 2007. *L'anthropologie Face à Ses Objets: Nouveaux Contextes Ethnographiques*. Paris: Éditions des archives contemporaines.

Marcus, G. E. 1998. *Ethnography through Thick and Thin*. Princeton, NJ: Princeton University Press.

Merry, S. E. 1996. "Legal Vernacularization and Ka Ho'okolokolonui Kanaka Maoli, The People's International Tribunal, Hawai'i 1993." *PoLAR: Political and Legal Anthropology Review* 19 (1): 67–82.

———. 2007. "Introduction—Conditions of Vulnerability." In *The Practice of Human Rights: Tracking Law between the Global and the Local,* edited by M. Goodale and S. E. Merry, 195–203. Cambridge: Cambridge University Press.

Musila, G. A. 2019. "Against Collaboration—or the Native Who Wanders Off." *Journal of African Cultural Studies* 31 (3): 286–93.

Muzalia, G. 2020. "'Businessisation of Research' and Dominocentric Logics: Competition for Opportunities in Collaborative Research." *Bukavu Series* (blog), Governance in Conflict Network, June 23. https://www.gicnetwork.be/businessisation-of-research-and-dominocentric-logics-competition-for-opportunities-in-collaborative-research/.

Rességuier, A. 2015. "'Small Things' in Humanitarian Work." *Mindfulnext* (blog). http://mindfulnext.org/small-things-in-humanitarian-work/.

Ricoeur, P. 1983. *Temps et Récit: Tome 1; L'intrigue et Le Récit Historique*. Paris: Éditions du Seuil.

Riles, A., and I. E. F. Jean-Klein. 2005. "Introducing Discipline: Anthropology and Human Rights Administrations." *PoLAR: Political and Legal Anthropology Review* 28 (2): 5–17.

Saillant, F., M. Kilani, and F. G. Bideau. 2011. *Manifeste de Lausanne: Pour Une Anthropologie Non Hégémonique*. Montreal: Liber.

Sardan, J.-P. 2008. *La rigueur du qualitative: Les contraintes empiriques de l'interprétation socio-anthropologique*. Vol. 3. Louvain-la-Neuve, Belgium: Academia Bruylant.

THREE

Research with Children Born of War

A Sensitive and Ethical Methodology

BETH W. STEWART

During the twenty-year war in northern Uganda, thousands of children were born into the rebel group known as the Lord's Resistance Army (LRA).[1] Their mothers (and often fathers) were abducted by the rebels and forced into marriage-like relationships in which the children were conceived (Stewart 2020). The fortunate ones survived and transitioned out of the LRA (escaped, were released, or were rescued), usually with their mothers, some with neither parent, and the odd few with both parents. Children born into the LRA[2] are part of a global population born of sexual violence and coercion during armed conflict, often referred to as "children born of war." More specifically, children born into the LRA were born of forced marriages in war, representing a specific pattern of sexual violence and coercion in conflict situations around the world. This chapter is based on a longitudinal study in northern Uganda with twenty-nine children born into the LRA who transitioned out of the war when they were between two and nine years old. After a brief overview of the topic and context, I review the study's methodology and methods. Using the case of one participant, I demonstrate how the mix of methods enabled the production of knowledge about the children's subjective sense of themselves and their lived experiences. This is followed by reflections on the disconnect between theorizing and conducting such research—on the difficulties, complexities, and impossibilities—and how the ethic of reciprocity offers a starting point for mitigating the problems. Ultimately, this chapter aims to present an ethical and sensitive methodology that I hope can inform and be adapted for research with children born of forced marriage in war in other contexts.

When I first met with mothers of children born into the LRA in 2011, they highlighted a lack of attention by nongovernmental organizations (NGOs) and researchers regarding the needs of their children. They expressed concern about their children's well-being and futures and provided a comprehensive list of the many complex issues they faced. A top issue was social exclusion in their communities and even families, which echoes the documented experience of children born of war in other contexts (Kahn and Denov 2019; Lee 2017; Erjavec and Volcic 2010; Coulter 2009; Rimmer 2006). The mothers of these children also listed other concerns, including access to education (Ojok 2020), access to their paternal clans, and psychosocial/spiritual support. This study with children born into the LRA began as a response to a gap in this research and the advocacy by their mothers.

Children born into the LRA are part of a global population of children born of war, including "persons of any age conceived as a result of violent, coercive, or exploitative sexual relations in conflict zones" (Carpenter 2007, 3). The small but growing body of literature addressing children born of war has been largely based on their mothers' perspectives, resulting in primarily descriptive scholarship incapable of explaining the unique subject position of the children. While this scholarship about children born of war offers valuable conceptual direction, the voices of children born of war were widely absent at the outset of this study in 2011 (Akello 2013; Seto 2013; Carpenter 2007; Das 2007; Watson 2007). Within the context of this growing field, however, new empirical work is emerging from studies in northern Uganda and other places affected by wartime sexual violence. However, those best informed about the problems are the children themselves: "Children and young people are capable of providing expert testimony about their experiences" (Thomson 2009, 1). Since this study began, the field of children born of war, including research in northern Uganda, has shifted toward centering the voices of the children (Lee 2017; Denov and Lakor 2017; Stewart 2017, 2015; Apio 2016; Ladisch 2015; Erjavec and Volcic 2010). This shift calls for a methodology that can effectively address the children's unique security and confidentiality concerns, be responsive to their cognitive development as young people, manage significant researcher-participant power discrepancies, build trust, and encourage meaningful knowledge production.

The Study

The study informing this chapter (Stewart 2017) was my doctoral research, initiated in response to a request relayed by my PhD supervisor, Erin

Baines, who had been working for years with mothers of children born into the LRA. The request from the mothers was for someone to give attention to their children (Baines 2017). The study subsequently set out to answer the following questions: How do the children experience their everyday social lives? How do they make sense of their experiences? What strategies and resources do they use or access to help navigate their everyday lives? What macro and micro processes lend insight into or explain these experiences? To answer these questions, I spent a total of eight and a half months in the urban center of Gulu town in northern Uganda over a period of five years from 2011 to 2016. This included a preliminary two-week visit plus a five-month stay with my family in 2011, followed by one-month visits in 2013, 2015, and 2016. During this period, I followed the lives of the twenty-nine young participants born into the LRA—who requested that they be referred to as children in the resulting publications despite the fact that they had moved toward or into adulthood during the course of the study. In 2011, most participants resided in Gulu with their mothers, save for two whose parents either remained in the bush or had been killed. The children were between the ages of two and nine when they transitioned out of the war.

A research assistant and a local organization supported the research in profound ways throughout the five years. My research assistant Aloyo Proscovia,[3] who resides in Gulu, served as a translator during the research activities that I conducted in person. In my absence, Proscovia also facilitated two to three additional group activities with the children each year, between 2012 and 2020. These meetings continued after the end of the study at the request of the children. My relationship with Proscovia is further explored in the coming pages.

I was partnered with a local organization, the Justice and Reconciliation Project (JRP), and worked closely with members of its Gender Justice Unit, from the start of the study in 2011. Through a memorandum of understanding, we agreed to terms that were mutually beneficial. Logistically, JRP helped me to find a research assistant and identify participants, also providing office space, access to drivers, plus a secure and private compound to use on weekends for research activities. In exchange, I made financial contributions to general office supplies, paid for resources specifically used for the study (e.g., the use of a vehicle and driver), and submitted a comprehensive report that was published by the organization (Stewart 2015). Perhaps the most valuable aspect of the partnership was the opportunity for Proscovia and me to discuss problems and concerns with JRP's Gender Justice Unit staff, who were already deeply familiar with the lives of children born into the LRA and their mothers. Together we identified and evaluated issues affecting the children, problem-solved situations raised by them or their mothers (while maintaining confidentiality), and discussed ethical concerns. There were inevitable trade-offs, including the likely possibility that the mothers and children expected benefits from me. Problems also arose from blurred boundaries of our partnership with JRP, which I discuss later in this chapter. Despite these challenges, both JRP staff and Proscovia were essential partners throughout the study. Without their cultural knowledge and skills (language, counseling, networking, organizing), their familiarity with the issues being studied, and their challenges to my inevitable ignorance and blind spots, this research could not have happened.

Based on their knowledge of the children's likely cultural preferences and comforts, Proscovia and JRP staff also informed the selection of methods used. Broadly, the study employed a child-centered methodology, which included a mix of participatory methods intended to be enjoyable activities that could facilitate collaboration between the children, myself, and Proscovia. The methods were sensitive to their cognitive development, education, and interests and included play, drawing, journaling, group discussions, interviews, and home visits. Proscovia served as a translator during the activities, which were mostly conducted in the Acholi language (Luo) and later translated and transcribed from audio recordings. Starting in 2013, Proscovia and I also conducted interviews with the mothers in their homes and with several key community members in 2015 and 2016. Reflecting the focus of the research questions, however, the vast majority of the research activities in this study were conducted with the children.

A Child-Centered Methodology

I chose to focus the research on the children's everyday lives and to center their voices in the research process to ensure that their stories directed the analysis. This section explains how I conceptualize child-centered research as a practice of decentering my Western adult perspective and valorizing the children's. I explain how selected methods were informed by participatory research, by ethnography, and in recognition of the importance of building respectful and trusting long-term relationships—a critical point that is raised throughout this volume (see Atim; De Nutte; and Schulz). Then, I offer an example of how knowledge was produced using a mix of selected methods.

My positionality as a middle-class, educated, White Canadian woman (and mother, which I discuss later in this chapter) inept in the local language required that I pay careful attention to the cumulative effects of colonialism, as outlined in the introduction of this volume. In the words of Linda Tuhiwai Smith (1999, 124), I have been "trained and socialized into ways of thinking, of defining and of making sense of the known and unknown" that rely on the simultaneous dismissal, silencing, and manipulation of indigenous knowledge and ways of knowing. Coming to Gulu with relatively abundant research funding and Western academic credentials further reproduced this hierarchy of knowledge and positioned me as an "expert" in a context that I knew very little about. Furthermore, writing in English (a colonial language) for a presumably largely Western audience about "vulnerable African children" carries the potential of turning their lives into spectacles for a Western audience, as Rey Chow (2003) warns. In the context of writing about Africa, such spectacles about "African children" are pervasive, as Binyavanga Wainaina (2005) so poignantly remarks in his scathing satire of Western representations of Africa. In the Western imagination, Wainaina argues, African children are either impoverished and hungry or delinquent. Anthropologist Jason Hart (2006) traces the project of "saving children" from Victorian-era philanthropy to the proliferation of the 1989 Convention on the Rights of the Child and argues that most research about children in the Global South depoliticizes their lives and is often rooted in (neo)colonial civilizing motivations of Western epistemology.

To challenge such colonial posturing in research, Hart suggests focusing on "empirical accounts of children's everyday lives amidst conditions shaped by both local and global forces" (2006, 7). Doing research with children at the level of their everyday lives challenges assumptions about childhood and children in Africa as vulnerable and passive.[4] Recognizing their social agency and participation in social and political life also means recognizing that from the viewpoint of children, everyday life looks different to what it looks like for adults (Prout 2002). Methods for such research should thus be age-appropriate, meaning they should reflect the cognitive and emotional development of the participants. Importantly, research methods for working with children born of war must consider the political and sociocultural specifics of contexts affected by political violence (Hart 2006). In this study, this meant conducting research in ways that were sensitive to the emotional and security needs of the children and their families, which included taking steps to hide their identities as children born into the LRA—both in their communities and in the data. The ethical imperative to "do no harm" (Wessells 2017, 269) through research extended to designing a research process that would ideally create opportunities for support and empowerment. The child-centered methods for this study were therefore selected to allow for subjective expression about the children's everyday lives, while also attending to their security, confidentiality, abilities, and potential for empowerment.

Both participatory research and ethnography informed the study's methodology. Participatory research helps to address the central question identified at the outset of this volume—"Who gets to speak, and on what kinds of terms?" A participatory approach prioritizes collaborative and inclusive research methods (Aldridge 2016), which helps to establish respectful, meaningful relationships with the participants in a study and to facilitate knowledge production grounded in their everyday lived experiences. In designing a safe and meaningful research methodology for engaging with war-affected youth in northern Uganda, Cheryl Heykoop (2014) stresses the value of participatory methods such as drawing and journaling and providing contemplative space to empower participants so that they can control when, what, and how much they wish to share. To a lesser extent, I also invoked ethnography to inform the study's methodology. While ethnography was born out of the troubled history of colonial anthropology, contemporary ethnography has developed in opposition to its past and is a methodology attuned to the dimensions of the everyday (Atkinson 2014, 5). Living in Gulu with my family, for example, was a choice made in recognition of giving attention to the everyday that requires residing in the field; the most powerful forces "of social life are not always on the surface, and are not always easily discovered" (O'Reilly 2008, 67–68). Other ethnographic-inspired methods included talking to people in the community about their war experiences and reconstruction processes, spending time with the children at their homes, sharing family meals, and visiting the mothers and other relatives at home.

Significantly, this research spanned five years. Christina Clark-Kazak (2011) recommends that researchers invest time and energy in relationships with young participants of marginalized war-affected populations. Doing so, she writes, can avoid essentializing their experiences and enable better understanding of the nuances and complexities of their subject positions. Taking time to build trust and respectful relationships over a five-year period was a critical aspect of the research process for this study. It encouraged meaningful and supportive connections between the participants, which still continue. Their relationships with each other and with Proscovia and myself were nurtured over time, which deepened my familiarity with their individual lives and families as well as with their cultural contexts.

One of the most important relationships to develop was the one between myself and Proscovia. Having someone I wholeheartedly trusted on the ground benefited the study in countless logistical ways and ensured that the study remained a regular part of the children's lives throughout the five years (and beyond). Trained as a counselor for people returning from LRA captivity, Proscovia adeptly served as the local point person for the study, and she became someone the children and some of the mothers turned to if they had problems. Her expertise and experience played a central role in the study and our friendship, discussions, mutual support, and shared concerns about the children were foundational to its success. Recognizing the financial precarity of the work, I have been paying Proscovia a monthly salary from 2011 up to the time of this writing in, 2022, with additional payments for her time, knowledge, and skills whenever I visit Gulu. While my means are limited, I have felt it is an important recognition of her ongoing work as support person to the study's participants while also acting as liaison for me to maintain local connections well beyond the official end of the study.

Next, I describe the primary methods applied in the study with specific examples and feedback from the children. Idro's storytelling in the next section demonstrates how the mix of these methods over five years led to the production of comprehensive data and analyses of the children's complex subjectivities.

PLAY

Play was central to establishing rapport, building trust, and providing a source of reciprocity. We held numerous day-long group workshops throughout the study, which always began with playful activities to set a positive tone. Recognizing the popularity of football among the participants, I always had a couple of footballs for the children to play with before, during, and after the research activities. I also brought badminton rackets and birdies for diversity. The children played more football after lunch, and at times I joined in. This would be followed by another game, such as a three-legged race or "telephone," before we started on data-gathering activities. The children unanimously reported that play and food were the best parts of the workshop days. One child reported, "[The project] brought me together with other friends. I can play with them, we can also tell stories among ourselves."

GROUP DISCUSSIONS

The primary goal of initial group discussions in 2011 was for the children to share and learn from each other, while data collection was a secondary goal. The discussions were pragmatically situated within workshops to flow with the natural ease of certain moments such as having lunch or after a fun activity. I hoped to create opportunities for storytelling, recognizing it as a culturally relevant participatory method that has been successfully used in other studies in northern Uganda (Schulz 2019, and in this volume; Baines 2017; Baines and Stewart 2011). Each discussion was followed by physical activities or relaxation before moving onto data-generating activities.

HOME VISITS

Inspired by ethnography, the home visits were an effort to nurture relationships with the goal of building a research environment that felt safe, respectful, and reciprocal (Chilisa and Tsheko 2014). Primarily social, these visits provided a great deal of information as I observed and became familiar with the children's family environments, living conditions, and relationships at home. According to the mothers, because they were all connected in some way with one NGO or another, my presence as a foreigner in their homes was not out of the ordinary. This was an important consideration in protecting the children's identities. We nonetheless also remained vigilant not to reference their identities unless we were certain that no neighbors or young children were listening. I almost always visited their homes with Proscovia, who translated my conversations with family members. We spent time helping to make meals, playing and drawing with the children, and chatting about everyday topics such as school, community issues and politics, food, health, and family dynamics.

INTERVIEWS

Proscovia and I conducted initial interviews with the children in 2011, four months into the fieldwork. These were semistructured with open-ended questions and conducted in carefully selected small groups of two or three, or individually, at private locations. The goal of the interviews was to expand on what each child had shared to date and to gain a more personalized sense of their everyday lives, while also using the focused time to strengthen our relationships. Proscovia and I sought to create a comfortable, respectful environment, and I offered them puzzle games and paper and colored pencils for the duration of the interview as a means of releasing tension. Difficult questions about their past were avoided unless the child raised the issue, and we asked for clarification. We approached each interview with a strategy unique to the child, mindful of the child's age, history, personality, and observed sensitivity. The children's responses to my questions in these initial interviews were usually short, so we allowed a good part of the dialogue to flow unstructured. In subsequent years, their responses were far more comprehensive and thoughtful, likely reflecting both greater maturity and comfort. By 2016, a number of the children chose to converse directly with me in English in the interviews.

After the first phase of fieldwork, I interviewed mothers and key community contacts. Initial interviews with mothers were semistructured with the primary goal of completing biographical details about their child's life—I used a list of essential questions (child's birth date, date of return, the child's health, *cen* [spiritual afflictions], experiences with traditional methods of reconciliation, siblings, and so on), but otherwise the conversations were unstructured, open ended, and usually lasted several hours. Subsequent interviews with the mothers involved only a few specific questions to fill in gaps in my data and were also unstructured, again lasting between two and four hours.

The interviews with community members included two school head teachers, a police spokesperson, a bishop who had been involved in the peace process, a local journalist, and two social workers. The goal of these community-based interviews was to get a sense of the broader narratives and concerns circulating in the community in which the children live. These interviews were unstructured, with only the topic of children born into the LRA as a guide.

DRAWING

Drawing was a primary method used as a participatory visual communication strategy (Literat 2013), which was supplemented by verbal explanations and participant observations. Logistically, drawing was valuable because it required minimal materials, and all able people can draw. To relieve concerns about lack of drawing skill, Proscovia and I stressed that the quality of the drawings was not important. The children had few opportunities in their lives to draw since blank paper and writing utensils were not common commodities in their lives (which helped to enhance the appeal of the activity). Most drawings were done during the many group workshops.

Drawing inherently values subjective and emotional ways of knowing (Rattine-Flaherty and Singhal 2007) and helped to capture the children's expressions of self and experiences of everyday activities, interactions, and places in a way that was more confidential than other visual methods such as photovoice.[5] Drawing is not bound by "the 'logic' of temporal sequence" (quoted in Literat 2013, 87) like oral and written representations, which hold the potential for metaphorical representation of complex emotions, perceptions, and identities, some of which may still be subconscious. Such subtle and nuanced expressions may be especially inaccessible to young people through oral and written communication because they require a certain level of "experiential maturity and comfort with language" (Literat 2013, 88; Boyden and Ennew 1997).

Stephany's drawing of the most important places and people in her life offers an example of how drawing produced knowledge about relationships between elements of her everyday lived experiences in a way that represents her complex emotions and sense of self. Stephany is a girl whose mother and father both remain in the LRA, which she left when she was two years old. In her drawing she depicted a school, a church, her mother, and her father. After the drawing sessions, she explained the image and why she drew her parents: "I like thinking about him. . . . I think that my father should be [here] with my mother." Stephany has no memory of her parents, only the knowledge that they are alive and with the LRA. Her drawing is of places in her everyday life that are visually connected with people who are present only in their absence through the abstract emotion of longing. This depiction of her parents' presence in her everyday life was verbally confirmed when she said she thinks of them. The children's verbal reflections about their drawings were central to our collaborative meaning-making and helped to advance, correct, and/or confirm the analysis of their drawings.

Sometimes, the drawings and their verbal explanations contributed to a bigger picture about the child; a broader understanding of their subjective sense of self. An example of this is my analysis of Junior's drawing in response to the prompt "Draw a time in your life when you felt like part of a family—past, present, or future." Junior's parents and only full sibling were killed in the bush. Upon his transition out of the war (he was captured by the Ugandan army), he was passed around his extended family with little care for his well-being and development. Referring to his drawing, he explained that he had drawn a recent safari trip with his uncle and cousins (see figure 3.1). It seemed unlikely, and I later learned that it never happened. On the drawing paper he had written in very large lettering "P6" to signify that he was in the primary 6 level at school, and his age was "16." In fact, Junior was not in school at this time and had only completed P2. As I got to know him better, I considered the safari drawing in the context of our many conversations and his further contributions. A sentiment captured in a drawing in his journal (see figure 3.2) suggested he missed his parents and longed to feel that he was part

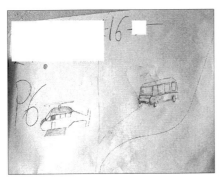

FIGURE 3.1. Drawing by Junior in response to "Draw a time in your life when you felt like part of a family—past, present, or future." Photo by Beth Stewart, October 22, 2011.

FIGURE 3.2. An unprompted drawing by Junior in his journal. Photo by Beth Stewart, December 27, 2011.

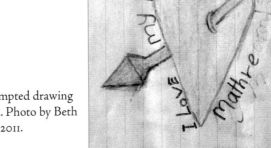

of a family. I came to recognize the safari drawing and the large declaration of his school level as representing his desire to belong, both among his peers and extended family.

JOURNALS

Journals were used as an unstructured participatory method, giving the children ownership of the contents of their journals. When first given these, they were told to write in it, draw in it, or leave it blank—it was entirely up to them to decide what to do with it. I later photographed their entries for documentation, but the children kept their journals. Additional context was provided through retrospective interviews with each of them so they could explain their entries. These conversations were critical collaborations of meaning-making that significantly contributed to the analyses of the journals. Like the conversations about their drawings during the workshops, the retrospective interviews also corrected my initial interpretations that sometimes reflected my subconscious and problematic assumptions about their victimhood. For example, six children drew violent images in their journals that included men with guns and people dying, all of which I initially thought may be representations of memories from their time inside the LRA. Through the interviews, however, I learned that only three of these were representations of their memories from the war, while the other three were drawings of scenes from movies they had recently watched.

Some of the children engaged with the practice of journaling more than others. Idro, for example, filled numerous journals throughout the years of the study and beyond, some of which I detail in the next section. The act of journaling provided the children with opportunities to share and construct narratives about themselves. Their entries provided snapshots of their everyday lives, making visible the ordinary (such as scenes from a movie) (Breheny, Horrell, and Stephens 2020), and also offering valuable glimpses of their thoughts and feelings, everyday experiences, relationships, and priorities, which helped me situate their lives within broader sociopolitical contexts (Stewart 2021).

Producing Knowledge: Idro

Idro's storytelling demonstrates how this mix of methods worked together over five years to offer a comprehensive expression of her subjective sense of her experiences and sense of self. Her stories were shared through journaling, drawing, unstructured interviews, home visits, and group discussions. Throughout the active study and subsequently when I was writing my dissertation, I shared my analysis of Idro's stories with her and asked for her feedback and corrections. Each time I visited Gulu, she and I met (she was almost fluent in English by the end of the study) to review my analysis and what I had written. Below is a collection of her thoughtful contributions that illustrate how these methods generated knowledge about how the children experience their everyday social lives and make sense of their experiences.

Idro's biographical information was collected from interviews with her and her mother (separately), home visits, and her journals. She was born in 1996 and was her mother and father's second child; the first died in the bush before Idro was born. She transitioned out of the war when she was seven with her mother and younger sister, and her father died in the LRA several years later. Her mother's family rejected them, and she did not know her paternal family, which meant she did not have a "home" in the Acholi sense—a paternal home village. Her mother's hut near Gulu was unsafe because her stepfather violently targeted her and her sister, who was also born into the LRA. Fortunately, Idro found a sponsor for boarding school, but she was eventually expelled as a result of periodic episodes in which she became violent and lost consciousness. She was then forced to return to where her mother and stepfather lived. Idro and her mother explained during an interview and a home visit, respectively, that the episodes were caused by a spiritual problem (*cen*): the spirits of dead people they walked over while in the bush had become attached to her spirit. Rather than remain around her stepfather, Idro found a man to live with and somewhere in the process acquired an incurable illness.

A sense of not belonging describes a significant aspect of how Idro experiences her everyday social life. Throughout the study, she expressed a deep sense of feeling excluded, which she attributed to the fact that she was born into the LRA. Due to the length of the study and her prolific journaling, I was able to trace this sense of exclusion across many areas in her life throughout the five-year period: at home as a result of her stepfather, at the school from which she was expelled, and in her mother's village where she and her sister had been rejected. In a poem she wrote in a journal titled "The Endless Suffering Caused By War," Idro refers to her sense of exclusion. Referencing the lack of a home or simply a safe place to return to at night, a common theme among children born into the LRA, she asks in her poem, "Where should we stay?" Accentuating this sense of place exclusion, her poem later states, "Nowhere to dwell, nowhere to stand, no shadow to cover us, no one beside us, we are hungry lonely on air." Poignantly, in 2016 Idro responded to a drawing-activity prompt during a workshop, "Draw yourself as an adult who was born into the LRA and as an adult who was born 'here,'" and she drew the image below, in which she compared how she perceived her life as a person born into the LRA to how she imagined her life would have been had she been born

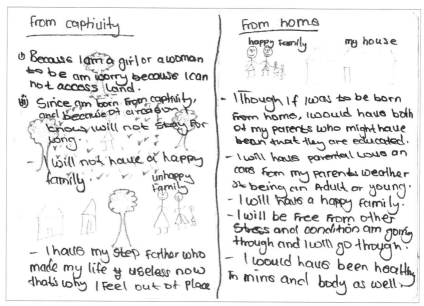

FIGURE 3.3. Drawing and text by Idro in response to "Draw yourself as an adult who was born into the LRA and as an adult who was born 'here.'" Photo by Beth Stewart, August 21, 2016.

"here" (see figure 3.3). She concluded, "I feel out of place," mirroring her other expressions of being denied a sense of belonging.

Idro's sense of exclusion, however, is only part of her story. Like the other children, she used a mix of methods (drawing, journaling, interviews, and discussions) to also tell stories to affirm who she believed herself to be, where she comes from, and who she aspires to be in the future. In her journal she wrote about her father: "I last saw him when I was young but I could only remember that he used to love me more than any other person." The other children also often recalled their time in the bush as a period when they felt a sense of belonging. Like Idro, they remember their fathers, and they remember being loved by them. By remembering their fathers in this way, they challenge the popular conception that depicts their fathers as savage rebels. These stories about their fathers also provide a narrative that insists that they come from culturally and socially legitimate families, in which children have two loving parents.

In her journal, Idro carefully framed her parents' marriage as legitimate. She explained that her mother waited for her father to escape the war and did not find another man. Idro wrote that her mother only remarried another man after she learned that Idro's father had been killed: "Two years later my mum heard a story that my dad was killed. . . . [Then] she decided to remarry to another man." This statement and framing not only legitimizes

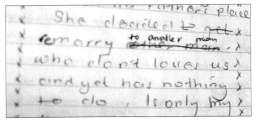

FIGURE 3.4. Excerpt of a journal entry by Idro. Photo by Beth Stewart, August 25, 2016.

the marriage but also acknowledges her mother as a culturally appropriate woman who waited before remarrying. It seemed significant that she made these corrections to her story (see figure 3.4)—not only did she carefully rephrase the statement but she did so with another pen, suggesting she returned to it at a later time after further consideration.

Similar to how she insists on the legitimacy of the family she was born into, Idro also depicts her mother as a strong and devoted Acholi mother: not *despite* the fact they remained in the bush for many years but because of it. In a group discussion, Idro reflected on her relationship with her mother: "There is a special relationship because of the past. For example, if maybe something has gone wrong, then they need to punish the children. . . . The mother will just say 'Ah, for me you don't punish my child. You don't know how much I suffered with this child.' So they protect you." Here, Idro suggests that her relationship with her mother is especially strong and special because of their past. She also suggests that she belongs with her mother. Many of the children suggest a deep sense of belonging in relation to their mothers. Reflecting a similar centrality in her life, another girl, Cora, drew only her mother when I asked them to draw the most important people in their lives. In an interview shortly after, Cora interpreted her drawing: "I drew a picture of my mom and our house. That one [pointing to hearts] is love. I love my mother."

My analysis of Idro's contributions reveals that she experiences a sense of exclusion from the places of her everyday life. In response, she creates a sense of who she is and where she belongs in relation to her mother and father. In doing so, she understands her experiences of exclusion to be based on misconceptions about who she is and where she comes from. In other words, she insists that she is more than the labels "LRA child" or "rebel child." Over the years, I have had many opportunities to discuss the analysis of her contributions to ensure that she agreed with my interpretations and to correct any errors or misunderstandings. Her stories were reflective of common themes among the other children's contributions, which led me to conclude, based on an observed pattern of expressions of exclusion, that children born into the LRA, like other children born of war, transgress the normative divide between private and public realms by forcing the private (sex) to be public (in war). Using various methods offered in the study, the children crafted narratives about themselves, and their creations of self represent a kind of reclamation of their private realm and an insistence on their personhood. While the children are unique individuals and their sense of who they are is never static, they share key life experiences that significantly contribute to their efforts to create a sense of who they are.

Ethical Challenges

Theorizing any methodology is to strive for ideal research practice. Careful conceptualization and design of an ethical methodology can help to mitigate potential harm resulting from the inevitable messiness of fieldwork, but the disconnect between theorizing and conducting research reveals the challenges, complexities, and limitations of realizing any ideal practice. This disconnect in my years-long research with children born into the LRA involved many ethical problems. In the following section I explore problems that arose from the length of the study and working with children in contexts of adversity, and I end with a review of my efforts toward ethical and meaningful reciprocity.

RELATIONSHIPS

The long-term nature of this research facilitated the development of trust and meaningful relationships between me, Proscovia, and the children. Idro's storytelling offers a glimpse into the richness of the children's contributions, which was only possible because of the endurance of the study. While I had designed a methodology aimed at mediating the intrinsic power differentials, which included a commitment to building long-term relationships, the inevitable complexity at times confounded ethical boundaries, emphasized our differences, and entangled our relationships in unintentional ways.

As the research progressed and our relationships developed, the children moved toward and into adulthood, my involvement in their lives and that of their families moved beyond the contours of the study, and the boundaries between research and friendship blurred. Social media connections meant that I was often (and still am) in regular contact with a number of the children. Some of their mothers also follow me on social media, although we rarely chat online. Such friendly and daily contact between myself and the children poses ethical challenges, such as revealing visual contrasts between our lives, which may increase expectations from me or fuel unrealistic fantasies about living as I do. Significantly, such connections also lead to questions about how this changes my ethical responsibilities toward the children, including the protection of their identities (Ellis et al.

2007) and the boundaries of what constitutes research data versus communication as friends (De Laine 2000).[6]

My identity as a mother in the field offered an initial sense of common ground between myself, Proscovia, and the mothers of the children, while also contributing to problematic assumptions on my part. In 2011, I lived in Gulu for five months with my children and partner—I was there as a mother and wife, later returning as a single woman/mother. Discussions about breastfeeding, challenges of discipline, and other parental concerns and joys were common when I visited the mothers. Proscovia herself was a young single mother, and throughout the study I encouraged her to bring her children to research activities (including our meetings with mothers), which meant that we almost always had an infant or toddler in tow. This arrangement supported her, and because children are so adored in the society, their presence helped to warm any environment. In a sense, these identity markers—mother, wife, single mother—fostered a sense, however superficial, of familiarity and shared experience. While feeling a sense of friendship with her young Congolese refugee participants, Christina Clark-Kazak (2013) reflects that the power asymmetries resulting from their different circumstances could never be ignored or overcome. Writing about how shared motherhood affects researcher-subject rapport, Brown and De Casanova (2009) similarly suggest that shared experiences of motherhood are "fictional" across significantly different living conditions. The more our relationships developed, the more I was prone to over-empathizing and to false notions of experiential closeness, both of which were grounded in my Eurocentric assumptions about mothering and child development, which inevitably shaped which issues I felt merited attention, sympathy, and concern. In such cases, Proscovia was essential in my reflexive practice to identify our cultural differences and decenter my ways of knowing and seeing.

Being a mother in the field also shaped my relationships with the children. This mother-child dynamic, while helpful in some ways, was also problematic as our relationships deepened. Idro's mother once shared with me that Idro had proclaimed that I was her first mother and that her actual mother was her second mother. The mother narrated this story in the context of emphasizing her and her daughter's gratitude for my commitment to Idro's well-being. As mentioned, Idro was the most prolific journal writer in the study. Between my visits to Gulu, she kept a private diary in which she wrote specifically to me, sometimes addressing me directly and often sharing her most private feelings, reflections, and experiences. Each time I visited Gulu, she had me photograph every page and instructed me to use it as research data. This dynamic accentuates the complex and often problematic negotiation of my multiple positionalities and responsibilities in relation to the children. It is possible that my role as mother influenced the attachment in our relationship—being a mother may have informed my behavior toward her, or my identity as a mother may have encouraged her to feel an attachment toward me. Four of the children use our social media connections to share their ongoing struggles with me. These are not requests for support; it seems that I am perceived as a safe person who knows a great deal about them but who is simultaneously removed from their community. They feel that I am someone with whom they can share and celebrate their personal achievements and to whom they can disclose deeply personal and private matters. At times, this has been emotionally difficult for me because it requires that I reengage with the issues of their lives while managing my own family's difficulties, and the juxtaposition of our lives and our troubles can create a profound sense of dissonance.

These ethical problems of long-term fieldwork reflect both the value and impossibilities of such relationships, and I recognize that I must accept the unease, knowing full well that many of our contradictions are unresolvable. Despite these inevitable limitations, being grounded in a methodology that encouraged reflexivity and self-awareness meant that investing time and effort into our relationships offered greater opportunities to contribute to the children's well-being and longer-term goals in ways that did not exacerbate the already significant power differentials (Clark-Kazak 2013).

"RESEARCH AS 'SOCIAL WORK'?"

In her piece "Research as 'Social Work'?" Clark-Kazak (2013) highlights the ethical and methodological challenges she faced in conducting research with Congolese youth in Uganda who have limited or no access to formal social services. Like Clark-Kazak, I sometimes felt as though I was doing social work. Sometimes the work proved to be beneficial—but not always.

A positive example was in 2011 when I learned that one of the girls in the study was not safe living at home. After discussing the problem with Proscovia and colleagues at JRP, we were able to help her get sponsorship to go to boarding school and connected her with a counselor with whom she worked for several months. Clark-Kazak (2013) cautions about the potential for ethical problems when engaging in advocacy for youth or when raising the expectations of the participants and interfering in their own relationships with organizations and services. I experienced such a case. Funding had run out at JRP to trace the unknown families of children born into the LRA, but the maternal family of the boy called Junior had not yet been found. As mentioned earlier, he witnessed the deaths of his parents and only sibling in the bush. He was subsequently taken to a reception center where he was claimed by a woman said to be his maternal grandmother. Two years later her claim was disputed by another woman, and because the competing claims could not be resolved, Junior was sent to live with his paternal family. Given this tumult and Junior's many laments about wanting to know his mother's family, it was clear to me that resolving his maternal identity was an important matter for him. During my visit in 2015, and with his permission, I offered to cover the costs incurred by one of JRP's staff members who was involved in the tracing. With the information she already had about his case, the task sounded fairly straightforward, and I was optimistic in the way I spoke to Junior about its progress. Unfortunately, the tracing stalled after a person who possessed essential information could not be located. Pursuing the case further would have required a significant and undefined time investment by the JRP staff member, who was unable to do so. My visit to Gulu ended, and I returned home, leaving Junior disappointed after having his hopes raised.

Conducting research with people who live in poverty poses other ethical dilemmas that triggered "knee-jerk" responses (Clark-Kazak 2013) based on my sense of the immediate urgency of a given situation. There were times, for example, when Proscovia and I arrived at a home where the family had not eaten for one or two days. We once visited Keila, who had been left home alone with a younger sister a few days prior because her mother had to take the other sibling, who was having severe respiratory problems, to the hospital. This family already lived day to day, depending on the meager income that the mother made selling charcoal. She borrowed money to take the child to hospital, and the girls were left at home with no money and no food. I brought them some beans, maize flour, and cooking oil. Idro's family also regularly experienced hunger, and I often brought beans and other basic foods when we visited. As I also did with other children, I sometimes provided small funds to assist with basic and urgent medical needs.

Farhana Sultana (2007) argues that in such cases, universities' institutional ethics frameworks can conflict with "good practice in the field" (383), which demands context-specific, relational, and politicized everyday actions. Research standards frown upon giving participants benefits beyond compensation for travel and time. Expectations for ethical practice in the field, Sultana (2007) argues, cannot be static across contexts. However, while my actions seemed pragmatic and ethical at the time, my good intentions may have impacted my relationships with the participants and complicated their consent in inscrutably subjective ways. Looking back at my field notes, I recognize that I also carried a sense of indebtedness to the participants for their involvement in the study from which I significantly benefit in academic, professional, and economic ways (Clark-Kazak 2009). In studies with marginalized populations such as this one, the researcher inevitably benefits more, "no matter how participatory the data collection," explains Clark-Kazak (2009, 136). As such, I may have fallen into the dynamic mentioned above of involving foreign support rather than supporting the participants' capacities to find their own solutions. Short-term interventions, such as my charitable responses, can reinforce identification with disempowering identities such as "vulnerable" or "victim" and exacerbate donor-recipient relationships between the researcher and participants (Clark-Kazak 2013). While I felt strongly at the time that it would have been unethical not to assist in some small way, my discussions with Proscovia helped to ensure that our support included capacity building to find solutions: "In our view, it is unethical for researchers merely to document the difficulties of refugees and their causes without, whenever possible, offering in return some kind of reciprocal benefit that may assist them in dealing with these difficulties and, where possible, in working towards solutions" (Mackenzie, McDowell, and Pittaway 2007, 310).

By performing (however unintentionally) the role of social worker, I may also have encouraged the children and their mothers to present themselves as more vulnerable than they were; what Mats Utas (2005) refers to as "victimcy." In a general sense, the children's continued involvement with the study for which I had been partnered with the grassroots organization JRP, could be considered as part of the significant involvement of NGOs and humanitarian assistance during the war and after, which perpetuated an economy largely dependent on foreign support (Branch 2008). This study began just four years postconflict, when there were still many registered aid organizations. In 2010, the NGO Forum-Gulu reported 120 members, but by 2016 this number had been halved (Buscher and Ashaba 2018). While officially partnered with JRP, the study's activities had little direct involvement from the organization after 2011. However, since I am a foreigner, the research was inevitably part of this system of foreign involvement in the lives of survivors. Tasker (this volume) notes how in the context of a high concentration of researchers, journalists, and NGOs in war-affected areas, the stories of survivors of sexual violence become a kind of currency. This potential transactional nature of my and JRP's interactions with the children, and especially their mothers, suggests that their participation may have been grounded in the expectation of benefits.[7] Atim (this volume) similarly notes that in northern Uganda, White researchers are sometimes conflated with aid workers and consequently as people with enough influence to access resources.

I cannot know to what extent these interactions affected our relationships and the stories shared. An illuminating example of this quandary occurred in 2011 when I asked the girls to draw a body map. We traced the body of one of the girls on a large piece of paper. They were then instructed to draw on the body harms they saw done to other children born of war. This question was beyond what I felt was the scope of the study, and I had no familiarity with using body maps as a research method. However, the boundaries of my partnership with JRP blurred when my colleagues at JRP's Gender Justice Unit saw an opportunity to potentially acquire important and urgent information from the children. After concerning reports from mothers of other children born into the LRA about stepfathers sexually assaulting the girls, my colleagues requested that I engage in this body map activity: one that had successfully been done with groups of women who returned from the LRA (Baines 2017). The Gender Justice Unit felt that a body map could potentially reveal information about incidents of abuse by stepfathers. We agreed to suggest to the girls that they draw harms done to *other* children born into the LRA—a strategy that would help remove the fear of outing themselves as victims of such abuses. Considering my lack of training and familiarity with this method, I regret using it and am grateful that the only problematic outcome seems to have been the production of confusing data for me to analyze.

The body map drawings were graphic depictions of war violence, and when the girls explained their drawings they giggled together and laughed, which I initially understood as a reaction to the discomfort they felt. Because the girls focused solely on violence in the war, the exercise was not helpful to my JRP colleagues and ultimately complicated rather than benefited my analysis of the data. In 2016, I asked one of the girls about the body map. She seemed to remember that their drawings were funny exaggerations of what they thought I expected. These concerns were involved in how I interpreted the data. The children's vulnerability was obvious, but I also had to question my subjective expectations about victims and vulnerability and whether I was interpreting the data through a biased lens. Doing so led me to ultimately discard the body map as evidence of violence either witnessed or experienced.

RECIPROCITY

Ethical conundrums like these arose regularly and challenged our ability to actualize the participatory principles laid out in the study's methodology. Conducting research with children born into the LRA is very context specific, which contributes to the disconnect between grand ethical principles and the practice of research. Good research practice, explains Chris Clark (2006) in relation to social work research, depends in large part on the moral character of the researcher. It is important that I understand the significance of how I conduct research, how knowledge is produced and presented, and the nature of my interpersonal relationships in the field: "Equity . . . flows through actions and thoughts—it is marked by genuineness and sincerity" (Sefa Dei 2005, xii). While power differentials in my relationships with children born into the LRA and their families and communities will never be balanced, reciprocity acts as "an ethical starting place" (Kovach 2009, 30) to partially overcome some of the challenges discussed above.

Indigenous scholar Margaret Kovach (2009, 149) explains that reciprocity can mean more than dissemination: "Giving back does not only mean dissemination of findings; it means creating a relationship throughout the entirety of the research." I took care to build trust and strong, respectful relationships and have remained committed to the research project for the five years of the study (and beyond) by returning five times and continuing to develop trust in my relationships with the participants and their mothers or guardians. Partly as an effort to give back, Proscovia continued to organize and facilitate regular group meetings over the years, which included some research activities (such as drawing prompts), but they primarily served as peer-support meetings. The children reported that they looked forward to the meetings and expressed the positive role the meetings played in their lives. "This project makes people to live happily," explained one boy, "so at least it helps to forget the past." Another child said, "[The study] helped me to change, to stop thinking too much about certain things and also it has helped me in many other ways. . . . It helped some of the thoughts to disappear from my head because it brought me together with other friends. I can play with them, we can also tell stories among ourselves." Similarly, another wrote in his journal, "I am very happy today because me and Proscovia and Beth and my friends we were so happy because we eat, we play, we discuss, we know ourselves." In the context of the chronic insecurity the children experience in their daily lives, these meetings provided some respite where they could speak openly about their identities as children born into the LRA, play, and enjoy a meal together.

Dissemination was and is also part of the process of reciprocity. As one girl insisted: "You go out and you tell the people, you put for them what we have been saying here. You push for them to see, also." Early analysis of the data revealed differences and commonalities among the children and illuminated their common sources of support and strength. Based on these sources of well-being, the children and I collaboratively identified other supportive interventions that could be undertaken by civil society groups and the government of Uganda—recommended in a report published and distributed by JRP (Stewart 2015). This collaboration happened during my 2015 month-long visit to Gulu over the course of a full-day group meeting and several one-on-one meetings, which I also used to verify the accuracy of the data and my analysis thereof. After reviewing the report during a group meeting with Proscovia at the end of 2015 (before it was published), one child commented approvingly, "The [report] is like our voice. It can help talk about us to the world." Another added, "The [report] explains the truth about us and our struggles with our life." As of 2020, the report has been JRP's most downloaded document from their website, and the organization has used it for its subsequent advocacy of children born into the LRA. Several of the children have gone on to speak on behalf of children born into the LRA at community sensitization events and at meetings with NGOs and other stakeholders. Three of them, that I am aware of, specifically referenced the report as a resource detailing their needs and concerns for anyone seeking further information.

My dissertation was also reviewed with the children. During my visit in 2016, I held two full-day workshops in which I presented some general themes identified in the data and reviewed some preliminary findings—open to input from the children. During this visit I also sought to clarify certain points, verify the data and my interpretations, and receive feedback about more specific analyses. While I was writing my dissertation, Proscovia organized several group meetings in which I had her review some of my interpretations and findings, and she also helped me to verify specific cases and stories. In 2018, after my doctoral defense, I returned to Gulu and presented the text and its contents to the children, and one-on-one to most of the mothers. The children spent an afternoon looking through it, enjoying seeing their quotes in printed text (by then, most of them were comfortable reading and speaking English), as well as their drawings. To this day, Proscovia holds a copy of the dissertation for the children to read whenever they wish. I also donated a copy of my dissertation to the Gulu University library so that it is accessible to local researchers.

Through visual, written, and verbal mediums, the twenty-nine children born into the LRA who were participants in this study shared valuable insights into their everyday lived experiences—often intimate, sometimes funny, and always meaningful. The research sought to challenge the representations of "vulnerable African children" that Wainaina (2005) identified by destabilizing both Euro- and adult-centric assumptions about childhood and about war-affected children in particular. In this sense, the study is a response to the call made by anthropologist Jason Hart (2006) to challenge constructions of war-affected children and Clark-Kazak's (2011) call to politicize war-affected young people rather than resorting to dominant apolitical categorizations. The methodology recognizes that children should be positioned in research as *the* experts about their lives. In the research process, analysis, and writing, I attempted to prioritize the voices of the children to make visible the meanings of their everyday lived experiences. As demonstrated by Idro's storytelling, the mix of methods offered flexibility and multiple means of producing knowledge. The participatory focus facilitated shared ownership of the research process and knowledge between me, Proscovia, and the children.[8] Furthermore, the five-year duration of the study gave us time to develop respect and trust—between myself and Proscovia, between ourselves and the children, and also among the children themselves. Despite our best intentions, ethical problems arose related to the complexities of our relationships and the challenges of conducting research with children in contexts of significant adversity. The disconnect between ideal participatory methodology and actualized research experiences was mitigated through sincere acts of reciprocity.

I hope this examination of the child-centered methods and approach used to produce knowledge about the lives of children born into the LRA can provide a framework for ethical and meaningful research with other populations of children born of war, especially those born of forced marriage in war. Such research will make positive contributions to our understanding of not just their lives but also how best to support the children and their communities in the process of postconflict recovery.

Notes

1. A local organization (Watye ki gen) recorded 952 children born into the LRA living in northern Uganda, but by the publication of their report (2015) they had not yet reached all areas, and many were either unaware of their efforts or were hesitant to come forward. From my own research, I estimate that approximately 2,500 to 3,000 children were born or conceived in the LRA. This accounts for the hundreds, and very possibly over a thousand, who died before getting out of the war (deaths at birth, from illness/malnutrition, abandonment, killed in battle, or lost) as well as those who died after transitioning out of the war. To date, there has been no effort to document the children who died before transitioning out of the bush.
2. I refer to this population of children as "children born into the LRA," rather than the more common refrain, "children born in captivity." I chose to do this, with approval from the study's participants, to avoid the limitations inherent in the term "captivity." Their experiences living among the rebels cannot uniformly be described as living in captivity.
3. Proscovia hereafter.
4. Hart (2004) argues that humanitarian discourse depoliticizes children and childhood rather than engaging with children's complex processes of identity construction and sociopolitical roles in their families, communities, and nation. Universal notions of childhood and childhood innocence mask "the possibilities of children's perspectives on and active participation in social life" (Olson 2004, 164).

5. Proscovia and I decided that equipping the children with cameras could attract unwanted attention and questions.
6. Consent has been given for the use of any details or quotes from such communications in this dissertation.
7. At the beginning of the study only two children had experience with another researcher. Reflecting the recent proliferation of research with children born into the LRA, by 2016 most of them had interacted with other researchers.
8. At a meeting at the end of 2016, the group decided to formalize and register as a community-based organization. They subsequently elected leaders, a treasurer, and a spokesperson; at their September 2017 meeting, they collectively finalized their group's constitution. They chose to call themselves Warom Child and Youth in Development. *Warom* means "we are the same." Throughout the research project, the children often insisted, "We are all the same." Their claim was a response to the exclusion they experienced in their everyday lives.

References

Akello, G. 2013. "Experiences of Forced Mothers in Northern Uganda: The Legacy of War." *Intervention* 112: 149–56.

Aldridge, J. 2016. *Participatory Research: Working with Vulnerable Groups in Research and Practice*. Chicago: Policy Press.

Apio, E. O. 2016. "Children Born of War in Northern Uganda: Kinship, Marriage, and the Politics of Post-conflict Reintegration in Lango Society." PhD diss., University of Birmingham.

Atkinson, P. 2014. *For Ethnography*. Thousand Oaks, CA: Sage.

Baines, E. 2017. *Buried in the Heart: Women, Complex Victimhood and the War in Northern Uganda*. New York: Cambridge University Press.

Baines, E., and B. Stewart. 2011. "'I Cannot Accept What I Have Not Done': Storytelling, Gender and Transitional Justice." *Journal of Human Rights Practice* 33: 245–63.

Boyden, J., and J. Ennew. 1997. *Children in Focus: A Manual for Participatory Research with Children*. Stockholm: Save the Children Sweden.

Branch, A. 2008. "Against Humanitarian Impunity: Rethinking Responsibility for Displacement and Disaster in Northern Uganda." *Journal of Intervention and Statebuilding* 2 (2): 151–73.

Breheny, M., B. Horrell, and C. Stephens. 2020. "A Participatory Journal/Dialogue Approach to Narrative Research Illustrated Using a Study of Informal Caregiving." *Qualitative Research in Psychology* 19 (2): 521–38.

Brown, T. M., and E. M. De Casanova. 2009. "Mothers in the Field: How Motherhood Shapes Fieldwork and Researcher-Subject Relations." *Women's Studies Quarterly* 37 (3/4): 42–57.

Buscher, S. K., and I. Ashaba. 2018. "Humanitarian Urbanism in a Post-conflict Aid Town: Aid Agencies and Urbanization in Gulu, Northern Uganda." *Journal of Eastern African Studies* 12 (2): 348–66.

Carpenter, C. 2007. *Born of War: Protecting Children of Sexual Violence Survivors in Conflict Zones*. Bloomfield, CT: Kumarian Press.

Chilisa, B., and G. N. Tsheko. 2014. "Mixed Methods in Indigenous Research Building Relationships for Sustainable Intervention Outcomes." *Journal of Mixed Methods Research* 83: 222–33.

Chow, R. 2003. "Where Have All the Natives Gone." In *Feminist Postcolonial Theory: A Reader*, edited by R. Lewis and S. Mills, 324–49. New York: Routledge.

Clark, C. 2006. "Moral Character in Social Work." *British Journal of Social Work* 36 (1): 75–89.

Clark-Kazak, C. 2009. "Power and Politics in Migration Narrative Methodology: Research with Young Congolese Migrants in Uganda." *Migration Letters* 6 (2): 131–41.

———. 2011. *Recounting Migration: Political Narratives of Congolese Young People in Uganda*. Montreal: McGill-Queen's University Press.

———. 2013. "Research as 'Social Work' in Kampala? Managing Expectations, Compensation and Relationships in Research with Unassisted, Urban Refugees from the Democratic Republic of Congo." In *Emotional and Ethical Challenges for Field Research in Africa*, edited by S. Thomson, A. Ansoms, and J. Murison, 96–106. London: Palgrave Macmillan.

Coulter, C. 2009. *Bush Wives and Girl Soldiers: Women's Lives through War and Peace in Sierra Leone*. Ithaca, NY: Cornell University Press.

Das, V. 2007. *Life and Words: Violence and the Descent into the Ordinary*. Berkeley: University of California Press.

De Laine, M. 2000. *Fieldwork, Participation and Practice: Ethics and Dilemmas in Qualitative Research*. Thousand Oaks, CA: Sage.

Denov, M., and A. Lakor. 2017. "When War Is Better Than Peace: The Post-conflict Realities of Children Born of Wartime Rape in Northern Uganda." *Child Abuse and Neglect* 65: 255–65.

Ellis, B. H., M. Kia-Keating, S. A. Yusuf, A. Lincoln, and A. Nur. 2007. "Ethical Research in Refugee Communities and the Use of Community Participatory Methods." *Transcultural Psychiatry* 443: 459–81.

Erjavec, K., and Z. Volcic. 2010. "Living with the Sins of Their Fathers: An Analysis of Self-Representation of Adolescents Born of War Rape." *Journal of Adolescent Research* 253: 359–86.

Hart, J. 2004. *Children's Participation in Humanitarian Action: Learning from Zones of Armed Conflict*. N.p.: Canadian International Development Agency.

———. 2006. "Saving Children: What Role for Anthropology?" *Anthropology Today* 221: 5–8.

Heykoop, C. 2014. "Our Stories Matter, Our Own Way: The Safe and Meaningful Engagement of Young People in Post-conflict Truth Telling in Northern Uganda." PhD diss., Royal Roads University.

Kahn, S., and M. Denov. 2019. "'We Are Children Like Others': Pathways to Mental Health and Healing for Children Born of Genocidal Rape in Rwanda." *Transcultural Psychiatry* 563: 510–28.

Kovach, M. 2009. *Indigenous Methodologies: Characteristics, Conversations, and Contexts*. Toronto: University of Toronto Press.

Ladisch, V. 2015. *From Rejection to Redress: Overcoming Legacies of Conflict-Related Sexual Violence in Northern Uganda*. N.p.: International Center for Transitional Justice.

Lee, S. 2017. *Children Born of War in the Twentieth Century*. Manchester: Manchester University Press.

Literat, I. 2013. "'A Pencil for Your Thoughts': Participatory Drawing as a Visual Research Method with Children and Youth." *International Journal of Qualitative Methods* 121: 84–98.

Mackenzie, C., C. McDowell, and E. Pittaway. 2007. "Beyond 'Do No Harm': The Challenge of Constructing Ethical Relationships in Refugee Research." *Journal of Refugee Studies* 202: 299–319.

Ojok, B. 2020. "An Examination of Schooling Attitudes and Responses to Children Born of War Following their Re-integration into the Post-conflict Settings of Northern Uganda." PhD diss., University of Birmingham.

Olson, K. R. 2004. "Children in the Grey Spaces between War and Peace: The Uncertain Truth of Memory Acts." In *Children and Youth on the Front Line: Ethnography, Armed Conflict and Displacement*, edited by J. Boyden and J. de Berry, 145–66. New York: Berghahn Books.

O'Reilly, K. 2008. *Key Concepts in Ethnography*. Los Angeles: Sage.

Prout, A. 2002. "Researching Children as Social Actors: An Introduction to the Children 5–16 Programme." *Children and Society* 162: 67–76.

Rattine-Flaherty, E., and A. Singhal. 2007. "Method and Marginalization: Revealing the Feminist Orientation of Participatory Communication Research." Paper presented at the NCA 93rd Annual Convention, November 15–17, 2007, Chicago.

Rimmer, S. H. 2006. "Orphans or Veterans: Justice for Children Born of War in East Timor." *Texas International Law Journal* 42: 323.

Schulz, P. 2019. "'To Me, Justice Means to Be in a Group': Survivors' Groups as a Pathway to Justice in Northern Uganda." *Journal of Human Rights Practice* 11 (1): 171–89.

Sefa Dei, G. J. 2005. "The Challenge of Inclusive Schooling in Africa: A Ghanaian Case Study." *Comparative Education* 413: 267–89.

Seto, D. 2013. *No Place for a War Baby: The Global Politics of Children Born of Wartime*. New York: Routledge.

Smith, L. T. 1999. *Decolonizing Methodologies*. New York: Zed Books.

Stewart, B. 2015. *We Are All the Same: Experiences of Children Born into LRA Captivity*. Gulu, Uganda: Justice and Reconciliation Project.

———. 2017. "'I Feel Out of Place': Children Born into the Lord's Resistance Army and the Politics of Belonging." PhD diss., University of British Columbia.

———. 2020. "The Figure of the Abducted Acholi Girl: Nation-Building, Gender, and Children Born into the LRA in Uganda." *Journal of Modern African Studies* 58 (4): 627–47.

———. 2021. "Place-Making and the Everyday Lives of Children Born into the Lord's Resistance Army." *Children's Geographies* 19 (1): 113–26.

Sultana, F. 2007. "Reflexivity, Positionality and Participatory Ethics: Negotiating Fieldwork Dilemmas in International Research." *ACME: An International Journal for Critical Geographies* 63: 374–85.

Thomson, P. 2009. *Doing Visual Research with Children and Young People*. New York: Routledge.

Utas, M. 2005. "Victimcy, Girlfriending, Soldiering: Tactic Agency in a Young Woman's Social Navigation of the Liberian War Zone." *Anthropological Quarterly* 78, (2): 403–30.

Wainaina, B. 2005. "How to Write about Africa." *Granta* 92 (1). htttps://granta.com/How-to-Write-about-Africa/.

Watson, A. M. 2007. "Children Born of Wartime Rape: Rights and Representations." *International Feminist Journal of Politics* 91: 20–34.

Wessells, M. G. 2017. "Children and Armed Conflict: Interventions for Supporting War-Affected Children." *Peace and Conflict* 231: 4–13.

FOUR

Sheltering Survivors and Localizing Research Ethics in Northeast Nigeria

LAWAN BALAMI AND UMAR AHMAD UMAR

In 1999, the World Health Organization (WHO) published guidelines to address ethical and safety concerns in gender-based violence (GBV) research. These global guidelines require all studies involving human subjects to adhere to certain ethical principles, which are based on the experiences of the International Research Network on Violence against Women. They were designed to inform the WHO Multi-Country Study on Women's Health and Domestic Violence against Women (WHO 2007). The first principle is respect for autonomy; research subjects must voluntarily and clearly consent to the research (WHO 2007; Mfutso-Bengo, Masiye, and Muula 2008). The second principle is beneficence and nonmaleficence, which means researchers must consider all the possible consequences of the research and balance the risks with proportionate benefits (Jahn 2011). The third principle involves adhering to the ethics of justice, which means equal and unbiased selection and rationing of benefits and risks among study participants (Cookson and Dolan 2000). Last, researchers should respect anonymity, privacy, and confidentiality. This is particularly important in research involving survivors of GBV, where the identities of the participants should not be linked with any of their personal responses (Fouka and Mantzorou 2011).

Research with survivors of gender violence during war and conflict presents ethical challenges hardly addressed by conventional guidelines. Because we worked as local research teams, our study mainly relied on international guidelines to help conduct exploratory qualitative research on the life stories of women and girl survivors of conflict-related sexual and gender-based violence (CRSGBV) in northeastern Nigeria. This was due to a lack of localized ethical research protocols to guide research studies with the survivors of Sexual and gender-based violence in Nigeria. At the development Research and Project Centre (dRPC), we resorted to modifying the international guidelines based on needs, research objectives, and contexts. The study suggests that implementing predesigned global principles in conflict settings can be challenging. We show how we compensated for gaps using self-judgment in the field and navigating barriers inadequately addressed by international guidelines like the WHO 2007. This chapter shares our reflections on localizing global standards for ethical research, including the challenges of working through household and community gatekeepers in internally displaced persons camps, dilemmas presented by financial incentives for participants, problems of translation into local languages, and communicating with illiterate participants. We argue that without such nuanced adaptations, research risks being counterproductive and harmful to participants.

Background and Context: Boko Haram Insurgency

The northeast region of Nigeria is one of the six geopolitical zones in the country. It consists of six states: Borno, Yobe, Bauchi, Adamawa, Gombe, and Taraba. It is a vast and extensive region inhabited by people of approximately seventeen different ethnic groups, but the major ethnic groups are Hausa, Fulani, and Kanuri. The northeastern region has 22.3 million predominantly Muslim inhabitants (Olisa 2013).

This region has a history of religious and ethnic conflict that goes back decades. However, the current insurgency by Boko Haram began in the mid-2000s (Walker 2012). The group was initially formed as a nonviolent sect in 2002, but this later changed as it initiated an active war against the Nigerian government in 2009. Boko Haram is an Islamic sect founded on the belief that Western education must be prohibited. A group of corrupt Muslims dominate Nigerian politics, particularly in the North. These beliefs are why Boko Haram wages war against the governing bodies in the North and the Federal Republic of Nigeria: to establish a "cleansed" Islamic state to be governed by sharia law. Fueled by a desire for vengeance against politicians, security agencies, and Islamic authorities, Boko Haram has killed thousands and displaced millions of civilians, especially in northeastern Nigeria. Its rampage is driven by religious radicalization, previous interreligious intolerance, poverty, and financial incentives.

Boko Haram engages in inhumane practices such as mass killings and the destruction of property. Their tactics include abduction of women and girls for forced marriage and forced hard labor but also to act as foot soldiers or suicide bombers (Matfess 2017). The sect has abducted over two thousand women and girls alone in the past few years. These abductions are often well planned and systematic, with some girls abducted from schools while others are forcefully taken from their homes as parents and siblings watch helplessly. Although many theories exist as to why the rebels kidnap young women and girls, experience shows that the primary reason for these abductions is forced marriage and sexual slavery.

As a result of the ongoing conflict, more than 2.5 million people have been exposed to multiple risks through displacement and migration over the past ten years (Amalu 2016). Thousands of women and girls have been abducted for child and forced marriage, sexual slavery, and forced labor (Zenn and Pearson 2014). As a consequence, the regional incidence of gender-based violence has rapidly increased. Indeed, United Nations High Commissioner for Refugees reports that there have been over 1,666 incidents of SGBV in Borno, Adamawa, and Yobe States from January to December 2019 (UNHCR 2020).

Research is essential for designing targeted interventions to support survivors of conflict-related sexual violence (Seagle et al. 2020). This may be counterproductive, however, with poor knowledge and lack of adherence to standard ethical guidelines by less experienced humanitarian actors and researchers (UNFPA 2016). Moreover, research has a unique set of dynamics and challenges regarding data collection, handling, and reporting. A myriad of specific ethical guidelines has to be considered and addressed before the commencement of any inquiry (WHO 2007). Although the general principles of research ethics used in nonemergency settings are similar to those in emergencies, some of the unique circumstances in emergencies may require case-specific ethical considerations (Mfutso-Bengo, Masiye, and Muula 2008). In conflict situations, the adherence to ethical standards cannot be overemphasized, as ethics promote the aim of the research and strengthen values essential to collaborative work like ours. They also help to ensure that researchers are held accountable to the public for their research (WHO 2007). Failure to adhere to ethical standards when working with survivors of CRSGBV can result in physical, emotional, and social harm to participants and may even be life threatening (Resnik 2015). Hence, before embarking on our research in northeastern Nigeria, it was important to exhaust all other data sources and to establish a demonstrable need to conduct primary data with survivors of CRSGBV (WHO 2007).

Research Methodology

This chapter draws from qualitative research and fieldwork conducted from June to August 2017 in internally displaced persons' (IDP) camps located on the outskirts of Maiduguri, Borno State.[1] These were Dalori camp, Muna camp, and Farm center camp. These IDP camps accommodate over thirty-five thousand IDPs and are the major entry points for returning survivors of CRSGBV from captivity (UNHCR n.d.).

The study received financial support from the Social Sciences and Humanities Research Council partnership and the Conjugal Slavery in War, a feminist collaborative research project that studies and documents enslavement, marriage, and masculinities to contribute to knowledge and understanding of forced marriage in war. Collaborating with community-based organizations like the Development Research and Project Center (dRPC), the partnership aimed to strengthen both individual and organizational capacity to prevent violence and advance the understanding of conjugal slavery as a weapon of war through evidence-based research. Conjugal Slavery in War supported dRPC to conduct exploratory qualitative research to document the life stories of women and girl survivors of CRSGBV. The dRPC research team comprised seventeen people: a research consultant, eight trained local female researchers from the Department of Social Sciences at the University of Maiduguri,[2] a field coordinator, a photographer, three interviewers, and three note takers.

The research team held in-depth interviews with seven survivors randomly selected from three IDP camps (as part of a larger set of interviews with fifty former Boko Haram captives). These included three women and four girls formerly abducted by Boko Haram. The participants were survivors of Boko Haram mass abductions for forced marriage, child labor, and radicalization. Most of the participants were abducted during invasions of small towns and villages. Some were taken directly from their homes in the presence of their families, while others were taken in transit while trying to escape to other towns. Six participants were forced to marry Boko Haram insurgents during captivity. The remaining woman who protested against forced marriage was adopted as a sex slave and subject to hard labor, including household chores. Some women who agreed to the marriage proposals rose to the ranks of combatants, performing infiltrative roles such as spying and suicide bombing. While this chapter concerns itself with the research process, we have analyzed the interviews in a previous report.[3]

Data was collected using an interview guide informed by previous desk reviews of research related to GBV among conflict-affected populations. The interview guide contained open-ended questions that gave participants the scope to express themselves within the confines of their comfort levels. The research consultant reviewed this and other instruments and pretested them by conducting preliminary interviews with similar respondents before administering them to the sampled survivors of CRSGBV.

During the interviews, specific attention was given to understanding the interviewees' feelings, fears, and emotions while in captivity. The respondents were asked to speak of their personal experiences and narratives related to other survivors. The interviews ranged from fifty to ninety minutes in duration and were conducted in the local languages of the region, which were predominantly Kanuri and Hausa. This was done to better understand exchanges between the interviewers and respondents.

ETHICAL CONSIDERATIONS

The WHO informed consent form for research involving vulnerable populations was adopted in this study (WHO 2015). Eligible respondents (formerly abducted women and girls) for the interviews were contacted through psychosocial support counselors who were informed of all aspects of the project, including purpose, risks, benefits, and all study safety measures to protect the research participants. The participants were informed that none of their personal information would be recorded. The selected participants were asked for consent before participation in the study, and the dRPC research team ensured no linkages of the interviewees' names to camp residents. The participants were also asked for separate consent to record interviews and discussions and informed of security measures to protect the recordings. Mothers with children fathered by Boko Haram members were asked questions related to their children, and verbal consent was also sought from them before commencing the interviews. Participant confidentiality was maintained throughout the full consent and discussion/interview process. For ethical reasons, we removed the names of the respondents from the transcripts to protect their anonymity. Identification labels were attached to quotations only for differentiation. Names of armed groups were also excluded from quotations to protect further attacks on the participants from insurgents.

The experience of dRPC documenting the women's stories opened doors for further stakeholder discussions. It served as a learning tool and opportunity to provide additional context and insight regarding the peculiar challenges of adhering to ethical principles while working with survivors of GBV (see CSiW 2019). However, in this chapter, we zoom in on dRPC's experience navigating the field and the ethical dilemmas and challenges encountered during recruitment, accessing, and interviewing the research participants.

Challenges with Adherence to Ethical Guidelines

This section presents some of the experiences and key challenges the dRPC research team encountered in conducting exploratory qualitative research—while adhering to ethical guidelines—on the life stories of women and girl survivors of CRSGBV.

The study involved nonliterate women. This in itself was challenging, as several modifications to facilitate communication and obtaining consent had to be made to the ethical protocols to meet the needs of the research target population. For example, the research team had to seek and obtain the consent of male head of household or community leaders before they could interview some of the participants. In some rural Nigerian communities, it is common for community leaders and household heads to permit certain things to be done in their communities/households. Although the practice is socially acceptable in some communities, it constitutes a potential breach of the ethical injunction of ensuring confidentiality in the research, especially in cases where perpetrators could be residents within the household or community (Bruno and Haar 2020). The participants might not have been able to decline requests for interviews if community leader / household heads had agreed to it.

The power of the community leader / household head to do and undo may have forced some participants to give their consent under duress or coercion, as more often than not, the consent or permission provided by household heads or community leaders may have been understood to automatically supersede the autonomy of the respondent to either participate or withdraw; the women might have felt morally obligated to participate following instructions from their elders. This was a great challenge as it is believed that too many modifications to conventional guidelines in GBV research, especially those related to confidentiality and anonymity, may invalidate a study (Bruno and Haar 2020).

Closely linked to the challenge above is the power wielded by IDP camp officials. Most survivors live in confined environments such as IDP camps where basic support services are offered and some form of protection by security personnel is provided. The atmosphere in the camps was tense. These environments with a strong military presence affected our interview processes since the participants might have agreed to take part in the study because camp officials endorsed it. Declining requests to be interviewed could have been interpreted as acts of disobedience.

It is noted that locations such as IDP camps form clusters from which researchers sample survivors to participate in SGBV studies, which may be convenient (UNICEF 2016). This, however, also comes with ethical complications since the survivors are identified, screened, and singled out by other community members to participate in the research. While the highest possible standards may be employed in the process, this practice conveys the impression that survivors are favored for attention and support compared to other community members, which further exposes the survivors to stigmatization (Fouka and

Mantzorou 2011). Additionally, when this practice is linked with incentives to cover transportation costs, it creates an atmosphere of envy toward survivors by community members (UNICEF 2016). Although counterproductive, researchers have little to no control over these actions as they are often handled by community structures such as women leaders and security personnel. This was also the case in our study since these structures are entry points for establishing contact with survivors. Research processes may thus fuel resentment and stigma around survivors due to poor ethics adherence (UNICEF 2016).

Studies have shown that researchers, especially during conflict and humanitarian crises, conduct studies down the social ladder—their subjects are economically disadvantaged individuals, those less literate and more stigmatized or discriminated against. This can create an informal hierarchy, making it difficult for participants to say no when approached for consent (Garcia-Moreno 2001). Although challenging, these cultural and context-specific characteristics cannot be completely dissociated from research involving vulnerable populations during times of humanitarian crises. There are also legitimate concerns regarding whether or not complete adherence to ethical standards is practical given all of the cultural, socioeconomic, and community factors at play (Habib 2019).

Managing Participants' Expectations

In our research, we realized that the practice of offering financial incentives to respondents for their participation in studies greatly influenced their interpretation of "benefits." Similarly, the practice has heightened their expectations of potential benefits from *any* data collection activity. While some studies suggest this is justifiable as it represents value for the information they are providing (Garcia-Moreno 2001), the greater consensus among researchers is that it is ethically compromising and introduces informant bias into the study (Hsieh and Kocielnik 2016; Resnik 2015). While avoiding incentives may seem routine and easy to apply on paper, it can be challenging to adhere to in a humanitarian situation. Take, for example, the scenario where a researcher is reading out an informed consent form to a hungry-looking female survivor with a hungry child. This scenario puts the researcher in a position where they may feel morally inclined to support the participant's immediate needs, especially if this support might facilitate their ability to contribute to the research process. Another consideration is that the major source of income in these populations is either farming or petty trading; time allocated to participate in the interviews may thus mean taking money out of the pockets of impoverished people. This further put researchers in a moral dilemma about whether compensation for time lost is ethically acceptable or not. Undoubtedly, all of this affects the interview process. During fieldwork, the researchers witnessed instances when participants failed to complete the interview when incentives were provided at the start. However, when incentives were offered at the end, the majority stay until completion. A widely debated issue is thus whether researchers may have sensitized participants to see the incentives as the only benefits of interest resulting from the research process (CSiW 2019; Garcia-Moreno 2001).

During humanitarian crises, research activities must be expedited. However, the bureaucratic processes involved in seeking ethical approvals from institutional review boards (IRBs) can significantly slow down the research activities (see Okyere, this volume; Bruno and Haar 2020). Although IRBs form an integral part of ethics in research, these delays may sometimes not be in the best interest of the beneficiaries, especially during emergencies where data collection feeds into interventions that aim to meet immediate needs. A study on the life stories of the CRSGBV survivors was conducted in northeastern Nigeria with no ethical review boards present. And in cases where such bodies are nonexistent, obtaining ethical approval may be almost impossible.

Recommendations for Ethical Standards Working with the Survivors of CRSGBV

Conventional ethical guidelines applied in health and sciences are insufficient to address context-specific and constantly varying ethical dilemmas that arise through research involving survivors of GBV in humanitarian crises (Garcia-Moreno 2001). The peculiar challenges experienced by these survivors place them in positions where they become vulnerable to harm, risk, and undue influence in research studies. This has, in some instances, been attributed to the failure of regulatory bodies leading to self-regulation by researchers (Fouka and Mantzorou 2011), poor knowledge and poor adherence to ethical guidelines for vulnerable populations (Rudra and Lenk 2020; Seagle et al. 2020; UNFPA 2016). As Walker discusses in this volume, there is a need for national or regional oversight of qualitative and evaluation research.

As a matter of urgency, the establishment of an ethical review board is needed, one that will regulate the conduct of research in the humanitarian context in Nigeria. The board should be mandated to review and monitor researchers' conduct with conflict survivors. There is also a need to develop standard ethical research protocols that are context specific, taking into consideration the peculiarities of northeastern communities.

WHO recommends that to avoid exposure of survivors to risk or harm, researchers should consider whether every other data source has been exhausted before embarking on data collection. This reduces exposure to risk or harm and reduces respondent fatigue from developing and compromising data quality (Lavrakas 2013).

Research protocols must always consider the potential benefits and risks of research activities to participants and their communities. Where there is an imbalance such that the risks outweigh the potential benefits, the activity must be aborted and, where possible, modified to a version that addresses the risks and concerns identified (IOM 2019). An example is when the perpetrator of GBV is a resident in the community where the research is to be conducted; in the absence of a safe space, interviewing in that community exposes the survivor to more harm.

Research protocols need to be revised and adapted to conform with global ethical and protection standards where potential harm exists. An initial step toward this can be achieved by community engagement and collaboration with local stakeholders to conduct independent reviews of the research protocols, identify research gaps, and determine the potential for exposure to risk for both participants and the community before commencement of the study (Bruno and Haar 2020; Contreras-Urbina et al. 2019). This is strongly tied to the concept of beneficence and nonmaleficence. The researcher needs to analyze how the activity may benefit or harm participants and strategize how best to prevent or minimize this potential (Fouka and Mantzorou 2011). These analyses, often overlooked, must be conducted before, during, and after any research activity (Seagle et al. 2020; WHO 2007).

Manifestations of risks due to poor adherence to research ethics while working with survivors of GBV often vary based on the context, preexisting cultural or social norms, and the region's security situation (Contreras-Urbina et al. 2019). These may range from effects such as psychosocial or emotional harm leading to mental trauma due to reliving traumatic experiences (Fouka and Mantzorou 2011) to wider effects such as negative community attitudes, including revictimization, rejection, stigma, and verbal and physical abuse. These effects often have socioeconomic implications for survivors such as denial of equal access to opportunities and resources (Fouka and Mantzorou 2011). Researchers therefore need to explore preexisting factors and assess how they may affect survivors following the research activity before it is conducted. Adhering to the principles of beneficence and nonmaleficence also entails avoiding multiple exposures of GBV survivors by duplicating efforts during data collection activities; the WHO recommends that humanitarian workers and researchers coordinate their efforts in this regard—avoiding what may be convenient for researchers or humanitarian organizations but detrimental to the health and well-being of participants (UN WOMEN 2010; WHO 2007). We believe adhering to these principles will go a long way toward minimizing the risk of emotional and physical harm to women and girls participating in any study (UN WOMEN 2010).

Information gathering among vulnerable populations, particularly survivors of GBV, should be guided by sound methodologies that provide detailed information to the target beneficiaries (WHO 2007). It is recommended that research activities be conducted with academically sound methodologies and, at the same time, have practical and contextual relevance (Bruno and Haar 2020). Participants should be adequately informed about the purpose of the research activity and potential benefits or harm. Contrary to the common practice of handing over informed consent forms to participants to read and append their signatures or thumbprints (WHO 2007), in certain contexts and before any form is signed, researchers must take time to communicate in a language best understood by the participants the purpose of the research activity and how the information will be used. Enough time should be allocated for thorough communication about the purpose of the research, and researchers also need to be clear that participation or lack thereof will not affect their access to services or benefits. Where incentives are provided, their nature should be made explicit before the interview (Resnik 2015; WHO 2007). In short, researchers need to be precise in explaining the research activity while not giving the participants any unrealistic expectations. The WHO recommends that a standardized informed consent form should communicate the background of the research activity, the objective of the interview, and the nature of the questions to be asked, including those that may involve remembrances of traumatic experiences, potential risks and benefits, ethical protocols for protecting participants, the autonomy of participation, and plans for dissemination of the findings (WHO 2007). An important consideration for informed consent in our research was that it was communicated in a language the participants most easily understood. Where language discord exists between a researcher and participants, an interpreter should be engaged to translate the document in an easily comprehended way. However, in the case of employing a translator, it is best to choose a professional interpreter or experienced researcher who is likely to conform to ethical standards. If both of these options are unavailable, a legal representative such as the IDP camp mental health and psychosocial support (MHPSS) counselor, Camp Coordination and Camp Management staff, a family member, or a guardian may provide such services (White et al. 2018).

Communicating the text contained in the informed consent form alone is not enough to validate informed consent; researchers need to confirm if respondents have a complete comprehension of the information provided and have confirmed their intention to willingly participate based on this knowledge. Only when this is accomplished can the consent be referred to as informed and ethically valid (Sugarman and Paasche-Orlow 2006; WHO 2007). Sudore et al. (2006) describe a technique known as "teaching to goal" in research involving vulnerable populations. The informed consent form is read to the respondents, who are also asked to read it to themselves or to repeat the words when they cannot read and write. Following this, they are asked a number of questions about the information provided and assigned a score, which determines whether or not the consent meets the criteria of being informed—after which data collection can proceed. If the participant fails, the process can be repeated, or the participant can withdraw from the study (Sudore et al. 2006; Sugarman and Paasche-Orlow 2006).

After all these steps have been implemented, the participants confirm their participation either in writing or verbally. While signatures may be the norm and have long been used as evidence for informed consent, this is highly discouraged when working with survivors of GBV since the signatures may serve as identifiers. The WHO recommends that the researcher signs a document confirming receipt of informed consent from each participant (WHO 2007).

Before, during, and after data collection, confidentiality is one of the most important methodological components to consider; however, researchers are inconsistent in their ability to apply and strictly adhere to this principle. This has been largely attributed to using global guidelines in varying contexts (Bruno and Haar 2020; Contreras-Urbina et al. 2019). Although contextual variations exist, confidentiality when conducting studies on survivors of GBV is nonnegotiable, and failure to adhere to this does not only depict a violation of ethics. It may also expose survivors and researchers alike to high levels of risk and harm (Contreras-Urbina et al. 2019). Where the safety and protection of participants are paramount, identities must be withheld and treated with the highest levels of confidentiality; no identifiers such as names or other markers are used in reports or publications resulting from the research activity (WHO 2007). At the onset of the proposal, protocols must therefore protect participants by ensuring confidentiality during data collection, transportation, storage, and reporting (Garcia-Moreno 2001). Interviews should be conducted in secure and safe environments (such as women's and girls' safe spaces) to avoid attention and ensure that participants' responses cannot be overheard (Shair, Akhter, and Shama 2019; WHO 2007). The WHO discourages taking photos and other identifying information to be used in reports or other publications when researching survivors of GBV. However, where this is necessary, it should follow ethical guidelines such as blurring faces and other features that can identify the survivor (WHO 2007).

When local researchers who are also residents in target communities are engaged to conduct interviews, confidentiality and adherence become even more important. In our study, the research team selected from the communities underwent intense ethics training and the risks attached to poor adherence. The team was also trained in strategies for navigating barriers to maintaining confidentiality as they interacted with survivors on a daily basis (WHO 2007). Research participants rightly worry about gossip and repercussions—harms that need to be mitigated by the team.

Hunt et al. (2016) suggest that when a study is initiated to facilitate emergency interventions, IRBs may standardize research protocol templates that can be modified in emergency contexts to avoid the bottlenecks of bureaucratic processes (Bruno and Haar 2020; Hunt et al. 2016). Using preapproved templates, they argue, will facilitate approval processes and help overcome some of the ethical challenges researchers face. Some educational projects have been exempted from IRB reviews in emergencies in certain countries (Mfutso-Bengo, Masiye, and Muula 2008); a similar approach can be applied to research involving survivors of GBV; however, considering the sensitive nature of the information, this should apply only in situations where researchers make use of preapproved research protocols.

The WHO recommendations state that where research on survivors of GBV involves data collection through the narration of past traumatic experiences, there is a need to provide first-line basic support services to cater for both emotional and physical injury that may result from triggering past events; these could range from MHPSS to treatment of physical injuries and other ailments (WHO 2007). Basic physical and mental health care should be accessible before commencing activities to reexpose survivors to traumatic experiences. The research activity feeds into developing programs that benefit survivors' immediate and emergency needs, such as interventions that prevent or address sexual violence (WHO 2007). Although this is highly recommended, it is not commonly practiced: as only 15 percent of reviewed studies have qualified personnel available to provide first-line basic support to survivors (Seagle et al. 2020). In settlements such as IDP camps where such services exist and are accessible, survivors may be referred with their consent to benefit from MHPSS counseling sessions and other needs. Where such services are absent or have yet to be established, such as in newly emerging humanitarian crises (WHO 2007), it is recommended that researchers acquire the required training and skills to provide first-line support for survivors' mental trauma and other basic needs (Lee et al. 2019). While these are good recommendations, in practice, the research team may not have the required expertise, and the survivor may not have access to MHPSS if the organizations providing the services do not have a professional affiliation with the research team. However, these options are relevant only when information cannot be obtained from other accessible data sources.

While there are unique challenges in researching children in humanitarian crises (Habib 2019), their vulnerability makes adherence to ethical standards even more critical (WHO 2007). General ethical guidelines have already been outlined in this chapter, but additional considerations must be taken into account. Foremost it is recommended when working with children to use simple language in the informed consent form; it should be short and precise and consider the child's cognitive development (Albersheim 2008). Children are also more likely to have limited knowledge of their rights, increasing their risk of falling prey to exploitation and exposure to physical and emotional harm (WHO 2007).

Even if children may not fully comprehend the ethical procedures involved in research, they must be involved at every step of the research process and allowed assent or dissent when it comes to participation in research activities (De Lourdes Levy et al. 2003). Assent entails an expression of agreement to participate in the study, while dissent is an expression of disagreement (Brown et al. 2017). Global variations exist regarding the legal age for consent in children; however, in Nigeria, a child can consent to participate in a study at fourteen (Federal Ministry of Health 2014). If the child does not have the legal status to consent, a parent or legal guardian with the child's best interest at heart may consent on their behalf (De Lourdes Levy et al. 2003). Cheah and Parker (2014), however, recommend an informed consent model in their study where assent is sought from the child as a prerequisite to consent from the adult; this, according to them, is more in line with global ethical standards as it involves the child in the decision process (see also De Lourdes Levy et al. 2003).

A highly skilled and qualified research team should be selected to conduct and supervise studies on GBV. Before commencing fieldwork, the team should have capacity building on core topics such as qualitative research techniques and ethical principles, particularly those that apply to survivors of GBV, GBV core concepts, basic MHPSS, and case management (Global Protection Cluster 2014). Researchers should avoid any intimidating behavior that may create an environment in which participants cannot express themselves freely or from which they are unable to withdraw (Garcia-Moreno 2001). Several cultural and demographic characteristics should also be considered when selecting the research team. The WHO recommends that researchers speak the same language as the survivor; where this is not possible, a professional translator should be sought (WHO 2007). The gender of the enumerators should also be factored into the selection criteria since survivors are mostly female and are more likely to open up to female researchers. Women should be given priority for selection as interviewers, while men can perform other functions such as supervisors (IOM 2019). However, gender alone should not be the only criterion for selection as other factors, such as experience and level of expertise, are also important.

Recommendations

Ethical considerations when researching survivors of GBV are complex and differ from other research activities in multiple ways. Unlike conventional studies, survivors who agree to participate speak out in a societal context of silence, fear, and shame. They are opening up about painful and personal experiences that could make them targets of stigma, rejection, and physical and emotional abuse (Garcia-Moreno 2001). Although global ethical guidelines exist, their application may differ based on different scenarios and contexts, which makes it even more challenging to have a one-size-fits-all protocol for GBV research. The complexity stems from working in precarious postconflict settings and speaking about GBV. As a result, researchers often have to resort to personal and moral judgments of what represents the best interest of participants and design new or modify existing protocols to address the dynamic challenges in this field of research. Additionally, research such as ours, which involves international researchers, is met with peculiar challenges. In our case, some of these were context-specific barriers, and how to navigate them was largely unknown to our international researchers.

This demonstrates the need to develop context-specific, localized protocols that are strong yet adaptable and detail flexible and alternative plans to address multiple ethical, safety, and security challenges. To achieve this, there is a need for strong collaboration between government at the local level, researchers and research organizations, and local and international stakeholders in developing, reviewing, and standardizing research guidelines, protocols, and methodologies. In drafting the required documents, specific attention should be paid to attending to survivors' economic and social needs, indirect coercion for consent, handling confidentiality in confined and densely populated settlements like IDP camps, and basic support services when conducting interviews. We believe that predeveloped and localized research protocols that focus on local issues will ensure cultural, economic, and social sensitivity in research on GBV survivors. This output could also guide the adoption of global ethical guidelines in conducting GBV research in regions like northeastern Nigeria.

Notes

1. We would like to show appreciation to Dr Judith Ann Walker, the Executive Director of dRPC Nigeria and Dr. Annie Bunting of York University Canada for the

support and guidance in rolling out this research activity. We equally appreciate the state government officials, women and girls, community, traditional and religious leaders, camp management and security agents who left their busy schedules to support field activities and participate in the Key Informant Interviews. The findings and conclusions in this chapter are those of the authors and do not necessarily represent the official position of dRPC.
2. The students were trained on research ethics and how to conduct in-depth interviews with female survivors of CRSGBV.
3. See Nigeria Country Report, August 2019, available on CSiW website: https://csiw-ectg.org/resources/publications/.

References

Albersheim, S. 2008. "Ethical Considerations at the Threshold of Viability." *BCMJ* 50 (9): 509–11.

Amalu, N. S. 2016. "Impact of Boko Haram Insurgency on Human Security in Nigeria." *Global Journal of Social Sciences* 14 (1): 35. https://doi.org/10.4314/gjss.v14i1.4.

Brown, H. R., E. A. Harvey, S. F. Griffith, D. H. Arnold, and R. P. Halgin. 2017. "Assent and Dissent: Ethical Considerations in Research with Toddlers." *Ethics and Behavior* 27 (8): 651–64. https://doi.org/10.1080/10508422.2016.1277356.

Bruno, W., and R. J. Haar. 2020. "A Systematic Literature Review of the Ethics of Conducting Research in the Humanitarian Setting." *Conflict and Health* 14 (1): 3–14. https://doi.org/10.1186/s13031-020-00282-0.

Cheah, P. Y., and M. Parker. 2014. "Consent and Assent in Paediatric Research in Low-Income Settings." *BMC Medical Ethics* 15 (1): 22. https://doi.org/10.1186/1472-6939-15-22.

Contreras-Urbina, M., A. Blackwell, M. Murphy, and M. Ellsberg. 2019. "Researching Violence against Women and Girls in South Sudan: Ethical and Safety Considerations and Strategies." *Conflict and Health* 13, article 55. https://doi.org/10.1186/s13031-019-0239-4.

Cookson, R., and P. Dolan. 2000. "Principles of Justice in Health Care Rationing." *Journal of Medical Ethics* 26 (5): 323–29. https://doi.org/10.1136/jme.26.5.323.

CSiW (Conjugal Slavery in War Project). 2019. *Nigeria Country Report—Conjugal Slavery in War*. http://csiw-ectg.org/nigeria-country-report/.

De Lourdes Levy, M., V. Larcher, R. Kurz, T. L. Chambers, F. P. Crawley, D. Gill, M. LoGiudice et al. 2003. "Informed Consent/Assent in Children: Statement of the Ethics Working Group of the Confederation of European Specialists in Paediatrics (CESP)." *European Journal of Pediatrics* 162 (9): 629–33. https://doi.org/10.1007/s00431-003-1193-z.

Federal Ministry of Health. 2014. *Federal Ministry of Health Guidelines for Young Persons' Participation in Research and Access to Sexual and Reproductive Health Services in Nigeria*. Abuja: Federal Ministry of Health. https://www.popcouncil.org/uploads/pdfs/2014HIV_YoungPersonsSRH-Nigeria.pdf.

Fouka, G., and M. Mantzorou. 2011. "What Are the Major Ethical Issues in Conducting Research? Is There a Conflict between the Research Ethics and the Nature of Nursing?" *Health Science Journal* 5 (1): 3–14.

Garcia-Moreno, C. 2001. *Putting Women First: Ethical and Safety Recommendations for Research on Domestic Violence against Women*. Geneva: World Health Organization. http://apps.who.int/iris/handle/10665/65893.

Global Protection Cluster. 2014. *Core Competencies for GBV Program Managers and Coordinators in Humanitarian Settings*. N.p.: Global Protection Cluster. https://www.refworld.org/pdfid/5c3704637.pdf.

Habib, R. R. 2019. "Ethical, Methodological, and Contextual Challenges in Research in Conflict Settings: The Case of Syrian Refugee Children in Lebanon." *Conflict and Health* 13 (1): 1–7. https://doi.org/10.1186/s13031-019-0215-z.

Hsieh, G., and R. Kocielnik. 2016. "You Get Who You Pay For: The Impact of Incentives on Participation Bias." *Proceedings of the ACM Conference on Computer Supported Cooperative Work* 27: 823–35. https://doi.org/10.1145/2818048.2819936.

Hunt, M., C. M. Tansey, J. Anderson, R. F. Boulanger, L. Eckenwiler, J. Pringle, and L. Schwartz. 2016. "The Challenge of Timely, Responsive and Rigorous Ethics Review of Disaster Research: Views of Research Ethics Committee Members." *PLoS ONE* 11 (6): 1–15. https://doi.org/10.1371/journal.pone.0157142.

IOM (International Organization for Migration). 2019. *Gender-Based Violence Knowledge, Attitudes and Practices Survey*. Geneva: International Organization for Migration. https://publications.iom.int/system/files/pdf/south-sudan-gender-based-kap.pdf.

Jahn, W. T. 2011. "The 4 Basic Ethical Principles That Apply to Forensic Activities Are Respect for Autonomy, Beneficence, Nonmaleficence, and Justice." *Journal of Chiropractic Medicine* 10 (3): 225–26. https://doi.org/10.1016/j.jcm.2011.08.004.

Lavrakas, P. 2013. "Respondent Fatigue." In *Encyclopedia of Survey Research Methods*. Sage Publications. https://doi.org/10.4135/9781412963947.n480.

Lee, C., A. J. Nguyen, E. Haroz, W. Tol, Y. Aules, and P. Bolton. 2019. "Identifying Research Priorities for Psychosocial Support Programs in Humanitarian Settings." *Global Mental Health* 6 (e23): 1–10. https://doi.org/10.1017/gmh.2019.19.

Matfess, H. 2017. *Women and the War on Boko Haram: Wives, Weapons, Witnesses*. London: Zed Books.

Mfutso-Bengo, J., F. Masiye, and A. Muula. 2008. "Ethical Challenges in Conducting Research in Humanitarian Crisis Situations." *Malawi Medical Journal* 20 (2): 46–49. https://doi.org/10.4314/mmj.v20i2.10956.

Olisa, I. D. 2013. "Insurgency in the North-East of Nigeria and Its Implications on Inter-State and Trans-Border Mobility." Unpublished paper.

Resnik, D. 2015. "Bioethical Issues in Providing Financial Incentives to Research Participants." *Medicolegal and Bioethics* 5: 35. https://doi.org/10.2147/mb.s70416.

Rudra, P., and C. Lenk. 2020. "Process of Risk Assessment by Research Ethics Committees: Foundations, Shortcomings and Open Questions." *Journal of Medical Ethics* 47: 343–49. https://doi.org/10.1136/medethics-2019-105595.

Seagle, E. E., A. J. Dam, P. P. Shah, J. L. Webster, D. H. Barrett, L. W. Ortmann, N. J. Cohen, and N. N. Marano. 2020. "Research Ethics and Refugee Health: A Review of Reported Considerations and Applications in Published Refugee Health Literature, 2015–2018." *Conflict and Health* 14 (1): 1–15. https://doi.org/10.1186/s13031-020-00283-z.

Shair, D., K. Akhter, and A. Shama. 2019. "The Role of Psychosocial Support in Coping with Incidents of Gender-Based Violence among Rohingya Refugees." *Intervention* 17 (2): 238–42. https://doi.org/10.4103/INTV.INTV_16_19.

Sudore, R., C. Landefeld, B. Williams, D. Barnes, K. Lindquist, and D. Schillinger. 2006. "Use of a Modified Informed Consent Process among Vulnerable Patients: A Descriptive Study." *Journal of General Internal Medicine* 21 (9): 1009. https://doi.org/10.1007/bf02743161.

Sugarman, J., and M. Paasche-Orlow. 2006. "Confirming Comprehension of Informed Consent as a Protection of Human Subjects." *Journal of General Internal Medicine* 21 (8): 898–99. https://doi.org/10.1111/j.1525-1497.2006.00542.x.

UNFPA (United Nations Population Fund). 2016. *Reporting Ethically on Gender Based Violence in the Syria Crisis.*

UNHCR (United Nations High Commissioner for Refugees). n.d. "Internally Displaced People." UNHCR, accessed October 25, 2022. https://www.unhcr.org/internally-displaced-people.html.

———. 2020. *Gender-Based Violence Prevention, Risk Mitigation and Response during COVID-19.* N.p.: UNHCR. https://reliefweb.int/report/world/gender-based-violence-prevention-risk-mitigation-and-response-during-covid-19.

UNICEF. 2016. *"Bad Blood": Perceptions of Children Born of Conflict-Related Sexual Violence and Women and Girls Associated with Boko Haram in Northeast Nigeria.* Abuja: UNICEF Nigeria; London: International Alert. https://www.international-alert.org/publications/bad-blood.

UN WOMEN. 2010. "Ethical Considerations in Monitoring Violence against Women." Virtual Knowledge Centre to End Violence against Women and Girls, last edited October 30, 2010. https://www.endvawnow.org/en/articles/174-ethical-considerations.html.

Walker, A. 2012. *Special Report: What Is Boko Haram?* Washington, DC: United States Institute of Peace. https://www.usip.org/sites/default/files/SR308.pdf.

White, J., T. Plompen, C. Osadnik, L. Tao, E. Micallef, and T. Haines. 2018. "The Experience of Interpreter Access and Language Discordant Clinical Encounters in Australian Health Care: A Mixed Methods Exploration." *International Journal for Equity in Health* 17 (1): 151. https://doi.org/10.1186/s12939-018-0865-2.

WHO (World Health Organization). 2007. *WHO Ethical and Safety Recommendations for Researching, Documenting and Monitoring Sexual Violence in Emergencies.* Geneva: World Health Organization. https://www.who.int/publications/i/item/9789241595681.

WHO (World Health Organization) Ethics Research Committee. 2015. "Templates for Informed Consent Forms." https://www.who.int/groups/research-ethics-review-committee/guidelines-on-submitting-research-proposals-for-ethics-review/templates-for-informed-consent-forms.

Zenn, J., and E. Pearson. 2014. "Women, Gender and the Evolving Tactics of Boko Haram." *Journal of Terrorism Research* 5 (1): 2–12. https://doi.org/10.15664/jtr.828.

FIVE

Research with Formerly Abducted Mothers and Fathers in Postconflict Northern Uganda

A Plea for Transparency

LEEN DE NUTTE

When setting up and implementing a research project, the researcher is ethically obliged to "guide, protect, and oversee the interests of the people he or she is studying" (Neuman 2011, 58). Moreover, research with participants who had experienced traumatic events due to collective violence is fraught with methodological and ethical challenges because of the many constraints in conflict and postconflict settings (Balami and Umar, this volume; Clark-Kazak 2021; De Haene, Grietens, and Verschueren 2010). Researchers run the risk of potentially violating the ethic to "do no harm" since they could expect participants to recount traumatizing experiences, the reliving of which can lead to distress, trauma, and even revictimization (El-Khani et al. 2013; WHO 2007). Research among people whose social positions are precarious, such as former child soldiers and victims of sexual and gender-based violence, can expose personal histories that they would prefer to keep hidden from their families and communities, and revealing these experiences could exacerbate their distress or initiate discrimination and marginalization (Apio 2016; Balami and Umar, this volume; Kohrt, Rai, and Maharjan 2015; Quirk, Bunting, and Kiconco, this volume).

Having few financial and social resources can also impede participants' autonomy in deciding to voluntarily participate in a research project (Atim, this volume; Mackenzie, McDowell, and Pittaway 2007; Schiltz and Büscher 2018). Participants may feel forced to participate and feel that they need to answer all the questions posed during interviews, hoping that full disclosure would increase their prospects of securing some kind of support. Sometimes they may not have (full) access to sufficient information to understand the implications of their participation (Wessells 2009; WHO 2007). On the other hand, scholars also point to the need to respect "participants' capacities for self-determination and their agency and resilience and [to] avoid paternalism" (Mackenzie, McDowell, and Pittaway 2007, 309). Participants could also perceive the research process as a way to have their voices heard and even become agents of advocacy for themselves and their peers (De Haene, Grietens, and Verschueren 2010; Wood 2006).

There will always be challenges associated with the potential extractive character of research, especially when projects are implemented in the Global South by researchers, institutions, and funders from the Global North (Clark-Kazak 2021; Okyere, this volume; Quirk, Bunting, and Kiconco, this volume; Van Den Berg 2020). All too often, researchers enter the research context with predefined projects, collect data, and disappear without further communicating their findings or generating "knowledge which has value to the communities from which it came" (Bunting and Quirk 2020, 9).

So how do we act given the unpredictability of the many methodological and ethical issues encountered before, during, and after fieldwork—which can be even more complicated in (post)conflict settings? Notwithstanding any number of guidelines and "best practices," "the bad news is that there are no definitive rules or universal principles that can tell you precisely what to do in every situation or relationship you may encounter, other than the vague and generic 'do no harm'" (Ellis 2007, 5). Researchers consequently need to reflect on the potential harm and benefits at every stage of the research process and be ready to adapt in ethical, moral, and responsive ways to unforeseen circumstances (Lahman et al. 2011).

Choices and decisions are continuously made by research teams and responded to by participants and their environments. Often, however, these choices and decisions are not openly shared in research publications—that is, "ethics and methods are usually addressed in relative brief and frequently perfunctory terms (assuming they are explicitly addressed at all), which reflects their status as a prelude to the main event" (Quirk, Bunting, and Kiconco, this volume). This lack of description and reflection limits the scrutiny and evaluation of research projects by all the parties involved or engaged in the research, such as participants, research brokers, ethical review boards, other scholars, community-based organizations (CBOs), nongovernmental organizations (NGOs), funders, and persons reading the publications. In this chapter, I want to plead for more transparency at all stages of the research process: openness about data collection, methods, analysis, and interpretation to enable the persons involved in the research and various audiences to "scrutinize [one's] work and the evidence used to support [one's] findings and conclusions" (Yin 2011, 19). Such open reflection can also support future researchers in anticipating similar ethical and methodological challenges (Clark-Kazak 2021). To illustrate the value of transparency, I shall be exploring some "ethically important moments and themes" that constitute the "difficult, often subtle, and usually unpredictable situations that arise in the practice of doing research" (Guillemin and Gillam 2004, 262), including several opportunities, challenges, choices, and decisions resulting from a relational and reflexive ethical stance in setting up, implementing, and phasing out a research project with mothers and fathers who became biological parents in captivity.

Research and Positionality

Over twenty armed groups have tried to gain power since Yoweri K. Museveni's army overthrew the Ugandan government in 1986 (Dolan and Hovil 2006). The armed conflict between the Ugandan government, led by President Museveni, and the Lord's Resistance Army (LRA), led by Joseph Kony, has received worldwide attention (Branch 2011; Dolan 2011). The LRA, which organized major massacres, killing and maiming countless civilians, also abducted thousands of children and youth to serve as child soldiers. In this context of captivity, the LRA set up a highly organized and controlled system of forced marriages and parenthood (Atim, Mazurana, and Marshak 2018; Carlson and Mazurana 2008; Watye Ki Gen and CAP International 2013). The Ugandan government also forced approximately 1.8 million people, who accounted for about 90 percent of the Acholi population, into internally displaced people's camps in which they experienced overcrowding and a lack of adequate security and protection, food, water, sanitation, livelihood, educational opportunities, and medical care (Finnström 2008; Harlachter et al. 2006). Many people still experience the economic, physical, psychological, and social consequences of this collective violence (Amanela et al. 2020; Mazurana, Marshak, and Atim 2019).

This chapter builds upon a previous eight-month stay in northern Uganda, where I did an internship and collected data for a master's thesis in Lira and Gulu districts in 2012 and 2013, and living in Uganda (mainly Kampala and Lira) from 2016 to 2021, when I was involved in the work of

CCVS-Uganda and collected data for my doctoral thesis (see below). I came to this context as an "outsider," a White, middle-class European female doctoral student funded by a European university. From the outset of the research project, I was involved as a researcher in the interuniversity research unit, the Centre for Children in Vulnerable Situations (CCVS). In 2015 I became increasingly involved in one of its practice centers, CCVS-Uganda, an international NGO providing mental health and psychosocial support services for war-affected individuals, families, and communities in Lango and the Acholi Sub-Region (Lira District, Oyam District, and Alebtong District, and by the time I left the organization at the beginning of 2021, Kitgum District), first as a representative of the board (2015–17) and later as the executive director (2018–21). My positionality, both openly and unknowingly, influenced the methodological and ethical decisions made throughout the research (Bodineau and Lipandasi, this volume; Quirk, Bunting, and Kiconco, this volume; Schulz, this volume), including processes of "getting in"; collaboration with research brokers; the autonomy, agency, and vulnerability of the participants; narration, power, and privilege; and completion of the fieldwork.

I draw upon doctoral research focusing on the long-term effects of collective violence resulting from the armed conflict between the LRA and the Ugandan government and specifically focuses on the upbringing of children in Kitgum District in northern Uganda. The study aims to yield a better understanding of the dynamics of change and transformation in physical and social settings and the practices and beliefs about children's upbringing in a context of (past) prolonged collective violence among specific target groups (see below). Furthermore, the project explores sources of formal and informal support for caregivers in the upbringing of children before, during, and after the conflict.

To explore the main research question, interviews and focus group discussions were conducted with various target groups living in the subcounties of Mucwini, Lagoro, and Omiya Anyima in Kitgum District.[1] These included eleven persons who became biological parents while in captivity under the LRA. Specifically, seven mothers and four fathers aged between twenty-six and thirty-eight years old when first interviewed. These participants were abducted when they were between eleven and sixteen years old and spent between five and twelve years in captivity. They became first-time parents when they were between fifteen to twenty years old, with the majority having had two children while in captivity. Also included were five persons who became caregivers living in internally displaced people's camps in northern Uganda and had lived there for at least three years, forty-three persons above the age of fifty ("elders") who were caregivers before, during, and after the collective violence (using both focus groups and follow-up interviews), and eight social workers who had at least three years' work experience in the development or humanitarian field. In addition to these recorded interviews and focus group discussions, I had numerous informal conversations with government leaders, community leaders, youth, social workers, fellow researchers, and caregivers of children/youth who were abducted by the LRA and never returned home.

The research team included me, the principal investigator; two White European female supervisors who are professors at Belgian universities; and five Ugandan research assistants. The supervisors were not part of the data collection team in the field but provided input to the data analysis, processing, and interpretation. The research assistants, two females and three males, were fluent in the local language and provided simultaneous translation during all the interviews and focus group discussions. One of the assistants was recruited because of the support he provided in another doctoral research project in the same location, while the others were selected because they had expertise as counselors in providing psychosocial support to the participants. Three were employed by an NGO providing mental health and psychosocial support services at the time of data collection. All of the research team members shaped the research process, as shall be illustrated in this chapter.

Four periods of fieldwork were undertaken to collect all the research data between 2014 and 2016, totaling eight months. During my first fieldwork in 2014, we explored the themes related to my research question. We piloted an interview guide that included questions about the participants' own upbringing, their experiences as caregivers before, during, and after captivity, and their perceptions of upbringing in the future. In my second period of fieldwork, in 2015, we conducted interviews and focus group discussions with the different target groups described above. The last two periods of fieldwork, in 2016, involved follow-up interviews and sharing all the personal collected accounts (i.e., member checks) with the formerly abducted mothers and fathers only. Given the often complex and rich interviews conducted during the first two fieldwork periods, we decided to extend the contacts with this target group and to follow up with two formerly abducted mothers during a period of about two years (July 2014 to July 2016) and the other mothers and fathers for one year (March 2015 to July 2016). Overall, we conducted at least four recorded interviews with each of the mothers and fathers.

Working with Research Brokers and "Getting In"

Gaining access to communities, individuals, and organizations is a basic requirement of fieldwork (Schiltz and Büscher 2018); it is crucial in identifying participants as well as implementing and validating recommendations (Ogora 2013). Although getting introduced to the field through an established organization can prove helpful in certain research projects (see Schulz, this volume), I deliberately chose not to be affiliated with any organization in Kitgum District because part of my research interrogated the support sources available to caregivers. Having participants who are mobilized by an organization could shape this information; participants could be hesitant to openly discuss the support they are receiving. It could also create the expectation of receiving additional support or feeling compelled to participate in the research (Quirk, Bunting, and Kiconco, this volume; Schiltz and Büscher 2018; Schulz, this volume). Given my position as an outsider, I had to work with different research brokers in the field who connected me to (potential) participants, including gatekeepers, research assistants, and participant mobilizers.

After receiving clearance from the ethical review board of Ghent University (through the Faculty of Psychology and Educational Sciences), I passed through several government offices in Uganda, which have gatekeepers positioned at different levels: the Uganda National Council for Science and Technology[2] on the national level, the chief administrative officer and the resident district commissioner on district level,[3] the local council III and the subcounty chief on subcounty level,[4] and the local council I at village level.[5] Following Ongwech (this volume), we noticed that "to get through, you have to make sure your letters are in order, visit the right people, and make the right calls. Courtesy calls are a must." Aside from these actors, there are many other players in the field, often with their own agendas and interests (Schiltz and Büscher 2018), such as persons who want to be part of the research project to get experience as research assistants or to secure financial gains. Although opportunities, restrictions, and risks are connected to using a formal political system, we noticed that it gave our research more credibility among local leaders and participants. After obtaining consent from the government offices on different levels, contact was sought with different groups of participants in various ways.

In collaboration with the research assistants and the Kitgum NGO Forum, I mapped out the organizations in Kitgum District that were providing or used to provide services to people experiencing challenges and difficulties resulting out of the collective violence that took place in northern Uganda. The social workers included in this research were mainly contacted from their workplaces. After duly informing them about all aspects of the study, they were asked to participate in a recorded one-on-one interview in English.

To establish contact with all the other participants, we organized a general informative meeting in every subcounty to which officials, representatives, potential participants, and anyone interested in learning more about the research were invited. These meetings occurred at the start of the first two fieldwork periods. They were designed to simultaneously inform a broader audience about the research and to alert potential participants who could attend as part of a larger group of people instead of singling them out (Kohrt, Rai, and Maharjan 2015; WHO 2007). This approach was necessary to avoid initiating or aggravating the stigmatization of specific target groups by exposing their histories to their wider communities. The participants who were forcibly recruited wanted to shield their engagement with the LRA from their families to avoid compromising their new marriages and/or protect the children born to them in captivity. As our research shows, this was especially a concern for the mothers who participated in the research since their experiences of being forcibly married and giving birth to children in captivity often complicated their postconflict marital relationships (Apio 2016; Atim, Mazurana, and Marshak 2018; De Nutte, De Haene, and Derluyn 2022; Kiconco 2015).

Furthermore, participants' choices to (at least partly) disclose or silence the context in which their children were born was framed within and repeatedly negotiated around various factors (De Nutte, De Haene, and Derluyn 2022). These included the age of the child (an informal assessment of the child's level of being "knowledgeable"/"clever"), the emotional impact of disclosure, the perceived stigmatization of the child leading to either wanting to frame the child's experiences (e.g., by explaining to the child why she or he was being stigmatized) or shielding the child from potential future stigmatization (e.g., by concealing or denying the context in which the child was born), the need for belonging and knowing one's identity, and the lack of resources and support in the upbringing of children (e.g., land, school fees, caregivers).

During the informative meetings at the subcounties, a participant mobilizer who brokered the first contact between me, my research assistants, and potential participants living in the respective subcounties was appointed. Two of these mobilizers were parish chiefs, and one was a local council I. In addition, because experiences of being forcibly recruited are highly sensitive, to the point where some people had not disclosed their full histories to their families and communities, snowball sampling was used to contact six mothers and fathers who became biological parents in captivity. Five of these participants were referred by our mobilizers.

In a few instances, gaining access at the family level was also necessary. For example, after reaching the home of one of the fathers who was forcibly recruited and initiating a follow-up interview, he received a call from his brother, who wanted to know who we were and what we were doing at his home. We also had to engage with the family members (a mother and two husbands) of some of our participants, mostly the mothers, to explain why they were taking part in the interviews. In all of these instances, the research project was framed within the general research question without going into detail regarding the specific target group the participant in question fitted within to minimize potential unwelcome social scrutiny (see above).

Although working with research brokers can increase the validity and reliability of research data, many scholars emphasize the ethical and methodological caveats (Gorin et al. 2008; Jacobson and Landau 2003). These may include hampered mutual understanding between researchers, brokers, and participants; a particular framing of participants' accounts by brokers; power differences between researchers and brokers; a complication of the voluntariness of consent as participants might feel obliged to take part in the research; and the influence of brokers' own expectations and interests on the research process (Clark-Kazak 2021; Mackenzie, McDowell, and Pittaway 2007; Schiltz and Büscher 2018). Indeed, brokers are active agents in the construction of relationships and information sharing between researchers and participants. Consequently, it is key that their role in the process is clearly described and reflected upon (Bunting and Quirk 2020; Schiltz and Büscher 2018).

Although it was necessary to work with research brokers to gain access to the research context, specifically to establish contact with participants living in the communities (i.e., persons who became biological parents in captivity, caregivers who raised children in the internally displaced people's camps, and elders), it was not possible to fully control which persons were or were not approached to take part in the research and what information was or was not passed on to potential participants (Ansoms 2013; Mackenzie, McDowell, and Pittaway 2007). Consequentially, some potential participants who were referred by the participant mobilizers did not fit the research selection criteria. Others had incorrect impressions about the nature of the research, which raised their expectations of receiving some kind of compensation or support. To address this concern, we met with most participants before the interview. In this meeting, as well as before the start and at the end of each interview, particular attention was paid to (re)informing the participants about the goals, benefits, and potential harms of their participation in the research. Informed consent was gained in a careful and continuous process—and had to be repeated—in each contact with the participants (Mackenzie, McDowell, and Pittaway 2007; Vervliet et al. 2015). In three instances, informal discussions were held with persons who did not fit the research criteria in order to minimize potential disappointment for people who had dedicated time to talk to us. Afterward, particular attention was paid to reinform the referring participant or mobilizer about the research aims.

The interviews conducted in the communities were audio-taped and later transcribed verbatim in English by an independent transcriber fluent in both

Acholi/Luo and English. This process revealed several occasions where one of my research assistants had added information that the participant had not given. Subsequent conversations with the research assistant yielded no definitive explanations for these unprompted additions. They may have been motivated by a desire to make the participants' accounts more comprehensive to an outsider or perhaps as a way to incorporate their own personal experiences since the research assistants also lived through the collective violence themselves. Since the interviews with the social workers were done in English, I transcribed these interviews myself.

In keeping with larger trends, the engagement of various research brokers was crucial to facilitating contact with participants in the communities, conversing with them, maintaining contact with them throughout the research process, and disseminating the research findings (see below). If England (1994, 84) states that fieldwork can be perceived as a "dialogical process in which the research situation is structured by both the researcher and the person being researched," the influence and often active involvement of the wider context in this process, including research brokers, family, and community members, cannot be underestimated and needs to be taken into account. In this research project, gaining access through both formal and informal channels was necessary to create an interactive environment in which participants and their wider context could be informed and provide input and feedback to the setup and process of the project.

Building the Research Relationship

Throughout my fieldwork, I invested a lot of time and energy in building relationships with my participants. This was partly because it was important to have regular contacts to clarify questions and expectations surrounding the project. Equally important was a concern with the often extractive character of research in the Global South (Bunting and Quirk 2020; Clark-Kazak 2021; Quirk, Bunting, and Kiconco, this volume) and, in this case, northern Uganda. By meeting regularly with and listening to participants, I was able to contextualize their stories better and demonstrated respect for the time and energy they put into the research. Although I duly considered the participants' questions for support and acted upon them in certain instances, I felt that this respect and time was frequently the only thing I could give in return (Wood 2006). Although elaborating a research relationship with the participants did not go as smoothly because of language barriers, high expectations, and power differences, I felt that participants started to feel more comfortable during the follow-up visits.

Meetings with the participants would generally take place where they felt most comfortable and at times that were most convenient to them. All six focus group discussions and twenty-five interviews took place at subcounty offices, which were often considered neutral zones. In addition, twenty-eight interviews were done at participants' homes; five were conducted at their workplaces, four at a family member's home, and eight at other locations (e.g., the home of another participant, a participant mobilizer, a hotel, or a shop). Participants who had to move from their homes to the interview location received modest compensation to cover their transport costs.

In most of the interviews, we matched the gender of the research assistants and participants because we wanted to be sensitive to the information that could (potentially) be shared, such as experiences of gender-based violence and forced marriages. However, we could not keep up this practice in the final round of interviews in 2016, as one of the male research assistants decided not to participate in the research after his second day. This was caused by his frustration that two participants did not show up for the planned interviews.

Several considerations informed the recurrent meetings. On the one hand, it was necessary to thoroughly explain the research and build trust to enable participation. On the other hand, protecting the participants' identities, stories, and privacy was essential. The latter proved challenging since we could directly contact only two of our participants living in the communities. All the other participants were mobilized through other research brokers (participant mobilizers or other participants). Some gave telephone numbers that were disconnected. Others relocated to another area. When we could not get in touch with participants, we tried to (re)establish contact through family or community members or visited them at their (new) homes. However, visiting participants at their homes involved the risk of making them feel obligated to participate in a process they were potentially not comfortable with, practically or emotionally. It also put their privacy at risk. We mitigated this risk by keeping the explanation of our research very broad, that is, referring to the general research project (i.e., children's upbringing during and after the collective violence in northern Uganda) in which various target groups were included instead of singling out the participants as persons who experienced abduction, forced marriage and parenthood. When following up with our participants, we did not receive any information indicating that sensitive information about their histories had been disclosed to the broader public.

To summarize, several challenges and opportunities resulted from the choice to have regular contact and recurrent interviews with our participants to develop a research relationship; we had enough opportunities to clear up any questions and expectations surrounding the project and to get a better understanding of the participants' narratives.

Power and Privilege

The power hierarchy between researcher and participants will always be ethically fraught (Lahman et al. 2011; Stewart, this volume). Coming in as a White, European doctoral researcher meant I had a privileged position, which invariably creates power imbalances between the researcher, research brokers, participants, and the wider community. Since I needed to acknowledge that my research relationships would inherently be hierarchical (England 1994; Schulz, this volume), some measures had to be taken to counterbalance this by ensuring that "participants [were] able to exercise some degree of control over the research process and the conditions of their involvement in it" (Mackenzie, McDowell, and Pittaway 2007, 310).

Addressing the Extractive Nature of Research

My research assistants, local leaders, and several participants repeatedly referenced previous examples of researchers and organizations who had come in, collected data, and disappeared without properly informing participants about the objectives of the research, what data was collected, or what would happen with the information they had provided. In this regard, Van Den Berg (2020, 41) suggests that "authentic and committed partnerships with those who contribute to knowledge production on the ground is fundamental to dismantling the extractive character of research." Reconsidering my engagement practice with the participants, research brokers, and other stakeholders (government and community leaders, NGO workers, other academics from the Global North and Global South) both challenged the power imbalance of the potential extractive nature of the research and contributed to deepening the data by meeting the participants, participant mobilizers, and officials multiple times over the course of two years of data collection for interviews, focus group discussions, and informal conversations, while also providing some basic support to participants and making sure that information emerging from the data collection was played back at various levels. This also opened up avenues for providing input and feedback to the setup and process. In addition, my engagement with CCVS and CCVS-Uganda enabled my research to be more practice- and policy-oriented.

However, notwithstanding these considerations, it is important to highlight two shortcomings to making the research more collaborative. First, the research was framed in a doctoral study funded by a European university, which meant the research setup had to be elaborated and approved by ethical review boards in Belgium and Uganda before entering the field, and specific kinds of dissemination channels such as peer-reviewed journals and scientific conferences are more valued (Bunting and Quirk 2020; Schulz, this volume;

Quirk, Bunting, and Kiconco, this volume). Second, my increasing involvement in the daily operations of CCVS-Uganda made me unable to pay sufficient attention to my doctoral studies. In an attempt to limit my extensive working hours, which were affecting my physical and mental health, combined with a commitment to make a more meaningful impact in people's lives, I fully engaged in the work of CCVS-Uganda and interrupted my doctoral trajectory from 2017 to 2021. On the one hand, this meant I could not keep in touch with the participants and research assistants as much as I would have wanted to after the last data collection period, in 2016. However, on the other hand, I could influence (to a certain level) the extension of CCVS-Uganda's services to some of the communities where we collected the research data.

Engaging with Participants' Questions for Support

Throughout the research process, it was necessary to simultaneously consider the participants' trauma and vulnerability as well as their strengths, resilience, and agency (De Haene, Grietens, and Verschueren 2010; Mackenzie, McDowell, and Pittaway 2007). Given that we asked participants to recount potentially traumatic experiences, we wanted to make sure that we could provide the necessary emotional support during and after the interviews and in between fieldwork periods (Amanela et al. 2020; Balami and Umar, this volume; Schulz, this volume). Crucially, four of my research assistants had a background in providing psychosocial services offered to all participants. It was clarified to the participants that using psychosocial services did not in any way influence their participation in the research project and that everything that was said during the sessions would be treated with confidentiality. During the data collection, psychosocial services were offered to six participants, of which four were formerly abducted mothers, one a father, and one a caregiver who raised children in the internally displaced people's camps. The sessions varied in length and included the participant's spouse and/or other family members in three instances.

Although the provision of basic counseling and follow-up was necessary, given the nature of our participants' experiences and the lack of mental health and psychosocial support services in the area, my research assistant's double role as translator and counselor also shaped the course of the interviews. For example, during transcription, it became apparent that she emphasized the presumed healing effects of narration in working through traumatic experiences (De Haene et al. 2012). This can be framed within the idea that recounting traumatic experiences is perceived to be a central mechanism of recovery for trauma survivors and that silencing the experiences is seen as less adaptive for the individual and the broader context (De Haene et al. 2012). In some instances, when participants chose not to expand on certain interview questions, the research assistant encouraged disclosure by telling them, "It would be good for you to talk about this" and "It will make you feel better." This could have put pressure on the participants to speak despite their wishes to remain silent to protect themselves and others.

Similarly, in providing care to our participants, my research assistants and I made sure to have regular debriefings to avoid being overwhelmed by the information that was shared during the data collection and engagement with participants in the counseling sessions. This was particularly important given that some of the research assistants lived through similar experiences, and hearing certain stories might also have caused them distress.

Notwithstanding the provision of emotional support, our participants living in the communities regularly raised questions about financial and material support (e.g., school fees, hospital bills, call credit) throughout the various contacts. I was often perceived as "the one knowing it all" and having access to money, connections, and opportunities. During and after the collective violence, many (international) aid organizations came in to provide various kinds of relief. The precarious environment of the internally displaced people's camps had given rise to a dependence on external donors (Harlachter et al. 2006; Wieling et al. 2017). However, beginning in 2013, when this research project was initiated, many scaled down (or closed down) their operations (Büscher, Komujuni, and Ashaba 2018). People's expectations of financial or material support after participating in research activities or organized meetings nevertheless continued (Ogora 2013). In postconflict northern Uganda, this dynamic is often fueled by research fatigue (Atim, this volume).

In an attempt to counter these perceptions, my positionality as a doctoral student was explained by one of the research assistants as one in which I wanted to learn but did not have access to many resources. However, my simultaneous positionality as a White European still gave rise to expectations. During the debriefing session in the final interviews with mothers and fathers who were abducted, five participants indeed shared that their decisions to participate in the interviews were (partly) based on the expectation of support, and for some, the expectation was still very much present until the last contact. This raises questions about whether research can ever be truly voluntary in low-resource settings and in a context where both formal and informal support structures are insufficient (Atim, this volume; Balami and Umar, this volume; Schiltz and Büscher 2018). For participants struggling to get by, how can they refuse to take part in a project if it has the potential to generate financial/material benefits?

On the other hand, the wish to participate in the research can also be seen as an expression of the participants' agency—of wanting to have their voices heard or to gain something from the research in order to change their situations (Vervliet et al. 2015). Interestingly, one participant claimed he had never been married and did not become a father while engaged with the LRA. At the time, we had already met him twice, and he had narrated experiences of being married and becoming a father in captivity. When we tried to explore why he changed his story, he insisted that he had never been married while in captivity. Did something happen that made him reluctant to share his story? Was he hoping for some kind of compensation or support after the interviews that he did not receive from the interview team?

Although participating "in a context in which local communities face extreme needs and precariousness, the question of how to deal as a researcher with expectations in terms of immediate change is central" (Schiltz and Büscher 2018, 132). Supporting research participants remains a gray zone in research ethics, and various practices are apparent in the field (Atim, this volume; Bodineau and Lipandasi, this volume; Kiconco 2015; Ogora 2013; Ongwech, this volume; Van Den Berg 2020). Notwithstanding the problematization that my privileged position brought about, I also acted from this position, as it enabled me access to leaders and organizations that could potentially provide various kinds of support (Ogora 2013). Apart from ensuring an option for emotional support (see above), I tried to build some kind of referral network for my participants, given that I chose to come in as an independent researcher. To this effect, I had meetings with several organizations and government leaders. At the outset of my third fieldwork, a district government leader informed me about a program that was being initiated to provide livelihood training to child mothers. After sharing this information with my female participants, some of them agreed to share their names with the office of this government leader. Unfortunately, after following up, I discovered the program fell through. Other connections I tried to facilitate also did not yield much as the organizations in question focused only on specific target areas or categories of beneficiaries. Consequently, the participants did not secure the benefits they sought through this research project.

My research assistants and I tried to provide basic support in specific situations. For example, one of our participants disclosed that her "husband" from captivity contacted her to find out about their daughter, who was born within their forced marriage in LRA captivity. He expressed interest in taking care of their daughter; however, no further contact was established. The participant requested call credit as she did not want to disclose this contact to her current (postconflict) husband or other family members. She was planning to return to live with her "husband" from captivity since her current husband was not caring for her and her daughter. On another occasion, we visited one of our participants at home only to learn that she had moved back to her parental home some months before without notifying her husband. He could not give us any information on how she was doing, which caused us concern about her well-being. We tried to locate her for a follow-up visit but failed to do so. My research assistant finally succeeded in making contact. The participant put forward the need for a reconciliation meeting, for which we provided transport, between the two families to clear up the issues between her and her husband which resulted in her moving back to her husband's home.

Member Checking

Another strategy to potentially address power imbalances between the researcher and participants was to explore member checking. Member checking is a "process in which collected data is 'played back' to the informant to check for perceived accuracy and reactions" and has been established as a reflexive process for all parties involved in the research (Cho and Trent 2006, 322). Member checking has a twofold objective (Goldblatt, Karnieli-Miller, and Neumann 2011). First, from a methodological standpoint, it minimizes misinterpretations of the narratives shared by the participants. Second, from an ethical viewpoint, it can be a way to increase active respondent participation by giving them more control over how their accounts are represented (Fernandez, Kodish, and Weijer 2003; Koelsch 2013). In addition, it also served as a valuable opportunity to "wrap up" the various interviews and to thank our participants for journeying with us. The member checks were carefully prepared to include broad themes touched upon by each mother and father who became a parent during LRA captivity, allowing them to make additions, deletions, or adjustments to the information they shared in previous interviews. The reactions to the member checking varied. Some participants perceived it as a chance to clarify and add to their stories. Others did not want to engage with the information they shared earlier on as it was too sensitive, or they interpreted the member check as a fault-finding mission. In the latter case, it seemed that the potential benefit of performing member checks as a means to increase the control of the mothers and fathers on how their accounts are represented had the exact opposite result, as it was seen as a way to rectify "errors" in the stories that were shared.

To summarize, my positionality and privileged position as a White, foreign researcher inevitably led to power imbalances between myself, the research assistants, our participants, and people in the broader research context. Several choices and decisions were made to counterbalance this by addressing the extractive nature of research, considering and engaging with participants' questions for support, trying to build a referral network, providing emotional support, and member checking.

Phasing Out

We cannot rush out of research relationships because breaking boundaries of trust may be harmful to participants (Vervliet et al. 2015). In an attempt to counterbalance the often extractive nature of research (see above), we provided enough time for debriefing in the final stage of the fieldwork. To "give back" to the community at large, formal and informal feedback sessions were organized featuring participants, social workers, government officials, and representatives. These sessions took place at the end of the data collection. We also held meetings at the end of every fieldwork period, similar to the meetings held at the beginning of the project but with the important addition of presenting preliminary research results. The simultaneous process of data collection, dissemination, and consultation provided opportunities for collaboration as various stakeholders (participants, research brokers, government and community leaders) were able to openly share their views on the research plans and outcomes, creating a broader support base for the data collected and deeper engagement between all the parties involved.

Some scholars even suggest that "where this is feasible, ongoing contact after the research, including opportunities for debriefing and the consideration of issues that might arise and remain after the research is concluded" (Mackenzie, McDowell, and Pittaway 2007, 306). Taking into account the sensitive nature of the research, one of the research assistants made three follow-up visits to check in on our participants. While this step was well intentioned, it ultimately complicated the phasing out of the research since the participants kept requesting additional support (Stewart, this volume). Overall, throughout the research project, up until the very end, managing participants' expectations remained difficult, despite recurrent information about the risks and benefits of the research and the attempts to provide some basic support ourselves. Notwithstanding mitigation through various choices and decisions made throughout the research project, it thus appeared that the participants experienced extractive research in this setting as we were not able to provide an answer to the varied needs they were experiencing (Atim, this volume).

The choices and decisions that a researcher makes in trying to perform methodologically and ethically sound research are bound by the project's objectives, the researcher's positionality, the relationships and interactions with research brokers and participants, and the opportunities and challenges situated in the broader research context. By elaborating on several major methodological and ethical issues and "ethically important moments" that I encountered while undertaking my fieldwork, I identified several opportunities, challenges, choices, and decisions. These resulted from a relational and reflexive ethical stance in setting up, executing, and phasing out my research project with mothers and fathers who became biological parents in captivity. I reflected on collaborations with research brokers, the influence of the broader context of participants (including family and community), regular contact with the participants, considering questions for support, and power and privilege. However, the choices and decisions made should be contextualized within the particular research setting and might not even be considered useful, ethical, or responsive in other contexts. For example, in some research projects, it might be more appropriate to gain access to participants through informal channels or have the data collected by an insider (see, for example, Atim, this volume). Nevertheless, these considerations may be useful to (future) researchers as starting points for reflection when entering and working in complex research settings (Clark-Kazak 2021).

Procedural ethics, such as those espoused by most ethical review boards, can only partially cover the methodological and ethical questions encountered in research with participants who experienced traumatic events as a result of collective violence (Clark-Kazak 2021; Vervliet et al. 2015). As such, "It has been argued [that] research ethics should move beyond these codes ... to the in-depth, long-term relationships that may develop between participants and researchers" (Lahman et al. 2011, 1399), into which "good ethical practice is rooted" (Thomson 2013, 148). The research relationships we built with our participants can be perceived as complex, intersubjective, and ever-changing spaces that influence and are influenced by the context in which they evolve (De Haene, Grietens, and Verschueren 2010; England 1994; Stewart, this volume).

In summary, over a period of one to two years, we journeyed together with mothers and fathers who became biological parents while in LRA captivity, "holding harm" (De Haene, Grietens, and Verschueren 2010) as we tried to increase the benefits and limit the risks of their participation in our research project by continuously reinforming them about the research, having recurrent meetings and discussions, respecting their potential wishes to keep their personal histories concealed from their families and communities, providing some basic support, and trying to increase their control in the representation of their accounts. While we implemented specific actions to make our research more collaborative, the setup of the project along the rules and expected outputs of a doctoral study, along with the many questions and expectations for support from our participants that we often could not provide a desirable answer to, could have created the perception and experience that the research was more extractive than it intended to be.

Even when we try to be as reflexive as possible, we shall never truly be prepared for the numerous ethical and methodological challenges that are part and parcel of doing research, especially in (post)conflict settings. Making difficult decisions, feeling uncomfortable and disappointed, often being unable to provide a satisfactory answer to participants' expectations, and trying to mitigate power differences are an inherent part of the research process, and it is not possible to lift the continuous tensions that we encounter as researchers. England (1994, 81) points out: "The openness and culturally constructed nature of the social world, peppered with contradictions and complexities, needs to be embraced not dismissed. This means that 'the field' is constantly changing and that researchers may find that they have to manoeuvre around unexpected circumstances. The result is research where the only inevitability seems to be unreliability and unpredictability." Researchers need to be open about the choices, decisions, achievements, and failures encountered in fieldwork and how they came about, as illustrated in this chapter. Not being transparent about choices and decisions potentially limits the scrutiny and evaluation of research projects by all parties who are included or engaged with the research. Although the ultimate obligation for implementing methodologically and ethically sound research lies with the researcher, institutions, such as ethical review boards and committees, need to stimulate and open up opportunities to safely reflect on and discuss these issues to prepare researchers to enter the field beyond considerations of procedural ethics. This can be done through in-depth and interactive reflections with ethical review boards and peer groups or engaging in equitable connections between stakeholders from the Global North and Global South: in other words, involving local partners from the start, implementing participatory research methods, and conducting practice-oriented research.

Notes

1. During the research project two of our participants moved to another location within Kitgum District.
2. If a new research project is initiated within Uganda, one has to file a request to the Uganda National Council for Science and Technology, which serves as an ethical commission.
3. The chief administrative officer and the resident district commissioner are, respectively, the head of the political system and the central contact person for security issues on the district level.
4. The local council III and the subcounty chief are, respectively, the head of the political system and the head of the community system on the subcounty level.
5. The local council I is the mayor of a certain village.

References

Amanela, S., T. F. Ayee, S. Buell, A. Escande, T. Quinlan, A. S. Ringterink, M. Schomerus, S. Sharp, and S. Swanson. 2020. *The Mental Landscape of Post-conflict Life in Northern Uganda: Part 2: Defining the Mental Landscape*. London: Secure Livelihoods Research Consortium. https://securelivelihoods.org/publication/the-mental-landscape-of-post-conflict-life-in-northern-uganda-part-2-defining-the-mental-landscape/.

Ansoms, A. 2013. "Dislodging Power Structures in Rural Rwanda: From 'Disaster Tourist' to 'Transfer Gate.'" In *Emotional and Ethical Challenges for Field Research in Africa: The Story behind the Findings*, edited by S. Thomson, A. Ansoms, and J. Murison, 42–56. London: Palgrave Macmillan.

Apio, E. 2016. "Children Born of War in Northern Uganda: Kinship, Marriage, and the Politics of Post-conflict Reintegration in Lango Society." PhD diss., University of Birmingham.

Atim, T., D. Mazurana, and A. Marshak. 2018. "Women Survivors and Their Children Born of Wartime Sexual Violence in Northern Uganda." *Disasters* 42: S61–S78.

Branch, A. 2011. *Displacing Human Rights: War and Intervention in Northern Uganda*. Oxford: Oxford University Press.

Bunting, A., and J. Quirk. 2020. "Introduction." In *Research as More Than Extraction? Knowledge Production and Sexual Violence in Post Conflict African Societies*, edited by A. Bunting, A. Kiconco, and J. Quirk, 5–9. London: openDemocracy. https://csiw-ectg.org/wp-content/uploads/2020/02/CSiW_Research_as_more_than_extraction.pdf.

Büscher, K., S. Komujuni, and I. Ashaba. 2018. "Humanitarian Urbanism in a Post-conflict Aid Town: Aid Agencies and Urbanization in Gulu, Northern Uganda." *Journal of Eastern African Studies* 12: 348–66.

Carlson, K., and D. Mazurana. 2008. *Forced Marriage within the Lord's Resistance Army, Uganda*. Medford, MA: Feinstein International Center. https://fic.tufts.edu/publication-item/forced-marriage-with-the-lords-resistance-army-uganda/.

Cho, J., and A. Trent. 2006. "Validity in Qualitative Research Revisited." *Qualitative Research* 6: 319–40.

Clark-Kazak, C. 2021. "Ethics in Forced Migration Research: Taking Stock and Potential Ways Forward." *Journal on Migration and Human Security* 9: 125–38.

De Haene, L., H. Grietens, and K. Verschueren. 2010. "Holding Harm: Narrative Methods in Mental Health Research on Refugee Trauma." *Qualitative Health Research* 20: 1664–76.

De Haene, L., P. Rober, P. Adriaenssens, and K. Verschueren. 2012. "Voices of Dialogues and Directivity in Family Therapy with Refugees: Evolving Ideas about Dialogical Refugee Care." *Family Process* 51: 391–404.

De Nutte, L., L. De Haene, and I. Derluyn. 2022. "'They Now Know That They Are Children of War': Forcibly Abducted Mothers and Fathers Balancing Disclosure and Silencing to Their Children Born of War in Northern Uganda." *Frontiers in Political Science* 4. https://doi.org/10.3389/fpos.2022.850969.

Dolan, C. 2011. *Social Torture: The Case of Northern Uganda, 1986–2006*. 2nd ed. New York: Berghahn Books.

Dolan, C., and L. Hovil. 2006. *Humanitarian Protection in Uganda: A Trojan Horse?* London: Humanitarian Policy Group, Overseas Development Institute. https://www.refworld.org/docid/4a5b32bf0.html.

El-Khani, A., F. Ulph, A. Redmond, and R. Calam. 2013. "Ethical Issues in Research into Conflict and Displacement." *The Lancet* 382: 764–65.

Ellis, C. 2007. "Telling Secrets, Revealing Lives: Relational Ethics in Research with Intimate Others." *Qualitative Inquiry* 13: 3–29.

England, K. R. L. 1994. "Getting Personal: Reflexivity, Positionality, and Feminist Research." *Professional Geographer* 46: 80–89.

Fernandez, C. V., E. Kodish, and C. Weijer. 2003. "Informing Study Participants of Research Results: An Ethical Imperative." *Ethics & Human Research* 25: 12–19.

Finnström, S. 2008. *Living with Bad Surroundings: War, History, and Everyday Moments in Northern Uganda*. Durham, NC: Duke University Press.

Goldblatt, H., O. Karnieli-Miller, and M. Neumann. 2011. "Sharing Qualitative Research Findings with Participants: Study Experiences of Methodological and Ethical Dilemmas." *Patient Education and Counseling* 82: 389–95.

Gorin, S., C. A. Hooper, C. Dyson, and C. Cabral. 2008. "Ethical Challenges in Conducting Research with Hard to Reach Families." *Child Abuse Review* 17: 275–87.

Guillemin, M., and L. Gillam. 2004. "Ethics, Reflexivity, and 'Ethically Important Moments' in Research." *Qualitative Inquiry* 10: 261–80.

Harlachter, T., F. X. Okot, C. A. Obonyo, M. Balthazard, and R. Atkinson. 2006. *Traditional Ways of Coping in Acholi: Cultural Provisions for Reconciliation and Healing from War*. Kampala, Uganda: Intersoft Business Services.

Jacobson, K., and L. B. Landau. 2003. "The Dual Imperative in Refugee Research: Some Methodological and Ethical Considerations in Social Science Research on Forced Migration." *Disasters* 27: 185–206.

Kiconco, A. 2015. "Understanding Former 'Girl Soldiers': Central Themes in the Lives of Formerly Abducted Girls in Post-conflict Northern Uganda." PhD diss., University of Birmingham.

Koelsch, L. E. 2013. "Reconceptualizing the Member Check Interview." *International Journal of Qualitative Methods* 12: 168–79.

Kohrt, B. A., S. Rai, and S. M. Maharjan. 2015. "Child Soldiers." In *International Encyclopedia of the Social and Behavioral Sciences*, edited by J. D. Wright, 430–38. Amsterdam: Elsevier.

Lahman, M. K. E., M. R. Geist, K. L. Rodriguez, P. Graglia, and K. K. DeRoche. 2011. "Culturally Responsive Relational Reflexive Ethics in Research: The Three Rs." *Quality & Quantity* 45: 1397–414.

Mackenzie, C., C. McDowell, and E. Pittaway. 2007. "Beyond 'Do No Harm': The Challenge of Constructing Ethical Relationships in Refugee Research." *Journal of Refugee Studies* 20: 299–319.

Mazurana, D., A. Marshak, and T. Atim. 2019. "The State of the War-Wounded in Northern Uganda: Data from 2013–2018 on Their Lives and Access to Healthcare." Working paper 70, Secure Livelihoods Research Consortium. https://

securelivelihoods.org/wp-content/uploads/War-wounded-Uganda-final-paper-online-1.pdf.

Neuman, W. L. 2011. "How to Review Literature and Conduct Ethical Studies." In *Qualitative Research and Educational Sciences: A Reader about Useful Strategies and Tools*, edited by G. Van Hove and L. Claes, 37–76. Harlow, UK: Pearson Education.

Ogora, L. O. 2013. "The Contested Fruits of Research in War-Torn Countries: My Insider Experience in Northern Uganda." In *Emotional and Ethical Challenges for Field Research in Africa: The Story behind the Findings*, edited by S. Thomson, A. Ansoms, and J. Murison, 27–41. London: Palgrave Macmillan.

Schiltz, J., and K. Büscher. 2018. "Brokering Research with War-Affected People: The Tense Relationship between Opportunities and Ethics." *Ethnography* 19: 124–46.

Thomson, S. 2013. "Academic Integrity and Ethical Responsibilities in Post-genocide Rwanda: Working with Research Ethics Boards to Prepare for Fieldwork with 'Human Subjects.'" In *Emotional and Ethical Challenges for Field Research in Africa: The Story behind the Findings*, edited by S. Thomson, A. Ansoms, and J. Murison, 139–54. London: Palgrave Macmillan.

Van Den Berg, S. 2020. "Selling Stories of War in Sierra Leone." In *Research as More Than Extraction? Knowledge Production and Sexual Violence in Post Conflict African Societies*, edited by A. Bunting, A. Kiconco, and J. Quirk, 40–42. London: openDemocracy. https://csiw-ectg.org/wp-content/uploads/2020/02/CSiW_Research_as_more_than_extraction.pdf.

Vervliet, M., C. Rousseau, E. Broekaert, and I. Derluyn. 2015. "Multilayered Ethics in Research Involving Unaccompanied Refugee Minors." *Journal of Refugee Studies* 28: 468–85.

Watye Ki Gen and CAP International. 2013. *The Lord's Resistance Army's Forced Wife System*. https://wpsncanada.files.wordpress.com/2012/05/wpsn-c-watye-ki-gen-and-cap-international-lra-force-wife-system-publication.pdf.

Wessells, M. G. 2009. "Do No Harm: Toward Contextually Appropriate Psychosocial Support in International Emergencies." *American Psychologist* 64: 842–54.

Wieling, E., C. Mehus, C. Yumbul, J. Möllerherm, V. Ertl, L. Achan, M. Forgatch, F. Neuner, and C. Catani. 2017. "Preparing the Field for Feasibility Testing of a Parenting Intervention for War-Affected Mothers in Northern Uganda." *Family Process* 56: 376–92.

WHO (World Health Organization). 2007. *WHO Ethical and Safety Recommendations for Researching, Documenting and Monitoring Sexual Violence in Emergencies*. Geneva: World Health Organization. https://www.who.int/publications/i/item/9789241595681.

Wood, E. J. 2006. "The Ethical Challenges of Field Research in Conflict Zones." *Qualitative Sociology* 29: 373–86.

Yin, R. K. 2011. *Qualitative Research from Start to Finish*. New York: Guilford Press.

SIX

Slavery and Its Meanings in the British World

Historiography, Knowledge Production, and Research Ethics

ANA STEVENSON AND REBECCA SWARTZ

Since the sixteenth century, philosophers, humanitarians, reformers, novelists, and politicians have embraced the language and analogy of slavery to describe innumerable sites of subjugation, exploitation, and oppression across the globe (Sklar and Stewart 2007; Roberts 2013; de Bolla et al. 2020). Ideas about liberty and freedom were central to Enlightenment thought; insistence upon the freedom of the individual exacerbated the process whereby its inverse—slavery—became a conceptual and literary device (Plasa and Ring 1994; Swaminathan and Beach 2016). These ideals may not have always been inherently gendered or racialized, yet their expression remained fundamentally exclusionary. Across an era when European men made universalistic proclamations that all men should be free, their contemporaries extended the transatlantic slave trade and the institution of chattel slavery across the Americas. The invocation of slavery and its meanings has extended to a series of other exploitative paradigms—from coercive labor practices such as indenture and convict transportation to the status of women, children, and refugees (Cunliffe [1979] 2008; hooks 1981; Neal 1987; Ferguson 1992; Miers 2003; Bhana 2008; Goyal 2017; Stevenson 2019; Swartz 2021).

The sheer prevalence of these ideas, we argue, has significant and ongoing consequences for historiography, knowledge production, and social science research methods. We come to these questions as feminist historians with research interests in histories of slavery in South Africa, Britain, Australia, and the United States. In this chapter, we consider the following question: What can contemporary social science researchers learn from historical methodologies and debates? We argue that awareness of the history and historiography of slavery, apartheid, and sexual violence is central to conducting research on these issues in the present day. This offers important insights into changes surrounding terminology and classification as it relates to historical and modern slavery and gender-based violence. Additionally, the contemporary mobilization of language surrounding slavery, apartheid, and their legacies highlight the challenges and disjuncture in the decontextualized application of these concepts. It is an ethical imperative to be sensitive toward these longer histories, both in the specific and broader contexts of social science research, in terms of content, method, and location. In other words, we argue that modern slavery and gender-based violence cannot be understood without reference to their historical contexts.

This chapter is particularly concerned with the ethical and political dilemmas that emerge when activists and scholars extend—or "stretch"—the definition of slavery to practices which go well beyond historical slave systems. Once many different practices are classified as "slavery," the distinctive forms of oppression and exploitation that defined enslavement can end up being diluted or marginalized.[1] Labeling all kinds of practices as "slavery" will always be politically appealing, at least tactically, but it also risks losing sight of distinctive systems. To make sense of the issues at stake here, this chapter examines how knowledge regarding slavery has historically been produced within the Atlantic world and then connects this history and historiography to slavery and its meanings within multidisciplinary research and activist contexts in our own times.

To interrogate the diverse historical meanings attributed to slavery and freedom, this chapter primarily focuses on the case of Sara Baartman. Although violence against women and girls in Africa has gained increasing international attention since the end of the Cold War, it was equally a historical feature of colonization. Indeed, Baartman's name has become synonymous with nineteenth-century racial, gender, and sexual exploitation at a global scale. Her story intrinsically highlights the depth of gender-based violence experienced by enslaved women across the British Empire. This chapter seeks to understand both her experiences and symbolic position within the Cape Colony's coercive labor practices, as well as in the context of nineteenth-century popular entertainment and twentieth-century knowledge production. It outlines the multidisciplinary scholarly debates that have considered Baartman's status as enslaved or free, both in terms of what little can be gleaned from contemporary accounts as well as through subsequent literature and historiography. Her situation fundamentally disrupted any clear interpretative paradigm between free and enslaved, illustrating just how amorphous these concepts were and continue to be. At the same time, this case study highlights a historical example of a total lack of research ethics—that is, a "negative example of 'what not to do'" when undertaking research (see Quirk, Bunting, and Kiconco, this volume). All too common are echoes across other cases that highlight the exploitation of African women and women of African descent for scientific research in other parts of the world.[2]

This chapter begins with the nineteenth-century British world before shifting to more recent paradigms. We are particularly concerned with debates regarding the meaning and boundaries of enslaved labor in British colonial and postcolonial contexts, which influenced colonial and contemporary tropes and ideas about slavery and freedom. Although Sara Baartman has been the subject of significant research, this scholarship has illustrated the degree to which she did not have a voice and was subject to coercion in the name of scientific knowledge production. Thus, the historiography about Baartman's life—pieced together using documents about her life written by others, rather than autobiographical sources—illustrates some of the tensions and traditions in these processes of naming coercive and exploitative labor regimes. Inspired by injunctions to historicize Baartman's experience, we aim to further historically contextualize her life by exploring it alongside and in conversation with the experiences of those who were also subject to slavery and coercion. Today, the ongoing mobilization of language surrounding the legacies of slavery and apartheid in South Africa, Uganda, and the United States draws attention to the unintended consequences that can emerge from decontextualized terminology. Thus, this chapter illustrates the wider history of the debates and knowledge production about slavery and freedom in the Global North and South. This follows an ethical imperative for multidisciplinary researchers to emphasize degrees of global unfreedom from both historical and contemporary perspectives.

Sara Baartman in the Era of Slavery and Abolition

The case of Sara Baartman raises an important issue for scholars of modern slavery and gender-based violence: that of research terminology. In both contemporary historical and interdisciplinary accounts of her life, Baartman's status as "enslaved" or "free" has been a matter of debate. And, as historian Catherine Hall reminds us, the very terms we use in our research are contingent and subject to change over time. According to Hall, neither Blackness nor Whiteness—nor masculinity and femininity—had any "essential meanings ... only discursive practices which articulated and organised particular sets of relations through the workings of knowledge and power" (Hall 2004, 50). What might appear to be a trivial issue of terminology had important implications for Baartman's life and subsequent historiographical interpretations. When discussing her story and its legacy, it is essential to keep in mind the historical contexts of transatlantic slavery and abolition, coerced labor in the Cape and across the British Empire, and the expansion of imperialist scientific practices at the beginning of the nineteenth century. It was through these broader developments and discourses that the "naming" of Baartman as either free or enslaved, object or subject of research, occurred.

Sara Baartman was born in the 1770s in the Dutch Cape Colony.[3] A member of the indigenous Gonaqua Khoekhoe group, she lived her first years in the Eastern Cape, working for Dutch farmer Cornelius Muller. With increased numbers of Europeans settling in and around Cape Town, there was a rising demand for domestic laborers to work in settlers' homes. When a trader from Cape Town passed by Muller's farm in 1795 or 1796, Baartman was sold to Pieter Cesars, who worked for a wealthy Cape businessman. As historians Clifton Crais and Pamela Scully put it, "He sold Sara as chattel: she was a slave in all but name" (Crais and Scully 2009, 24). In Cape Town, where she would live for around a decade, Baartman worked for Cesars's employer, Jan Michiel Elzer. After Elzer passed away, Baartman worked for Pieter Cesars, and later his brother Hendrik Cesars, as a domestic laborer. Hendrik Cesars and his wife were part of Cape Town's growing Free Black community: their ancestors had likely come to the Cape as slaves, but both were born as free people. When Cesars ran into financial problems, he began to use Baartman to "entertain" sailors in Cape Town. He also met Alexander Dunlop, a Scottish doctor who worked at the Slave Lodge. Together—and both facing financial pressures—they devised a scheme to take Baartman to England, where her exhibition could earn them significant amounts of money (Crais and Scully 2009).

Thus, prior to Baartman's travel to the imperial metropole, where issues regarding slavery and abolition were the subject of widespread public debate, her status as free or unfree was already complex. When the Cape was initially colonized in 1652, Dutch East India Company officials made it clear that indigenous peoples' laws and customs had to be respected and that they should not be enslaved (Ward 2009). This resulted in a situation where indigenous people were forced into labor, yet the legal category of "slave" was not applied to them. This in itself has been subject to historiographical debate, with South

African feminist historian Yvette Abrahams asserting that the "slave owning culture" of the Dutch Cape meant it was "not unnatural that slavery should be a theme of white/Khoisan interaction from the start" (1996b, 91–92). Despite not being legally classified as enslaved, individuals of Khoesan descent could be forced into "apprenticeships." The 1809 Caledon Code also placed restrictions on their freedom of movement; Khoekhoe people had to have a fixed place of abode and carry passes in order to legally move around the colony. The use of passes to "manage" and coerce labor helped to open the door to twentieth-century apartheid laws, under which Black South Africans were equally subject to coercive pass laws.

These issues of terminology and classification would continue to shape Baartman's trajectory as she traveled to Britain. As Baartman was of Khoesan descent, her travel outside of the colony was not legal, and her travel papers conveniently relabeled her from a "Hottentot [sic]" woman to a "Free Black" (Crais and Scully 2009, 56–57). An individual's legal status, whether enslaved or free, could also be subject to change when moving between the periphery and metropole or between European and North American countries and back again (Drescher 2009). Ultimately, Baartman "lived on the edge of slavery and freedom as defined under Dutch and later British rule" (Scully and Crais 2008, 309).

Once Baartman arrived in London in 1810, there was considerable controversy in the British public sphere regarding her status as enslaved or free (Abrahams 1996b; Qureshi 2004; Scully and Crais 2008; Hall 2012). Soon Baartman was displayed for popular entertainment, her body being used to represent racial difference. According to historian Sadiah Qureshi, London had become the metropolitan center for these popular entertainments. At the turn of the nineteenth century, their scale and expanse would transform dramatically, with colonized peoples often at the forefront of many such exhibitions (Qureshi 2011). Displaying people and animals as the spoils of imperial expansion was not the only hallmark of these popular entertainments. Across the nineteenth century, the "ancient practice of exhibiting anomalous bodies" would consolidate into a highly profitable transatlantic institution (Thomson 1996, 2). These entertainments became increasingly central to popular culture during an era when scientific research began to eclipse religious explanations for natural phenomena and instead establish teratology, the study of congenital abnormalities, based upon physical differences (Thomson 1996). It was in this sense that scientific knowledge operated as "a means of popularizing empire, providing a route through which a wider class of Europeans came into contact with and intervened in the imperial narrative" (Sivasundaram 2010, 154). These exhibitions and other popular entertainments increasingly became what Diarmid A. Finnegan and Jonathan Jeffrey Wright describe as "spaces of global knowledge" (Finnegan and Wright 2015, 10). Given their status as pseudoscientific sites of engagement with contemporary knowledge production, the classification of those on display was an essential part of how these popular entertainments functioned.

A controversial court case concerning Baartman's status was also held in London in 1810. For the evangelical abolitionists and humanitarians who sought to intervene, the specter of slavery and its meanings offered a useful paradigm through which to convey aspects of Baartman's life, both at the Cape and in Europe. This interpretation of Baartman as an enslaved person could make her the subject of a particular kind of humanitarian campaigning, aimed to provoke pity and emotion for her treatment in the metropolitan public sphere.[4] Prominent members of the antislavery lobby expressed their objection to Baartman's display through the norms of transatlantic antislavery discourse, in which abolitionists and other reformers were willing to use the meaning of slavery both directly and expansively. According to an October 1810 letter to the *Morning Chronicle*, Baartman's display was "contrary to every principle of morality and good order" and was furthermore an "offence to public decency, with that most horrid of all situations, *Slavery*" ("An Englishman" 1810; Hall 2012, 66–68; Qureshi 2004, 238–41). Another October letter to the *Examiner* described Baartman as a slave, who should be immediately released, as she is "entitled to all the rights and privileges of a British subject" (A Constant Reader 1810).

The existence of a contract would determine the outcome of Baartman's 1810 court case, again emphasizing the degree to which chattel slavery—as distinguished from other coercive labor regimes—was at the heart of the matter. A contract was indeed produced, yet its existence prior to the legal proceedings remains highly questionable (Qureshi 2004). Ultimately, the court found that Baartman had consented to both her travel and display and had accepted payment for the work. This was particularly troubling to antislavery campaigners who routinely relied on the image of the "victimised female, passive object of the white man's lust" (Hall 2012, 66). Yet Baartman's voice remained absent in the ensuing London court proceedings. She was interviewed—amid debate if this should be done in Dutch or English—but her words were not printed verbatim (Scully and Crais 2008).

During an era when the meaning of slavery was continually being made and remade across the British and Atlantic worlds, this language functioned to alert contemporaries to the exploitation inherent in an individual's situation. Slavery was seen as the worst form of exploitation; it was far less complicated to explain than other forms of coerced labor, which existed along a continuum from unfree to free (Roediger [1991] 1999). But the lack of clarity inherent in these designations also complicated the interpretative paradigm through which subsequent historians and interdisciplinary researchers have interpreted Sara Baartman. Anne McClintock argues that race, class, and gender must be understood as "articulated categories"; "they come into existence *in and through* relation to each other" (1995, 5). In the sections that follow, we demonstrate that the very dynamics of terminology and classification that were unclear during Baartman's life have continued, leading to speculation regarding consent, and the politics of her representation in popular and academic knowledge production.

After the initial exhibitions in London, other exhibitions featuring Baartman then toured various British cities as well as Ireland. Baartman was taken to Paris, where she was to be exhibited by an animal trainer, S. Reaux. Georges Cuvier, a comparative anatomist at the Musee d'Histoire Naturelle, took an interest in her body, subjecting Baartman to close and nonconsensual inspection (Qureshi 2011). When she died, Cuvier conducted extensive "research" on her body, resulting in a publication on Khoekhoe anatomy (Qureshi 2011).[5] This was despite recorded evidence of Baartman refusing Cuvier's research demands during her life. As Anne Fausto-Sterling emphasizes, this approach to scientific inquiry was considered completely unexceptional—and in fact quite "forward-looking"—at the time (Fausto-Sterling 1995, 20). These interactions exemplify the degree to which nineteenth-century scientific inquiry was, according to Sujit Sivasundaram, "molded by the European imperial age. Its methodology—its commitment to laws, collections, and classifications—made sense of, and arose out of, imperialism" (Sivasundaram 2010, 154). When she was first displayed in England and later in France, Baartman became an object of research; whether through the public gaze and imagination or, later, through her use as a "scientific" specimen. Indeed, these modes of scientific interaction persisted well into the twentieth century and beyond. In fact, a cast of Baartman's body was displayed in the Musée de l'Homme until the 1970s.

It is important to raise the issue of Sara Baartman's own identification as enslaved or free: how did she, as the subject of this transnational story, see herself? Historians such as Yvette Abrahams, Sadiah Qureshi, and Pamela Scully and Clifton Crais have pieced together the remnants of the historical records that exist to capture Baartman's lived experience at the Cape of Good Hope, as well as her final years in England and France. Other sources illuminate the experiences of the Khoisan and enslaved people alongside whom Baartman lived and worked, thus informing and enriching what can be known about her life. The lives of many other women who were coerced and enslaved at the Cape across the eighteenth and nineteenth centuries sometimes emerge within the records of court cases, offering glimpses of the degree of violence enacted upon enslaved women by slave owners, including men and women (Scully 1995; Gqola

2007; Murray 2010; Tsampiras 2016; Thornberry 2018). More often, however, enslaved women's voices were equally silenced in the Cape Colony, eclipsed by that of enslaved men or even slave owners (Murray 2010).

As social science researchers working on modern slavery and gender-based violence are increasingly aware, the labeling of research "subjects" as outside knowledge-making can have important ramifications for the individuals and communities at the center of research interventions. So, too, can the unexamined use of particular terminology—for example, "victims" or "survivors." Yet such ethical questions were largely overlooked at the time of Baartman's trial; very few historical records remain to illuminate her everyday life, and none offer a true glimpse of her own words or her own voice. What little can be known comes from archival records, wherein Baartman's voice remains absent, meaning that her life has been read through multiple, sometimes competing or contradictory disciplinary lenses.

This historical context—first, of coercive labor practices at the colonial Cape under both Dutch and British regimes, and second, of transatlantic slavery and antislavery campaigning in England—was fundamental to how Sara Baartman was understood and positioned in the early nineteenth century. Coupled with new discourses regarding colonists' attitudes toward indigenous women as well as that of scientific knowledge production, her case highlights the ethical importance of attuning ourselves to the broader contexts in which we embed our research. While Baartman has emerged as a figure and symbol in South African historiography and broader feminist scholarship regarding the position of Black women in the nineteenth and twentieth centuries, this discussion necessarily reiterates the degree to which the interpretation of her life story has been fundamentally shaped by the contexts in which she lived. It also illustrates the necessity of questioning the taken-for-granted categories that are used in contemporary research, as they similarly arise out of diverse and often competing contexts and knowledge regimes.

Historiography and Knowledge Production in the Twentieth and Twenty-First Century

The story of Sara Baartman is but one instance of how slavery and its meanings have shaped knowledge production across the centuries. During Baartman's life, as already mentioned, there was considerable debate regarding her status as enslaved or free. Sometimes the terminology or classification of "slave" was used to highlight the uncertainties surrounding her legal status as well as her position in the context of scientific knowledge production. The debates that shaped her life again emerged at the center of these two trajectories within twentieth- and twenty-first-century historiography and knowledge production. One trajectory has been dedicated to greater specificity; the other has been concerned with expansive definitions and understandings. This has ongoing consequences for knowledge production surrounding modern slavery and gender-based violence. One consequence of the new consciousness born of the interactions between scholarship and activism has been new approaches to social sciences research methods and ethics.

Across the 1980s and 1990s, feminist and postcolonial scholarship observed the global dimensions of the synergies between representations of gender, race, and class. Indeed, feminist scholars increasingly argued that gender must be included in discussions of race- and class-based oppression (King 1988; Crenshaw 1989, 1991; Collins 1990; Bozzoli 1983). Baartman's public exhibition across Europe as the "Hottentot Venus" gained disproportionate scholarly significance at this juncture, morphing her into what sociologist Zine Magubane describes as an "icon" of racial and sexual difference (Magubane 2001, 817). The "theoretical groundswell" that began after historian Sander Gilman's 1985 article, which compared the symbolism surrounding Baartman with the figure of the nineteenth-century prostitute, "cannot be separated from the growing popularity of poststructuralist analyses of race and gender." Yet many of the most theoretical analyses, Magubane argues, failed to question who actually "counted as Black," why people of African descent ever became "icons of sexual difference," and how different historical and cultural contexts shaped Baartman's "very different interpellation into French versus British medicine and science." The result was that much of the era's scholarship has disconcertingly situated Baartman *outside* history" (Magubane 2001, 817–18; Gilman 1985).

These criticisms increasingly emphasized the need for historically, culturally, and socially informed analyses of Sara Baartman. As American-based historians and biographers Clifton Crais and Pamela Scully observe, the academic outpouring on Baartman from the 1980s onward effectively overlooked the early years of her life, in favor of focusing on "those brief, if momentous, years she spent in Europe displayed as the Hottentot Venus." The result was that "Sara's story became *the* story of what men (especially white men) do to women (especially black women), and thus part of the politics of global feminism" (2009, 24). Renewed scholarship about Baartman emerged against a background of scholarly debates about slavery and apartheid in southern Africa, as well as the political upheavals of the 1980s and 1990s.

Among Southern African scholars, these decades also witnessed debates about coercive labor regimes at the Cape. Historians' positions on Khoesan slavery in subsequent texts have no doubt been influenced by well-known liberal Cape historian W. M. Macmillan, who wrote that Khoesan at the beginning of the nineteenth century were "doubtfully better off even than the slaves" (Macmillan 1927, 65). Comparisons between labor regimes remained a significant area of investigation for subsequent generations of historians. In her classic study of the interaction between Khoesan people and Christianity, historian Elizabeth Elbourne describes the status of Khoesan people in the early nineteenth century as follows: "Although the Khoekhoe were technically 'free,' their status in many respects at the turn of the century in the Eastern Cape approximated that of slaves, particularly in rural areas where the mobility of so-called Hottentots, as well as their ability to get out of contracts, was severely limited by local legislation, including vagrancy legislation, and by quasi-legal custom" (2002, 82–83). Elbourne thus argues that the treatment of laborers in the Cape, whether enslaved or free, was fundamentally shaped by the culture of a slave-owning society.

The question of whether or not Baartman was enslaved at the Cape became a central concern for this revisionist scholarship, and her legal status has received much scrutiny. Yvette Abrahams was one of the first to insist that focusing on "her conditions of labour" was absolutely essential to historicizing Baartman as a person, rather than merely as a symbol, in order to adequately place her at the center of her own historical and social context (1996a, 13; 1998). Citing Abrahams, Sadiah Qureshi also alludes to the possibility of Baartman's enslavement; the diminutive use of the moniker "Saartjie ('little Sara' in Dutch) in contemporary accounts," she suggests, is evidence in support of Baartman's enslavement because "diminutives were often used to differentiate slaves or collared [sic] people from their white counterparts, effectively assigning them the status of children" (2004, 235). Following South African literary scholar Pumla Dineo Gqola, scholars have increasingly found it useful to "read and position Sarah Baartman as a slave, rather than as an indentured worker" (Gordon-Chipempere 2011, 3; Gqola 2010).

Thus, as Caribbean scholar Natasha Gordon-Chipembere observes, academic conversations about Baartman in the Global North tend to be "radically different" from conversations among scholars in the Global South. This has significant repercussions in terms of both historiography and knowledge production because Baartman's "womanhood has [often] been 'read' within the paradigms of the North American slave experience" (2011, 2–3). Such an approach can have the effect of reifying historical experience of chattel slavery across the Americas, particularly in the United States, while sidelining the specificity of historical slave systems elsewhere (Abrahams 1996b; Quirk 2011).

The analysis of slavery, indenture, forced labor, and coercive labor practices across southern Africa has been equally defined by linguistic indeterminacy about the nature of each. Nigel Worden and Clifton Crais's edited collection *Breaking the Chains: Slavery and Its Legacy in the Nineteenth-Century Cape*

Colony (1994) and Gerald Kraak's *Breaking the Chains: Labour in South Africa in the 1970s and 1980s* (1993) epitomize this trajectory; the former describes slave emancipation and its aftermath in the colonial Cape, while the latter focuses on coerced labor during apartheid (Worden and Crais 1994; Kraak 1993). This is despite the fact that South African historians have been wary of a lack of conceptual clarity regarding different labor forms in the past, calling attention to a tendency to describe all forms of unfree labor using similar terms (Malherbe 1991). Relatedly, historian Mahmood Mamdani argues for Africanist scholars to move beyond "a history by analogy" and instead "establish the historical legitimacy of Africa as a unit of analysis" ([1996] 2018, 8–11).

Beyond academia, too, the ethical issues that have emerged from questions about terminology and classification have had important political consequences. Slave memory and heritage have often been suppressed in twentieth-century South Africa, where increasingly pervasive social and political segregation had made Whiteness the most desirable social attribute (Worden 2009). Worden argues that during the apartheid years "distinct slave heritage was played down in the interests of common struggle" (2009, 27). This was further complicated by the use of the term "slavery" to describe the different forms of oppression wrought by the apartheid state. This makes the mobilization of slave identity for a figure like Baartman even more interesting, as it speaks to a process of reclamation that was rooted in the politics of postapartheid South Africa as much as it was in the early nineteenth century. Postapartheid nation-building attempts also used capacious definitions of slavery in order to highlight shared experiences of colonial and apartheid oppression. Worden points out, however, that the simple equation of Khoesan treatment and slavery has not been uncomplicated. In the early 2000s, as Khoe and San leaders began to make claims to indigenous status and rights in South Africa, these "possibilities were not open to those who claimed slave ancestry. To be descended from a slave was to be an outsider and thus part of a colonial history, albeit on the receiving end" (Worden 2009, 28).

Much of the revisionist scholarship about Sara Baartman also illuminated the campaign for her remains to be repatriated to South Africa from the Musée de l'Homme in Paris. This campaign had been spearheaded by the Griqua National Conference through the 1990s and supported by Nelson Mandela since 1995. It successfully culminated in Baartman's remains being returned in April 2002 and laid to rest in the town of Hankey, Eastern Cape, on August 9, National Women's Day (Qureshi 2004; Gordon-Chipembere 2011; Henderson 2014). Even then, President Thabo Mbeki used language of coercion and slavery when speaking at her reburial in Hankey. For Mbeki, Baartman's story was the story of African people, "a story of our reduction to the status of objects that could be owned, used and disposed of by others," and thus "a story of the loss of our ancient freedom." Mbeki also connected her history to the specter of gender-based violence in South Africa, saying, "[The] women of our country have borne the brunt of the oppressive and exploitative system of colonial and apartheid domination. Even today, the women of our country carry the burden of poverty and continue to be exposed to unacceptable violence and abuse" (2002).

For Abrahams, Qureshi, and Gqola, the most ethical and productive methodological approach to returning Baartman to history has been to focus on her labor status in the context of broader historical debates about Khoisan slavery. Gordon-Chipembere "insists upon a historically specific Southern African context as the landscape and the time frame in which to access Sarah Baartman." Her argument that "regardless of legal definitions, the Khoisan were exposed to conditions that would clearly be defined as slavery" explicitly embraces the most expansive conceptualization of its meanings. In contrast, much contemporary knowledge production has instead regarded Baartman "externally, perceived through an archived, colonial lens that does not bring the reader any closer to the personhood of Sarah Baartman" (Gordon-Chipembere 2011, 3–4). As Siphiwe Gloria Ndlovu reflects, "Saartjie Baartman's body told the story of how brown women had for centuries suffered emotional, physical, and epistemic violence at the hands of white men, history, and science." Yet in making these observations, Ndlovu argues there is a need to reconceptualize Baartman as a woman not shaped by the European colonial archive but with a personal history (2011, 18). This knowledge production made continual recourse to racialized experiences of slavery and gender-based violence.

Humanitarianism and Activism in the Era of Slavery and Apartheid

Humanitarians, abolitionists, and reformers of the eighteenth and nineteenth centuries were less consistently concerned with the minutiae of what constituted legal enslavement and more preoccupied with the existence of many degrees of exploitation and coercion. As Srividhya Swaminathan and Adam R. Beach emphasize, the "multiple meanings" associated with slavery in the eighteenth-century British imagination contradict most contemporary historiographical understandings of the era's reliance on labor regimes grounded in chattel slavery. For many, slavery existed along "a continuum of experiences attached to different labour conditions" (Swaminathan and Beach 2016, 1). These complicated questions of terminology and classification remained unresolved in the production of knowledge well into the twentieth century.

Such trends operated on both local and global levels. When the United Nations adopted the *1956 Supplementary Convention on the Abolition of Slavery,* the *Slave Trade, and Institutions and Practices Similar to Slavery*, it introduced the phrase "practices similar to slavery" to the global humanitarian lexicon. This offered the groundwork for former colonies, many of which had recently become independent nation-states, to reconsider the meaning of colonialism in the context of international law. A decade later, Special Rapporteur on Slavery Mohamed Awad's 1966 *Report on Slavery* used the rephrased descriptor "slavery-like practices" to describe colonialism, apartheid, and racism (Allain 2012; Bunting and Quirk 2017). This generated an expansive—rather than a restrictive—paradigm for interpreting what constituted slavery. It has become powerful for humanitarians, activists, and even scholars to continue to connect many forms of exploitation, including labor and sexual exploitation, along a historical continuum from slavery to the present. Indeed, Pumla Dineo Gqola conceives of "slavery, colonialism, and apartheid ... as moments along a continuum, and not as separate, completely distinct, and mutually exclusive periods" (2010, 6).

An instructive example of these interrelated trends emerged in an activist pamphlet coissued by the Federation of South African Women (FEDSAW) and the African National Congress (ANC) Women's League during the 1950s. Published in Johannesburg in both English and Sesotho, *Women in Chains* (1956) was developed in the context of the apartheid government's intention to extend pass laws to Black women following the election of the National Party in 1948 and the gradual expansion of the apartheid regime thereafter. In August 1956, a multiracial protest of twenty thousand women marched to the Union Buildings to present Prime Minister J. G. Strijdom with an antipass petition (Gasa 2007). The women of FEDSAW led what became known as the Women's March on Pretoria. "It is the duty of every woman to support the struggle of the African woman," the *Women in Chains* (1956) pamphlet proclaimed, "to proclaim abroad to women all over the world this latest attempt of the Nationalist government to enslave further the African people." Thus, FEDSAW and the ANC Women's League challenged the labor exploitation and oppression of Black South African women under apartheid by mobilizing the language of slavery.

Across the subsequent decades, slavery continued to be one of the key concepts that activists used to challenge power across temporal, geographic, and national sites. Increasingly, slavery and its meanings have become paired with apartheid and its meanings in a manner that reflects the terminology of the United Nations' 1956 Supplementary Convention on the Abolition of Slavery (Jacobs and Soske 2015; Stevenson 2018). For example, the process of using both slavery and apartheid as language to challenge power has recently transpired in contemporary East African politics, activism, and cultural production. In 2017, President Yoweri Kaguta Museveni proposed to amend Article 102 (b) of the 1995 Constitution of the Republic of Uganda, which limits presidential candidates to seventy-five years of age. Museveni has been the country's president since 1986 and seems unwilling to step down. In 2011, Museveni prevailed in the presidential elections after amending constitutional presidential term limits in 2005. Despite objections from opposition parties and the public, a parliamentary majority voted to remove the age limit for presidential candidates on September 12, 2017. Museveni, who was seventy-seven years of age at the time of the 2021 elections, appears poised to remain president for life. The Ugandan musician and independent parliamentarian Robert Ssentamu Kyagulanyi, also known as Bobi Wine, responded with the song "Freedom" (2017) to highlight the injustices that parliamentary policies have placed on Ugandan citizens. Wine began his career in popular music in 2000, yet only since his election to politics in 2017, as the member of Parliament for the Kyaddondo East Constituency in Kampala, has the live performance of political music been prohibited by the Ugandan Police Force (Lwanga 2020).

"This is a message to the government expressing exactly what's on the peoples' mind," the lyrics to "Freedom" begin (Wine 2017). The context in which Wine makes these claims is to describe the Ugandan Bush War, the 1980s civil war in which Museveni overthrew President Milton Obote. Although Obote had been a liberation leader during the 1960s, his leadership of postcolonial Uganda was dominated by significant political instability, violence, and the destruction of democratic institutions (Brett 1995). Indeed, the Bush War and subsequent civil conflicts have been and continue to be significant sites of gender-based violence (Liebling and Kiziri-Mayengo 2002). Wine observes that Museveni has become what he fought against by doing what he promised he would not do once in power. This entails a very distinctive lyrical approach:

> We are living in a dance similar to the one of slave trade; this oppression is worse than apartheid.
> The gun is the master, citizen slave; the pearl of Africa is bleeding, Question:
> What was the purpose of the liberation; if we can't have a peaceful transition?
> What was the purpose of the constitution; when the government disrespect[s] the constitution? (Wine 2017; Lwanga 2020, 204)

Describing twenty-first-century Ugandans as "citizen-slaves," Wine compares Museveni's rule to the transatlantic slave trade, as well as slavery more broadly, and the resulting political tensions to South Africa's struggle against apartheid. "Freedom" was banned from Ugandan television and radio stations soon after its release. However, the song gained popularity on social media, especially YouTube. Ethnomusicologist Charles Lwanga argues that this song, driven by its underlying political approach, has achieved political significance insofar as Wine's performances generated a series of by-elections that have culminated in political success for opposition parties (Lwanga 2020, 133, 6).

The power that Bobi Wine commands by connecting the legacies of slavery across the British and Atlantic world to the present moment also reverberates in North American politics, activism, and cultural production. Filmmaker Ava DuVernay's Netflix documentary *13th* (2016) makes similarly compelling links between the contemporary prison-industrial complex and the history of chattel slavery in the United States. So, too, has the 1619 Project of the *New York Times Magazine*, which first appeared in August 2019, reframing the arrival of the first enslaved Africans in the colony of Virginia in 1619—rather than the nation's revolutionary era—as the founding moment of the United States. The director of the 1619 Project, Pulitzer Prize–winning journalist Nikole Hannah-Jones, also uses slavery and its meanings expansively. The result is to describe southern plantations where enslaved people of African descent lived and labored as "forced-labor camps"; freed people not as sharecroppers but as subject to a form of "apartheid"; and the effects of racism not merely as violence but as "racial terrorism" (Hannah-Jones 2019). The potency of these connections has become even more urgent in the wake of the ongoing Black Lives Matter protests around the globe. Across 2020, activists and journalists continued to articulate continuities between Atlantic slavery, Jim Crow in the United States, and apartheid in South Africa (Windsor 2020).

At the same time, however, many scholars have become more precise with respect to concerns about what constitutes slavery, why different labor practices do or do not represent enslavement, and who gets to decide on whether a particular labor regime constitutes slavery. Often motivated by ethical concerns, historical scholarship in the twenty-first century has aimed toward what Swaminathan and Beach describe as "a carefully graded terminology of 'unfree' and 'coerced' to draw distinctions between the extreme race-based chattel slavery found in the Atlantic system and other forms of labour exploitation" (Swaminathan and Beach 2016, 1). Historians and anthropologists are often dedicated to using historical, cultural, and social contexts to bring significant nuance to these discussions (e.g., Cunliffe [1979] 2008; Davis 1983; Neal 1987; Ferguson 1992; Miers 2003; Bhana 2008; Goyal 2017; Stevenson 2019; Swartz 2021). For example, historical anthropologist Benedetta Rossi suggests that it is important to consider the many elements that broadly define experiences of slavery in West Africa. Her schema captures any "historical forms of enslavement" in the term slavery but bifurcates the concept further based on related practices. Consequently, *classificatory slavery* relates to "stigmatization on the ground of inherited or putative slave status," *metaphorical slavery* includes "forms of exploitation akin to slavery," and the "exogenous discourses opening new fields of thought and action around the notion of slavery" are termed *extraverted slavery*. The latter three categories, Rossi argues, "should not be seen as types of slavery but as different phenomena variously related to it" (2009, 5–6).

Yet other scholars find debates about the minutiae of terminology and classification to be missing the point, with potential ethical implications. Legal scholar Ariela Gross (2008), for example, asks: "When is the time of slavery?" The answer to this rhetorical question may be *now*, yet her more nuanced argument emphasizes the need to create historical narratives that identify the differing trajectories of Black slavery and White freedom in the United States. This requires an emphasis on how persistent legal injustices of the Jim Crow laws followed the abolition of chattel slavery, as well as an understanding of how both have engendered persistent legal inequalities for African Americans (Gross 2008; Robinson 2000; Blackmon 2008; Brooks 2008; Mbembe 2017). These examinations, often the product of activist-scholars, exemplify when the analysis of that which is no longer slavery and its meanings are less analogical and far more grounded in historical causation. It is an approach that evokes the history of chattel slavery as a labor regime across the British and Atlantic worlds, while also refocusing attention toward those who were literally enslaved or whose experiences aligned more closely with literal enslavement than with its analogies and metaphors of coercion and exploitation.

The use of slavery and its meanings has become a global narrative in which the connections between free master and unfree worker, man and woman, and imperial metropole and settler colony have been played out for centuries. These connections illuminate not only the triangulations borne of the transatlantic slave trade but also the transnational extent of colonial and settler brutality. While many commentators, activists, and scholars have found there to be power in approaching these concepts in an expansive manner, there is equal power in exploring different forms of exploitation on their own terms. When these interpretive paradigms have been turned toward the status of women, there has been an imperative to focus on the nuances and complexities of race, gender, class, and enslaved status, as each relates to gender-based violence. At the heart of such discussions are questions about labor and self-ownership, which can occlude the historically, culturally, and socially specific differences which contribute to women's oppression across the globe. A historiographical approach emphasizes that each of these interpretive paradigms are equally sites of knowledge production.

The unresolved issues of terminology and classification have important ethical implications for both historical and contemporary research about slavery and connect to current debates regarding the decolonization of knowledge. For historians, much of the scholarship explored throughout this chapter advocates a methodological approach that is highly attuned to the limitations of the archive. Increasingly, the injunction to read the colonial archive "against the grain," whether through rich or fragmented records, is not enough.[6] There has been a growing insistence that something more is required to understand the nature and meaning of gender-based violence (Gqola 2015). Following Hayden White's postmodernist insistence that the boundaries between fact and fiction are more indistinct than empiricist histories allow, others purposefully bring historical, cultural, and literary scholarship together in order to "arrive at a greater understanding of the relationship between slavery, gender and violence" (Murray 2010, 446; White [1973] 2014).

Many of the historians who seek to reevaluate the lives of Khoisan women insist upon an alternative, imaginative methodological approach. For example, Yvette Abrahams has advocated a "liberatory history" grounded in the natural world to advance another step closer to Sara Baartman (Abrahams and Omsis 2011, 32). Siphiwe Gloria Ndlovu argues that this demands "coming to knowledge and different ways of thinking about and remembering the past" and should ultimately involve "practicing an 'ethics of care'" toward women such as Baartman: an ethos that would make it possible to concede that not everything can be—or should be—knowable (2011, 28, 23). For social scientists, the historical uncertainties and slippages surrounding terminology and classification offer insight into the degree to which similar uncertainties persist today, particularly in contexts of conflict and gender-based violence.

The paradigms that have been created and sustained through knowledge production have the potential to stay with us, as historians and social scientists, when we enter the field—whether it be to delve into the archive or assemble case studies, collect qualitative and quantitative data through surveys and interviews, or gather a lifetime's worth of experience through oral history. Although historiography and methodology are different modes of scholarly inquiry, changing methods of interpretation have been indelibly linked to the shifting ethical approach to Sara Baartman. Many historical and sociological concepts have been used in an attempt to get closer to her lived experience. This emphasizes the need for scholars to be self-reflexive toward research ethics and to constantly rearticulate a commitment to ethical data collection in which participants are active. It is difficult—but ultimately necessary—to disaggregate the logics of those who have come before us, because these very logics continue today.

Notes

Our thanks to the editors and reviewers for their valuable feedback and guidance as we developed this chapter. We are also very grateful for the contributions of research assistant Gertrude Nakibuule.

1. For example, some scholars problematize the implications of women's rights reformers describing free White women as enslaved, even while acknowledging the implications of gender-based oppression, see: bell hooks, *Ain't I a Woman: Black Women and Feminism* (Boston: South End Press, 1981); Angela Y. Davis, *Women, Race & Class* (London: The Women's Press, 1983).
2. For broader approaches to medical history, medical humanities, and bioethics, see Holloway (2011), Horwitz (2013), Owens (2017), and Masakure (2020).
3. Given the paucity of records relating to Sara Baartman in the Cape, many of the details of her life—including date of birth—are subject to debate in the literature. Similarly, scholars use many different spellings for her name. See: Gordon-Chipembere, ed. *Representation and Black Womanhood*.
4. On humanitarianism and emotions, see Ballantyne (2016).
5. Historian Nell Irvin Painter does not use quotation marks around the word *science* when discussing nineteenth-century scientific research, "even theories and assertions of the most spurious, pernicious, or ridiculous kind," stating that it can be productive to "note the qualifications of yesterday's scientists than to brand as mere 'science' their thought that has not stood the test of time" (Painter 2010, x).
6. For reading the colonial archive "against" and "along" the grain, see Stoler (2009).

References

Abrahams, Y. 1996a. "Was Eva Raped? An Exercise in Speculative History." *Kronos* 23 (1): 3–21.
———. 1996b. "Disempowered to Consent: Sara Bartman and Khoisan Slavery in the Nineteenth-Century Cape Colony and Britain." *South African Historical Journal* 35 (1): 89–114.
———. 1998. "Images of Sara Bartman: Sexuality, Race, and Gender in Early-Nineteenth-Century Britain." In *Nation, Empire, Colony: Historicising Gender and Race*, edited by R. R. Pierson, H. Chaudhuri, and B. McAuley, 220–36. Bloomington: Indiana University Press.
Abrahams, Y., and K. Omsis. 2011. "'My Tongue Softens on That Other Name': Poetry, People, and Plants in Sarah Bartmann's Natural World." In *Representation and Black Womanhood: The Legacy of Sarah Baartman*, edited by N. Gordon-Chipembere, 31–46. Basingstoke, UK: Palgrave Macmillan.
Allain, J. 2012. "The International Legal Regime of Slavery and Human Exploitation and Its Obfuscation by the Term of Art: 'Slavery-Like Practice.'" *Cahiers de la recherche en droits fondamentaux* 10: 27–42.

Ballantyne, T. 2016. "Moving Texts and 'Humane Sentiment': Materiality, Mobility and the Emotions of Imperial Humanitarianism." *Journal of Colonialism and Colonial History* 17 (1). Project Muse.

Bhana, K. S. 2008. "Indenture in Comparative Perspective." *Safundi: The Journal of South African and American Studies* 9 (2): 215–24.

Blackmon, D. A. 2008. *Slavery by Another Name: The Re-enslavement of Black Americans from the Civil War to World War II*. New York: Anchor Books.

Bozzoli, B. 1983. "Marxism, Feminism and South African Studies." *Journal of Southern African Studies* 9 (2): 139–71.

Brett, E. A. 1995. "Neutralising the Use of Force in Uganda: The Role of the Military in Politics." *Journal of Modern African Studies* 33 (1): 129–52.

Brooks, P. E. 2008. *Boycotts, Buses, and Passes: Black Women's Resistance in the US South and South Africa*. Amherst: University of Massachusetts Press.

Bunting, A., and J. Quirk, eds. 2017. *Contemporary Slavery: Popular Rhetoric and Political Practice*. Vancouver: UBC Press.

Collins, P. H. 1990. *Black Feminist Thought: Knowledge, Consciousness, and the Politics of Empowerment*. London: Routledge.

A Constant Reader. 1810. Letter to *The Examiner*, April 14.

Crais, C., and P. Scully. 2009. *Sara Baartman and the Hottentot Venus: A Ghost Story and a Biography*. Princeton, NJ: Princeton University Press.

Crenshaw, K. 1989. "Demarginalizing the Intersection of Race and Sex: A Black Feminist Critique of Antidiscrimination Doctrine, Feminist Theory and Antiracist Politics." *University of Chicago Legal Forum* 1 (8): 139–67.

———. 1991. "Mapping the Margins: Intersectionality, Identity Politics, and Violence against Women of Color." *Stanford Law Review* 43 (6): 1241–99.

Cunliffe, M. (1979) 2008. *Chattel Slavery and Wage Slavery: The Anglo-American Context, 1830–1860*. Athens: University of Georgia Press.

Davis, A. Y. 1983. *Women, Race and Class*. London: Women's Press.

de Bolla, P., E. Jones, P. Nulty, G. Recchia, and J. Regan. 2020. "The Idea of Liberty, 1600–1800: A Distributional Concept Analysis." *Journal of the History of Ideas* 81 (3): 381–406.

Drescher, S. 2009. *Abolition: A History of Slavery and Antislavery*. Cambridge: Cambridge University Press.

Elbourne, E. 2002. *Blood Ground: Colonialism, Missions, and the Contest for Christianity in the Cape Colony and Britain*. Montreal: McGill-Queen's University Press.

"An Englishman." 1810. *Morning Chronicle*, October 12.

Fausto-Sterling, A. 1995. "Gender, Race, and Nation: The Comparative Anatomy of 'Hottentot' Women in Europe, 1815–1817." In *Deviant Bodies: Critical Perspectives on Difference in Science and Popular Culture*, edited by J. Terry and J. Urla, 19–46. Bloomington: University of Indiana Press.

FEDSAW (Federation of South African Women) and the ANC (African National Congress) Women's League. 1956. *Women in Chains*. Johannesburg: Federation of South African Women and the African National Congress Women's League. Wits Historical Papers. http://historicalpapers-atom.wits.ac.za/women-in-chains-published-jointly-by-fedsaw-and-n-c-womens-league.

Ferguson, M. 1992. *Subject to Others: British Women Writers and Colonial Slavery, 1670–1834*. New York: Routledge.

Finnegan, D. A., and J. J. Wright, eds. 2015. *Spaces of Global Knowledge: Exhibition, Encounter and Exchange in an Age of Empire*. Farnham, UK: Ashgate Publishing.

Gasa, N. 2007. "Feminisms, Motherisms, Patriarchies and Women's Voices in the 1950s." In *Women in South African History: Basus'iimbokodo, Bawel'imilambo / They Remove Boulders and Cross Rivers*, edited by N. Gasa, 207–29. Cape Town: HSRC Press.

Gilman, S. L. 1985. "Black Bodies, White Bodies: Toward an Iconography of Female Sexuality in Late Nineteenth-Century Art, Medicine, and Literature." *Critical Inquiry* 12: 204–42.

Gordon-Chipembere, N., ed. 2011. *Representation and Black Womanhood: The Legacy of Sarah Baartman*. Basingstoke, UK: Palgrave Macmillan.

Goyal, Y. 2017. "The Logic of Analogy: Slavery and the Contemporary Refugee." *Humanity: An International Journal of Human Rights, Humanitarianism, and Development* 8 (3): 543–46.

Gqola, P. D. 2007. "'Like Three Tongues in One Mouth': Tracing the Elusive Lives of Slave Women in (Slavocratic) South Africa." In *Women in South African History: Basus'iimbokodo, Bawel'imilambo / They Remove Boulders and Cross Rivers*, edited by N. Gasa, 21–41. Cape Town: HSRC Press.

———. 2010. *What Is Slavery to Me? Postcolonial/Slave Memory in Post-apartheid South Africa*. Johannesburg: Wits University Press.

———. 2015. *Rape: A South African Nightmare*. Auckland Park, South Africa: Jacana Media.

Gross, A. 2008. "When Is the Time of Slavery: The History of Slavery in Contemporary Legal and Political Argument." *California Law Review* 96: 283–322.

Hall, C. 2004. "Of Gender and Empire: Reflections on the Nineteenth Century." In *Gender and Empire*, edited by P. Levine, 46–76. Oxford: Oxford University Press.

———. 2012. *Macaulay and Son*. New Haven, CT: Yale University Press.

Hannah-Jones, N. 2019. "The 1619 Project." *New York Times Magazine*, August 14. https://www.nytimes.com/interactive/2019/08/14/magazine/black-history-american-democracy.html.

Henderson, C. E. 2014. "AKA: Sarah Baartman, the Hottentot Venus, and Black Women's Identity." *Women's Studies* 43 (7): 946–47.

Holloway, K. F. C. 2011. *Private Bodies, Public Texts: Race, Gender, and a Cultural Bioethics*. Durham, NC: Duke University Press.

hooks, b. 1981. *Ain't I a Woman: Black Women and Feminism*. Boston: South End.

Horwitz, S. 2013. *Baragwanath Hospital, Soweto: A History of Medical Care 1941–1990*. New York: New York University Press.

Jacobs, S., and J. Soske, eds. 2015. *Apartheid Israel: The Politics of an Analogy*. Chicago: Haymarket Books.

King, D. K. 1988. "Multiple Jeopardy, Multiple Consciousness: The Context of a Black Feminist Ideology." *Signs: Journal of Women in Culture and Society* 14 (1): 42–72.

Kraak, G. 1993. *Breaking the Chains: Labour in South Africa in the 1970s and 1980s*. London: Pluto Press.

Liebling, H., and R. Kiziri-Mayengo. 2002. "The Psychological Effects of Gender-Based Violence following Armed Conflict in Luwero District, Uganda." *Feminism & Psychology* 12 (4): 553–60.

Lwanga, C. 2020. "Audible Publics: Popular Music and the Politics of Participation in Postcolonial Uganda." PhD diss., University of Pittsburgh.

Macmillan, W. M. 1927. *The Cape Colour Question: A Historical Survey.* London: Faber & Gwyer.

Magubane, Z. 2001. "Which Bodies Matter? Feminism, Poststructuralism, Race, and the Curious Theoretical Odyssey of the 'Hottentot Venus.'" *Gender & Society* 15 (6): 816–34.

Malherbe, V. C. 1991. "Indentured and Unfree Labour in South Africa: Towards an Understanding." *South African Historical Journal* 24 (1): 3–30.

Mamdani, M. (1996) 2018. *Citizen and Subject: Contemporary Africa and the Legacy of Colonialism.* Princeton, NJ: Princeton University Press.

Masakure, C. 2020. *African Nurses and Everyday Work in Twentieth-Century Zimbabwe.* Manchester: Manchester University Press.

Mbeki, T. 2002. "Speech at the Funeral of Sarah Bartmann." Department of Foreign Affairs, Republic of South Africa, August 9. http://www.dirco.gov.za/docs/speeches/2002/mbek0809.htm.

Mbembe, A. 2017. *Critique of Black Reason.* Durham, NC: Duke University Press.

McClintock, A. 1995. *Imperial Leather: Race, Gender and Sexuality in the Colonial Contest.* New York: Routledge.

Miers, S. 2003. "Slavery: A Question of Definition." *Slavery & Abolition: A Journal of Slave and Post-slave Studies* 24 (2): 1–16.

Murray, J. 2010. "Gender and Violence in Cape Slave Narratives and Post-narratives." *South African Historical Journal* 62 (3): 444–62.

Ndlovu, S. G. 2011. "'Body' of Evidence: Saartjie Baartman and the Archive." In *Representation and Black Womanhood: The Legacy of Sarah Baartman*, edited by N. Gordon-Chipembere, 17–30. Basingstoke, UK: Palgrave Macmillan.

Neal, D. 1987. "Free Society, Penal Colony, Slave Society, Prison?" *Australian Historical Studies* 22 (98): 497–518.

Owens, D. C. 2017. *Medical Bondage: Race, Gender, and the Origins of American Gynecology.* Athens: University of Georgia Press.

Painter, N. I. 2010. *The History of White People.* New York: W. W. Norton.

Plasa, C., and B. J. Ring, eds. 1994. *The Discourse of Slavery: Aphra Behn to Toni Morrison.* Abingdon, UK: Routledge.

Quirk, J. 2011. *The Anti-slavery Project: From the Slave Trade to Human Trafficking.* Philadelphia: University of Pennsylvania Press.

Qureshi, S. 2004. "Displaying Sara Baartman, the 'Hottentot Venus.'" *History of Science* 42 (2): 233–57.

———. 2011. *Peoples on Parade: Exhibitions, Empire, and Anthropology in Nineteenth-Century Britain.* Chicago: University of Chicago Press.

Roberts, J. 2013. *Slavery and the Enlightenment in the British Atlantic, 1750–1807.* New York: Cambridge University Press.

Robinson, R. 2000. *The Debt: What America Owes to Blacks.* New York: Penguin.

Roediger, D. R. (1991) 1999. *The Wages of Whiteness: Race and the Making of the American Working Class*. London: Verso.

Rossi, B., ed. 2009. *Reconfiguring Slavery: West African Trajectories*. Liverpool: Liverpool University Press.

Scully, P. 1995. "Rape, Race, and Colonial Culture: The Sexual Politics of Identity in the Nineteenth-Century Cape Colony, South Africa." *American Historical Review* 100 (2): 335–59.

Scully, P., and C. Crais. 2008. "Race and Erasure: Sara Baartman and Hendrik Cesars in Cape Town and London." *Journal of British Studies* 47 (2): 301–23.

Sivasundaram, S. 2010. "Sciences and the Global: On Methods, Questions, and Theory." *Isis* 101 (1): 146–58.

Sklar, K., and J. B. Stewart, eds. 2007. *Women's Rights and Transatlantic Antislavery in the Era of Emancipation*. New Haven, CT: Yale University Press.

Stevenson, A. 2018. "The Gender-Apartheid Analogy in the Transnational Feminist Imaginary: *Ms. Magazine* and the Feminist Majority Foundation, 1972–2002." *Safundi: The Journal of South African and American Studies* 19 (1): 93–116.

———. 2019. *The Woman as Slave in Nineteenth-Century American Social Movements*. Cham, Switzerland: Palgrave Macmillan.

Stoler, A. L. 2009. *Along the Archival Grain: Epistemic Anxieties and Colonial Common Sense*. Princeton, NJ: Princeton University Press.

Swaminathan, S., and A. R. Beach, eds. 2016. *Invoking Slavery in the Eighteenth-Century British Imagination*. London: Routledge.

Swartz, R. 2021. "Child Apprenticeship in the Cape Colony: The Case of the Children's Friend Society Emigration Scheme, 1833–1841." *Slavery & Abolition: A Journal of Slave and Post-slave Studies* 42 (3): 567–88.

Thomson, R. G., ed. 1996. *Freakery: Cultural Spectacles of the Extraordinary Body*. New York: New York University Press.

Thornberry, E. 2018. *Colonizing Consent: Rape and Governance in South Africa's Eastern Cape*. Cambridge: Cambridge University Press.

Tsampiras, C. 2016. "'Stubborn Masculine Women': Violence, Slavery, the State, and Constructions of Gender in Graaff-Reinet, 1830–1834." *Radical History Review* 126: 107–21.

Ward, K. 2009. *Networks of Empire: Forced Migration in the Dutch East India Company*. Cambridge: Cambridge University Press.

White, H. (1973) 2014. *Metahistory: The Historical Imagination in Nineteenth-Century Europe*. Baltimore: Johns Hopkins University Press.

Windsor, M. 2020. "'Apartheid and Jim Crow Are Really No Different': Why George Floyd's Death Reverberated in Africa." *ABC News*, July 12. https://abcnews.go.com/International/apartheid-jim-crow-george-floyds-death-reverberated-africa/story?id=71556630.

Wine, B. [Robert Kyagulanyi Ssentamu]. 2017. "Freedom," single. Africha Entertainment.

Worden, N. 2009. "The Changing Politics of Slave Heritage in the Western Cape, South Africa." *Journal of African History* 50 (1): 23–40.

Worden, N., and C. Crais. 1994. *Breaking the Chains: Slavery and Its Legacy in the Nineteenth-Century Cape Colony*. Johannesburg: Witwatersrand University Press.

TWO

Organizations, Institutions, and Knowledge Production

SEVEN

Conducting Participatory Research with Male Survivors of Wartime Rape in Northern Uganda

PHILIPP SCHULZ

In this chapter I offer ethical and methodological reflections on a process of conducting participatory research with male survivors of wartime sexual violence in postconflict northern Uganda.[1] Drawing on personal experiences of field research,[2] I reflect on possibilities and challenges for researchers and practitioners seeking to conduct research with populations in vulnerable situations and aim to share experiences of carrying out research in ethically sensitive and participatory ways.

As part of a doctoral dissertation research project examining male survivors' conceptualizations of justice (Schulz 2017), I conducted research with forty-six male survivors of wartime rape across the subregion of Acholiland in northern Uganda. The study aimed to examine male sexual violence survivors' conceptions of justice and to investigate how and to what extent prescribed transitional justice processes in Uganda address male sexual and gendered harms. The data collection was organized around four participatory workshop discussions with survivors who are members of a survivor support group—the Men of Courage—and guided by a participatory research approach. Framed by a commitment to conducting research *with* survivors, rather than *on* them, this approach sought to equip research participants with a level of agency during the data collection process, to contribute toward a longer-term and multifaceted process of gradually shifting the locus of power from the researcher to the researched. The research was therefore intended as an exercise in knowledge production geared toward the terms of the researched. Although not fully adhering to the methodological principles of participatory (action) research (PAR), a specific methodology that is increasingly employed across the social sciences (Cornwall and Jewkes 1995), I was nevertheless guided and inspired by its underlying principles and ideals (see Robins 2011; Lundy and McGovern 2006), especially those focused on collaboration, empowerment, and reciprocity. While the research process did contain several actionable elements, as elaborated upon further below, this element was not as strongly pronounced as the defining characteristic of PAR would require—so I primarily speak of participatory research and parenthesize (or obscure) the "action" component for the purpose of this chapter.

The research was conducted in close collaboration with the Refugee Law Project (RLP). Situating the study within an ongoing organizational process of working with male sexual violence survivors made it possible to engage with survivors in more ethically integral and mutually collaborative way. Derived from these experiences, I propose a participatory research framework and close institutional affiliations as avenues for managing and responding to some of the methodological and ethical challenges associated with conducting research into conflict and violence in African contexts. Through such approaches, the unequal power dynamics and exploitative tendencies that often characterize research in conflict zones can, at least in part, be responded to and engaged with.

Yet, it is fundamentally important to acknowledge that these steps and strategies can never ultimately dismantle the unequal power distributions that inevitably characterize research under these circumstances and which henceforth require constant reflexivity and critical engagements with positionalities and power on the side of researchers (Thapar-Björkert and Henry 2004). To this end, in this chapter I will also engage with limitations to this approach and with the inevitable asymmetrical power relations that continue to shape the research encounter as described here. These can never be fully avoided, but they can and need to be acknowledged and engaged with.

I begin by presenting the overall background to the study, before introducing participatory research and its main methodological and ethical tenets. The core of the chapter then analyzes how these methodological principles were put into practice in the particular context of my research project. That section thereby introduces different data collection techniques as guided by a participatory framework and reflects on the possibilities as well as limitations of this approach. That discussion specifically emphasizes the importance of collaboration, participation, and reciprocity to facilitate a relational and participatory research process but also acknowledges challenges to the implementation of my study.

Background: Researching Sexual Violence against Men in Northern Uganda

Across time and space, male-directed sexual violence during conflict is much more common than is frequently assumed. This is true both in northern Uganda (Schulz 2018) and elsewhere globally. However, the dynamics surrounding these crimes and the experiences of male survivors remain notoriously underexplored. In northern Uganda, during the early years of the conflict (also see Atim, this volume; Ongwech, this volume), sexual violence against men was geographically widespread and linked to systematic warfare patterns of violence (RLP 2014). During this phase of the conflict, and in response to various armed uprisings and rebellions—including one led most prominently by the Lord's Resistance Army under the command of Joseph Kony (also see Stewart, this volume)—the National Resistance Army of the Ugandan government directed various brutal military operations against both armed groups and civilian populations in northern Uganda. Embedded within this context, government soldiers committed widespread sexual violence against men, including penetrative anal rape, locally referred to as *tek-gungu*, which locally translates as "to bend over" (*gungu*) "hard" or "forcefully" (*tek*) (Finnström 2008). Across the Acholi subregion, this terminology "became widely used among the community because of the numerous cases of male rape attributed to the government soldiers" (JRP 2013, 22). Despite their widespread prevalence, accounts of sexual violence against men in Acholiland are subjected to various intersecting layers of silences and marginalization (Schulz 2018) and henceforth remain consistently underexplored, thereby mirroring the limited global attention paid to wartime sexual violence against men more generally (Dolan 2015).

This marginalization of sexual violence against men is particularly evident in relation to transitional justice processes, both in northern Uganda and also globally. Even though past decades have witnessed increasing efforts toward justice in response to conflict-related sexual and gender-based violence (Mertus 2004), few efforts have been made to redress male sexual and gendered harms (Schulz 2020a). Barely a handful of studies have thus far examined the nexus between transitional justice and sexual violence against men, and existing research is characterized by narrow conceptions of justice and persistently lacks empirically grounded survivors' perspectives. As a consequence, the various ways in which male survivors of sexual violence seek to respond to their violations and what justice means to them have been insufficiently explored.

This vacuum of justice in response to sexual violence against men is particularly pronounced in northern Uganda. A variety of previous, existing, and proposed transitional justice measures in northern Uganda—including criminal prosecutions, a transitional justice policy, and localized justice mechanisms (such as traditional reconciliation ritual and ceremonies)—consistently fail to account for crimes of gender-based violence more broadly (Okello and Hovil 2007), and for crimes of male rape in particular (Schulz 2021). To illustrate, the Ugandan government's transitional justice policy—the country's guiding transitional justice framework that emerged as a result of the 2008 Juba Peace Agreement (Anyeko et al. 2012)—is reflective of these gender blind spots (JLOS 2019). In the criminal justice arena, the recent verdict against Dominic Ongwen at the International Criminal Court (Atingo 2021) and ongoing proceedings of the International Crimes Division under the High Court of Uganda against Thomas Kwoyelo include charges of sexual and gender-based violence toward women and girls (Ogora 2020). However, these investigations do not take into account crimes of sexual violence against men. Conditioned by larger silences and taboos, Uganda's transitional justice landscape is strikingly insensitive and irresponsive to sexual violence against men and male survivors' experiences. In brief, the research underpinning the reflections in this chapter unveiled that situated within this prevailing vacuum of justice in response to sexual violence against men in northern Uganda, male survivors sought to engage with their experiences on their own terms. This unfolded primarily within the context of survivors' groups that create pathways through which male survivors can exercise agency and achieve justice on the micro level (Schulz 2021).

Participatory (Action) Research—Methodological and Ethical Principles

Researchers working in fragile or violence-affected contexts are increasingly reflecting upon questions of power, ethics, and the politics of knowledge production (Bunting, Kiconco, and Quirk 2020; Mwambari 2019; Cronin-Furman and Lake 2018; Schulz 2020b; Wood 2006), with a specific focus on hierarchical research relationships and discrepancies of authority and control inherent to research processes in these contexts (Malejacq and Mukhopadhyay 2016). In recent years, collaborative and participatory research processes have become increasingly prominent as potential avenues for addressing and partially mitigating some of these inequities and challenges. One of the most important models has been that of participatory (action) research (PAR) (Fals-Borda 1987; Robins and Wilson 2015; Lundy and McGovern 2006). Centralizing research participants' collaboration, participation, and empowerment, these approaches to research inter alia intend to "ground knowledge production in the everyday lives of those most affected" (Robins and Wilson 2015, 236), as well as to challenge power discrepancies and exploitative methodological approaches (Pittaway, Bartolomei, and Hugman 2010; Bunting 2015), much in line with the overall focus and objective of this volume.

Participatory research is designed to be normatively, methodologically, and ethically rooted in emancipatory work, primarily *with* and *by* marginalized and oppressed populaces, and seeks to challenge "the historical colonizing practices or research and ownership of knowledge" (Stewart 2017, 36). This emphasis on research *with* or *by*, rather than research *on*, is therefore fundamentally important for and constitutive of participatory research. As Budd Hall writes, participatory research is "fundamentally about who has the right to speak, to analyze and to act" (1992, 16). This, Beth Stewart argues, requires that researchers "remain reflexive and aware of power relations at every stage" of the research (2017, 36).

In their implementation of a participatory research project, Lundy and McGovern (2006) similarly explain that "action research methods are framed by a commitment to social justice . . . , challenging structures of oppressing and acting *with* ordinary people to bring about social change" (49). Bunting further clarifies that participatory research "ideally, is designed to include, at all stages of the project, the community in which the research is taking place" (2015, 71). The key principles of PAR thus include community participation, local ownership, and local control (Lundy and McGovern 2006, 51). This type of research thereby aims to shift the locus of power from the researcher to the researched. According to Robins and Wilson (2015), "Participatory research focuses on a process of sequential reflection and action. . . . Local knowledge and perspectives are not only acknowledged, but form the basis for research and planning" (226).

In seeking to understand what "justice" means from the perspectives of male survivors themselves, my study was oriented along those principles and similarly translated into "an exercise in knowledge production on the terms of the researched" (Robins 2011, 137). Robins further notes that community participation is important to "challenge international prescriptive tendencies and to ensure that voices from the grassroots are heard" (136), both of which drive the rationale behind my study. The research process adopted throughout this study was primarily intended as a collaborative and mutually reciprocal exercise in knowledge production; yet unequal power relations between the research participants and me persist (Schulz 2020b) and ethical and methodological challenges remain, as elaborated in further detail as part of the concluding discussion.

In addition to these methodological guiding principles, PAR is similarly characterized by specific normative criteria, particularly in that it "rejects the liberal value of neutrality in social research and aims to advance the goal of a particular community" (Robins and Wilson 2015, 228). Lundy and McGovern (2006) likewise emphasize that PAR "rejects the position that research should be objective and value-free, and that researchers should remain detached and neutral. It is an overtly political paradigm that engages researchers on equal terms with marginalized groups, in a collaborative initiative to bring about social justice and social change" (51). Maintaining neutrality or value-free engagement is a task that is not only often impossible but also undesirable, if not even unethical, especially in relation to research with populations in marginalized, victimized, and vulnerable situations (Zahar 2009). Remaining entirely neutral or value-free in light of the often heartbreaking stories and experiences of male survivors was not something I managed, nor something I aspired to. Instead, I often found myself reacting emotionally to these stories, thus failing to stay value-free or neutral in response to what my interlocutors chose to share with me (see Schulz and Kreft 2021, 498). Rather than staying entirely value-free, my normative aim was instead to foreground and elucidate the harmful experiences of marginalized and victimized male survivors of sexual violence in northern Uganda.

While the research design employed throughout this project thus aligns with some of the core methodological and ethical principles of participatory research in a variety of ways—in terms of centralizing collaboration, participation, and reciprocity—my methodological approach nevertheless also differs from it in various ways. In "conventional" PAR, community members typically become fully involved in the study's entire decision-making processes, and local stakeholders need to be "fully involved in the initiation, design, [and] decision-making" of the project (Lundy and McGovern 2006, 52). Robins and Wilson emphasize that the "identification of the goals and the nature of the PAR is a joint project of the community and the researcher," and that researched communities "must determine the goals and methods" (2015, 230). In my research, I preidentified the goals and research questions of the study beforehand, through extensive desk research rather than a full democratic and collaborative process with survivors. This reflected the unequal distribution of power skewed in favor of the researcher in terms of research focus and agenda setting. This was largely because the study was conducted as part of a doctoral dissertation and that henceforth the research questions and aims and objectives pretty much had to be defined beforehand.

Nevertheless, the exact focus of my research—on justice in response to sexual violence against men—and the corresponding research question were discussed and confirmed in close communication with RLP during my preliminary visit to the field in May 2015, and then with representatives of survivors' groups in 2016, before the data collection commenced. Similarly, while the research design and data collection techniques were proposed by me, they were also thoroughly discussed, approved, and slightly adapted for context and purpose in collaboration with RLP and by the chairpersons of the survivors' groups. Especially important here were the communal and participatory dimensions of the workshop discussions with survivors, where it was crucial to ensure that data collection techniques were in synch with the priorities as articulated by RLP and the survivors' associations. While my study thus aimed to be as participatory as possible, it did not fully qualify as PAR to the extent that research conducted by, for instance, Robins (2011) or Lundy and McGovern (2006) do. Furthermore, the "action" element of PAR—which in the literature is arguably only ill-defined and somewhat ambiguous in its meaning and scope—fell somewhat short. Although the process did contain several "actionable" elements toward the participating communities of survivors—primarily in the form of jointly drafting a constitution for the survivors' group, as described below—this element was not as strongly pronounced or distinct as the defining characteristics of PAR would require.

Fully adhering to the principles of PAR within the framework of a postgraduate research project, however, proved to be difficult for a variety of reasons. First, the limited time frame of a three-year period and financial constraints present practical barriers to a fully collaborative process of consistently designing, conducting, and writing the study in collaboration with victims' communities. Robins and Wilson (2015) likewise argue that in practical terms, the dearth of funding for PAR studies represents a challenge to the emergence of PAR in transitional justice scholarship. Similarly, the institutional checks and balances of many social science graduate schools, including the requirements of "first year" progress seminars, result in strong pressures to ensure that the aims, design, and objectives of the study are rigorously identified and defined prior to the actual field research and data collection period. Institutional review boards and research ethics committees likewise demand clearly identified research questions, goals, objectives, and research designs before granting ethical approval. There are consequentially strong institutional pressures to make some key decisions prior to engagement with victim communities in the first place (see Boser 2007). Of course, doctoral dissertation research *can* be designed and conducted collaboratively, more in line with PAR principles than my study was and does not necessarily have to be solitary. There are, indeed, fascinating examples of participatory research by doctoral students and early-career researchers (see, for instance, Stewart, this volume; Marzi 2021). Yet the institutional structures and requirements of postgraduate and doctoral research often make it inherently complicated to fully design these projects as PAR.

Despite these constraints and besides the distinctions between my study and holistic PAR, I remain inspired and guided by a participatory approach and particularly by a commitment to "ground knowledge production in the everyday lives of those most affected" (Robins and Wilson 2015, 236). This study therefore constitutes a sustained effort of actively engaging with male survivors of sexual violence as participants in the research in an ethnographic and participatory sense that is steered away from research as exploitative or extractive (Bunting, Kiconco, and Quirk 2020) but that is rather based upon meaningful relationships (Fujii 2018; Tynan 2021) and that grounds knowledge production in the everyday lived realities of survivors—thereby feeding into ongoing debates about decolonization of knowledge production (Tynan 2021). At the same time, the knowledge and information gathered for and through this research project are also immediately relevant for the objectives of the participating groups of survivors, as further specified below.

Yet, of course, in research with marginalized and/or victimized populaces, such as those in this study, power asymmetries nevertheless prevail, clearly geared in favor of the researchers (Cronin-Furman and Lake 2018), "no matter how participatory the data collection" (Clark-Kazak 2009, 136) is designed (see Stewart 2017). In the concluding discussion below, I further reflect on this by taking into account my own positionalities vis-à-vis the research participants in this project, especially regarding race, class, and socioeconomic background, and how this sits in relation to the research approach and process.

Conducting Participatory Research with Male Survivors of Wartime Rape in Uganda

The findings underpinning this study specifically draw from ten months of field research in May 2015, between January and July 2016, and in June and September 2018. Prior to the actual data collection period, I spent a month in northern Uganda in May 2015 to reassess and validate the previously identified research gaps, refine the proposed research questions in collaboration with local partners, and maintain prior contacts with key informants and local organizations. After the data collection, analysis, and write-up of the dissertation, in June 2018, I spent another three weeks in Gulu with my interlocutors, primarily to return and distribute copies of my dissertation and to organize a workshop to share my findings with my research participants and collaborators. The goal of this later trip was to give back to the community that shaped this research.

At the same time, the affiliation with RLP, as mentioned above, made it possible to enter into an established and sustainable process of conducting research and working with male survivors. For the past ten years, RLP has engaged with male survivors of sexual violence in an inclusive, empowering, and ethically sensitive way (Dolan et al. 2017). More specifically, RLP has been working with different organized victims' groups and associations across the country, composed of male survivors of sexual violence (RLP 2014; Edström et al. 2016).[3] One of these groups is located in northern Uganda and composed of Acholi male survivors of sexual violence: the Men of Courage umbrella association. The structure of this association is made up of smaller, localized subgroups in separate locations across the subregion of Acholiland. All findings directly focused on male survivors' experiences and perspectives derive from workshop discussions with voluntarily participating members of these three groups.

The collaboration with RLP, thereby joining an established process of engagement, was instrumental not only in getting into contact with male survivors but also in developing mutual trust between me and collaborators at RLP and with research participants, who are members of the survivors' groups. As Norman (2009) emphasizes, trust must be developed over time and sequentially. Due to its prolonged and sustained engagement with male survivors of sexual violence, RLP has been able to establish a strong mutual trust between the organization and its staff and the groups of survivors—and Ongwech, in his contribution to this volume, reflects more fully on the nature of RLP's work with conflict-affected communities in general. A study on male survivors developed in cooperation between RLP, the Institute for Development Studies, and the Men of Hope Refugee Association Uganda emphasizes that this engagement "is dependent upon it linking to and involving those who are at the heart of the change they wish to see" (Edström et al. 2016, 37). The research participants in my study similarly acknowledged this collaborative relationship and appreciated RLP's continuous and sustainable support: "If it were not for RLP, we as survivors would not be where we are now. They have really supported us so much and we appreciate that a lot," one survivor explained.[4]

By becoming an integral component of this process, some of the trust the survivors have in the institution (and its staff) was transferred to me as an affiliated researcher. During the workshops, various survivors emphasized that they felt reassured and comfortable enough to participate in the discussion specifically because they were conducted in cooperation with RLP and accompanied by staff with whom the survivors engaged with over a prolonged period. "We feel confident to participate in this because it is done together with RLP," one survivor attested. Another aspect that arguably influenced this process of developing mutuality, connection, and trust was our shared sexual and gender identities as heterosexual men. Several of the survivors emphasized that they felt more comfortable engaging with me because of my gender identity, which they assumed would better help me to understand their gender-specific harms and experiences. At the same time, our shared gender identities and sexual orientations underpinned my relationships with my male RLP colleagues and often framed part of how and what we spoke about. This is not to suggest that only male researchers can conduct this research, but in this particular sociocultural context and with this particular group of survivors, our gendered positionalities arguably shaped the process.

An affiliation alone, however, cannot establish the necessary trust or relationship needed for this type of work. Therefore, to further build trust, I also regularly engaged with representatives and members of the group on an informal basis prior to (as well as after) each workshop, to ensure that the survivors who participated in the discussions had an opportunity to meet in advance and get to know me, my approach, and the nature of the project. Similarly, prior to the data collection period, I met the chairperson of the Men of Courage group during the Second South-South Institute in May 2015 on sexual violence against men and boys in Cambodia. We talked at length about my research and my intention of conducting the study in the following year. When I first met him again on one of my first days in northern Uganda a few months later, he was excited to see me and specifically stated that he viewed my prior engagement and our conversations in Cambodia as a clear sign of my commitment, which for him helped to establish a trusting relationship.

This engagement and contact with the survivors continues to this day, and whenever I am in Uganda, I visit the survivors—many of whom have become close acquaintances. Thanks to social media, we are also able to stay in touch frequently despite the physical distance between Uganda and Germany. At the same time, my collaboration with RLP as an institution continues to this day beyond this particular project. For my current postdoctoral research project, exploring male survivors' agency, I am again officially affiliated with RLP. I also stay in regular and close contact with the two colleagues at RLP who supported my work and who have become close friends ever since. The cooperation and affiliation with RLP also made it possible to conduct the research with male survivors in the presence of experts in the field, which was instrumental in potentially addressing certain ethical considerations. In particular, one of my RLP colleagues is a trained psychological counselor who regularly provides counseling sessions for conflict-affected communities in northern Uganda. By joining the workshops, he was available and able to provide immediate psychological and psychosocial service to respondents in case it was necessary.[5] The World Health Organization's guide (WHO 2007) on ethical and safety recommendations for researching, documenting, and monitoring sexual violence in emergencies specifically emphasizes the importance of the availability of basic services, including psychosocial support, when interviewing victims of sexual violence.

Despite these substantial methodological and ethical aspects, my collaboration with RLP also involved more practical components. For instance, having a desk in the Gulu office made it possible to become part of the daily working routine, and the organizational and institutional infrastructure facilitated practical aspects such as travel to the field. At the same time, my cooperation with RLP was not a one-way street characterized by its support of my research but was rather based upon mutual collaboration. Especially in the early months of my affiliation with RLP, I regularly assisted and supported my colleagues' daily work-related activities, frequently traveled to the field to implement RLP's programming, and thus actively supported the organization's work.

This cooperation thus helped me become part of RLP's established process of working with male sexual violence survivors and to directly see the impact that this work can have. Active participation also fostered a sense of being part of a team, rather than being an outsider, which greatly influenced my ability to cooperate with colleagues. These different levels of involvement in RLP's work were not just unique opportunities to obtain a deeper understanding and appreciation of the local context. Rather, I view them as part of my active role in a collaborative process, which thus constitutes elements of "giving back" to a process I benefited from immensely, something which is of particular concern to scholarly discussions about conducting ethical research and reimagining less extractive modes of knowledge production (Tynan 2021), as outlined in the introduction to this volume.

At the same time, and despite these numerous positive aspects of my affiliation with RLP, closely collaborating with a nongovernmental organization and/or with the assistance of research collaborators, or "brokers" (Parashar 2019; Mwambari 2019) of course also entails methodological and practical implications, including possible drawbacks. Engaging with research participants—and in particular with groups of victims and survivors—through the mediation of nongovernmental organizations or civil society organizations (or through "brokers") almost inevitably carries with it certain expectations on the side of research participants, for instance with regard to potential service provision or financial/material gains due to participation in the study. At the same time, in the context of my study, it may very well be that participants felt at least partly compelled to participate, due to the fact that it was carried out in affiliation with RLP and that they would not have chosen to participate if it were not for their and my respective linkages to RLP. To engage with these concerns, we made sure to repeatedly emphasize that participation in the workshop discussions was entirely voluntary, and that even though the study was conducted in affiliation with RLP, it was an independent endeavor and that, therefore, it was not linked to RLP's programming and service provision.

Workshop Discussions with Male Sexual Violence Survivors

Situated within this broader context of engagement and collaboration, and as mentioned above, male survivors' perspectives on justice and their experiences specifically derive from four participatory workshop discussions with a total of forty-six male survivors who are members of three different survivors' groups. The survivors were from different parts across Acholiland, and were all between fifty and eighty years of age. To preserve survivors' anonymity and uphold confidentiality, the exact locations of these groups will not be revealed.

For these workshop discussions, we only included male survivors who are part of survivors' support groups, but no survivors outside the context of such groups. This sampling strategy was underpinned by various ethical considerations, which were prioritized over questions of representation and generalizability, as described in greater detail below. Specifically, the Men of Courage umbrella group has clearly defined political and societal agendas and follows a commitment to advocate for justice on behalf of male survivors (RLP 2014). As such, the participating survivors were expected to have had a certain interest in partaking in the workshops on this theme. The fact that the research project's main focus aligns with one of the group's key objectives suggests that some of the research insights can potentially also be used for the group's benefit and purposes, even if in indirect ways. Moreover, the group's relationship with RLP, its integration in an existing support structure, and its role in a collaborative process fostered a research environment that could respond to some of the ethical challenges of conducting research on this topic and of engaging with male sexual violence survivors.

In practical terms, one participatory workshop was conducted with each of the subgroups, in addition to a final workshop, which brought together representatives from each of the three groups. As specified above, for each of these workshops, only voluntarily participating members joined the discussion—which we thoroughly established during prior engagements and discussions with members of the groups. The workshops were conducted in familiar locations where the groups usually conduct their meetings, which were members' homesteads or a nearby school compound, chosen as safe locations by survivors themselves. The fourth workshop, which brought together representatives of all three subgroups, was organized in RLP's office in Gulu. While some of the respondents in this fourth exchange had already participated in one of the previous three workshops, other participants had not yet been part of prior discussions. Participants were provided with refreshments (drinks) and their travel costs to the respective locations were reimbursed. The workshops were designed to be open and participatory, rather than structured and confrontational. We thus made a conscious effort to avoid an imposed group interview or focus group discussion format, to enable a participatory process as much as possible. For the first three workshops, I began with one guiding question: What does justice mean to you?[6] This then facilitated a discussion between the research participants, RLP colleagues, and me. If necessary, clarification and/or follow-up questions were asked, some of which were prepared in advance, and some arose contextually from the conversation. I therefore served in a facilitative capacity, rather than as the research director (see Robins 2011), while participants had a certain level of agency over the workshop process and the direction of the discussion. All four workshops were conducted in Acholi, with two RLP colleagues translating for my benefit—demonstrating my positionality as an obvious outsider to this context.[7] To preserve anonymity and at the request of the participants, the workshops were not recorded, and I took handwritten notes of the translated content instead. Because of the workshops' focus on questions of justice, I did not include any direct questions about their harmful experiences of sexual violence. In each of the discussions, however, survivors themselves always situated their perspectives in relation to their individual experiences of harm, and openly spoke about their sexual violations. Various survivors expressed that "talking has really helped, and it was important to get this out." We never interrupted these elaborations but rather let survivors speak freely and then connected their input back to the focus of the discussions on justice.

The fourth workshop began with a short presentation about the Ugandan government's draft transitional justice policy (JLOS 2019). This was designed to facilitate and frame an informed discussion about contextual transitional justice developments in Uganda. In preparation for this workshop, I compiled a summary of the draft transitional justice policy. The summary was translated into Acholi, since some workshop participants were not proficient in English. The summary was also designed to translate the technical language of the policy document into more accessible language. Copies were provided to the participants on the day of the workshop. Following the presentation, we then asked survivors to position their views and perspectives on justice in relation to the draft policy and the proposed transitional justice measures. The discussion then followed a similarly open structure comparable to the previous workshops and was directed by the same guiding question. In this setup, I partially positioned myself with a certain level of expertise on the subject matter, which in turn further fuels or exacerbates the power dynamics at play between myself as the intervening researcher and the research participants. At the same time, however, this presentation also served to pass on relevant information on sociopolitical developments in the country that are of relevance and interest to the survivor groups' objective of advocating for justice on behalf of male survivors.

The fourth workshop was also followed by a meeting for members of the groups to work toward the future development of their separate groups and the Men of Courage umbrella association. Survivors determined this meeting and its content themselves. A month in advance of the last workshop, my RLP colleagues and I spoke to the group's chairperson to plan the upcoming discussion and to determine to what extent and how the groups could benefit from getting together in one space. The three separate groups are united under the Men of Courage umbrella but do not necessarily engage with one another on a regular basis—with the exception of some of the chairmen of the subgroups occasionally meeting at RLP-organized events. Against this backdrop, and based on previous deliberations within the groups, we therefore fostered a space for members of the groups to get together and facilitate the future development and organization of their group. During the meeting, members confirmed their commitment to further formalize the structure of the groups in order to officially register as an association at the local government level.

Toward this end, a constitution was needed for the Men of Courage umbrella group. During this meeting, we began to work jointly on developing a constitution, which I, together with representatives of the group and colleagues at RLP, continued to work on after the workshop. Providing this space for the group thereby constituted an aspect of actively involving research participants in the process within a participatory manner, and formed an actionable part of my process of "return[ing] to the community something of real value, in forms determined by participants themselves" (Pittaway, Bartolomei, and Hugman 2010, 234). Unfortunately, however, the further development of the document halted by the time I wrapped up my research, and in 2018, when I returned again to northern Uganda, the constitution had yet to be finalized.

In addition to this aspect of "giving back" to those involved in the research process, as another crucial element of practicing reciprocity, in June 2018 I had a chance to return copies of my dissertation to my research collaborators at RLP and representatives of the survivors' groups who participated in this study. This, too, was intended to return the final output of the collaborative research process to those who actively participated in it, whose stories the work is based on, and who, through their courage of sharing their experiences, made this work and these insights possible in the first place. Similarly, the book project based on this work and derived from the initial dissertation is available open access (Schulz 2021) and thus (at least in theory) available to the groups of survivors but also interested communities in northern Uganda and beyond at large. Due to pandemic-related travel restrictions, I have not been able to share copies of the book immediately upon publication in November 2020, but was finally able to return to Uganda with copies of the book for my research collaborators and members of the survivors' groups in early May 2022—thereby returning the insights of the stories to whom they belong.

Overall, various participants stated that the workshops were empowering and emancipatory. "I am glad you are giving us a chance for telling the truth and we shall use the information accordingly," one survivor proclaimed. Directly linked to the focus of the study, another survivor attested that this "research is also justice, because the truth will come out during research." In relation to such viewpoints and expectations specifically but also during the research more generally, I attempted to manage my informants' expectations with regard to the actual expected outcome of the study. I continuously emphasized that the research was for an academic study and that I could not promise that any of this would ensure that "the truth will come out," nor that survivors would immediately benefit.

Limitations

Despite these possibilities of engaging with the survivors' groups, only including male survivors of sexual violence who are members of institutionalized survivors' associations may also imply methodological limitations for the representativeness of the findings. In particular, some of my arguments cannot be directly extended to individual male survivors who are not part of these groups. Survivors who are not linked to institutionalized groups may have differing perspectives on transitional justice compared to survivors in groups with clearly defined political and societal agendas and a commitment to advocate for justice (RLP 2014). These relative limitations of representation, however, stand in contrast to the ethical considerations underpinning my sampling strategy, as elaborated above. Ultimately, I prioritized ethical sensitivity and integrity over greater representation and generalizability.

At the same time, and as discussed at length above, while the research process was designed to be as participatory as possible, and contained certain actionable elements for the participating survivors—such as the draft constitution and elements of reciprocity—my approach does not fully qualify as PAR as conceptualized in the literature (Cornwall and Jewkes 1995).

Specifically, while the survivors did actively participate in the data collection, I was not able to fully involve them in designing and setting out the study objectives in the first place. Furthermore, while I actively worked toward "giving back" and returning something of value to the communities of survivors who participated in the study, the "action" elements of PAR were present but arguably limited. These are limitations to my approach and the way I was able to implement it that ought to be acknowledged here.

Implications and Ways Forward

In this chapter, I have sought to reflect on my experiences of conducting research with male survivors of wartime sexual violence, guided by a participatory research approach that is focused on collaboration and reciprocity and intended to be a relational approach to conducting research (Fujii 2018) with groups in marginalized and victimized situations. In essence, a participatory approach enabled me to actively engage groups of survivors in the study and thus to carry out research *with* local communities, rather than *on* them. This, I argue, can help in a longer-term process of slowly and gradually shifting the locus of power and agency solely/primarily from the researcher and more toward research participants. This is necessary for situating researchers and research participants on more equal footing and to recalibrate power relationships in favor of the researched, thereby actively working toward reimagining processes of knowledge production, as per the objective of this volume at large and as laid out in the introduction.

Second, the chapter discussed the possibilities and limitations of institutional affiliations and collaborations in conducting research. In the context of my study, and despite certain constraints of collaborating with nongovernmental organizations, conducting the study in affiliation with the RLP enabled me to situate the research as part of a collaborative, sustainable, and ongoing progress of working *with* male survivors (Edström et al. 2016). This facilitated strong relationships of trust and enabled me to conduct the study in a relational framework (Fujii 2018). Likewise, such an approach facilitates more engaged research, in contrast to interventionist and extractive approaches characterized by researchers quickly "coming in," gathering data, and "getting out" without sufficient follow-up, as is often the case for external researchers bound by time and resource constraints and/or driven by self-serving interests.

Such an approach requires time and resource commitment on the side of the researcher that only fairly mirrors the commitment and energy invested into the research process by collaborating partners and research participants. These practices can move us closer to ethical and mutually beneficial research for all partners involved, therefore contributing to a longer-term and multifaceted process of recalibrating unequal power relations inherent in traditional-dominant approaches to empirical research in (post)conflict zones and instead moving beyond extraction (see introduction).

Nevertheless, despite these measures and approaches, unequal power relations persist—in the context of this study specifically (Schulz 2021) and in research on violence, conflict, and security in conflict-affected and violence-ridden contexts at large (Malejacq and Mukhopadhyay 2016; Thapar-Björkert and Henry 2004). These power asymmetries are inherently structural, built into the research conduct from the start, and can therefore never be avoided or dismantled, "no matter how participatory the data collection" (Clark-Kazak 2009, 136) is and how emancipatory a study is set up (Speed 2006). In the context of my study, these power relations between me and my research participants were evident at every point, starting from the conceptualization and design of the study, which was carried out primarily by me, to my status as an intervening outsider. Another prominent and ever-present way in which these inequities manifest refers to the highly differential socioeconomic and cultural backgrounds of my study participants, my RLP collaborators, and me, which constantly underpin any engagement, whether in the research context or beyond. Inspired by Baines (2016), I am therefore constantly mindful that outside, Western scholars "will always be self-limited in their ability to listen to and write outside the yoke of colonialism" (28).

What we as external researchers in these contexts can and indeed *must* do is to first of all openly acknowledge our own positionalities and the power relations and privileges that come with it (Parashar 2019; Mwambari 2019), and then actively work toward engaging with them, addressing them, and trying to minimize power asymmetries wherever and whenever possible. One way to do that is through adopting participatory and collaborative processes (Bunting 2015), which in turn open up alternative avenues of redesigning knowledge production processes (see introduction).

Notes

1. Ethical approval has been obtained from: Ulster University Research Ethics Committee (REC/15/0112), Gulu University Research Ethics Committee (GUREC/33/05/2016), and the Ugandan National Council for Science and Technology (UNCST) (SS4021).
2. Although I borrow the commonly used terminology of "field research" and "the field" I do echo critiques of "the field" as a limited and often colonial and extractive imagination of where and how research takes place (Shepherd 2017).
3. The other two groups are called the *Men of Hope* and *Men of Peace*, and are located in Kampala and Nakivale refugee settlement respectively.

4. At the same time, the groups also want to evolve and emancipate themselves from this institutional affiliation, to become more independent; see further below.
5. At no point during the research process, however, was it necessary for my colleagues to offer such psychosocial support or assistance to the research participants.
6. The approach of asking this particular question was previously discussed with RLP colleagues, and deemed as appropriate to initiate and guide the conversation.
7. Having two colleagues present at the workshops to translate allowed for rigorously double-checking exact translation and interpretations of the viewpoint of survivors as articulated during the sessions.

References

Anyeko, K., E. Baines, E. Komakech, B. Ojok, L. Ogora and L. Victor. 2012. "'The Cooling of Hearts': Community Truth-Telling in Northern Uganda." *Human Rights Review* 13 (1): 107–24.

Atingo, J. 2021. "Watching the ICC Judgement of LRA Commander Dominic Ongwen with Ugandan Victims of Enforced Marriage." *Africa at LSE*, February 17. http://eprints.lse.ac.uk/109018/.

Baines, E. 2016. *Buried in the Heart: Women, Complex Victimhood and the War in Northern Uganda*. Cambridge: Cambridge University Press.

Boser, S. 2007. "Power, Ethics and the IRB: Dissonance over Human Participant Review of Participatory Research." *Qualitative Inquiry* 13 (8): 1060–74.

Bunting, A. 2015. "Monitoring Gender Equality and Violence in Conditions of Structural Inequality and Violence." In *Disability, Rights Monitoring, and Social Change: Building Power out of Evidence*, edited by M. Rioux, P. C. Pinto, and G. Parekh, 67–79. Toronto: Canadian Scholars' Press.

Bunting, A., A. Kiconco, and J. Quirk. 2020. *Research as More Than Extraction? Knowledge Production and Sexual Violence in Post-conflict African Societies*. London: openDemocracy. https://cdn-prod.opendemocracy.net/media/documents/CSiW_Research_as_more_than_extraction.pdf.

Clark-Kazak, C. 2009. "Power and Politics in Migration Narrative Methodology: Research with Young Congolese Migrants in Uganda." *Migration Letters* 6 (2): 131–41.

Cornwall, A., and R. Jewkes. 1995. "What Is Participatory Research?" *Social Science & Medicine* 41 (12): 1667–76.

Cronin-Furman, K., and M. Lake. 2018. "Ethics Abroad: Fieldwork in Fragile and Violent Contexts." *PS: Political Science & Politics* 15, no. 1 (April): 607–14.

Dolan, C. 2015. "Letting Go of the Gender Binary: Charting New Pathways for Humanitarian Interventions on Gender-Based Violence." *International Review of the Red Cross* 96 (894): 485–501.

Dolan, C., T. Shahrokh, J. Edström, and D. Kabafunzaki. 2017. "Engaged Excellence or Excellent Engagement? Collaborating Critically to Amplify the Voices of Male Survivors of Conflict-Related Sexual Violence." *IDS Bulletin* 47 (6): 1–25.

Edström, J., C. Dolan, T. Shahrokh, and O. David. 2016. *Therapeutic Activism: Men of Hope Refugee Association Uganda Breaking the Silence over Male Rape in Conflict-*

Related Sexual Violence. IDS Evidence Report 182. Brighton, UK: Institute for Development Studies.

Fals-Borda, O. 1987. "The Application of Participatory Action-Research in Latin America." *International Sociology* 2 (4): 329–47.

Finnström, S. 2008. *Living with Bad Surroundings: War, History, and Everyday Moments in Northern Uganda.* Durham, NC: Duke University Press.

Fujii, L. A. 2018. *Interviewing in Social Science Research: A Relational Approach.* London: Routledge.

Hall, B. L. 1992. "From Margins to Center? The Development and Purpose of Participatory Research." *American Sociologist* 23 (4): 15–28.

JLOS (Justice Law and Order Sector). 2019. *National Transitional Justice Policy.* Kampala: Justice Law and Order Sector / Ministry of Justice of the Republic of Uganda.

JRP (Justice and Reconciliation Project). 2013. *The Beasts at Burcoro: Recounting Atrocities by the NRA's 22nd Battalion in Burcoro Village in April 1991.* JRP Field Note XVII. Gulu, Uganda: Justice and Reconciliation Project.

Lundy, P., and M. McGovern. 2006. "Action Research, Community 'Truth-Telling' and Post-conflict Transition in the North of Ireland." *Action Research* 4 (1): 49–64.

Malejacq, R., and D. Mukhopadhyay. 2016. "The 'Tribal Politics' of Field Research: A Reflection on Power and Partiality in 21st-Century Warzones." *Perspectives on Politics* 14, no. 4 (December): 1011–28.

Marzi, S. 2021. "Participatory Video from a Distance: Co-producing Knowledge during Covid-19 Using Smartphones." *Qualitative Research* (August): 1–17.

Mertus, J. 2004. "Shouting from the Bottom of the Well: The Impact of International Trials for Wartime Rape on Women's Agency." *International Feminist Journal of Politics* 6 (1): 110–28.

Mwambari, D. 2019. "Local Positionality in the Production of Knowledge in Northern Uganda." *International Journal of Qualitative Methods* 18 (1): 1–2.

Norman, J. 2009. "Got Trust? The Challenge of Gaining Access in Conflict Zones." In *Surviving Field Research: Working in Violent and Difficult Situations*, edited by C. L. Sriram, J. C. King, J. A. Mertus, O. Martin-Ortega, and J. Herman, 71–89. London: Routledge.

Ogora, L. 2020. "Ongwen's Trial Has Highlighted SGBV Crimes, Says Gender Activist in Uganda." *International Justice Monitor*, January 9. https://www.ijmonitor.org/2020/01/ongwens-trial-has-highlighted-sgbv-crimes-says-gender-activist-in-uganda/.

Okello, M. C., and L. Hovil. 2007. "Confronting the Reality of Gender-Based Violence in Northern Uganda." *International Journal of Transitional Justice* 1 (3): 433–43.

Parashar, S. 2019. "Research Brokers, Research Identities and Affective Performances: The Insider/Outsider Conundrum." *Civil Wars* 21 (2): 249–70.

Pittaway, E., L. Bartolomei, and R. Hugman. 2010. "'Stop Stealing Our Stories': The Ethics of Research with Vulnerable Groups." *Journal of Human Rights Practice* 2, no. 2 (July): 229–51.

RLP (Refugee Law Project). 2014. *Julius Okwera: A Survivor's Journey through Pain, Despair and Hope!* Kampala: Refugee Law Project, School of Law, Makerere University.

Robins, S. 2011. "Addressing the Needs of Families of the Missing: A Test of Contemporary Approaches to Transitional Justice." PhD diss., University of York.

Robins, S., and E. Wilson. 2015. "Participatory Methodologies with Victims: An Emancipatory Approach to Transitional Justice Research." *Canadian Journal of Law & Society* 30, no. 2 (May): 219–36.

Schulz, P. 2017. "Conflict-Related Sexual Violence against Men and Transitional Justice in Northern Uganda." PhD diss., Ulster University.

———. 2018. "The 'Ethical Loneliness' of Male Sexual Violence Survivors in Northern Uganda: Gendered Reflections on Silencing." *International Feminist Journal of Politics* 20 (4): 583–601.

———. 2020a. "Examining Male Wartime Rape Survivors' Perspectives on Justice in Northern Uganda." *Social & Legal Studies* 29, no. 1 (February): 19–40.

———. 2020b. "Recognizing Research Participants' Fluid Positionalities in (Post-)Conflict Zones." *Qualitative Research* 21, no. 4 (2020): 550–67.

———. 2021. *Male Survivors of Wartime Sexual Violence: Perspectives from Northern Uganda.* Berkeley: University of California Press.

Schulz, P., and A.-K. Kreft. 2021. "Researching Conflict-Related Sexual Violence: A Conversation between Early-Career Researchers." *International Feminist Journal of Politics* 23 (3): 496–504.

Shepherd, L. 2017. "Research as Gendered Intervention: Feminist Research Ethics and the Self in the Research Encounter." *Crítica Contemporánea: Revista de Teoría Política*, no. 6: 1–15.

Speed, S. 2006. "At the Crossroads of Human Rights and Anthropology: Toward a Critically Engaged Activist Research." *American Anthropologist* 108, no. 1 (March): 66–76.

Stewart, B. 2017. "'I Feel Out of Place': Children Born into the Lord's Resistance Army and the Politics of Belonging." PhD diss., University of British Columbia.

Thapar-Björkert, S., and M. Henry. 2004. "Reassessing the Research Relationship: Location, Position and Power in Fieldwork Accounts." *International Journal of Social Research Methodology* 7, no. 5 (February): 363–81.

Tynan, L. 2021. "What Is Relationality? Indigenous Knowledges, Practices and Responsibilities with Kin." *Cultural Geographies* 28, no. 4 (July): 597–610.

WHO (World Health Organization). 2007. *WHO Ethical and Safety Recommendations for Researching, Documenting and Monitoring Sexual Violence in Emergencies.* Washington, DC: World Health Organization.

Wood, E. J. 2006. "The Ethical Challenges of Field Research in Conflict Zones." *Qualitative Sociology* 29 (3): 373–86.

Zahar, M.-J. 2009. "Fieldwork, Objectivity, and the Academic Enterprise." In *Surviving Field Research: Working in Violent and Difficult Situations*, edited by C. L. Sriram, J. C. King, J. A. Mertus, O. Martin-Ortega, and J. Herman, 191–212. New York: Routledge.

EIGHT

Research Ethics Governance and Epistemic Violence

The Case for a Decolonized Approach

SAMUEL OKYERE

The Rhodes Must Fall protest at the University of Cape Town in 2015 and other protests that have emerged in its wake have revitalized long-standing sociocultural and political movements against the legacies of imperialism and colonialism (Pimblott 2020, 211; Bhambra, Gebrial, and Nişancıoğlu 2018). Following in the footsteps of those who were at the vanguard of this struggle, such as Aimé Césaire and Léopold Sédar Senghor, the recent university campus–based decolonization campaigns have aimed to topple memorials honoring imperialists, slave traders, and racist ideologues and advocated more inclusive pedagogies, epistemologies, and ethnicities in higher education and wider society (Bhambra 2014; Ahmed 2012). Research and knowledge production are among the key areas identified as reflecting endemic institutional racism, white supremacy, and other deleterious effects of colonialism and imperialism.

These ideological legacies have been observed at all stages of research: from the conception and planning of projects, access to funding opportunities, methodological and philosophical frameworks, fieldwork practices, and publications and dissemination activities through to intellectual property ownership (Garrafa and Lorenzo 2008). The legacies can be even more acute in collaborative research, knowledge exchange, and partnerships between Global North and Global South institutions and partners (Binka 2005; Last 2018;

Walsh, Brugha, and Byrne 2016; Matenga et al. 2019). As El Refaei (2020, 12) observes, these partnerships are sometimes said to have the aim of "building African capacity," a framing that ignores the fact that African capacity already exists and needs to be recognized on its own terms in the same way as that of the Global North partner.

Even where the influence of "the colonial matrix of power" (Quijano and Ennis 2000, 541, cited in Mignolo 2007, 485) surrounding such partnerships is duly acknowledged, measures to promote parity, inclusivity, and other redress mechanisms do not always materialize. Agendas, ways of working, and program management are still largely driven and dominated by partners based in the Global North (Bradley 2008, 675). The power differentials can be most apparent in funding access and arrangements. Global South partners often have to endure incredibly patronizing, paternalistic "due diligence" bureaucracies to access their share of collaboratively won funding lodged in the Global North partners' accounts (Bradley 2008; Landau 2012; El Refaei 2020).

Over the last couple of decades, many scholarly works criticized these processes, which Binka (2005, 207) describes as "scientific colonialism" (see, e.g., Chinn 2007; Khupe and Keane 2017; Smith 2012; Kovach 2009; Seifert 2018; Roy 2011; Mignolo 2009; Nhemachena, Mlambo, and Kaundjua 2016). These contributions have primarily focused on the methodological and philosophical aspects of the problem: notably by advocating for the use of indigenous- and Global South–derived methodologies, philosophies, and practices to counterbalance the dominance of Western-centric research ideas and methods. A related issue that has received comparatively little attention is the operation and reproduction of coloniality in research governance structures and practices such as ethics approval processes.

This chapter contributes to addressing the gap through reflections on my experience of securing ethical approval at a UK university for research studies in Ghana and Nigeria and on my experiences during the fieldwork in both countries. The chapter highlights the subtle and overt ways in which the criteria for evaluating ethical considerations, such as consent and risk, can be laced with ethnocentrism and "othering." Further, it demonstrates the epistemic violence inherent in some of the obligations that research ethics committees (RECs) in Global North institutions place on research in the Global South. More broadly, the chapter underscores how RECs discharge subjective powers that ultimately determine the forms of knowledge, ideas, and values that are produced, heard, or suppressed. It concludes with a call for greater decolonial scrutiny of research governance systems and processes as part of the wider effort to decolonize research and education.

RECs, Ethical Approval Processes, Power, and Coloniality

According to the Economic and Social Research Council, a key body for social research in the United Kingdom, the primary function of RECs is to review research involving human participants to ensure that people's dignity, rights, and welfare are protected (ESRC 2005, 44). RECs typically scrutinize research designs, fieldwork plans, participant recruitment, engagement plans, and other aspects of research projects to judge whether these adhere to predefined standards for meeting informed consent, privacy, safety, anonymity, and other ethical principles (Strathern 2000; Boulton and Parker 2007; Murphy and Dingwall 2007). Ethical approval processes are usually straightforward. Approval is either granted in the first instance, or applications are requested to effect changes, after which approval is granted.

RECs generally comprise conscientious people who are often well versed in the relevant regulations and research practices. They are often led by researchers who understand the challenges researchers face in the field and therefore try their best to both mitigate risks and manage the ethics application process. Their concerns are not always limited to safeguarding participants' rights but can also extend to a desire to support the efforts of their colleagues to attain high standards of dignity, autonomy, and respect in their work. When they spot weaknesses in applications, they could be more inclined to provide meaningful advice for resolving them instead of simply using flaws as a reason to refuse approval.

Despite these good intentions, RECs and prior ethical reviews have been the focus of immense criticism. Dixon-Woods et al. (2007) observe that RECs occupy an authoritative position from which they discharge remarkable subjective power because judgments on what is ethical or not tend to reflect members' expertise, personal values, and discretionary judgments rather than objective universally accepted moral standpoints. Expanding on this, Boser (2007, 1063) expresses concern about the enormous powers wielded by RECs to decide whether a study can go ahead or not. For Porter (1999, 13), the system of prior ethical reviews can convey the erroneous impression that researchers are more knowledgeable or better placed than their participants to determine suitable standards of informed consent, anonymity, and other ethical considerations.

Decolonial, indigenous, critical race scholars, and advocates for virtue and communitarian ethics similarly argue that the dominant systems of ethical review utilized in the Global North promote a narrow understanding of ethics and ethical (mal)practice (patterson 2008; Tuck and Guishard 2013; Naudé 2019; Guishard et al. 2018; Cannella and Lincoln 2018, 84). They largely reflect Western, White-privilege normative assumptions of risk, consent, benefits, and burdens that too often ignore and undermine understandings and practices of these in indigenous communities and populations in the Global South (Porter 1999, 13; Tuck 2009; Smith 2012; George, MacDonald, and Tauri 2020). Talk of taking a more "culturally sensitive" approach to research and ethics in the Global South often means nothing more than tweaking Western-centric practices for use in these spaces, while indigenous and Global South researchers are also increasingly forced to conform to Western-derived ethical regimes due to inequalities in funding and other resources (Chattopadhyay and De Vries 2008).

These concerns underpin Denzin's (2008a, 97) long-standing criticism that social science institutional review boards in the United States (the equivalent of RECs in the UK and elsewhere) promote a particular form of ethical conduct that is not conducive to a transdisciplinary, global, postcolonial world. These critics do not dispute the need for rigorous ethical oversight in research with indigenous and historically oppressed communities. The focus of their concerns is the tendency of Global North–based RECs, partners, and researchers to assume that their systems, processes, and practices are necessarily more rigorous, refined, and reliable than those located in the Global South and expect that these standards will be applied in research in these communities (Chilisa 2005; Guta et al. 2012). This obligation is often defended as a means of "protecting" or "saving" vulnerable communities from unethical research practices. Cannella and Lincoln (2018, 173) liken this language to the colonial and imperial narrative of "saving" supposedly naive and uncivilized Black and Brown peoples.

Sabati (2019) adopts a similar tone in her argument that RECs in the Global North uphold "colonial unknowing." Their assessments of risks and harms in research focus primarily on physical, medical, and psychological harms with no regard to epistemic violence and other harms to which American and European researchers and institutions have contributed through colonization, imperialism, and racial injustices (Benton 2016). Morris (2015) gives a practical example of how dominant American and European ethical approaches still overlook and undermine the realities of social life, family, and community in research in the Global South. She argues that the conventional view on informed consent assumes that "research participants are individuated subjects who are more-or-less autonomous of social ties and obligations, literate, adult, and accustomed to relating to others in the context of formal contractual agreements," although this assumption does not hold good in some indigenous and Global South communities (Morris 2015; as cited in Butz 2008, 242). As the chapter discusses in the next section, similar problems emerged during research in Ghana and Nigeria when I attempted to apply ethical practices developed for research in the UK to these communities, as required by my UK-based university's ethical code of conduct.

Securing Ethical Approval for Research in Nigeria and Ghana

This chapter contains my reflections on the process of securing ethical approval at a UK-based university for research studies in Ghana and Nigeria and on my experiences during fieldwork in the two countries. The Ghana research formed part of my doctoral studies in 2010, and the aim was to explore the narratives and lived experiences of a group of children who were engaged in income-earning activities at an artisanal gold mining site in Kenyasi, a rural district in the country's Brong-Ahafo region. The Nigeria study was carried out in 2018 with the aim of exploring the understandings of and attitudes to child sexual abuse and sexual health inequalities in Cross River State in Nigeria. I was prompted to write this chapter in part due to my concern about how very little had changed in the eight-year period between the two studies despite the many warnings about the problems linked to importing ethical practices modeled for research in the UK and elsewhere in the Global North into communities in the Global South. Indeed, despite the move toward ethics in practice or situational ethics, the obligations placed on researchers to import ethical practices have been strengthened rather than scaled back.

I was aware at the outset that both studies presented a range of ethical and practical issues. Some target participants were children, classed by default as vulnerable because of perceptions about their (im)maturity. They were also deemed to be an "at risk" population because of their involvement in activities considered exploitative and hazardous. In the case of the Ghana study, I was aiming to collect data at an artisanal gold mining site. This is an environment popularly imagined as a den of social misfits, illegality, violence, and criminal behavior, magnifying safety concerns. Furthermore, child sexual abuse and child exploitation are considered to be sensitive subjects. I fully expected that all this would flag ethical concerns; so in both cases, I devoted time to extensively researching related ethical issues and measures to mitigate potential harms.

In the case of the Ghana study, I consider myself fortunate that at the time of applying for ethical approval in 2010, the list of expectations and demands for ethical approval was becoming more attuned to sociological and qualitative research methods. This, along with the detailed consideration set out in my application, meant I did not face any major challenges in the process. Nevertheless, a number of areas were nonnegotiable in the eyes of the REC due to the specific vulnerabilities of my target participants. The ethics form included, as was standard, an undertaking that participation of all children in all research studies required formal permission from their parents, guardians, or other responsible adult gatekeepers. To secure any child's participation, I had to contact the child's parents or guardians in the first instance to inform them of the study and then to seek their consent to speak with their child. Once the parent agreed, I could go through the same information with the child to check whether they might be interested in taking part in the research. If the child agreed to do so, the next step was to go through the participant information forms and other details to ensure that both the child and adult gatekeepers were sufficiently informed before any data collection could begin.

The same preconditions for recruitment of child participants were made by the REC when I applied for ethical application to conduct the Nigeria study eight years later, with attendant problems in the field, too, as will be discussed. This time the ethical approval process had been further complicated by exasperatingly bureaucratic form-filling requirements (see Bosk and De Vries 2004; Hammersley 2009; Whelan 2018; Petrova and Barclay 2019). However, the reams of forms I had to complete were not my main concern. Indeed, I fully expected that I would have to make a robust and lengthy case for the fieldwork in light of the topic, the relative vulnerability of some potential participants, and other dynamics surrounding the study. At times, I even found the process useful in the ways suggested by Hedgecoe (2008) and Guta, Nixon, and Wilson Michael (2013). Revisiting the study's motivations, methodology, participant recruitment practices, and other aspects as required to complete the ethics forms provided an opportunity to strengthen them where necessary before embarking on the fieldwork.

However, this second ethical approval process extended beyond fundamental considerations of consent, respect, and dignity. This time it was heavily clouded by considerations of risk, fear, and litigation. Approval was now largely contingent on university and insurance officials, an arena in which explicit and implicit prejudices about the research setting and other operations of coloniality became apparent. There was a general requirement that all research carried out overseas had to undergo extra travel safeguards. The university's stated guidance was that judgments on the safety of the proposed research site would be made based on information about the country as published on the UK Foreign and Commonwealth Office website.

Based on this criterion, there were no restrictions against travel from the UK to Cross River State in Nigeria, as I stated on the application together with my plans for fieldwork safety. However, as hinted in the introduction to this book, certain issues unfairly receive greater "visibility" and "legibility," although they may be far removed from the wider realities in a given context.

A very different reality emerged from the insurance assessment that formed part of the review. Feedback from the insurance assessors was that Nigeria was a "dangerous country" facing "kidnaps and terror attacks," so I needed to provide mitigations for these, among other safety concerns, before approval could be granted. This characterization of Nigeria as a "dangerous country" was totalizing and prejudicial and it also marked an arbitrary shift in the university's criteria for judging safety and travel risks for overseas research.

As I had stated in the original application, beyond advisories and commonsense safety measures such as being careful in public spaces, respecting local laws, using approved transport forms, and so on, the Foreign and Commonwealth Office had no other concerns relating to travel to the part of Nigeria where the study was based. Hence, while I acknowledged that it is impossible to fully estimate the nature and diversity of risks that can occur during fieldwork (Strathern 2000; Morris 2015), I was nonetheless concerned about bringing questions about kidnapping and terror attacks into the discussion. Having already provided what I considered to be a comprehensive assessment of the real risks for traveling to and living and working in Cross River State, together with contingency measures for emergencies, I felt the most important things were to watch out for "ethically important moments" and being responsive to events as they developed during fieldwork (Guillemin and Gillam 2004, 261; Calvey 2008).

I felt I was being asked to "make up" and respond to risks irrelevant to the proposed research setting, an act that would contravene the advice from Ritchie and Lewis (2003, 70) that researchers should avoid stigmatizing and making prejudicial assumptions about research communities. Attributing unfounded risks to the research setting would have made me complicit in "unethical" conduct even before commencement of the fieldwork. It would mean I was also helping to establish a precedent that might then be applied to others traveling to Cross River State and similar locations for research. I was faced with a dilemma because ethical approval for the study seemed contingent on complying with this demand by the REC. Here, I was reminded of the accusations of ethical "imperialism" (Schrag 2010), or how RECs discharge subjective powers which ultimately determine the forms of knowledge; that certain ideas and values would be heard and others suppressed was clear to see (Boden, Epstein, and Latimer 2009, 733).

In the end, I decided not to comply with the request. Instead, I responded that while terror attacks and kidnappings had been carried out by Boko Haram, these were in a tiny stretch of the country and over one thousand kilometers away from Calabar in Cross River State, where the study was based. I added that media and popular commentary on Nigeria tend to ignore the fact that it is a huge country with a population of over two hundred million most of whom live in peace in much the same way as people do in most UK cities and towns. As such, while I understood the concerns about risk and safety underpinning the request to reflect on terrorism and kidnapping, they were not merited in the context of my study, and my presumption was that there had been a misunderstanding. This explanation that the assessment was at risk of becoming an instance of "ethics creep" (Haggerty 2004) was accepted and the application approved.

Compliance Dilemmas

Once in the field, further evidence of how the obligations Global North–based RECs place on researchers traveling for studies in the Global South can undermine or delegitimize values and expertise in these communities also became apparent. As I discuss elsewhere (Okyere 2018), I discovered that adhering to the undertaking to which I had committed myself was going to be extremely difficult. A challenge that soon became apparent was the requirement to involve parents and adult gatekeepers in securing access to child research participants for the purpose of informed consent.

In the Ghana study, I discovered that many children working at the Kenyasi artisanal gold mining site had traveled independently almost two hundred miles to Kenyasi to seek income-earning opportunities in an attempt to fund their education, pay for apprenticeships, or further other interests. For these youths, there were no parents or guardians to consult. Still intent on abiding by the RECs prescribed mode for recruiting children, I initially decided to exclude these youths from the study and engage only with children whose parents or adult gatekeepers were accessible. However, this plan soon unraveled. The parents appreciated that I had come to see them about their children's potential involvement in the study. However, most of them were also bemused by my actions. They repeatedly informed me that my overture was unnecessary and that I could engage with the children in their own capacities.

Indeed, as I subsequently discovered, some youth working at the site were outraged at my insistence on seeking their parents' permission to involve them in the study when they had themselves offered to do so. They saw this as a discourtesy because they were deemed by their own parents and community to be young adults, not children. Most of them were in their late teens and were seen as capable and mature enough to take up work at an artisanal gold-mining site. Hence, despite my explanation that this was a requirement by my university, they took umbrage at being treated as if they were not mature or capable enough to make independent informed decisions about being interviewed or observed during their work. Some who initially offered to participate, in fact, pulled out when I told them I needed to secure the consent of their parents. It was obvious that the REC's requirement that I ought to involve parents and gatekeepers in seeking consent, for children's participation had regretfully offended the very people whom the measure was meant to benefit.

I had a similar experience eight years later in Calabar, Cross River State. While sex with individuals below the age of eighteen years is criminalized by the state, girls under eighteen can still be found working as prostitutes across Calabar. These girls and sex workers in general face stigmatization and extortion; they are subject to harassment by clients, police, and members of the public alike. During the fieldwork, some people described them as thieves, "dirty" people, and victims of witchcraft or demonic possession. Others described them as "bad girls" who are beyond help instead of deserving of support by the police and other officials. For these reasons, many young prostitutes work independently and keep their identities and involvement in sex work secret from friends, neighbors, and relatives. Indeed, many do not class themselves as prostitutes but assert they are looking for relationships with "sponsors" or "blessers": relatively well-to-do men who can provide for their needs.

Because of these aforementioned factors, it became evident early on in the fieldwork that a participant recruitment mode that required the involvement of parents, guardians, and adult gatekeepers was a nonstarter. Furthermore, similar to the Ghana study, I found that the normative assumptions about childhood, maturity, and consent that underpinned the obligation placed on me by the REC were not wholly workable in the research context. Young girls who were approached for interviews declined because of the requirement that their adult "guardians" would have to be involved in the consent process. They told me it undermined their desire to keep their activities a secret and that it was also an affront to the independent status afforded them by their parents and communities. The normative ideas about childhood, maturity, consent, risk, safety, and vulnerability that informed the ethical decisions and demands by my UK-based university may have been well meaning, but their underlying assumptions were poorly suited to potential respondents in Ghana and Nigeria for all kinds of reasons.

Discussion and Conclusion

This chapter underscores the instrumentality of RECs and ethical review processes in the reproduction of colonial subjectivity and knowledge, one of the four elements of what Quijano and Ennis (2000) describe as the colonial matrix. It also highlights the prejudices inherent in ethical approval processes and how the obligations placed by RECs in Global North institutions on researchers heading out for research in Global South communities can be epistemically violent and hence "unethical" when applied in these communities.

The requirement that parents and guardians ought to be always involved in securing the consent of their children or guards and their involvement in the study presupposed that there were always parents and guardians to be consulted. It also assumes that parents believe they should be consulted. I was therefore attempting to apply a practice modeled for childhood research in the UK, where children typically live with parents or in care and at a place where a different attitude toward children's maturity, autonomy, and other assumptions existed. This mandatory demand was and is explained as a child protection and child safeguarding measure. Some may argue that it is prudent, given the relative vulnerability of the children concerned and the nature of the activities they were involved in.

Yet viewed more critically, the demand is also a mode of transmitting and establishing Western-centric normative views on childhood and child protection that are erroneously promoted as "universal." Under this model, anyone under age eighteen is reduced to an incompetent individual in need of adult guidance. Children biologically are of course comparatively immature relative to adults. However, a blanket position on their incompetence and immaturity, especially based exclusively on their calendar age, is also highly problematic (James and James 2004; Clark-Kazak 2009). This assumption did not fit with how childhood, maturity, or competence were imagined by adults and children alike in both studies. In the Ghana study, the findings revealed that children aged fourteen and over are not unequivocally viewed as "immature" or "incompetent," as those of this age are typically construed in ethical risk assessments.

This is not to say the vulnerabilities of children or even adults are not recognized in the community where the study took place. Instead, those classed as young adults are not seen as incompetent in the same way as babies or preteen children, for instance. Indeed, one of the main findings of the study was that the community's belief in the relative maturity of the youth in question largely explained the social permissibility of their income-earning activities in artisanal gold mining. It was also a factor in the case of independent child migrants whose parents allowed them to independently undertake the nearly two-hundred-mile round trip to seek income-earning opportunities at places such as Kenyasi and elsewhere in southern Ghana. The same understandings of maturity, competence, and safety were also found to be an important factor in why parents and guardians in Calabar did not object when their teenage children went out at night and came home late.

Viewed through these lenses, it was clear to see why a decision about taking part in an activity that primarily involved talking about their work was seen by parents and the youth as something which the latter were more than competent enough to handle. Therefore, without denying the genuine concern that underpinned the requirement, the chapter nonetheless argues that the situation also underscores foregone conclusions about childhood, consent, and maturity inherent in my university's ethical clearance processes even for research in Global South communities (Chilisa 2005; Guta et al. 2012). It can be construed as an inadvertent promotion or privileging of Western-centric ideals under the cloak of safeguarding children's best interests, neutrality, and objectivity and hence a form of epistemological violence.

The experiences presented here also show the power of social construction wielded by RECs or their power to determine what knowledge, ideas, and values are heard and which are suppressed. At one point I was not convinced that the Nigeria study would receive approval due to the doubts about security and other issues which the ethical approval process had imposed on the country despite the fact that it was largely safe and peaceful. Refusal of ethical approval can befall all studies regardless of their location. However, in this instance, the project's fate hinged on assumptions of fear, risk, and (in)security rooted in stigmatizing and totalizing discourses about race, communities, and life in the Global South that can, in turn, be traced to colonization and imperialism (Wilson 2017; Flint and Hewitt 2015; Chowdhury 2019).

To conclude, the mere fact of REC directives and ethical governance being unhelpful or unsuited to a particular context does not necessarily make these systems unethical. Instead, to borrow from Fricker's analysis of epistemic violence (2007, 1), their unethical nature lies in the fact that they produce or sustain a form of injustice in which whole societies are wronged in their capacities or abilities as knowers. As earlier noted, dominant approaches to research ethics and ethical governance as a whole are firmly rooted in colonial Global North scientific rationalities and legal concerns with a long history of delegitimizing Global South persons, institutions, and ways of knowing. Despite their stated good intentions, judgments of propriety, (il)legality, expertise, and acceptable conduct—which are all crucial to whether a project receives approval or not—are underpinned by this historical and persistent baggage.

Notable efforts have been made to bridge the divide, but the epistemological, moral and legal values of Global South communities are still at a major disadvantage at various stages in ethical governances and practices. The system's unjust and hence unethical nature thus lies in the fact that it can and does delegitimize others' virtuous values, customs, and ways of knowing while maintaining an unfair advantage held by the powerful in structuring what are deceptively presented as collective or universal social understandings (Fricker 2007, 147). This meets Byskov's (2020, 118) criteria proposed for determining whether a measure is epistemically unjust and therefore unethical where it produces unfair outcomes: unfair judgments of epistemic systems, abilities, and capacity; unfair denial of knowledge or expertise; unfair exclusion and denial of stakeholder rights and involvement; and unfair existing advantage or disadvantage.

Since completing the two studies, insurance, risk, and neoliberal concerns have become even more integral to social research ethical considerations (James 2020). Social justice concerns that ostensibly inform the intensification of these measures risk becoming even more peripheral in decisions about applications. There is, therefore, a need to emphasize this goal and advocate for a situated ethics better suited to the diversity of social research (Guillemin and Gillam 2004; Perez 2019, 149). Challenging the persistence of colonial and imperial ideologies is an important step in this direction.

References

Ahmed, S. 2012. *On Being Included: Racism and Diversity in Institutional Life.* Durham, NC: Duke University Press.

Benton, A. 2016. "African Expatriates and Race in the Anthropology of Humanitarianism, Critical African Studies." 8 (3): 266–77. https://doi.org/10.1080/21681392.2016.1244956.

Bhambra, G. 2014. *Connected Sociologies.* London: Bloomsbury Publishing.

Bhambra, G., D. Gebrial, and K. Nişancıoğlu, eds. 2018. *Decolonizing the University.* London: Pluto Press.

Binka, F. 2005. "Editorial: North-South Research Collaborations; A Move towards a True Partnership?" *Trop Med Int Health* 10 (3): 207–9. https://doi.org/10.1111/j.1365-3156.2004.01373.x.

Boden, R., D. Epstein, and J. Latimer. 2009. "Accounting for Ethos or Programmes for Conduct? The Brave New World of Research Ethics Committees." *Sociological Review* 57, no. 4 (November): 727–49. https://doi.org/10.1111/j.1467-954X.2009.01869.x.

Boser, S. 2007. "Power, Ethics, and the IRB: Dissonance over Human Participant Review of Participatory Research." *Qualitative Inquiry* 13, no. 8 (November): 1060–74. https://doi.org/10.1177/1077800407308220.

Bosk, C., and R. De Vries. 2004. "Bureaucracies of Mass Deception: Institutional Review Boards and the Ethics of Ethnographic Research." *ANNALS of the American Academy of Political and Social Science* 595, no. 1 (September): 249–63. https://doi.org/10.1177/0002716204266913.

Boulton, M., and M. Parker. 2007. "Informed Consent in a Changing Environment." *Social Science & Medicine* 65 (11): 2187–98. https://doi.org/10.1016/j.socscimed.2007.08.002.

Bradley, M. 2008. "On the Agenda: North-South Research Partnerships and Agenda-Setting Processes." *Development in Practice* 18 (6): 673–85. https://doi.org/10

.1080/09614520802386314.

Butz, D. 2008. "Sidelined by the Guidelines: Reflections on the Limitations of Standard Informed Consent Procedures for the Conduct of Ethical Research." *ACME: An International Journal for Critical Geographies* 7 (2): 239–59. https://www.acme-journal.org/index.php/acme/article/view/805.

Byskov, M. F. 2020. "What Makes Epistemic Injustice an 'Injustice'?" *Journal of Social Philosophy* 52 (1): 114–31. https://doi.org/10.1111/josp.12348.

Calvey, D. 2008. "The Art and Politics of Covert Research: Doing 'Situated Ethics' in the Field." *Sociology* 42, no. 5 (October): 905–18. https://doi.org/10.1177/0038038508094569.

Cannella, G., and Y. Lincoln. 2018. "Ethics, Research Regulations, and Critical Social Science." In *The SAGE Handbook of Qualitative Research*, edited by N. Denzin and Y. Lincoln, 5th ed., 172–94. Los Angeles: Sage.

Chattopadhyay, S., and R. De Vries. 2008. "Bioethical Concerns Are Global, Bioethics Is Western." *Eubios Journal of Asian and International Bioethics* 18 (4): 106–9.

Chilisa, B. 2005. "Educational Research within Postcolonial Africa: A Critique of HIV/AIDS Research in Botswana." *International Journal of Qualitative Studies in Education* 18 (6): 659–84.

Chinn, P. 2007. "Decolonizing Methodologies and Indigenous Knowledge: The Role of Culture, Place and Personal Experience in Professional Development." *Journal of Research in Science Teaching* 44 (9): 1247–68.

Chowdhury, R. 2019. "From Black Pain to Rhodes Must Fall: A Rejectionist Perspective." *J Bus Ethics* 170 (2): 287–311. https://doi.org/10.1007/s10551-019-04350-1.

Clark-Kazak, C. 2009. "Towards a Working Definition and Application of Social Age in International Development Studies." *Journal of Development Studies* 45 (8): 1307–24.

Denzin, N. 2008a. "IRBs and the Turn to Indigenous Research Ethics." In *Access, a Zone of Comprehension, and Intrusion*, edited by B. Jegatheesan, 97–123, Advances in Program Evaluation 12. Bingley, UK: Emerald Group Publishing.

———. 2008b. "The Elephant in the Living Room: Or Extending the Conversation about the Politics of Evidence." *Qualitative Research* 9 (2):139–60.

Dixon-Woods, M., E. Angell, R. Ashcroft, and A. Bryman. 2007. "Written Work: The Social Functions of Research Ethics Committee Letters." *Social Science and Medicine* 65 (4): 792–802.

El Refaei, E. S. 2020. "Global Research Partnerships: Beyond the North-South Divide? Local Engagement." Refugee Research Network, Paper No. 4 (March). https://carleton.ca/lerrn/wp-content/uploads/LERRN-Working-Paper-No.-4-Research-Partnerships.pdf.

ESRC (Economic and Social Research Council). 2005. *Research Ethics Framework*. Swindon, UK: ESRC.

Flint, A., and V. Hewitt. 2015. "Colonial Tropes and HIV/AIDS in Africa: Sex, Disease and Race." *Commonwealth and Comparative Politics* 53 (3): 294–314. https://doi.org/10.1080/14662043.2015.1051284.

Fricker, M. 2007. *Epistemic Injustice: Power and the Ethics of Knowing*. Oxford: Oxford University Press.

Garrafa, V., and C. Lorenzo. 2008. "Moral Imperialism and Multi-centric Clinical Trials in Peripheral Countries." *Cad Saude Publica* 24 (10): 2219–26.

George, L., L. Te Ata o Tu MacDonald, and J. Tauri. 2020. "An Introduction to Indigenous Research Ethics." In *Indigenous Research Ethics: Claiming Research Sovereignty beyond Deficit and the Colonial Legacy*, edited by L. George, L. Te Ata o Tu MacDonald, and J. Tauri, 1–15. Bingley, UK: Emerald Publishing.

Guillemin, M., and L. Gillam. 2004. "Ethics, Reflexivity, and 'Ethically Important Moments' in Research." *Qualitative Inquiry* 10 (2): 261–80. https://doi.org/10.1177/1077800403262360.

Guishard, M. A., A. Halkovic, A. Galletta, and P. Li. 2018. "Toward Epistemological Ethics: Centering Communities and Social Justice in Qualitative Research." *Forum Qualitative Sozialforschung / Forum: Qualitative Social Research* 19 (3). https://doi.org/10.17169/fqs-19.3.3145.

Guta, A., S. Nixon, J. Gahagan, and S. Fielden. 2012. "'Walking along beside the Researcher': How Canadian REBs/IRBs Are Responding to the Needs of Community-Based Participatory Research." *Journal of Empirical Research on Human Research Ethics* 7 (1): 17–27. https://doi.org/10.1525/jer.2012.7.1.17.

Guta, A., S. Nixon, and G. Wilson Michael. 2013. "Resisting the Seduction of 'Ethics Creep': Using Foucault to Surface Complexity and Contradiction in Research Ethics Review." *Social Science and Medicine* 98 (December): 301–10.

Haggerty, K. D. 2004. "Ethics Creep: Governing Social Science Research in the Name of Ethics." *Qualitative Sociology* 27:391–414. https://doi.org/10.1023/B:QUAS.0000049239.15922.a3.

Hammersley, M. 2009. "Against the Ethicists: On the Evils of Ethical Regulation." *International Journal of Social Research Methodology* 12 (3): 211–25.

Hedgecoe, A. 2008. "Research Ethics Review and the Sociological Research Relationship." *Sociology* 4 (25): 873–86. https://doi.org/10.1177/0038038508094567.

James, A., and A. James. 2004. *Constructing Childhood: Theory, Policy and Social Practice*. New York: Palgrave Macmillan.

James, F. 2020. "Ethics Review, Neoliberal Governmentality and the Activation of Moral Subjects." *Educational Philosophy and Theory* 53 (5): 548–58. https://doi.org/10.1080/00131857.2020.1761327.

Khupe, C., and M. Keane. 2017. "Towards an African Education Research Methodology: Decolonizing New Knowledge." *Educational Research for Social Change* 6 (1): 25–37. http://www.scielo.org.za/scielo.php?script=sci_arttext&pid=S2221-40702017000100004.

Kovach, M. 2009. *Indigenous Methodologies: Characteristics, Conversations, and Contexts*. Toronto: University of Toronto Press.

Landau, L. 2012. "Communities of Knowledge or Tyrannies of Partnership: Reflections on North-South Research Networks and the Dual Imperative." *Journal of Refugee Studies* 25 (4): 555–70. https://doi.org/10.1093/jrs/fes005.

Last, A. 2018. "Internationalization and the Academy: Sharing across Boundaries?" In Bhambra, Gebrial, and Nişancıoğlu *Decolonising the University*, 208–30.

Matenga, T. F. L., J. M. Zulu, H. Corbin, and O. Mweeba. 2019. "Contemporary Issues in North-South Health Research Partnerships: Perspectives of Health Research Stakeholders in Zambia." *Health Res Policy Sys* 17 (1): 7. https://doi.org/10.1186/s12961-018-0409-7.

Mignolo, W. 2007. "Delinking: The Rhetoric of Modernity, the Logic of Coloniality and the Grammar of De-coloniality." *Cultural Studies* 21 (2–3): 449–514. https://doi.org/10.1080/09502380601162647.

———. 2009. "Epistemic Disobedience, Independent Thought and Decolonial Freedom." *Theory, Culture & Society* 26 (7–8): 159–81. https://doi.org/10.1177/0263276409349275.

Morris, N. 2015. "Providing Ethical Guidance for Collaborative Research in Developing Countries." *Research Ethics* 11 (4): 211–35. https://doi.org/10.1177/1747016115586759.

Murphy, E., and R. Dingwall. 2007. "Informed Consent, Anticipatory Regulation and Ethnographic Practice." *Social Science & Medicine* 65 (11): 2223–34.

Naudé, P. 2019. "Decolonizing Knowledge: Can *Ubuntu* Ethics Save Us from Coloniality?" *J Bus Ethics* 159: 23–37. https://doi.org/10.1007/s10551-017-3763-4.

Nhemachena, A., N. Mlambo, and M. Kaundjua. 2016. "The Notion of the 'Field' and the Practices of Researching and Writing Africa: Towards Decolonial Praxis." *Africology: The Journal of Pan African Studies* 9 (7): 1–22.

Okyere, S. 2018. "'Like the Stranger at a Funeral Who Cries More Than the Bereaved': Ethical Dilemmas in Ethnographic Research with Children." *Qualitative Research* 18 (6): 623–37. https://doi.org/10.1177/1468794117743464.

patterson, d. 2008. "Research Ethics Boards as Spaces of Marginalization: A Canadian Story." *Qualitative Inquiry* 14 (1): 18–27.

Perez, T. S. 2019. "In Support of Situated Ethics: Ways of Building Trust with Stigmatised 'Waste Pickers' in Cape Town." *Qualitative Research* 19 (2): 148–63.

Petrova, M., and S. Barclay. 2019. "Research Approvals Iceberg: How a 'Low-Key' Study in England Needed 89 Professionals to Approve It and How We Can Do Better." *BMC Med Ethics* 20 (7): 1–13. https://doi.org/10.1186/s12910-018-0339-5.

Pimblott, K. 2020. "Decolonising the University: The Origins and Meaning of a Movement." *Political Quarterly* 91 (1): 210–16. https://doi.org/10.1111/1467-923X.12784.

Porter, E. 1999. *Feminist Perspectives on Ethics*. London: Longman.

Quijano, A., and M. Ennis. 2000. "Coloniality of Power, Eurocentrism, and Latin America." *Nepantla: Views from South* 1 (3): 533–80. muse.jhu.edu/article/23906.

Ritchie, J., and J. Lewis. 2003. *Qualitative Research Practice: A Guide for Social Science Students and Researchers*. London: Sage Publishers.

Roy, A. 2011. "Slumdog Cities: Rethinking Subaltern Urbanism." *International Journal of Urban and Regional Research* 35 (2): 223–38.

Sabati, S. 2019. "Upholding 'Colonial Unknowing' through the IRB: Reframing Institutional Research Ethics." *Qualitative Inquiry* 25 (9–10): 1056–64. https://doi.org/10.1177/1077800418787214.

Schrag, Z. 2010. *Ethical Imperialism: Institutional Review Boards and the Social Sciences, 1965–2009*. Baltimore: Johns Hopkins University Press.

Seifert, M. 2018. "Performing the Hyphen." *Revista Brasileira de Estudos da Presença* 8 (4): 691–718. https://doi.org/10.1590/2237-266078758.

Smith, L. T. 2012. *Decolonizing Methodologies: Research and Indigenous Peoples.* 2nd ed. New York: Zed Books.

Strathern, M. 2000. "Accountability and Ethnography." In *Audit Culture: Anthropological Studies in Accountability, Ethics, and the Academy,* edited by S. Marilyn, 279–304. London: Routledge.

Tuck, E. 2009. "Suspending Damage: A Letter to Communities." *Harvard Educational Review* 79 (3): 409–28.

Tuck, E., and M. Guishard. 2013. "Un-collapsing Ethics: Racialized Sciencism, Settler Coloniality, and an Ethical Framework of Decolonial Participatory Action Research." In *Challenging Status Quo Retrenchment: New Directions in Critical Research,* edited by T. Kress, C. Malott, and B. Porfino, 3–28. Charlotte, NC: Information Age Publishing.

Walsh, A., R. Brugha, and E. Byrne. 2016. "'The Way the Country Has Been Carved Up by Researchers': Ethics and Power in North-South Public Health Research." *Int J Equity Health* 15: 204. https://doi.org/10.1186/s12939-016-0488-4.

Whelan, A. 2018. "Ethics Are Admin: Australian Human Research Ethics Review Forms as (Un)Ethical Actors." *Social Media + Society* (May) 4 (2): 1–9. https://doi.org/10.1177/2056305118768815.

Wilson, K. 2017. "Re-centering 'Race' in Development: Population Policies and Global Capital Accumulation in the Era of the SDGs." *Globalizations* 14 (3): 432–49.

NINE

Research Ethics in Complex Humanitarian Settings

The Case of USAID/Nigeria's Evaluation of Its Northeast Nigeria Portfolio

JUDITH-ANN WALKER

Concerns about violations of human rights abuses in humanitarian settings are increasing as the complexity, scope, and duration of humanitarian emergencies deepen in the Global South. Multiple platforms and associations exist within the humanitarian aid community to try to ensure that ethical guidelines are followed when it comes to both vulnerable beneficiaries and host nations. Especially important here are indicators around ethics and rights, which have emerged as key tools for evaluating conduct in relation to humanitarian aid. Independent activist platforms such as Devex and Watchlist on Children and Armed Conflict have led the way in shaping the watch agenda. Watchlist on Children and Armed Conflict is a network of nongovernmental organizations (international, national, and local) working together to end violations against children in armed conflicts and to guarantee their rights. Watchlist provides monthly updates generated from the experiences of member organizations and engages the United Nations (UN) Security Council's children and armed conflict agenda with data, recommendations, and stories. In addition to these ongoing institutionalized accountability initiatives, flashpoint events such as the 2018 case of Oxfam inaction over allegations of sexual exploitations of minors in the Republic of Haiti have sparked global attention, driving new calls for accountability and resulting in bilateral agencies, in this case the British government, tightening guidelines on humanitarian assistance (Edwards 2018).

Both high-profile flashpoints and civil society mobilizations have directed attention toward ethical violations around service delivery. Ethical violations within humanitarian research have not received the same level of concern or scrutiny. Indeed, the impetus for strengthening research ethics in humanitarian emergencies comes largely from implementers and funders of research and the results of their work, such as scientific studies and evaluations. Funders of evaluations who focus on ethics in research include the European Union, Global Affairs Canada, and Nordic humanitarian-assistance programs. But perhaps the most significant contributor to this field is the World Health Organization (WHO), which produces guidelines for ethics in research with human participants.

Recent reviews by donor agencies point to challenges in the application of standard ethical research guidelines in the high-risk and unstable research environment of humanitarian emergencies. The conditions presented by complex humanitarian emergencies (CHEs) are even more challenging for the application of standard research guidelines. The UN defines a CHE as "a humanitarian crisis in a country, region, or society where there is total or considerable breakdown of authority resulting from internal or external conflict and which requires an international response that goes beyond the mandate or capacity of any single and/or ongoing UN country program" (Brown et al. 2008).

Thought leaders, think tanks, and scholars have broadened the classic UN definition to characterize CHEs as a cacophony of overlapping natural and human-made disasters. These tend to be long running and multicountry in scope, oftentimes with historical roots triggered by modern catalysts (Anderson and Gerber 2018). In such situations it is not uncommon for humanitarian agencies to view traditional research ethics guidelines as an unwanted intrusion that is likely to slow down service delivery. Monitoring, evaluating, and learning of program performance may be deemed unnecessary or inversely correlated to emergency needs of displaced and at-risk people. Indeed, Holly Reed noted that ethical codes tended to place limits on research and operations in Liberia, but "the very process of establishing codes was useful because it created a dialogue between donors and agencies about ethics" (National Research Council 2002, 4). This issue is located in a wider debate between normative theory versus empirical research in the field of bioethics (Anderson and Gerber 2018).

Learning from recent humanitarian crises in Liberia and other conflict hotspots, the humanitarian aid community convened several learning forums and roundtables in the late 1990s and early 2000s in an effort to develop minimum standards and guidelines for research in humanitarian emergencies (Anderson and Gerber 2018). Central to these discussions is the reaffirmation of research ethics in new standards and guidelines, such as the joint policy of operations and the principles and policies of humanitarian operations that have informed practices in the CHE of Liberia (Black 2003). These guidelines aimed to avoid a trade-off between ethical and time-sensitive research.

The most significant issue here is evaluation research, which can be defined as research "conceived and commissioned by humanitarian agencies in order to answer operational questions" (Anderson and Gerber 2018, 97). This chapter examines the case of USAID/Nigeria's northeast Nigeria portfolio of evaluations of its humanitarian programs. The portfolio is distinct in several ways. First, it is scientifically robust, with significant technological applications, yet remains wholly silent on research ethics. Second, USAID/Nigeria is the most significant bilateral funding agency in Nigeria's Northeast. Also, of the myriad humanitarian agencies in Nigeria's Northeast, USAID/Nigeria's contribution to the Official Development Cooperation basket in Nigeria is the second largest.[1] Last, USAID/Nigeria is also the only funding agency that has outsourced monitoring and evaluation of the northeast portfolio to an independent contractor working through a mechanism of third-party monitoring. The chapter examines USAID/Nigeria's evaluations of third-party monitoring of US government–funded programs in the Northeast to explore the pattern and manner in which evaluation research is conducted devoid of ethics.

Boko Haram and the CHE in Northeast Nigeria

The roots of the conflict in the Northeast can be traced to dual disasters, both human-made and caused by climate change (Sayne 2011). In a real sense, the CHE in the Northeast can be viewed as internal to the dynamics of Borno State, an old empire where tradition and modernity collide in a context of inequality, poverty, and gender subjugation. The conflict sparked by Boko Haram in Maiduguri, the capital of Borno, in 2002 has now engulfed three states in Nigeria's Northeast as well as in nearby Chad, Niger, and Mali. Eighteen years of insurgency in Borno, Adamawa, and Yobe States, coupled with natural disaster unleashed by climate change in the Lake Chad basin, have created a scale of emergency and have devastated livelihoods, security, and all aspects of social life; all these factors recommend the Northeast as a severe and classic case of a CHE.

According to USAID data, in Nigeria 8.7 million people are in need of humanitarian aid in the Northeast. The data also show that there are an estimated 2.9 million internally displaced people in Nigeria (USAID/Nigeria 2021). With a population of 182.2 million, Nigeria tops the list of the three African countries with the largest number of internally displaced people. The other countries are the Democratic Republic of Congo and Sudan. Since 2009, the Boko Haram Islamic insurgency has affected 14.8 million people in northeast Nigeria. The UN Development Programme estimates that the conflict has claimed thirty-five thousand lives as of 2020 (UNDP 2021).

Yet another feature found in CHEs is the abduction of girls and women as well as sexual violence, which characterized the insurgency from its inception. However, it was the abduction of 276 girls from Chibok, Borno State, on April 14, 2014, and of 110 girls in Dapchi, Yobe State, on February 19, 2018, both from boarding schools, that brought the northeast Nigeria emergency closer to typical CHEs.

Insurgents' focus on humanitarian aid workers as targets for the disruption of humanitarian assistance is also typical of CHEs. This disruption means that the needs of the affected go unmet. The 2020 report of the Coverage, Operation, Reach, and Effectiveness (CORE) group notes that "humanitarian access in the conflict-affected states of northeast Nigeria has been highly constrained since the start of the current humanitarian response in 2016. An estimated 1.2 million Nigerians living outside the government-controlled areas in those states are completely cut off from humanitarian assistance, while several million more are obstructed to varying degrees in their ability to reach—and be reached by—critical aid" (Stoddard et al. 2020).

The northeast conflict also differs from the early definitions of CHE: the insurgency is fundamentally a subregional phenomenon, with Nigeria as the epicenter for West African *Salafia* movements, which have been growing undetected there since the 1990s. Recent affiliation with the Islamic State of Iraq and Syria (or ISIS) suggests a global movement challenging the internal-insurgency hypothesis. But perhaps the most significant way in which northeast Nigeria challenges classical concepts of CHEs is how humanitarian assistance from global agencies is matched and indeed surpassed by the Nigerian governments' (federal and state) resources and programs.

Another feature of complexity of Nigeria's Northeast crisis is that as communities return to areas managed by liberated local governments, both humanitarian and development-assistance projects are being carried out, in most cases led by the government in collaboration with the international humanitarian-assistance community. Against this background, it is important to note donors' recognition of the leadership role of the national and subnational governments in both the humanitarian and development projects in the region. Not surprisingly, CORE's 2020 report captures the voice of the humanitarian-assistance community in Nigeria's Northeast by noting that "with humanitarian assistance representing less than one per cent of Nigeria's US$500 billion economy, 'it is unrealistic to think we have an influence over the government" (Stoddard et al. 2020, 10).

The CORE report speaks to the difficulty of applying classical definitions of stages in humanitarian emergencies to Nigeria's Northeast. This is because, within the Northeast, many locations move through stages of emergency, relief, and recovery and back to acute emergency within a short period of time as territory is liberated and lost. As insurgents advance, attack (and in some cases hold) territory, retreat, and advance once again, humanitarian-assistance donors find themselves programming for emergency relief, stabilization, recovery, resilience, and development all at the same time and within the same geography.

Against this background, hundreds of international humanitarian agencies traverse northeast Nigeria providing humanitarian assistance. Olojo, writing on this issue, notes that "by 2018, Maiduguri hosted at least 150 nongovernmental organisations (NGOs) involved in humanitarian work. Some of these organisations were challenged by state authorities over accountability issues. More than half were operating without legal registration. . . . Ethics and trust issues are also crucial in such settings" (2019). In addition to the international NGOs, several multilaterals and bilaterals, such as USAID/Nigeria, have a significant presence and portfolio in northeast Nigeria.

Research Methodology

This is a case study of evaluations of USAID humanitarian-assistance programs engaging women and girls as human participants in the CHE of northeast Nigeria. While several studies and reports have been produced on research ethics in situations of crisis, conflict, emergencies, and disasters, few studies exist on research ethics of nonepidemiological evaluation research in the context of CHE. Against this background, this chapter takes its point of departure from the broad literature on research ethics in situations of humanitarian emergencies and aligns with normative underpinnings of this body of work which hold that research ethics in such contexts are valued, good, just, and right while also supportive of good science (Puri et al. 2015).

Drawing from the broader literature on research in humanitarian emergencies and from the narrow group of studies focusing specifically on research ethics for purposes of evaluation in CHE, two normative requirements are distilled and proposed as essential for evaluations in CHE settings. The literature review below identifies the following key factors: adoption of an organizational policy on research ethics, and intentional design of research ethics in evaluation protocols.

This chapter frames two research questions derived from the literature review: (1) To what extent did USAID adopt an organizational policy on research ethics with regard to its northeast humanitarian portfolio? (2) To what extent did the design of evaluation protocols incorporate research ethics in an intentional manner? These questions are explored in the case study of USAID evaluations of the CHE in northeast Nigeria.

These questions are examined through a desk-based content analysis of four data sources related to the USAID evaluation of the work of a contractor (DevTech) in the Northeast. The four data source areas are (1) DevTech's request for proposals for field based monitors (FBMs), which was accessible in the public domain on open access platforms; (2) the technical concept notes of northeast monitoring, evaluation, and learning (MEAL) missions issued from May 14, 2019, through October 2, 2020; (3) the list of DevTech guiding documents and templates issued to FBMs; and (4) the DevTech job descriptions and job specifications. The job descriptions outlined tasks for the mission, and the job specifications outlined core competencies required for FBM staff to carry out the mission.

In addition, for purposes of full disclosure, data was also drawn from DevTech's communications with the author of this chapter, who represented one of the firms assessed, shortlisted, and accepted for field based monitoring. DevTech's communications with the author's organization related to bids. This communication was deemed as being for the "sole use of the intended recipient(s)," that is, the author's organization. No restriction was placed on the purpose for which the communication could be used, and no nondisclosure agreement was signed.

Ethics in Monitoring and Evaluating Humanitarian and CHE Settings

The WHO leads the broad discussion of research ethics, and of ethics in cases of emergencies, disasters, and crises. For the WHO, research ethics in situations of humanitarian emergencies is "a system or code of moral values that provides rules and standards of conduct" (WHO 2007, 7). The WHO goes on to argue:

> The three primary ethical principles that should guide all inquiries involving human beings (including methods used to collect information) are as follows: 1) Respect for persons, which relates to respecting the autonomy and self-determination of participants, and protecting those who lack autonomy, including by providing security from harm or abuse. 2) Beneficence, a duty to safeguard the welfare of people/communities involved,

which includes minimizing risks and assuring that benefits outweigh risks. 3) Justice, a duty to distribute benefits and burdens fairly. In emergency settings, dependency, loss of autonomy, breakdown of community/social systems and ongoing security threats are the norm. (2007, 7)

While the wider literature on research ethics in humanitarian emergencies as well as specific studies on evaluation in CHEs address diverse details, these works agree on the fundamental proposition that effective research must be driven by a commitment to ethics expressed in organizational policy and driven by research design. Put simply, good research in humanitarian emergencies and also in conditions of CHEs is associated with good ethics, which must be adopted by organizers of such research.

Learning communities focusing on evaluations in situations of humanitarian emergencies, such as the Active Learning Network for Accountability and Performance in Humanitarian Action (ALNAP), provide manuals, recommendations, and guidelines for organizations implementing ethics for humanitarian-evaluation researchers (Buchanan-Smith, Cosgrave, and Warner 2016). ALNAP advocates for the adoption of ethical considerations for evaluation in humanitarian emergencies and argues that such principles should always follow the principle of "do no harm." In short, "the starting point should be to consider how engaging in the evaluation process might affect those taking part or being consulted" (Buchanan-Smith, Cosgrave, and Warner 2016, 56). ALNAP cautions that evaluators in humanitarian emergencies must be intentional in their awareness and mitigate any potential raise in expectations that participation in research will lead to more aid. In the same 2016 publication, ALNAP goes on to make the case for evaluations in humanitarian settings to be conducted in a "conflict-sensitive" manner (Buchanan-Smith, Cosgrave, and Warner 2016, 56). ALNAP's perspective of conflict sensitivity is further developed in a 2017 work challenging blueprint evaluation models by making the case for mainstreaming appreciative inquiry, revision, pause, and reflection into research processes in order not to exacerbate tensions in humanitarian settings (Christoplos et al. 2017).

With a perspective similar to that of ALNAP, Puri et al. identify the implementation of the "do no harm" principle as the ethical standard of practice for evaluation research in humanitarian emergency situations. In this regard they go on to recommend detailed research-design issues to incorporate ethics (Puri et al. 2015). Other design issues that are viewed as ethical violations include not using operational research methods, and not using control groups.

In a 2020 piece, Bruno and Haar undertake a systematic review of the literature. They note: "While key concepts within all research settings such as beneficence, justice and respect for persons are crucially relevant, there are considerations unique to the humanitarian context. . . . Humanitarian crises are prevalent throughout the globe and studying them with the utmost ethical forethought is critical to maintaining sound research principles and ethical standards." In their review, they identify four key context factors of CHEs that impinge on research in such settings: population vulnerability, the challenge of applying standard research protocols, inadequate informed consent processes, and ease of coercion. The authors argue that these factors can be mitigated when research organizers become dedicated to the application of ethical protocols. Their systematic literature review identifies nine major themes in the ethics of research in humanitarian settings, in order of significance: an ethics-review process; community engagement; the dual imperative, or necessity that research be both academically sound and practically relevant; informed consent; cultural considerations; risk to researchers; child participation; mental health; and data ownership.

Specific studies on research ethics in CHEs share a similar perspective with more general works focusing on humanitarian emergencies. Despite the unpredictability and challenges of CHEs, scholars concerned with research in CHE also point to the normative imperative of the research agency adopting an ethical framework operationalized through a policy and research design. In a 2009 piece on research on CHE, Pringle and Cole spell out key ethical considerations of a standard ethical code as follows: "(1) the research is not at the expense of humanitarian action; (2) the research is justified in that it is needs-driven and relevant to the affected populations; and (3) the research does not compromise the humanitarian principles of neutrality, impartiality and independence. These primary considerations are in harmony with the humanitarian goals of saving lives, alleviating suffering, and témoignage [testimonial]" (115).

In summary, the literature on evaluation research in humanitarian emergencies, as well as the works that address evaluation research in CHEs, revolves around two key recommendations. These are that ethics must be formally adopted by the assessment organization and that ethics must be incorporated into the design of the research methodology.

Ethics in USAID/Nigeria's Policy on Evaluation in Northeast Nigeria

This discussion identifies key USAID/Nigeria policy documents establishing the framework for evaluation of the northeast portfolio. USAID/Nigeria's policy related to its humanitarian-assistance work in the Northeast is spelled out in the 2015–20 *Integrated Country Strategy*; the *Country Development Cooperation Strategy, 2015–2020*; and the *Country Development Cooperation Strategy (CDCS), August 11, 2020–August 10, 2025.*

The 2015–20 *Cooperation Strategy* notes that "in the Northeast, what was once a civil protest against the profound level of corruption in government has now morphed into a deadly insurgency.... As a result, USAID is now responding ... and providing humanitarian assistance to the millions affected by the Boko Haram insurgency in the northeast" (USAID/Nigeria 2015–2020, 9). It also outlines USAID/Nigeria's Northeast program: "While the responsibility to overcome the Boko Haram insurgency, deter communal violence, and satisfy the core grievances of marginalized communities rests with the GON, USAID will continue to provide humanitarian assistance" (55).

The *Cooperation Strategy* for the contemporary period, 2020–25, divides USAID/Nigeria's Northeast work into two goals with implications for humanitarian assistance. The first is defined as a special development objective of achieving greater stability and early recovery in the Northeast. Stability and resilience were to be achieved through the USAID/Nigeria Mission's four strategic development priorities: good governance, conflict mitigation and sensitivity, resilience, and inclusion. Central to the achievement of these objectives is what USAID defines as the provision of basic public services to support the Northeast: "As the region moves along the continuum from humanitarian assistance to early recovery and eventually towards longer-term development in line with the other DO goals, the provision of basic public services will underpin that transition" (USAID/Nigeria 2020–2025, 36). The second goal, a dedicated humanitarian-assistance focus, was to be achieved equitably and efficiently through interagency cooperation. USAID/Nigeria spells out this focus in the following terms: "The size of the humanitarian needs and the regional nature of the insurgencies that drive the humanitarian situation dictate an international effort to address the situation. USAID is the key leader in this humanitarian response—both in absolute dollar terms and in shaping the response" (USAID/Nigeria 2020–2025, 35).

Both the 2015–20 and 2020–25 *Cooperation Strategy* documents contain some detail on the research approach of MEAL. The 2015–20 *Cooperation Strategy* is anchored on purposeful MEAL, with emphasis on program and performance management and accountability. There is no mention of research ethics, a code of ethics, or engagement of third-party monitors in the 2015–20 document. However, the 2020–25 *Cooperation Strategy* notes that "limited monitoring by Mission staff will be supplemented by third-party monitoring because of extensive restrictions on official travel due to various security issues across the country" (37). No mention is made of research ethics in the detailed discussions laying out the new USAID/Nigeria MEAL strategy. However, one reference was made to ethics when laying out the USAID/Nigeria strategy with regard to conflict: "Broader development programming will take conflict-sensitive approaches and incorporate Do-No-Harm principles across all sectors. Through incorporating this priority across its Objectives, USAID will continue to create opportunities for the meaningful participation of women, youth, and faith-based organizations to advance religious freedom and tolerance, and to prevent and mitigate conflicts, including mitigating risks for mass atrocities" (14). No further information is provided on how this will be carried out.

Ethics in the Design of USAID/Nigeria's Evaluation of Its Northeast Portfolio

This section of the chapter examines the extent to which the process and design of the northeast portfolio evaluation incorporated measures, tools, and approaches that take key principles of research ethics into consideration. The first point to note here is that the 2015–20 *Cooperation Strategy* makes no mention of third-party monitors and speaks mainly in terms of the USAID/Nigeria Mission–directed MEAL portfolio and the new training programs being rolled out for MEAL staff at the mission. Despite this omission, by September 2016, USAID/Nigeria awarded the four-year MEAL contract to DevTech Systems Inc. to provide MEAL activities for the USAID/Nigeria portfolio, which included the Northeast.

DevTech described the Nigeria MEAL engagement as follows: "The activity goal is to transform USAID/Nigeria into a premier practitioner of program monitoring and evaluation (M&E) rooted in a learning and adaptive culture. Through the Learning Program (TLP) DevTech provides continuous, on-the-ground, on-demand and systematic support to all USAID/Nigeria teams, sectors, and implementing partners (IPs) on performance monitoring, data verification, impact and performance evaluations, project and activity level monitoring, evaluation and learning plans, organizational learning, capacity building and knowledge management" (Nigeria MEAL Activity).

The DevTech request for proposals (RFP) issued in 2018 noted that

> USAID/Nigeria Mission staff experience significant challenges monitoring activities in several states because of security threats and frequent security status changes. MEL is seeking to recruit qualified local data collection firms to implement a Field Based

Monitoring (FBM) Platform in North Eastern (NE) states of Nigeria in order to provide support to the Mission to meet its monitoring requirements. . . . The Monitoring, Evaluation, and Learning (MEL) Activity of DevTech Systems, Inc. provides continuous, on-the-ground, on-demand and systematic support to all USAID/Nigeria teams, sectors, and implementing partners (IPs). This support covers performance monitoring, data verification, impact and performance evaluations, project and activity level monitoring, evaluation and learning plans, organizational learning, special studies, capacity building and knowledge management. (DevTech Systems 2018)

With regard to the requirements for assessing firms responding to the 2018 RFP, DevTech listed technical assessment criteria with no mention of past experience developing, holding staff accountable to, or administering codes of ethics in research. Under selection criteria, DevTech stated:

The firm must demonstrate extensive relevant technical experience in: (a) research and mobile data collection in NE Nigeria either specializing in one technical sector or working across the sectors of interest to USAID and (b) management of research and mobile data collection teams to include mobile data collection, data quality assurance and reporting; and (2) Experience in the traditional development sectors (education; health, population and nutrition; peace, democracy and governance; agriculture, economic growth and environment) will be considered equal to the firm's research and data collection experience working in humanitarian emergency response / disaster assistance sectors and modalities (protection, shelter, food security, etc.).

When laying out competency expectations for staff of firms, DevTech's requirement was that "key personnel should show significant educational and/or work experience in the organizations' area of expertise in any of the traditional development sectors (education; health, population and nutrition; peace, democracy and governance; agriculture, economic growth and environment)" (DevTech Systems 2018). Despite the fact that the DevTech RFP addressed research capacity requirements in depth, asking for bidding firms' specific methods employed and analytic skills retained, no mention was made of research ethics.

The package of DevTech guiding policy documents provided to all new firms engaged as FBMs contained thirteen core templates, none of which included guidelines on research ethics issues or concerns. These guiding documents were "Daily Framework Debriefing Template," "DevTech CV Proposal," "DevTech FBM Attendance Sheet," "FBM Data Collection Tool Minimum Requirements," "FBM Debriefing Presentation Template," "FBM Site Visiting Reporting Template," "FBM Task Order Budget Template, Revised," "FBM 2 Page Summary Template," "Disclosure of Real or Potential Conflict of Interest for USAID Evaluations," "Success Story Guideline for USAID Partners," "USAID 1420 Biodata Form," "USAID Conflict of Interest Form," and "USAID Graphics Manual and Partner Co-branding Guideline."

Table 9.1 presents findings over the period from May 14, 2019, to October 2, 2020, to address the question of whether research ethics featured in DevTech technical concept notes, which outlined each mission, or could be found in job descriptions of the key personnel for the mission and job specifications of experience and qualifications to accomplish it.

Table 9.1. Research ethics in DevTech concept notes

Total number of DevTech concept notes reviewed	Number of concept notes reviewed targeting women/girls	Number of concept notes reviewed referencing research ethics	Job description with tasks on ethics for key personnel	Job specifications requiring past experience in research ethics
17	16	1	0	1

Source: Review of technical concept notes from May 14, 2019, to October 2, 2020.

Importantly, the only technical concept note that referenced ethical guidelines in MEAL was the most recent, issued on October 2, 2020, which stated: "Principle 1: Do no harm and be conflict-sensitive. To protect USAID staff, partners, and beneficiaries, data collection plans and methods should be consistent with public health guidelines and be conflict-sensitive. Data collection partners should have adequate safety plans, and infection prevention and control (IPC) measures. Data collection should not exacerbate the spread of COVID-19" (DevTech Systems 2020a).

Notwithstanding the mention of "do no harm" in this concept note, none of the three job positions recommended by DevTech for implementing the mission contained tasks or responsibilities related to ethics. The positions were program manager/coordinator; field monitor (conflict management and mitigation specialist or peace resolution expert) and field monitor (conflict management and mitigation communication specialist / data collector); and finance and administrative officer.

All key tasks were technical and focused on the use of technology in data collection. The program manager/coordinator, for example, was expected to have "experience in reviewing and drafting success stories." Other key tasks included the following: "maintain responsibility and oversight for coordinating logistics and travel and ensure proper security measures are in place where necessary; travel with the teams and supervise all field activities; and be responsible for reviewing all data for accuracy and integrity in advance of monitoring report writing for both teams of field monitors."

Interestingly, for the first time, a concept note for an assignment was accompanied by a job requirement—or, in the language of human resources management, a job specification for a position of field monitor—which referenced research ethics. Under the section of "relevant experience," DevTech said the position holder "must have experience in project management in conflict mitigation and management, peacebuilding and or development expert. At least 5 years of experience in peacebuilding and Do No Harm related work" (DevTech Systems 2020d).

The DevTech requirement that field monitors have experience in work related to "do no harm" aligns well with principle 1 of the October 2, 2020, accompanying concept note. This signals a recognition of research-related ethics in the MEAL portfolio. However, it is noticeable that none of the duties of the field monitors had any relevance to the ethical standards of "do no harm." The three duties of the field monitors were "work in collaboration with team members to produce communications materials that tell the conflict management and mitigation partners' successes; administer monitoring protocol to elicit information on the activity's successes and areas for improvement; and edit monitoring report as needed."

Humanitarian Accountability and Ethics Blindness

Findings of ethics blindness in the DevTech MEAL portfolio in Nigeria's Northeast are, in many ways, not surprising given that USAID/Nigeria made only a passing reference to research ethics in the 2020–25 *Cooperation Strategy* and was wholly silent on this issue in the 2015–20 *Cooperation Strategy*. Therefore, given the deprioritization of research ethics for USAID/Nigeria at the policy level, it was unlikely that DevTech, as a contractor, would have embraced the challenge of incorporating research ethics into its evaluation brief in the Northeast. USAID, and indeed DevTech, chose to adopt an approach to MEAL which focused on technological application (on- and offline) for data collection that failed to take ethics into consideration.

USAID/Nigeria's dual humanitarian/development programming strategy in the Northeast, coupled with the contracting out of the MEAL task, was not cause for exemption from ethics in evaluation. Rather, both programmatic realities demand a greater need to focus on ethics for upward accountability to tax payers, downward accountability to beneficiaries (direct and indirect), and horizontal accountability to the humanitarian community in Nigeria and to host governments, as well as to the numerous ethical review boards and panels that exist across northeast Nigeria.

The assumption that US government humanitarian assistance in the Northeast does no harm and may even be empowering and emancipating women and girls cannot be accepted or asserted without the evidence. Researchers, whether USAID/Nigeria staff or MEAL contractors equipped with a code of ethics, will be better guided to address research dilemmas as they arise as well as conflicts with Nigerian government humanitarian agencies and community leaders wishing to protect displaced women and girls against humanitarian staff and interventions in their capacity as traditional leaders.

But more importantly, the United States government's portfolio of projects in the Northeast executed by multiple implementing partners must also be evaluated in accordance with project-wide ethical standards and protocols. The current focus in the MEAL program is technical and technology focused and emphasizes real-time reporting, staying clear from assessing implementing partners' ethics and value propositions on women and girls in CHE settings.

USAID/Nigeria issued another RFP dated September 24, 2020, for MEAL services for the period 2020–25 that were in line with the 2020–25 *Cooperation Strategy*. It is notable and somewhat troubling that while the bid package contains guidelines on care for property, there is no similar guideline on care for human subjects or participants in CHE settings. Indeed, there is no distinction between MEAL requirements in CHE zones versus non-CHE zones in Nigeria and no differentiation on evaluation considerations for development- versus humanitarian-program assessments. While the Compliance with the Trafficking Victims Protection Reauthorization Act (H18) in the RFP package could have offered a pathway toward elaborating on ethics, this was not the case (USAID 2020).

To the extent that the new USAID RFA stated that USAID was prepared to consider extraneous nonvalue for money factors in assessing bid responses, it is possible that the successful bidding contractor could include protocols on ethics in the northeast portfolio. However, this potential was circumscribed by the fact that USAID strictly defined these noncost/price factors to the exclusion of ethical codes. Thus, the opportunity captured in this USAID guide to bidders seems not to offer a gateway for incorporating a code of ethics for evaluation in the Northeast. The mission's RFP stated that "USAID will conduct a Best Value source selection based on evaluation factors listed below. These factors will serve as the standard against which all technical information will be evaluated and identify the determination factors that Offerors should address.... For overall evaluation purposes, all technical evaluation factors other than cost or price, when combined, are significantly more important than cost/price" (USAID 2020).

In conclusion, this case study offers important insights into the methodology and epistemology of evaluation with implications for humanitarian, and indeed development, accountability. As the donor of the second-largest contribution to the Official Development Cooperation basket in Nigeria and with a significant intervention in Nigeria's Northeast, the USAID/Nigeria Mission must find a way to align its technical data requirements and grant-making approach with a not-so-new normative reality of ethics in aid. While the literature does recognize that codes of ethics can slow down real-time evaluation in disaster settings, codes also demonstrate respect for public agencies and the norms of the environment and are a standard against which USAID/Nigeria, its contractors, and its grantees should be held. Without application of ethical code, USAID programs run the risk of being technically sound but with limited community resonance, decreased normative value, and the potential for rejection by community and government agencies with custodial authority over women and girls in CHEs. Against this background, findings of the CORE assessment quoted above are relevant again. When respondents were asked which agencies were best able to deliver aid in the Northeast, USAID/Nigeria was not mentioned, and when they were probed about the type of mechanism for effectively delivering aid, community consultation emerged as strikingly significant (Stoddard et al. 2020). This suggests that ethical codes can have transactional value when engaging stakeholders in zones of CHE, as the codes point to respect and commitment to local communities.

What are the implications of this case study for the theory of ethics in CHEs? Findings from this study call for a deepened and more intensive searchlight on donor accountability in the arena of research. In the absence of high-profile violations of research ethics (flashpoint cases), such as the Oxfam operational staff in Haiti, contributions to the discourse on research ethics in CHEs has mainly been by academics for academic research. The epistemology of literature on research ethics for program evaluation is dated and underdeveloped. Even in cases where the international humanitarian aid community work to advance guidelines for application in CHEs, there is only a passing reference to research ethics for evaluation.[2] In the absence of such a searchlight, ethics-blind practices such as the one documented in this chapter go unnoticed and are even perceived as normal by global and local stakeholders.

Notes

1. It comes second only to the World Bank (USAID/Nigeria 2015–20, 57).
2. An example of guidelines that fail to address ethics in evaluation research is the Humanitarian Charter and Minimum Standards in Humanitarian Response, by the Sphere Project (2011). The Sphere Project was initiated in 1997 by a group of NGOs and the International Red Cross and Red Crescent Movement to develop a set of universal minimum standards in core areas of humanitarian response. Other examples of guidelines that fail to address ethics are the Inter-agency Network for Education in Emergencies' Minimum Standards for Education: Preparedness, Response, Recovery; the Small Enterprise Education and Promotion Network's Minimum Economic Recovery Standards; and the Livestock Emergency Guidelines and Standards.

References

Anderson, M., and M. Gerber. 2018. "Introduction to Humanitarian Emergencies." In *Health in Humanitarian Emergencies*, edited by David Towners, 1–8. Cambridge: Cambridge University Press. https://www.cambridge.org/core/books/health-in-humanitarian-emergencies/introduction-to-humanitarian-emergencies/D2A8592F97497D7C786B4EF4B19E081F/core-reader.

Black, R. 2003. "Ethical Codes in Humanitarian Emergencies: From Practice to Research?" *Disasters* 27 (2): 95–108.

Brown, V., P. J. Guerin, D. Legros, C. Paquet, B. Pécoul, and A. Moren. 2008. "Research in Complex Humanitarian Emergencies: The Médecins Sans Frontières/Epicentre Experience." *PLoS Med* 5 (4): e89. https://doi.org/10.1371/journal.pmed.0050089.

Bruno, W., and R. J. Haar. 2020. "A Systematic Literature Review of the Ethics of Conducting Research in the Humanitarian Setting." *Conflict and Health* 14:1–17. https://www.ncbi.nlm.nih.gov/pmc/articles/PMC7245798/.

Buchanan-Smith, Margie, John Cosgrave, and Alexandra Warner. 2016. *Evaluation of Humanitarian Action Guide*. London: ALNAP. https://www.alnap.org/system/files/content/resource/files/main/alnap-evaluation-humanitarian-action-2016.pdf.

Christoplos, Ian, Paul Knox-Clarke, John Cosgrave, Francesca Bonino, and Jessica Alexander. 2017. *Strengthening the Quality of Evidence in Humanitarian Evaluations*. Summary Method Note, May 2017, ALNAP Discussion Series. London: ALNAP. https://www.alnap.org/system/files/content/resource/files/main/alnap-eha-method-note-5-2017.pdf.

DevTech Systems. 2016. "Nigeria Monitoring, Evaluation and Learning Activity, 2016–2020." DevTech Systems Nigeria. https://devtechsys.com/projects/Nigeria-Monitoring-Evaluation-and-Learning-Activity/ (page discontinued).

———. 2018. "Request for Proposals: Third Party Monitoring Data Collection Activities." DevTech Systems Nigeria. Shared with the dRPC.

———. 2020a. Field based monitors concept notes, March 11, 2019, to March 10, 2021. October 2. DevTech Systems Nigeria. Shared with the dRPC.

———. 2020b. Job descriptions for mission, including job specifications, issued between May 2019 to October 2020. DevTech Systems Nigeria. Shared with the dRPC.

———. 2020c. List of DevTech guiding documents and templates issued between May 2019 to October 2020. DevTech Systems Nigeria. Shared with the dRPC.

———. 2020d. Proposed field based monitors scope of works. DevTech Systems Nigeria. Shared with the dRPC.

———. 2020e. Technical concept notes of northeast MEAL missions issued between May 14, 2019, to October 2, 2020. DevTech Systems Nigeria. Shared with the dRPC.

Edwards, S. 2018. "Accountability in the Aid Sector: Humanitarians Can No Longer Be above the Law." Devex, February 27. www.devex.com.

National Research Council. 2002. *Research Ethics in Complex Humanitarian Emergencies: Summary of a Workshop*. Holly Reed, rapporteur. Washington, DC: National Academies Press.

Olojo, A. 2019. "Humanitarian Aid in Nigeria's North-East. Helping or Hurting?" Institute for Security Studies, July 31. https://issafrica.org/iss-today/humanitarian-aid-in-nigerias-north-east-helping-or-hurting?utm.

Pringle, J. D., and D. C. Cole. 2009. "Health Research in Complex Emergencies: A Humanitarian Imperative." *Journal of Academic Ethics* 7 (1): 115–23.

Puri, J., A. Aladysheva, V. Iversen, Y. Ghorpade, and T. Brück. 2015. "What Methods May Be Used in Impact Evaluations of Humanitarian Assistance?" IZA Discussion Paper No. 8755. https://www.iza.org/publications/dp/8755/what-methods-may-be-used-in-impact-evaluations-of-humanitarian-assistance.

Sayne, A. 2011. *Climate Change Adaptation and Conflict in Nigeria*. Washington, DC: US Institute of Peace.

Stoddard, Abby, Paul Harvey, Monica Czwarno, and Meriah-Jo Breckenridge. 2020. *Humanitarian Access SCORE Report: Northeast Nigeria Survey on the Coverage, Operational Reach, and Effectiveness of Humanitarian Aid*. N.p.: CORE.

UNDP (United Nations Development Programme). 2021. *Assessing the Impact of Conflict on Development in North-East Nigeria*. Abuja: United Nations Development Programme. https://www.undp.org/sites/g/files/zskgke326/files/migration/ng/Assessing-the-Impact-of-Conflict-on-Development-in-NE-Nigeria---The-Report.pdf.

USAID. 2020. "Request for Proposal (RFP) SOL_72062020R00012—Monitoring, Evaluation and Learning (MEL) Support Activity." September 24, 2020.

USAID/Nigeria. 2021. *Nigeria—Complex Emergency*. Fact Sheet 2, March 12. https://reliefweb.int/report/nigeria/nigeria-complex-emergency-fact-sheet-2-fiscal-year-fy-2021.

———. N.d. *Country Development Cooperation Strategy (CDCS), August 11, 2020–August 10, 2025*. N.p.: USAID/Nigeria. https://2017-2020.usaid.gov/sites/default/files/documents/CDCS-Nigeria-August-2025.pdf.

———. N.d. *Country Development Cooperation Strategy, 2015–2020*. N.p.: USAID/Nigeria. https://2012-2017.usaid.gov/sites/default/files/documents/1860/Nigeria_CDCS_2015-2020.pdf.

WHO (World Health Organization). 2007. *WHO Ethical and Safety Recommendations for Researching, Documenting and Monitoring Sexual Violence in Emergencies*. Geneva: World Health Organization. https://www.who.int/publications-detail-redirect/9789241595681.

TEN

Video Documentation and Video Advocacy

The Story of the Documentary
Bringing Up Our Enemies' Child

OTIM PATRICK ONGWECH

In May 2007, a team of legal officers and social workers from the Refugee Law Project (RLP) traveled to the Kyaka II refugee settlement in Kyegegwa, western Uganda, to deliver an information session. Formally called a "psycho-legal clinic," this week-long camp offered refugees on-site counseling, legal advice, and other services, such as referrals to specialized care. Such clinics had become routine for the RLP officers. They had conducted them in different parts of Uganda many times before. But what they heard in Kyaka II startled them.

A group of men spoke about what it is like to raise children born from the rape of their wives by their enemies. The children had been conceived in the men's country of origin, the Democratic Republic of Congo (DRC), during flight. Now it was peacetime. Families were together and safe in the camp; yet these men were continuing to experience immense pressure, trauma, and psychological torture from the presence of these children.

The men spoke of how their relationships with their wives had crumbled and of how this heavy burden affected the normalcy of a family living under one roof. These cases were and are numerous; most households in Kyaka II were working through similar experiences. And they were doing this largely on their own. No institution or organization was addressing their issues. Only the local churches offered a safe space where they could access some counseling and therapeutic services. In their pain, the church had become their only consolation.

The field team related this discovery to the rest of RLP upon their return. It was a turning point for the organization. The intense deliberations that followed were, in retrospect, when the idea of building advocacy around conflict-related sexual violence (CRSV) first took root in RLP. It came at a propitious time. The Juba Peace Agreement (2006) had been signed the year before, and the conflict in northern Uganda was coming to an end. But Adam Branch (2011, 10) viewed events differently: "Tragically, the violence of the LRA [Lord's Resistance Army] insurgency and counterinsurgency has not ended but has only shifted to Democratic Republic of Congo and South Sudan, with a rising toll of killed and displaced." There were also "silent" stories circulating of male survivors of wartime rape, though one would have been hard pressed to find a single victim who was willing to speak openly about his ordeal.

For an organization working around forced migration and conflict, these developments offered an opportunity for linking sexual violence and armed conflict together and bringing them into policy discussions. We could now more easily gather evidence of the effects of rape as a weapon of war, as well as explore related themes like the use of commercial sex as a survival tool during conflict and in its aftermath.

Apart from simply documenting these phenomena, we saw that we could play a role in helping communities to heal. One way we thought to do this was by introducing video documentary work into our operations. This chapter explores how RLP has, since 2008, innovatively used video to facilitate a process of communal healing, a technique our institution has dubbed "social therapy." The method is a residual remedy for critical mental health issues associated with the lived realities of postconflict communities. This project has become my career, and RLP's journey in this area has become my own. The day we heard that field presentation from Kyaka II was my first day on the team.

The Path to Video Advocacy

RLP was founded in 1999 as a community outreach project of the School of Law, Makerere University in Kampala, Uganda. We focused on action-oriented research, visiting refugee communities and settlements to establish issues of concern, and we employed a strong, community-led approach to knowledge production. This means that we validated our questions as well as our findings with those involved before we engaged policymakers, development partners, and other key stakeholders for action. This bottom-up approach, which we still use, hands the process to communities and gives ownership to those most affected.

RLP did not always have an audiovisual unit. In October 2006, when I joined RLP's Research and Advocacy department as a data management consultant, its main method for disseminating information was a working paper series. These were popular among stakeholders, and a new release would often precipitate a new intervention by someone somewhere. But as I became more involved in field research, I found myself wanting a tool that could more directly convey the evidence we were gathering. Chris Dolan (2009, 30) agrees: "I felt that our findings would be stronger and more accessible if supported with visual documentation." This is the sort of evidence that pen and paper do not capture effectively.

The answer for me, as it has been for many other researchers, was video. According to MacDougall (1998, 297), "Images and written texts not only tell us things differently, they tell us different things." Using audiovisual equipment to accurately document and capture data enables us to relay what we see, feel, hear, smell, and touch more vividly. For certain audiences this makes our advocacy message more believable. Lawrence (2020, 2) describes this power well when he says that "filmmaking for fieldwork is more than using a camera and sound devices to gather data on location. It is about a collection of procedures and skills involved in cinema praxis that can inspire our thinking and transform our ability to understand the world." Blending videography and photography with social research is a powerful tool for communication that can and should complement the more traditional production of text.

In 2008, I was sponsored by the international NGO Witness to attend an intensive training course at the Video Advocacy Institute of Concordia University in Canada. This endowed me with new skills and empowered me to achieve my desires at RLP. It also gave me a camera, which I won for a video advocacy idea on internally displaced persons (IDPs) titled *What about Us?* (2009). I was set to engage in video advocacy. Now all I needed was internal buy-in for integrating videos into RLP's work and a funder willing to support creative methods of using storytelling to address social issues affecting forced migrants.

The production of *What about Us?* demonstrated the effectiveness of this new tool. RLP's then director, Dr. Chris Dolan, welcomed the work for its ability to amplify the voices of forced migrants. The film generated such momentum that even Uganda's state minister of disaster preparedness and refugees felt obliged and pledged the commissioning of a profiling exercise of the urban IDPs. *What about Us?* was produced at a time when communities in northern Uganda were just starting to recover from the government's two-decade-long struggle with the insurgents of the Lord's Resistance Army. The communities were grappling with issues around postconflict trauma, resettlement, gender, and CRSV, among many others. Chris Dolan (2009, 57) acknowledged that "while the same period saw relatively large numbers of the IDPs in Teso and Lango return home, the IDPs in the Acholi sub-region remained far more skeptical about the peace process."

Within this broader context, *What about Us?* told the human-interest story of how many people from the Acholi ethnic group left their homes for IDPs camps in the north, while untold others fled to urban settings such as Kampala for safety. In thirty-two minutes, the film highlighted the plight of this second group and their twenty-two-year struggle to survive in the nation's urban slums. The widely disseminated video dispelled the assumption that as soon as conflict ends, everything returns to normal. Screening it garnered support and brought stakeholders into discussion.

Several videos followed on the success of *What about Us?* with each new production inspiring the next. *Gender against Men* (2009) boldly exposed the gender-based violence experienced by refugees and IDPs during their forced migration. It was a revelation to the country and the world at large that male rape had happened in Uganda during the Lord's Resistance Army conflict. The film left no doubt that this was an issue that needed attention. *Gender against Men* was publicly launched at the National Theatre after being first validated in front of a group of male survivors of rape in northern Uganda. It was then distributed widely, both physically and virtually, with millions of views across various spaces. For this work we received Documentary of the Year at the Kenya International Film Festival in 2009. *Gender against Men* was key in reaching international audiences. It also confirmed that IDPs were facing similar issues that refugees were despite the different circumstances: sexual violence was a cornerstone in both contexts. The platform we created to openly talk about CRSV set a stage for a national discussion around accountability and facilitated truth-telling regarding what transpired for victims of war in northern Uganda.

RLP was, as an organization, continuing to transform while all this was happening. It was concentrating more and more on CRSV and sexual and gender-based violence (SGBV), and by this point several studies, campaigns, and conferences on these topics had taken place. RLP was also in the midst of a restructuring. When I had joined, it was organized into three departments: Legal Aid and Counseling, Education and Training, and Research and Advocacy. It was now reorganizing itself around a series of programmatic themes: Access to Justice; Gender and Sexuality; Mental Health and Psychosocial Wellbeing; and Conflict, Transitional Justice, and Governance. A video unit was also set up within this last thematic area, and I received a new title: video advocacy officer. With an expanded team of five, videographers started to accompany researchers and other program staff on their field visits in order to make video advocacy an integral component of their work.

In 2010, we conducted a major new research project into SGBV and women's rights in northern Uganda. This included focus groups with men; one issue they repeatedly brought up was that this project was only aimed at benefiting women. It was clear they, too, had suffered SGBV, and some of them were in urgent need of physical medical help and psychological rehabilitation. This research result gave us a chance to dig further into the revelations that the *Gender against Men* documentary had first unearthed.

The film *They Slept with Me* was released the next year (2011). It became a success in further creating awareness around male survivors of sexual violence in Uganda. This narrative-driven documentary was used in several public screenings and spaces, and the discussions that followed further confirmed that male rape had taken place during the conflict. Even though this is a taboo subject in many African societies, the documentary inspired other community members to open up about their experiences. This catalyzed a community-wide discussion on solutions and generated a list of demands for justice.

Production on *They Slept with Me* began in earnest when we encountered a man who was willing to give a full personal account of his sexual violation. He was an exception. Many members of the community felt unable to speak about their personal experiences in public, even though they continued to suffer emotional and physical pain from their gruesome experiences. The following was related by Chris Dolan (2009, 45), a key informant: "The army's second division used to do this male rape, known as *Tek Gungu*, on any men who were arrested in the rural villages, over a period of six or seven months. Many of them subsequently committed suicide. To be victim of Tek Gungu was regarded as worse than being killed. There was a period when these events even entered into the songs people sang. Eventually local leaders protested and the whole unit was transferred." Many victims, we learned, had never opened up or sought medical help or psychosocial support. But we persisted, and with help of some other organizations, we were able to identify three male survivors who agreed to speak.

As a team, we were aware that sharing this content would undo many myths surrounding male survivors. It would prove that male rape had happened but had never been addressed. And so, after completing the rough cut and carefully cross-checking the facts and narratives, we returned to the community to validate our work. While setting this up, we spoke at length to ensure that expectations stayed in check. We made our goals clear: we wanted to use the video to raise awareness and identify the needs of the victims so that we could build advocacy around those affected. After all was done and agreed, RLP asked the film's central protagonist if his family could attend the screening so they could understand what had happened to him. In response, he suggested showing the film to the entire community. Excited about this opportunity, we moved fast to make the necessary arrangements.

Men, women, youth, and community leaders attended the screening. It took place on an open-air stage. RLP gave a short introduction and then handed the microphone over to the film's protagonist so that he could speak about why he participated in this documentary. The community watched and got inspired by the story. After the screening, three men and one woman took the microphone and spoke about their own experiences. These confessions were emotionally affecting, and though it was late in the night, people continued to listen. And in the weeks that followed, community members came to the RLP offices to speak privately or called to tell us what they were going through both physically and psychologically.

The screening of the video created awareness in the community and helped many to heal—it was communal psychological healing. RLP was able to gather these victims into groups for counseling and also refer those requiring medical rehabilitation for treatment. RLP coined a new term for the entire process: "social therapy." This describes a community's psychological healing after watching a documentary about their collective traumatic experience and being inspired to deliberate openly about their plight.

By 2011, most RLP staff had embraced the use of video as a tool of advocacy. We could feel its effectiveness during screenings in communities and at RLP functions. Video advocacy had become central to our strategy, and this was recognized in 2015 when it was decided to separate the video unit that was originally under the aegis of the Research and Advocacy department (which became Conflict, Transitional Justice and Governance) and reconstitute it as branch of RLP's operations: Media for Social Change. We had come a long way. Yet the one question we had not yet touched on was the revelation that began our journey down this path and that introduced this article: What does it mean to bring up your enemies' child? We had learned an immense amount in the preceding years, were encouraged by the impact of our videos so far, and had developed a method that worked. It was time to replicate that success with the residents of Kyaka II. But it would still be another six years before that documentary would see the light of day.

Bringing Up Our Enemies' Child

Bringing Up Our Enemies' Child (BUOEC) is a forty-two-minute documentary that traces the emotional and psychological highs and lows faced by the husbands of women with children born of rape. It is a narrative-driven film that raises many pertinent questions. Above all, it asks: How does a man care for his physically, emotionally, and spiritually injured wife while, at the same time, keeping his mental frustration and trauma in check as he goes about nurturing his "enemy's" child?

For many such men, including the main protagonist of the film, their connection to the child stems from their understanding of family. For their wives, the "enemy's child" is her child, and for their own biological children the child born of rape is a sibling. But for the men themselves the emotional connection starts from a place of anger, not love. A man in this position faces many challenges as he tries to discern how (or even whether) to care for this child. What *BUOEC* explores is whether a man in these circumstances can possibly grow to love this child.

The phrase "our enemies' child" therefore has many meanings. It refers to a child born of a seed implanted during rape, a product of coercion, and a child whose very existence torments the victim(s). It is also a permanent reminder of what happened: the rape and the war itself. The same child is simultaneously a blood relation to the mother's children and a presence that becomes an axis of tension, uncertainty, anxiety, confusion, desperation, and conflict. As pointed out by Megan, Grimm, and Kunz (2007, 14): "Sexual violence also occurs during times of peace, but takes particular forms and is motivated for different reasons during armed conflict. In some conflicts it has been used strategically to advance military objectives, such as the clearing of a civilian population from an area, and has occurred with varying degrees of official knowledge and support."

"Our enemies' child" is also a metaphor and a reminder for the scars left behind on the parents and families raising children born of rape. In part these are part of the physical, psychological, and emotional pain inflicted on women during and in the aftermath of war. They also include the ripple effects of wartime sexual violence on those surrounding these women, such as their families, communities, and societies. As the main protagonist in *BUOEC* says: "It is the child who is bringing trouble between me and my wife. If it was not for being a Christian, I could have divorced or chased away my wife because that child is the one who brings us problems." Who are the real targets of sexual violence? Two major narratives dominate discussions around CRSV. Both have their blind spots. First, Ugandan culture views women as insignificant. For the rapists, the rape of women is primarily a vehicle for humiliating men, their husbands, by proxy. The cultural narrative does not recognize the pain and suffering of women, and in this way the immediate target of the act makes the woman a secondary victim. Second, the international discourse on gender sees rape as a violation of women's rights and as an expression of patriarchy. It does not recognize the pain of men and fails to understand that in the rape of women, men can be victims.

Culturally, the gender identity of the children significantly impacts the magnitude of the tensions that men grapple with. The majority of the affected families in Kyaka II are from the Banyamulenge ethnic group, a minority population found along the borderlands of Burundi, Rwanda, the DRC, and Uganda, with a good number now in Tanzania. In patriarchal societies such as those of the Banyamulenge, girls are expected to leave the household when they marry and be a source of bride wealth. Boys, on the other hand, are expected to inherit. This makes the idea of male children born of rape more complicated. Are they allowed to become competitors in the inheritance stakes? Would accepting this become the ultimate concession to the enemy? The anxieties provoked by these questions have the potential to trigger rage and aggression within the home. In many postconflict societies of Africa's Great Lakes region, such tensions are key (albeit unacknowledged) triggers of SGBV in homes.

The law can, in several ways, aggravate these dynamics. Rights and access to abortion, or lack thereof, are key. Many refugees who were forcibly impregnated during flight would likely opt for abortion, if it were available, at the very least to safeguard their marital relationship and family. This is not a legal option in Uganda. Women who would otherwise choose to rid themselves of such unwanted pregnancies find themselves stuck as mothers. In some cases these women are subsequently rejected by their spouses and turn to prostitution to meet their survival needs. This, again, is unlawful in most African countries. The law shows no leniency in light of the coercive environment, while perpetrators in these times of conflict get away with their crimes due to the absence of evidence. This leaves women caught between the law and reality.

Through identifying such complexities, *BUOEC* highlights the urgent importance of deconstructing some of our most ingrained mantras related to CRSV: "rape as a weapon of war"; "wars fought on women's bodies"; "rape, the most forgotten crisis"; and "rape, one of the greatest conspiracies of silence." To what extent do these oft-repeated statements block us from seeing, understanding, or speaking of the heavy burden placed on men as a result of such events?

Participatory Video and the Making of BUOEC

I have met filmmakers who criticize the style and quality of video advocacy films. But films like ours should be judged on different merits. Video advocacy is about highlighting and addressing social issues affecting a constituency and, through film, targeting a precise audience to find possible solutions. It is about keeping the story firmly in the hands of those affected by involving them in production and then pushing for positive policy change by following up on the action points generated during dissemination. This participatory methodology opens up new spaces and platforms for communities to use creative tools for improving societal standards.

The RLP video team and I had gained substantial experience with deploying video advocacy as a tool for social change by the time we returned to Kyaka II. We had successfully used film for "social therapy" among the male survivors of sexual violence in northern Uganda. I was excited to roll out the same methodology and test its effectiveness in another community dealing with distinct but related issues.

ACCESS

Doing so was not without its challenges. One major issue was the bureaucratic hurdles set up to control access. The United Nations High Commissioner for Refugees has been mandated by the Office of the Prime Minister (OPM) as custodian of refugees in Uganda. It is responsible for attending to refugees' needs. However, refugees' safety and security are guaranteed by the Settlement Administration—a team of officers reporting to OPM. All visits to settlements must receive written authorization from the OPM's commissioner for refugees in Kampala. Cameras are furthermore prohibited without a special permit. This restraint is meant to safeguard refugees who are facing persecution in their country of origin.

Beyond this, film teams require clearance from the Uganda Communication Commission, Media Council, the Uganda Police Force, and several other government institutions, including at times the local authorities. Finally, RLP requires clearance from bodies such as the Uganda National Council for Science and Technology in order to include video documentation within the framework of a research project. RLP benefits from its strong and positive relationship with many of these institutions, but ensuring that all the documentation is in order before filming is still a time-consuming and difficult task.

Even with the right documentation, gaining access also requires the film team to build and maintain personal relationships with various gatekeepers. For example, during visits to the settlement the team was always sure to pay a courtesy call to the camp commandant before traveling back to Kampala. Courtesy calls are a must. Even though the team may have received permission from OPM in Kampala, it would still need to defer to the "president" of the settlement and do what he expects. His ego must be massaged, and he must be invited to be involved in a way that works for both parties. With *BUOEC*, we kept the invitation limited because these were very sensitive issues. We knew clients would not speak freely in the presence of the authorities. So we shared our concept papers, told the president we were having a workshop, and invited him to send representatives to witness the said workshop. We also placed courtesy calls to other local councils and offices to keep people on our side and to pick up important security information.

Inside the settlements, the refugees themselves also have clear leadership structures. Known as Refugee Welfare Committees (RWCs), these are largely equivalent to the local councils used in villages. RWCs are the primary avenue for resolving grievances, and OPM's administrators intervene only when these fail to solve the problem. This makes the settlement design and setup comparable to a country within a country. My task as a filmmaker was to navigate these systems and get the camera into the affected community to document its story.

TRUST BUILDING

In February 2017, my team of four and I visited the site for three days to reconnect with RLP's contacts in the settlement. We were engaging with men about their issues; all five of us were men. We attended Sunday worship at the local church and convened two meetings to discuss our project. We followed this with a second visit in late April to have a more formal conversation with a manageable group of community members. Twenty-one individuals were included: the camp's commandant and gender officer (two); church leaders (three); Banyamulenge community elders and representatives (seven); parents of children born out of rape, as well as victims or survivors of rape (four); and RLP staff (five). This workshop endeavored to respond to issues raised and deliberated over emerging concerns.

We had earlier also conducted pre-visits with the community at large to build trust. We always try to get acquainted with the people before we start pulling out cameras. We explained the project to different groups of villagers, including the RWCs, so that they understood what we were trying to do. Taking the time to do this is important because if you do not educate community members first, they can become agitated once the equipment comes out. And even if they allow you to continue, they will be uncomfortable in front of the lens.

Creating a trusting atmosphere in which people feel able to speak freely also requires attention to local social dynamics and, of course, language skills. During our visits we learned that Banyamulenge social norms often put men and women into separate social spaces. We saw this, for example, in the sitting arrangement in the church: women and infants sat separately from men and from children. When it came to interviews, each gender felt more comfortable interacting with the same gender. Age also played a role: elders never truly opened up in front of someone who looked younger than them in appearance.

FIGURE 10.1. Author/filmmaker with pastor.

FIGURE 10.2. Author/filmmaker with pastor.

FIGURE 10.3. Author/filmmaker with pastor.

Video Documentation and Video Advocacy

As the lead filmmaker, I found myself in the center of most engagements and field documentation, yet I did not understand the dialect spoken by the Banyamulenge people. This was frustrating for me personally as I had to rely on translators and was concerned that key messages might be misinterpreted. But we had set up our team in light of this limitation, and we made sure that the Mulenge-speaking people in our office were on board. Having somebody who knows the local language is great for breaking the ice and getting people to open up. So preparation is key, and rushing this sort of trust-building work only causes problems. Once everybody is settled, pressing the record button is straightforward.

FILMING

Once you have dealt with the authorities and visited the community and your teams know what they are going to do, it is now time to approach the interviewees. These are usually victims or survivors. One needs to be very careful around expectation management. Once people start talking about issues that they believe no one can solve, the first question they usually have is "Are you going to be able to solve this?" You need to have an answer ready. Sometimes I provide referrals, or I think of partners who can come in and fill the gap; sometimes I must tell them that I cannot make any intervention at all.

There are ethical considerations around paying for interviews, and in general I'm against the practice. But at the same time, if I'm going to film someone, I'm going to take up a whole day of their time. I will make many requests. I might tell them to take off their shirt and then put it back on. I might be filming their eyes at close range while they're cooking. It's very distracting and at times uncomfortable. There is no standard way to put a value on the amount of disruption we cause, but we do believe we should at least compensate people for their time. We usually base compensation on what people would otherwise be doing. If a respondent is a carpenter, we try to calculate how much money they would have earned had we not interrupted their work. If the respondent is a farmer, we ask how many acres they might have otherwise tilled that day. It is just an estimate, but a humane one.

We always try to clarify the compensation at the end. If you do it at the beginning, it will look like we are buying information, and we do not want them to try to please us with the answers they give. The consent forms also have a stimulating effect on respondent behavior. Paper consent forms register differently in respondents' minds, especially if they are from rural settings. In rural settings, they equate signatures to monetary values. I have given you my signature; what do I get in return? Because of this, we use on-camera consent at the start of an interview.

Sustained engagement with your main character(s) is key to creating a successful documentary. You sit down with them not once, not twice, but several times and then let them flow. You always need to be ready because you are never sure when something important will come out. It does not work to prompt them in an interview or to say that they need to speak on such-and-such a topic. Everything vanishes when you do that. Instead, you simply have to engage with them several times to make sure you capture all the ideas they have.

Your exit strategy is as important to production as your planning. You have gone into a community with all this equipment. You have set up cameras everywhere. Now the community is looking expectantly at you. They see very sophisticated equipment going into homes and know there is a lot of value there. Your exit strategy is one reason why you made those courtesy calls and hopefully got their contact numbers. You might need security.

Postproduction includes ethically dealing with the content, including anonymization, and ensuring participants' safety and security among many others.

VALIDATION

Filmmakers must always set time aside to return to the community members that participated for validation. This exercise ensures the information presented in the film is accurate and does not misrepresent their narratives or interests. Again, the local authorities are important for this process. They may be able to identify gaps that were missed during production and that need to be included to complete the story. After watching the draft and incorporating the edits, the film is now ready for launch and public viewing.

DISSEMINATION

The distribution of a participatory video must have at least one launch within the community. This encourages community ownership, a goal of the project in and of itself, while enabling community members to become the film's first promoters. This experience also causes the film to stick in the minds of the community, thereby making it a touchstone of discussion for as long as the issue lasts.

Effective mobilization of the community for a film launch includes inviting leading figures, key experts, and other stakeholders involved in the film's issues. Radio announcements, posters, and written invitations should create further publicity. Finding a venue spacious enough to facilitate the right environment for screening and deliberation is mandatory, and equipment should always be doublechecked before the show begins. A successful launch also requires the presence of a skilled moderator who understands the film's issues and who can guide the discussion after the screening ends. Other events, such as exhibitions, can be organized in parallel with the main film launch. This move helps mobilize the public and generates much-needed attention.

A committee should be set up following the launch that can make follow-up recommendations based on what its members saw in the film. That way, the community will feel empowered to own its issues and seek solutions. This committee can, for example, take recommendations to relevant government offices and seek redress. Such a committee is also a type of monitoring and evaluation tool—a built-in accountability mechanism that encourages learning for new projects using similar methods.

Finally, having walked successfully through the community participatory process, the filmmaker may go a step further to start up a global campaign for action. By liaising with the committee and the community members, they can start an awareness campaign on social media and find new allies for the cause such as policymakers, authorities, and those who can provide international support.

Key Concerns not Mentioned in BUOEC

The politics of marginalization against the Banyamulenge minority in the DRC, which extends to the rest of Africa's Great Lakes region, is a gray area that I intentionally avoided in the film due to the complexity surrounding the genesis. Several narratives have various reasons for the horrendous violence toward them. Participants (all Banyamulenge) I engaged during the preproduction workshop attributed the violent discrimination to the involvement of the youth in the installation of the current Rwanda regime. The backlash consists of the events taking place during aftermath of the 1994 Rwandan genocide:

> I was not someone meant to flee ... because they started prosecuting us which affected all the Banyamulenge as a result of witch-hunt from all the tribes living around us who became our enemies. These were called the Bemba and it's as if they had conspired with the others. Therefore they overpowered us because for them they worked with the government soldiers [DRC's army] and they were getting help from government soldiers and they were armed. It then became necessary for us to flee because things had turned into a different level. (protagonist, *BUOEC*)

Although I was more interested in discovering how to mitigate the negative impact caused by the presence of children born of rape in the community, Banyamulenge also experienced ongoing anxiety arising from the presence of their perpetrators (from the Banyamulenge's country of origin), who are now living with them in Kyaka II also as refugees and continue to threaten them in the settlements. Being a close community that is hesitant to intermarry with other tribes has worsened the already bad situation, prompting other communities to gang up against them for targeted rape as a means of "forced integration" into the DRC society. My casual attempt to raise this with the Settlement Administration was dismissed "as a group constantly looking for preferential treatment everywhere they go."

A Munyamulenge committee member at a workshop (2017) in Kyaka II settlement said:

> We as Banyamulenge don't have power to stop this violence, therefore we are calling upon Refugee Law Project and other organizations to advocate for our rights. The reason we cannot control it is because those who violate our rights are the government, together with other tribes in Congo, though we are only talking on the issues of foster parent taking care of children born as result of rape. Our tribe's major issue is only the insecurity.... People are just taking advantage of stealing our properties and eating [our cows]. While we see them enjoying our belongings, we don't have where to report. There is also violence even right now as I am speaking. People are still burnt in their homes back in Congo and others are fleeing because of the issues. Discriminations are still occurring here in Uganda. Our fellow refugees are discriminating against us. Now we are thinking [about] where to go because we are homeless and country-less.

Adam Branch (2011, 20) portrayed such intervention as defending humanity against predatory African sovereignty.

CRSV and children born out of rape create dynamics that put a unique strain on families. It breaks some apart. However, as *BUOEC* shows, some families defy all societal stereotypes and remain as one unit. In the center of all this is the man that silently deals with invisible regalia hidden in and as names of these children born of rape but reminds generations of their sad history. The use of audiovisual and multimedia tools goes a long way in both escalating and reversing such traumatic memories, depending on the aim. For *BUOEC*, it was designed to rehabilitate and facilitate recovery. Through video advocacy, victims and survivors of CRSV use storytelling to ably overcome individual and societal plights. By collectively sharing experiences and engaging in deliberations after the screening of testimonies and lived realities, the community participation necessitates interrogation and management of mental health, especially in men raising children born of rape. These are unspoken of but are a major cause of depression and violence in homes. The woman is more likely to talk about it, but there is a need for a collective approach to sexual violence from the public sphere that will interrogate the causes of this violence on a firsthand basis from inside homes rather than hearing about discussions of violence secondhand from organizations' platforms and conferences.

Implicit in this solution is an assumption that men and women value their family life—their emotional interactions with each other and with their children—and that they are willing to confront societal norms around issues that threaten that life. Clearly, these norms and issues need to be documented and discussed if we are to solve such complex matters. Hopefully this will break down monumental assumptions about how both women and men behave and how societies interpret such complexities: this will help us to respond much more effectively to the issue(s) in question rather than just simply demonize one-half of society and glorify the other.

The film is therefore sympathetic to both men's and women's positions in such situations but stresses that children from rape, like all children, need to be loved. This dynamism propels us to learn how such possibilities can shape the gender discourse around children born of war. Only then can we start involving international bodies and players to forge a consensus around the subject of families and children born of rape.

References

Branch, A. 2011. *Displacing Human Rights: War and Intervention in Northern Uganda.* Oxford: Oxford University Press.

Dolan, C. 2009. *Social Torture: The Case of Northern Uganda, 1986–2006.* London: Berghahn Books.

Lawrence, A. 2020. *Filmmaking for Fieldwork: A Practical Handbook.* Manchester: Manchester University Press.

MacDougall, D. 1998. *Transcultural Cinema.* Edited and with an introduction by Lucien Taylor. Princeton, NJ: Princeton University Press.

Megan, B., K. Grimm, and R. Kunz. 2007. *Sexual Violence in Armed Conflict: Global Overview and Implications for the Security Sector.* Geneva: Geneva Centre for the Democratic Control of Armed Forces.

Refugee Law Project. 2009. *What about Us?* Documentary, Refugee Law Project, 32 min. https://www.refugeelawproject.org.

———. 2009. *Gender against Men.* Documentary, YouTube, 44 min. https://www.youtube.com/watch?v=mJSl99HQYXc.

———. 2011. *They Slept with Me.* Documentary, YouTube, 12 min. https://www.youtube.com/watch?v=6dxaFqezrXg.

———. 2021. *Bringing Up Our Enemies' Child.* Documentary, YouTube, 42 min. https://www.youtube.com/watch?v=qMCHhWEBpuE.

ELEVEN

Resolving Justice

Frictions between Community-Based Organizations and the United Nations Women, Peace and Security Agenda

HEATHER TASKER

Methods are integral to both research ethics and the politics of representation. These issues intersect in important ways that render scalar conceptions of justice for gendered violence in conflict: tensions between spaces constructed as "global" and spaces positioned as "local" are produced through different invocations of authority, integrity, and politics. In this chapter, I reflect on the results of a survey project conducted with civil society organizations (the "Justice Survey") and what they tell us about justice in postconflict contexts from the perspective of those who work closely with survivor communities. The perspectives that emerge from the Justice Survey sometimes connect, but more often conflict, with international languages and agendas. This exploration provides insights into the politics of knowledge production, how expertise is assessed and established, and the costs associated with marginalizing the perspectives of those working most directly with affected communities.

To explore these intersections and tensions, I compare the perspectives of justice workers shared through an international survey with the ways in which the United Nations Security Council constructs normative responses to gender and sexual violence in conflict through its Women, Peace and Security (WPS) resolutions. The Conjugal Slavery in War (CSiW) collaborative research partnership launched a project in September 2017 to examine the perspectives, experiences, and challenges of community-based justice workers in six conflict-affected and postconflict countries. The Justice Survey was first prompted through insights from Mambo Zawadi of SOFEPADI, the Democratic Republic of Congo, who strongly believed that little attention is paid to the struggles and perspectives of local community-based organizations (CBOs) and that these were minimized through concentrated attention on international humanitarian actors (personal communication 2016). In recent years there have been developments to better support community organizations, including through direct funding and capacity building (Global Affairs Canada 2017). These interventions are, however, subject to critiques similar to the WPS resolutions and the advancement of solutions deemed relevant and important by Global North actors. These problems may be important to local actors as well, but the question of what is being left out in such initiatives is important to explore and address.

Issues related to poverty, reparations, and education dominate conceptions of justice for those working directly with survivors, while the WPS resolutions emphasize gender mainstreaming and the prevention and redress of militarized and tactical sexual violence. These different conceptions of justice and peacebuilding have material impacts for survivors and the organizations working to advocate their needs. To access funding, international credibility, and support, justice needs to be framed in terms that are intelligible to the "international community," which speaks much the same language as that employed by the WPS resolutions. This affects who is able to speak about issues of gendered violence and justice and in what ways, who is determined to provide expertise on these issues, and who at times may foreclose alternative perspectives and modes of achieving justice.

I begin this chapter with a review of the Justice Survey: the political imperatives that led to its development, the form it takes, and its relationship to researching conflict-related gender violence more generally. I move from here to a consideration of ethics in researching gendered violence in postconflict contexts to highlight issues of representation. Next, I examine the development and key focus areas of the WPS resolutions and how these contrast with local priorities. Using the metaphors of friction (Tsing 2004) and scale, I consider points of abrasion and opportunity, contrasting the perspectives of CBOs with United Nations (UN) agendas. "Scale" refers to hierarchized social, political, and economic spaces wherein sociospatial politics are both produced and contested (Hameiri and Jones 2017). The scale metaphor is also useful in relation to the Justice Survey itself, in which we ask participants to reflect on the mode or level of justice most helpful to survivors and the spaces they operate in—locally, nationally, internationally—as well as the opportunities and pitfalls associated with each mode. Throughout this chapter, questions of representation are posed: Who speaks for whom, who gets to hear which concerns, how do different frames of violence determine who and what gets heard, and to what effect?[1]

Researching Conflict-Related Gender Violence

Stories and experiences from survivors of gendered violence have international salience and market value. They are increasingly sought by researchers, journalists, nongovernmental organizations (NGOs), and politicians. Large international campaigns such as End Rape Now and the #MeToo movement have raised issues of sexual violence within the public sphere across contexts and borders, and this increased awareness results in public pressure to take action. When this universalizing imperative overshadows nuanced and locally derived understandings of the causes and consequences of gendered violence, however, support measures are often ineffective at best and damaging to communities and survivors at worst. Hilhorst and Douma (2018), for example, describe the sometimes deleterious effects on community organizations and interpersonal relationships resulting from the rush in eastern DRC for organizations, both established and newly formed, to "help" women who had been raped in conflict. This raises ethical questions; it also runs the risk of overburdening survivors and contributing to a political climate in which stories of sexual violence can help advance careers at the expense of the dignity and support of survivors (Boesten 2017; Loken, Lake, and Cronin-Furman 2018). Even more problematically, there is a danger of gendered violence being invoked to justify external military intervention (Mertens and Pardy 2017; Heathcote 2018).

Rule-of-law building initiatives have expanded significantly in recent years in postconflict contexts with the aim of liberalizing justice systems, increasing access to legal support and establishing a rules-based order in societies recovering from violent upheaval (Lake 2018; Sesay 2019). In effect, these programs often provide real benefits in shifting understandings of what is considered violent and criminal, enhancing understanding of human rights, and achieving progressive decisions in cases of serious violence for offenses such as rape and other forms of gender-based violence (Lake 2018). Conversely, these initiatives sometimes further entrench unequal access to power and resources and can prove to be inaccessible to the most vulnerable community members (Sesay 2019). As Sesay (2019) found in Sierra Leone and Liberia, some rule-of-law building initiatives may both solidify unequal systems of and access to justice while simultaneously delegitimizing customary law that previously had important influence in social life. Customary law is not to be fetishized or positioned as necessarily more just than liberal legal orders; indeed, Lake, Muthaka, and Walker (2016) make it clear that customary law is often gender discriminatory and, in favoring social cohesion over individual rights, provides limited redress for deeply personal harms. In promoting one view of how justice can be obtained over another perspective, some rule-of-law building projects fail to enhance achievement of justice or to contribute to sustainable peacebuilding. To counter these risks, it is imperative that multifaceted understandings of justice are respected and multiple avenues to achieve justice be supported.

The Justice Survey was a CSiW initiative that aimed to better understand the key perspectives, priorities, concerns, and challenges for community-based justice workers in six conflict-affected countries: the Democratic Republic of Congo, Liberia, Nigeria, Sierra Leone, Uganda, and Rwanda. The first phase of the research began in July/August 2018 and was conducted entirely online. Questions in the survey with CBO staff explored what justice means to and for survivors of sexual and gendered violence; helpful and accessible justice mechanisms for victims (local, national, or international courts); the most urgent needs of survivors (reparations, medical care, access to education, and government apology), and the most significant barriers to justice (stigma, poverty, language, and locations of courts). The survey was first developed in Survey Monkey and made available in French and English. CSiW partners[2] sent the link to their networks of contacts, encouraging recipients to forward the survey to expand its reach. CSiW partners were responsible for selecting the most appropriate organizations and regions to distribute the survey, thus drawing on their expertise and knowledge within their countries.[3]

It became apparent that the online format did not meet with expectations due to ongoing and underappreciated internet accessibility challenges. As Quirk, Bunting, and Kiconco (this volume) make clear, data collection is never merely a technical activity; it is imbued with challenges, setbacks, and politics such as internet inaccessibility and misapplied assumptions about language. This research was no exception, and it is thanks to ongoing collaboration and open conversations with CSiW partners that we had the necessary information to change course. Phase two of the research, launched in the spring of 2019, utilized the Kobo Toolbox platform allowing for offline data collection on iPads distributed to CSiW partners. Using iPads makes the survey more accessible, as they do not require an internet connection, and researchers are able to provide translation for participants not fluent in French or English. This second phase is still ongoing, and Nigeria is the first partner country to have completed the research, which means Nigerian responses are perhaps overrepresented in this chapter despite ongoing efforts to represent all countries and perspectives. In total, we received 172 completed surveys.[4] Individual priorities for justice vary somewhat among the participants and between regions; however, there are also some core recurring themes, namely an emphasis on the material needs of survivors, a belief that impunity and corruption are serious problems, and a multifaceted view of justice that includes but extends beyond formal legal processes. These findings are discussed in greater detail in the "Scalar Tensions" section.

In developing the Justice Survey, we hoped to gain a better understanding of how CBOs understand and represent the justice needs of survivors of sexual and gender-based violence, both in war and postconflict contexts. We wanted to understand how CBOs assess different avenues of redress for survivors; what policies, processes, and institutions work well; and which are not helpful and why. We also wanted to learn more about the nuances and complexities of what justice means in postconflict contexts. A central challenge exists in this approach: Why did we administer the survey to justice workers with CBOs rather than ask the survivors themselves about their conceptions of justice and justice needs? The critique of this question is very valid; abstraction from the voices and perspectives of survivors can serve to silence or misrepresent their experiences. For crimes such as sexual violence, which already carry significant stigma and often have a silencing effect on survivors, are we not inadvertently reinforcing these processes by asking representatives of survivors to speak on behalf of their justice needs?

Important critical scholarship has shown that the burden on survivors to tell and retell their stories carries the risk of retraumatization (Theidon 2007), and the sharing sometimes becomes performative for Western researchers or aid workers rather than cathartic and healing for survivors (Bunting 2017). We are able to minimize risks to survivors by drawing on experiences they have already shared rather than requesting that they repeat firsthand accounts. Teddy Atim (this volume) explains that immediately following conflict-related violence, survivors are often traumatized, and their concerns are rightly focused on meeting their immediate needs and personal safety. Participants may feel research fatigue when researchers flock to communities requesting interviews, focus groups, and meetings following a period of violent upheaval (Atim, this volume). Researchers who fail to properly understand the context they are working in or the gendered and sociocultural realities of research participants risk doing more harm than good; even the best-intentioned and best-informed researchers must be aware of the relative power they wield and the possible constraints on survivors' full and informed consent to participate in research (Quirk, Bunting, and Kiconco, this volume). While institutional ethical protocols may be in place, these provide no guarantee that researchers will not put participants at risk (Walker, this volume; Balami and Umar, this volume).

Excellent research has been done with survivors of sexual violence in postconflict contexts; research that develops through personal relationships between researchers and survivors brings nuance and complexity to situations too often shrouded in spectacle and homogenization. Much exemplary work has been facilitated by partnerships between researchers and CBOs (see, for example, Schulz 2018, 2019; Aroussi 2018; Dunn 2017; Bunting 2018). For these reasons, we felt it was important to amplify the perspectives of individuals who facilitate and conduct research, support survivors, and advocate gender justice both within and beyond their own communities. Rather than silencing survivors, we are committed to a research methodology that values the expertise of frontline workers who are already tasked with representing survivors, be it in policy consultations, criminal trials, or securing and providing services. Importantly, some justice workers as well as researchers and activists are themselves survivors of conflict-related sexual and gender-based violence, which lends further nuance to the determinations of expertise and advocacy around justice needs (see Schulz, this volume, for reflections on collaborating with survivor support groups and Atim [this volume] for discussions on working as an "insider-outsider"). For these reasons, it is crucial to attend to the understandings of justice needs and priorities of CBOs.

CBOs are well placed to contribute to understandings of the political-economic context in which conflict and postconflict gendered violence occurs and the ways in which contextual components either align with or depart from the development of international criminal justice for gendered violence. For example, recent critical literature has drawn attention to the overuse of discourses such as "rape as a weapon of war" (Meger 2016; Crawford 2013; Buss 2009) and the need to "stop impunity" (Engle, Miller, and Davis 2016; Houge and Lohne 2017; St. Germain and Dewey 2013). This research offers valuable critical perspectives on how international nongovernmental organizations (INGOs), the United Nations (UN), the International Criminal Court (ICC), and other international bodies draw on concepts for specific policy aims or to further larger agendas. However, this critical literature tends to prioritize empirical findings from Northern academic researchers over consideration of the needs, priorities, and perspectives of organizations embedded in the communities that are directly impacted by both international agendas and critical academic research. This is not to say that academic research must necessarily align itself with the approaches taken by local CBOs, or that empirical work may not counter the perspectives held by representatives of these organizations. Rather, it is to draw attention to the myriad ways that knowledge about conflict-related sexual and gender-based violence is produced, which perspectives are privileged, and how even critical work can sometimes further marginalize the contributions made by community-based justice workers by focusing solely on bodies with the highest international visibility.

Feminist engagement with issues of sexual violence in conflict has expanded significantly in recent years, and has reached a point where some scholars are encouraging feminists to research elsewhere, arguing that the emphasis on sexual violence occludes other wartime harms (Henry 2016; Baaz and Stern 2018; Engle 2014). Critical scholars such as Buss, Engle, and Halley argue that focus on rape as a violation of international law serves to detract from structural causes of violence and emphasize individual accountability over systemic considerations (See Meger 2016, for a recentering of the structural, political, and economic factors in war-related rape.) So-called international criminal law feminism emphasizes combating impunity as a key strategy to end sexual and gendered violence in conflict (Engle 2014) and that imposing rule of law is crucial for postconflict recovery and necessary restructuring (Houge and Lohne 2017). While research and UN resolutions on gendered violence in conflict have flourished in recent years, a significant gap remains between how violence is talked about by international actors and the more grounded, concrete measures necessary to prevent and redress violence in contextualized and appropriate ways.

Ethical Methodologies

In considering methods and ethics in research, it is important to recognize that academic research and the work of CBOs exist within hierarchical and politically complex environments. CBOs are tasked with navigating political climates in which funding is tied to a politics of representation that demands certain stories and constructions of gendered violence. Women and girls are often included in stories of war and conflict as a means of presenting the scale of atrocities or showing the suffering of victims but not as agentic citizen-actors (Hilhorst and Douma 2018). In the global context, where attention spans are limited, and the twenty-four-hour news cycle dominates, it is always a challenge to claim space, funding, and political attention for the needs of survivors. How organizations therefore present the needs of survivors to policymakers, to INGOs, or in international research projects (like the Justice Survey) tells us not only about the needs of survivors but also, importantly, about the needs and concerns that justice workers think are most important to an international audience. Opportunities arising from research of this nature are twofold; we can learn a great deal about complex and nuanced conceptions of justice and unmet justice needs and also about the strategic priorities of CBOs attempting to navigate international research and advocacy networks to invest in the people whom they work each day to support.

In the first phase of the research using the online platform, I was responsible for the majority of the analysis. The responses were thus read through my North American academic lens as a White Canadian doctoral student. The second phase of the research seeks to partially address this limitation. As part of this phase the Nigerian responses were analyzed in collaboration with a CSiW partner organization, development Research and Project Centre (dRPC); staff members Dr. Lawan Balami and Umar Ahmad Umar (see their chapter in this volume); and fellow doctoral candidate Rahina Zarma. This adaptation provided insights and made nuances apparent in the results that would not have been intelligible had I conducted the analysis alone. It is a routine division of labor that sees Global South partners collect data and Global North researchers analyze and interpret it (Alatas 2003). More complexity and richness can be gleaned from responses if all the collaborators are involved in the analysis phase of the research, with different modes of expertise and experience rounding out the interpretation. For example, Balami and Umar clearly positioned the importance of religious and traditional leaders as potential partners for reintegrating women formerly abducted by Boko Haram. The role of these leaders is not routinely recognized by INGOs or humanitarian organizations and so, without Balami and Umar's contributions, these community members would not have their perspectives included in the surveys. Community stigma is also more easily understood in deeper context for both survivors and other community members, as well as the challenges they are living through and the historical and political circumstances contributing to the conflict. Without deeper context and different perspectives to drive decision-making each step of the way, one runs the risk of simply reproducing what has been done before in other locales and replicating not only methods but findings at the expense of added knowledge.

In reflecting on the ethical implications of the methods we as researchers choose to employ in our work, it becomes apparent that no choice we make is, or should be, neutral. The decisions about who we talk to, when and where we talk to them, and how we analyze and disseminate the results are all political actions with implications far beyond our individual projects and careers. For these reasons, conversations about methodological concerns are crucial for understanding different perspectives on ethical research, and these conversations, like the research itself, must include as many diverse voices as possible.

We can demonstrate respect for survivors of gendered violence by taking seriously the concerns and priorities of those who work most closely in supporting them, often at great personal risk (Amnesty International 2017). While there are numerous and important critiques of formal legal processes, particularly for international criminal justice, in the academic literature (Bunting 2018; Buss 2009; St. Germain and Dewey 2013), the respondents to our survey are still waiting for some semblance of justice for the survivors they support. Important problems with the international criminal justice system, such as the remoteness of proceedings and lack of contextual specificity, were identified by the Justice Survey participants. Serious issues within local justice mechanisms, such as corruption and high social status serving to protect perpetrators, were *also* revealed to be of similar concern. Researchers can work in collaboration with CBOs to identify impediments to justice at all institutional levels and support their advocacy to address these barriers.

Regions where sexual and gender-based violence frequently occurs with impunity also tend to be regions where CBOs who work to address these issues are not respected by governments and militaries or are themselves silenced (Amnesty International 2019). The risks to local activists are significant. One survey respondent from eastern Democratic Republic of Congo shared the following when asked about relations between government and CBOs: "This will take time for these community organizations to adapt to the realities of the country. Because if they do their job exactly, they will be hunted down, they will not have the free field to actually perform their tasks" (Survey 21, DRC—translated from French).[5] In this instance, we see how ongoing conflict and insecurity not only impact the ability of CBOs to offer comprehensive services to survivors but may also directly threaten the safety of those working in these organizations.

A better understanding of the challenges CBOs face with different justice mechanisms focuses attention on forms of justice outside the ones limited to individual experiences, opening up space to analyze systemic and structural barriers. Likewise, examining points of overlap and disjuncture between perspectives from local actors and the dominant international agenda opens up spaces to consider differential priorities and the opportunities and drawbacks they represent. The friction produced through scales of justice work can be productive, frustrating, or often both. What is critical throughout these processes is to examine and work against entrenched hierarchies of power relations, to reevaluate how we come to know what we do, where this knowledge originates from, and—perhaps most importantly—what is being left out or silenced in reproducing these frames. By amplifying the perspective of justice workers, we demonstrate respect for their expertise, which in turn signals a commitment to working collaboratively to address gendered violence across organizations and regions.

Resolving Gendered Justice at the UN

The last three decades have seen increased attention to and funding for projects aimed at improving gender equality and combating violence against women in conflict-affected and fragile contexts. Few initiatives have been as influential or widespread in this goal as the Women, Peace and Security (WPS) resolutions of the UN, the National Action Plans based upon them, and the many organizations, researchers, and practitioners working on the development and implementation of these initiatives. The political imperatives within the WPS resolutions have significant impact on the advocacy work done by CBOs and INGOs, on positioning the WPS agenda as important to understanding how sexual and gendered violence is framed internationally, and on affecting what is possible within communities and what may be minimized or left out as a result of their influence.

The UN Security Council Resolution 1325 (UN Security Council 2000) was the first in a series of resolutions concerned with WPS and marked the beginning of attempts by the Security Council to recognize the inextricability of women from sustainable peacebuilding by "*reaffirming* the important role of women in the prevention and resolution of conflicts and in peace-building, and *stressing* the importance of their equal participation and full involvement in all efforts for the maintenance and promotion of peace and security, and the need to increase their role in decision-making with regard to conflict prevention and resolution" (UN Security Council 2000, 1).[6]

The WPS resolutions seek to acknowledge the unique harms suffered by women and girls during times of war. In the twenty years since UNSCR 1325, there have been nine further resolutions addressing WPS. Each builds on the others, clarifies issues of concern, and specifies gendered harms in war and postconflict opportunities for women (Heathcote 2018). Central to this overall architecture is an elaboration of the ways in which women are harmed during war and the risk of these harms to international peace and security, as is the purview of the Security Council. The language used in the WPS resolutions reflects normative discourse in their denunciation of violence against women and their assertions of the importance of women participating in peace processes (Shepherd 2016). In the development of normativity in the resolutions subsequent to 1325, we can see a specific shift in discussions of gender-based harms in war. Early resolutions emphasized the inclusion of women as peacebuilders and humanitarian imperatives such as refugee protections, while the later resolutions show a stronger emphasis on combating impunity and concerns with weaponized rape and terrorism:

> *Recognizing* the differential impact on the human rights of women and girls of terrorism and violent extremism, including in the context of their health, education, and participation in public life, and that they are often directly targeted by terrorist groups, and *expressing deep concern* that acts of sexual and gender-based violence are known to be part of the strategic objectives and ideology of certain terrorist groups, used as a tactic of terrorism, and an instrument to increase their power through supporting financing, recruitment, and the destruction of communities. (UN Security Council 2015)

This focus on sexual and gendered violence as strategic and tactical within the WPS resolutions converges with broader UN policy on rape in war as strategic and a weapon of war. Connecting sexual violence with terrorism, extremism, and other acts of war paradoxically opens up space for militarized responses (Quirk, Bunting, and Kiconco, this volume; Mertens and Pardy 2017; Isaksson 2014).

In Res. 1325, we see a focus on the status of women and girls as potential victims due to gender-based precarity resulting from conflict and displacement, whereas in later resolutions there is a shift to considering intentional acts of war that place women and girls at increased risk. Aroussi (2011, 2017) argues that 1325 was developed to address gender inequality in transitional, postconflict societies in empowering ways. The elements most often highlighted (and that have been expanded and focused on in subsequent resolutions) represent women as victims of sexual violence in war rather than emphasize their capacity as political actors and peacebuilders. This focus on strategic and tactical sexual violence diverts focus from structural and political inequalities that contribute to SGBV in times of relative peace as well as war—and from SGBV in war that is not necessarily weaponized (Aroussi 2011). In positioning sexual violence in war as a threat to international peace and security to be addressed militarily, certain acts may be prevented or redressed, but many causes of gendered violence in both war and peace remain entrenched (Baaz and Stern 2013). Shepherd (2016) expands upon this by arguing that much implementation of WPS agendas serves to "make war safe for women," rather than developing demilitarization strategies to end and prevent conflict more broadly.

To fully consider the ways these international framings of conflict-related sexual and gender-based violence impact survivors' experiences and opportunities of justice, I now turn to the ways that the WPS agenda both coincides and diverges with the experiences of CBOs working directly with victims. By bridging these scales of action, we are better able to understand how justice operates on different registers and the multitude of meanings and potentials within the concept.

Frictions in Gendered Justice

Björkdahl and Höglund (2013) draw on the concept of friction, first developed by Tsing (2004), to elucidate the tensions and conflictual nature of peacebuilding projects that intersect international and local actors. Friction as a concept is developed through notions of hybridity and a recognition of the multiple scalar concerns that manifest in distinct locations, mutually influencing and informing one another. Hybridity in postconflict contexts is marked by power relations, and "also holds an ability to translate and negotiate difference as it moves away from binary combinations such as the global and the local, and thus conceptualise the global/local as 'both/and' rather than 'either/or'" (Björkdahl and Höglund 2013, 294). Friction, then, is produced within spaces marked by hybridity when competing interests and concerns come into contact and tension with one another. These tensions can be either productive or destructive (Björkdahl et al. 2016).

Through employing the friction metaphor, we can begin to understand how the strategic and shifting priorities of the WPS resolutions; UN approaches to weaponized rape and sexual violence; and calls for anti-impunity, accountability, and justice are all interwoven, mutually constitutive, and fraught with competing understandings and conceptualizations. The different components and considerations relating to the WPS resolutions intersect, sometimes conflict, and frequently enable a web of concerns that are not above power relations and epistemological hierarchies despite their avowed feminism. Hellmüller (2013) argues that the focus on liberal state-building processes serves to ignore or only belatedly consider the peacebuilding priorities of local communities, emphasizing that while hybridized spaces incorporate multiple "levels" of concerns, the interplay between actors and the friction produced remains heavily in favor of the international realm. This echoes Basini and Ryan's (2016) critique, which argues that the emphasis on the liberal state to bring about gender justice is inherently limited and disempowering to communities, leaving little support for alternative ways of conceptualizing and enacting peace and justice.

As discussed in the previous section, the securitization of sexual violence operates in a way that decontextualizes, dehistoricizes, and depoliticizes sexual violence, positioning it as distinct from other violence in both war and peace. Indeed, respondents in the Justice Survey identified concerns with international criminal law as at times replicating the same colonial structures that contributed to the propagation of conflict-related harms. The focus on tactical sexual violence in the WPS resolutions occurs seemingly at the expense of considering systemic inequalities and the ways that these limit women's participation. The word "poverty," for example, does not once appear in any of the ten WPS resolutions, despite its being widely recognized as a serious barrier to women's political participation as well as increasing their vulnerability in times of conflict. For example, Haushofer et al. (2019) found that unconditional cash transfers—the disbursement of funds directly to individuals without stipulations on how it is spent—reduced rates of intimate partner violence by 73 to 82 percent in Kenya. Baaz and Stern (2013) found that soldiers in the Congolese national army enacted their frustration and anger over poverty and lack of opportunity through gender-based violence. Respondents to the Justice Survey identified poverty and lack of economic means as a barrier to justice and as aggravating the experience of violence: "Because they are poor, they remain vulnerable to their perpetrators of sexual assaults" (Survey 36, Sierra Leone), while economic empowerment was considered crucial to overcoming hardship. Of the 172 respondents 81 percent considered financial reparations[7] and 86 percent considered financial support to be important or very important for survivors. When we contrast that with more symbolic elements of justice such as government apology (59 percent), the ongoing material needs of survivors are made clear, and having these needs met is crucial for achieving a sense of justice.

Research partnerships are themselves implicated in financial challenges and considerations. CSiW was funded by the Social Science and Humanities Research Council (Canada), and one of the stipulations of this funding was that funds were not to be used to support service provision of operational costs for partners, including community-based partners. While sensible in theory, this can be difficult to apply in practice. For many partners, there is no sharp divide between research and service provision; they know research participants through the services they offer, research questions arise based on community needs, and results inform how CBOs will operate. Participatory research especially may involve both therapeutic and research activities (see Schulz, this volume). The political economy of knowledge production, in this case, draws distinctions between "research" and "service" in ways that do not wholly recognize how research can be used to better the lives of individuals, not only in years to come but through a process of participation (Schulz, this volume). Short-term and project-based funding, shifting political imperatives from donors, and increasing competition for too few grants force CBOs to operate in a state of precarity. By constantly having to seek out short-term grants and tailor activities to a fickle international political climate, CBOs struggle to meet sustainable daily operations. Without long-term and sustainable funding for service provisions and necessary infrastructures, there is little space and opportunity to engage in meaningful research despite community-based researchers having the knowledge and ability to contribute to and direct this work. This creates a dearth of contextually relevant knowledge about the causes and consequences of conflict-related sexual and gender-based violence in international politics: capacity and understanding may be there, but without the opportunity to systematically and rigorously "prove" it through empirical research, it stays within communities and has limited sway in international politics.

True (2015) argues that lack of engagement with structural issues demonstrates an inability or ignorance of the root causes of sexual violence in conflict, narrowing the focus of the WPS agenda to one of protection rather than prevention. By extension, survivor support is positioned as increasing the resilience of individual survivors (Taylor 2018), rather than as a mode of justice that survivors have a right to. Despite extensive research showing that reparations in the form of financial support, education, and health care are desperately needed, only four of the ten resolutions mention reparations (UNSCRs 2122, 2106, 1888, 2467). Of these, only UNSCR 1888 and 2467 go beyond briefly stating that victims of sexual violence and/or violations of individual rights should have access to reparation. UNSCR 1888 connects the need for reparations to disarmament, demobilization, and reintegration processes and humanitarian assistance, demonstrating an understanding of the inextricability of postconflict support for survivors with enduring peace. This recognition of continuums between conflict and postconflict and the complexities of experiences and support needs, is a crucial step in offering a more nuanced perspective of harms in war than is demonstrated elsewhere in WPS resolutions subsequent to 1325. Resolution 2467 (2019) demonstrates an evolution in the Security Council's recognition of the importance of reparations to survivors of gendered violence in conflict. Linking reparations to anti-impunity efforts, 2467 emphasizes that women should have reparative support when appropriate and positions the lack of reparations as contributing to social marginalization. Importantly, 2467 also recognizes reparation needs for children born of war.

In both UNSCRs 1888 and 2467, reparations play a secondary role to investigation, prosecution, and punishment in that reparative provisions are positioned as an outcome of successful prosecution rather than a state or international responsibility regardless of whether criminal convictions have been secured.[8] The material needs of survivors do not disappear in instances where there is insufficient evidence to prosecute, or when individual accountability cannot be determined. Respondents to the Justice Survey unequivocally stated that reparations are central to conceptions of justice, both outside of and in addition to formal legal proceedings. The respondents identified lack of medical care, education, and financial support as very important or important barriers to achieving justice, and they identified reparations as very important for achieving a sense of justice for survivors: "At its core the form of justice should help restore their dignity and rights as full citizens. Justice is reparations, both material and symbolic" (Survey 2, Uganda).

The WPS resolutions emphasize that impunity and lack of accountability compound sexual violence in conflict, as can be seen in the first WPS resolution, 1325, and the 2019 resolution, 2467:

> *Emphasizes* the responsibility of all States to put an end to impunity and to prosecute those responsible for genocide, crimes against humanity, and war crimes including those relating to sexual and other violence against women and girls, and in this regard *stresses* the need to exclude these crimes, where feasible from amnesty provisions. (UN Security Council 2000, 3)

> *Urges* Member States to strengthen access to justice for victims of sexual violence in conflict and post-conflict situations, including women and girls, who are particularly targeted, including through the prompt investigation, prosecution and punishment of perpetrators of sexual and gender-based violence. (UN Security Council 2019, 6)

This is important, as the emphasis on criminal accountability and combating impunity advances notions of liberal normativity, punishment rather than prevention, and decontextualize offenses, particularly in relation to and reliance on the ICC and other ad hoc and special tribunals ulterior to national court systems (Bunting 2018; Hellmüller 2013). Again, this was a challenge explicitly discussed by numerous Justice Survey respondents. International legal mechanisms are distant and decontextualized, and respondents prefer to see justice served within their communities: "In certain regions, local justice systems are different from the international hence people are more likely to conform to local laws. Also the local judicial system is closer and in direct contact with the victims and perpetrators at the grassroot level and this serves as an advantage" (Survey 3, Nigeria). However, respondents across national contexts routinely identified impunity, lack of accountability, and an absence of political will to prosecute as major barriers to achieving a sense of justice and also facilitating ongoing violence, particularly for those in powerful or privileged positions. Corruption and impunity at the local level is seen as a serious impediment to achieving justice: "Some of them feel that some certain people are too powerful to be punished, so even if they should report to the authority, nothing will be done" (Survey 71, Nigeria).

While respondents to the Justice Survey discussed impunity and lack of accountability as significant barriers to achieving justice, notions of justice went far beyond criminal prosecutions and were more likely to include health care, financial reparations, access to education, and jobs. Justice for community-based workers carries a strong focus on the well-being and psychological recovery of victims, as well as an emphasis on the more material outcomes of justice, such as reparations, skills training, and medical care. Indeed, in phase one of the English survey results, the priorities of victims that were rated as very important were, in order, medical treatment, access to formal justice mechanisms, psychosocial support, safety, and security. The components least likely to be considered very important were "government apology" and "memorialization." In the second phase of the research in Nigeria, safety and security were rated as most important for survivors, with 91 percent considering it very important. This is not surprising, given the ongoing insecurity and conflict in northeastern Nigeria, but it is still important to emphasize since it draws out the contextual specificity of justice needs in relation to conflict contexts. And yet, less tangible concepts such as impunity and political will were also often invoked by respondents as important for victims or as barriers to achieving a fair outcome. It thus seems that the conditions and potential for justice are being highlighted, with impunity and lack of political will as barriers to the construction of space for justice.

Bunting (2018) draws out how conceptions of justice as the primary prerogative of courts, particularly international courts like the ICC, are limited due to the decontextualization inherent in criminal prosecutions occurring far from where events initially occurred. She states that while international courts are limited in what they can achieve, they are still important for meaning-making around gendered violence and as spaces for justice (2018, 2). While international criminal trials are important for developing discursive understandings of gendered violence in war, this opportunity is confined to liberal understandings of harm. There are limited opportunities for meaningful community redress when those who commit atrocities are tried and imprisoned far from their communities, particularly when those most impacted by violence emphasize the complexity and continuing repercussions of ongoing violence in a way that cannot be captured by formal justice mechanisms.

Through this research, we can see how differently concepts like impunity and justice are used by local and international actors and hold different meanings for people based on their respective positions. While community-based organizations strategically draw on the WPS resolutions, there are also other pressing concerns not contained in UN policy relating to gender and war. The WPS resolutions' emphases on the ICC, ad hoc tribunals, and mixed tribunals as crucial for achieving justice run counter to the perception of survey respondents who state that formal justice mechanisms, when divorced from reparative processes, hold limited opportunity for rebuilding society in postconflict contexts. While CBOs rely on formal legal mechanisms for certain components of justice, justice goes far beyond international trials and prosecutions, which are inaccessible for survivors in many cases: "The local justice, if administered properly, serves as a courage to deter perpetrators, but the international justice seems foreign to victims" (Survey 8, Liberia).

Considering how international normative practices and principles have come to inform and intersect with localized perceptions of violence and justice, it is important to consider the technologies and practices through which this occurs. Christensen (2018) argues that the symbolic and material investment by justice actors has served to shape the field of international criminal law plus the development of justice discourses which shape the potential and end goals of international criminal law. In examining the input of academics, INGOs such as Human Rights Watch and Amnesty International, and justice actors (lawyers and judges working in international law), Christensen charts the way different perspectives and emphases have served to build the field of international criminal justice. Similar to Houge and Lohne's (2017) work, Christensen shows how a field is shaped through conceptual framings from key actors who have "buy-in." Importantly, Christensen, Houge, and Lohne do not consider the roles that community-based organizations play in shaping the discursive field of international criminal law, although our survey showed that regional actors are highly invested in developing both local and international approaches to justice for survivors; indeed a number of CSiW partners have worked with ad hoc tribunals and the ICC to develop jurisprudence around conflict-related gendered crimes. Community-based organizations are uniquely situated in the intersections between the economy of knowledge production, legal mobilization, and the political economy of SGBV in conflict-affected societies, with deep understanding of the tensions and challenges circulating within justice imperatives.

The respondents in the survey reported a clear disconnect between the normative role of justice systems and the reality of what is available to victims: "Most victims always feel neglected by communities, governments, and justice mechanisms" (Survey 4, Uganda). Whitney Taylor (2018) discusses legal mobilization and the ambivalence that accompanies legal claims in a context where few have faith in the legal system. Similar sentiments exist in the regions where we administered the Justice Survey: "There are no proper justice mechanisms" (Survey 25, Sierra Leone) even though many individuals rely on them for both recognizing the experiences of victims and providing necessary services and measures for recovery: "They [victims] should value the justice system and exercise patience" (Survey 84, Nigeria).

The perceived bureaucracy of the international system was daunting, and some respondents felt localized approaches were preferable, since "the national protects the survivor. International may help, but it has too many bureaucracies" (Survey 30, Liberia). Another respondent indicated that local justice was the most effective because "immediate help is given to the victim, whereas for international justice, the time factor is of importance. Justice delayed is justice denied" (Survey 10, Sierra Leone). Conversely, for respondents who indicated a preference for international justice mechanisms, this was most often based on the belief that local justice does not properly uphold the rights of survivors and that corruption is a serious problem: "Political affiliations or 'orders from above' may disturb justice accessed by the victim" (Survey 10, Sierra Leone).

Here again we see tensions within complex postconflict environments where the legal system does not yet function the way CBOs would like it to and yet is relied upon to secure justice for victims. It is in this ambivalent space where we also see concerns about the international system and the role it might play in filling some of the gaps that exist both regionally and nationally. In one regard, the international system gives recognition and a larger platform for the experiences of victims to be acknowledged, as well as opportunities for reparations. However, decontextualization seems to contribute to hesitation by a number of respondents who would rather see their own national systems take up the role of administering justice in situated and localized ways, centering survivors in the process:

> In certain regions, local justice systems are different from the international, hence people are more likely to conform to local laws. Also, the local judicial system is closer and in direct contact with the victims and perpetrators at the grassroot level, and this serves as an advantage. (Survey 3, Nigeria)

> "Meaning-making" by survivors should be central in shaping any justice response. Many international and even local justice processes tend to be "out of context" . . . to survivors. (Survey 5, Uganda)

These tensions between international legitimacy and national ownership were also apparent in the Justice Survey through responses expressing ambivalence about the respective roles of international and national justice mechanisms. While the international mechanisms were, in some cases, seen as placing issues of SGBV in the spotlight and granting them global attention, international courts were also viewed as decontextualized and not attuned to local circumstances. In this, we see a similar concern to that expressed by Basini and Ryan (2016) in that international discourse around SGBV is useful up to a point but less so when issues are claimed at the international level in ways that do not translate or are less relevant locally. In this, I do not mean to romanticize or fetishize the local as a distinct, static location removed or somehow isolated from international concerns or politics (Tsing 2004). Indeed, as demonstrated, participants in the Justice Survey are invested in international processes and keen to share perspectives to advance conceptions of justice internationally. Rather, it is to consider how, where, and by whom international priorities are produced and then implemented, "vernacularized,"[9] or not, in distinct locales (Merry 2006, 2009; Levitt and Merry 2009). Elucidating these processes serves to uncover the actors behind resolutions and campaigns, to bring forward how their concerns connect and diverge with those working to support survivors within communities, and to advance a nuanced and multiscaled conception of what justice for SGBV in conflict can mean.

"Localization" has increasingly become a buzzword and key priority in humanitarian and peacebuilding projects. The embedding of international projects and approaches to community settings, with adjustments for context and appropriateness, has been touted as a central feature of nexus approaches to humanitarianism, development, and peacebuilding (Barakat and Milton 2020). Increasing difficulties in accessing conflict-affected areas, targeting humanitarian staff, and the proliferation of humanitarian needs have prompted reliance on local partner NGOs over INGO involvement in "crisis" contexts (Barakat and Milton 2020).[10] This has often resulted in increased security risks and danger to local organizations (Tronc, Grace, and Nahikian 2019; Pascucci 2019), and unfair burdens are placed on local organizations that continue to work through the most devastating upheavals after INGOs pull their staff (Mambo Zawadi, personal communication 2016). Turns toward localization can, at the best of times, integrate local knowledge and expertise with international resources, increase capacity within communities, and contribute to longer-term peacebuilding and achievements of justice. This demonstrates the productive and beneficial potentials of "friction" where different knowledge and skill sets come into contact and produce something meaningful that would not be possible in isolation (as per Björkdahl et al. 2016). However, when introduced as a principle to whitewash rather than correct unequal realities (who stays versus who can leave, who shoulders the highest security risks, and whose knowledge is valued more) through the guise of less top-down programming, it increases risks to local actors while doing nothing to disrupt power imbalances (Carpi 2022). Indeed, as Maha Shuayb powerfully wrote in a 2022 piece for the *New Humanitarian*, increased demands for "local perspectives" further entrench inequality by tokenizing community-based actors as "experts" on specific issues, provided that what they share coincides with the already dominant understanding of the problem at hand; there is little space to challenge what international organizations consider factual.

Toward Deeper Collaboration

As Global North researchers, we can combat these identified inequalities by engaging in meaningful partnerships, by shifting leadership responsibilities, and by taking better direction from our Global South colleagues. This is not always an easy feat; academia trains us to venerate the accomplishments of individual scholars and to place academic experts on a pedestal, leaving little space to start from a place of not knowing and having partners to guide you—to ask how you can contribute rather than attempting to explain others' realities. Quirk, Bunting, and Kiconco challenge all of us to move beyond extraction research: to refuse to legitimate research that pulls out and removes from communities information seen as useful or interesting to academic researchers while offering nothing back. I build on this challenge with one of my own; rather than only offering "something" back to communities, it is our responsibility to ensure that what is offered is meaningful, important, and useful to our collaborators. Moves to decolonize academic research and increased opportunities for collaborative projects offer a glimmer of hope, but as individual researchers we must both recognize and accept that for the time being our careers may be impacted by attempts to do research more ethically and to engage in slow research. Meaningful collaborations take time and may not result in the high volume of publications our disciplines mark as signs of "success."

Increased attention to and outrage over conflict-related sexual and gendered violence in recent decades have resulted in attempts to prevent and redress violence at multiple levels and scales, with local and global actors at times working in concert and sometimes divergently. Shared concerns over impunity and corruption in the justice system contrast with international attention on weaponized rape at the expense of the ongoing material needs of survivors, as highlighted by CBOs. Likewise, international legal mechanisms themselves hold both promise and limitations, offering sites to explore the ambivalence some local actors hold toward international organizations more generally and highlighting the simultaneous risks of decontextualization with opportunities for awareness raising and support in achieving justice aims. To take seriously the productive potential of these tensions, the expertise of those working most directly with survivors and advancing peace in their communities, must be recognized and incorporated into policy, especially when the latter conflicts with international priorities.

As researchers, we have an ethical imperative to ensure that the perspectives and experiences of those working to obtain justice are amplified, understood, and acted upon. Research questions and methods can be adapted to help shift how we construct and relay expertise, and the politics of knowledge production is itself an important site of inquiry. Throughout, we have the duty and responsibility to ensure that we minimize harm to those who have already been made vulnerable by gendered violence and conflict, to organize against extractive and exploitative research, and to work in collaboration and partnership against violence and for the advancement of justice.

Notes

1. These reflections have developed through the process of administering and analyzing the survey, and through helpful conversations at the CSiW Institute '*Enslavement, Conflict, and Forced Marriage in Africa*', June 25th–28th 2018, University of Witwatersrand, South Africa.
2. SOFEPADI, Democratic Republic of Congo; SEVOTA, Rwanda; Women's Forum, Sierra Leone; ADWANGA, Liberia; development Research and Project Centre (dRPC), Nigeria; Women's Advocacy Network and Refugee Law Project, Uganda.
3. CSiW country teams previously conducted in-depth interviews with survivors of conflict-related forced marriages and related violence. See csiw-ectg.org for reports detailing their findings.
4. Nigeria: 102; Sierra Leone: 27; DRC: 18; Liberia: 11; Uganda: 13; Rwanda: 1.
5. Survey responses have been lightly edited for ease of reading.
6. All emphases in UN Resolutions are preserved from the originals.
7. Reparations are distinct from financial support in that reparations are implemented in recognition of harms suffered and wrongs committed. They are intended to repair these harms. More general financial support does not necessarily have the same recognition of wrongs having occurred.
8. While there are opportunities for victims to access reparations when perpetrators have been convicted by the International Criminal Court, the pool of funds is small compared to the number of victims entitled to make claims. Accessing reparations is also a long and temporally constrained process, and only those most directly impacted can benefit. There is little to no reparative support available for communities; for intergenerational harms, etc. See Redress 2017 report for further discussion.
9. Merry's (2009) and Levitt and Merry's (2009) work on vernacularization con-

cerns how international normative practices and principles are translated and made intelligible and useful in different localized contexts.
10. See Fassin and Pandolfi (2010) for discussion of how emergency and crisis are understood and developed.

References

Alatas, S. F. 2003. "Academic Dependency and the Global Division of Labour in the Social Sciences." *Current Sociology* 51 (6): 599–613.
Amnesty International. 2017. "Attacks on Human Rights Activists Reach Crisis Point Globally." Amnesty International, May 16. https://www.amnesty.org/en/latest/news/2017/05/attacks-on-rights-activists-reach-crisis-point-globally/.
———. 2019. *Laws Designed to Silence: The Global Crackdown on Civil Society Organizations*. London: Amnesty International.
Aroussi, S. 2011. "'Women, Peace and Security': Addressing Accountability for Wartime Sexual Violence." *International Feminist Journal of Politics* 13 (4): 576–93.
———. 2017. "Women, Peace, and Security and the DRC: Time to Rethink Wartime Sexual Violence as Gender-Based Violence?" *Politics & Gender* 13 (3): 488–515.
———. 2018. "Perceptions of Justice and Hierarchies of Rape: Rethinking Approaches to Sexual Violence in Eastern Congo from the Ground Up." *International Journal of Transitional Justice* 12 (2): 277–95.
Baaz, M. E., and M. Stern. 2013. *Sexual Violence as a Weapon of War? Perceptions, Prescriptions, Problems in the Congo and Beyond*. London: Zed Books.
———. 2018. "Curious Erasures: The Sexual in Wartime Sexual Violence." *International Feminist Journal of Politics* 20 (3): 295–314.
Barakat, S., and S. Milton. 2020. "Localisation across the Humanitarian-Development-Peace Nexus." *Journal of Peacebuilding & Development* 15 (2): 147–63.
Basini, H., and C. Ryan. 2016. "National Action Plans as an Obstacle to Meaningful Local Ownership of UNSCR 1325 in Liberia and Sierra Leone." *International Political Science Review* 37 (3): 390–403.
Björkdahl, A., and K. Höglund. 2013. "Precarious Peacebuilding: Friction in Global–Local Encounters." *Peacebuilidng* 1 (3): 289–99.
Björkdahl, A., K. Höglund, G. Millar, J. van der Lijn, and W. Verkoren, eds. 2016. *Peacebuilding and Friction: Global and Local Encounters in Post-conflict Societies*. Milton Park, UK: Routledge.
Boesten, J. 2017. "Of Exceptions and Continuities: Theory and Methodology in Research on Conflict-Related Sexual Violence." *International Feminist Journal of Politics* 19 (4): 506–19.
Bunting, A. 2017. "Narrating Wartime Enslavement, Forced Marriage, and Modern Slavery." In *Contemporary Slavery: Popular Rhetoric and Political Practice*, edited by A. Bunting and J. Quirk, 129–57. Vancouver: UBC Press.
———. 2018. "Gender Politics and Geopolitics of International Criminal Law in Uganda." *Global Discourse* 8 (3): 422–37.
Buss, D. E. 2009. "Rethinking 'Rape as a Weapon of War.'" *Feminist Legal Studies* 17 (2): 145–63.

Carpi, E. 2022. "The Epistemic Politics of 'Northern-Led' Humanitarianism: Case of Lebanon." *Area* 54 (2): 330–42.

Christensen, M. J. 2018. "The Symbolic Economy of International Criminal Justice: Shaping the Discourse of a New Field of Law." In *Strengthening the Validity of International Criminal Tribunals*, edited by J. Nicholson, 74–98. Leiden, Netherlands: Brill Nijhoff.

Crawford, K. F. 2013. "From Spoils to Weapons: Framing Wartime Sexual Violence." *Gender & Development* 21 (3): 505–17.

Dunn, H. 2017. "The Transitional Justice Gap: Exploring 'Everyday' Gendered Harms and Customary Justice in South Kivu, DR Congo." *Feminist Legal Studies* 25 (1): 71–97.

Engle, K. 2014. "The Grip of Sexual Violence: Reading United Nations Security Council Resolutions on Human Security." In *Rethinking Peacekeeping, Gender Equality and Collective Security*, edited by G. Heathcote and D. Otto, 23–47. Basingstoke, UK: Palgrave Macmillan, 2014.

Engle, K., Z. Miller, and D. M. Davis, eds. 2016. *Anti-impunity and the Human Rights Agenda*. Cambridge: Cambridge University Press.

Fassin, D., and M. Pandolfi. 2010. *Contemporary States of Emergency: The Politics of Military and Humanitarian Interventions*. Princeton, NJ: Zone Books.

Global Affairs Canada. 2017. "Canada's Feminist International Assistance Policy." Government of Canada. https://www.international.gc.ca/world-monde/issues_development-enjeux_developpement/priorities-priorites/policy-politique.aspx?lang=eng.

Hameiri, S., and L. Jones. 2017. "Beyond Hybridity to the Politics of Scale: International Intervention and 'Local' Politics." *Development and Change* 48 (1): 54–77.

Haushofer, J., C. Ringdal, J. P. Shapiro, and X. Y. Wang. 2019. "Income Changes and Intimate Partner Violence: Evidence from Unconditional Cash Transfers in Kenya." Working Paper No. w25627, National Bureau of Economic Research.

Heathcote, G. 2018. "Security Council Resolution 2242 on Women, Peace and Security: Progressive Gains or Dangerous Development?" *Global Society* 32 (4): 374–94.

Hellmüller, S. 2013. "The Power of Perceptions: Localizing International Peacebuilding Approaches." *International Peacekeeping* 20 (2): 219–32.

Henry, N. 2016. "Theorizing Wartime Rape: Deconstructing Gender, Sexuality, and Violence." *Gender & Society* 30 (1): 44–56.

Hilhorst, D., and N. Douma. 2018. "Beyond the Hype? The Response to Sexual Violence in the Democratic Republic of the Congo in 2011 and 2014." *Disasters* 42: S79–S98.

Houge, A. B., and K. Lohne. 2017. "End Impunity! Reducing Conflict-Related Sexual Violence to a Problem of Law." *Law & Society Review* 51 (4): 755–89.

Isaksson, C. 2014. "Fighting for Gender Equality: Why Security Sector Actors Must Combat Sexual and Gender-Based Violence." *Fletcher Forum World Affairs* 38: 49–72.

Lake, M. 2018. *Strong NGOs and Weak States: Pursuing Gender Justice in the Democratic Republic of Congo and South Africa*. Cambridge: Cambridge University Press.

Lake, M., I. Muthaka, and G. Walker. 2016. "Gendering Justice in Humanitarian Spaces: Opportunity and (Dis)empowerment through Gender-Based Legal De-

velopment Outreach in the Eastern Democratic Republic of Congo." *Law & Society Review* 50 (3): 539–74.
Levitt, P., and S. Merry. 2009. "Vernacularization on the Ground: Local Uses of Global Women's Rights in Peru, China, India and the United States." *Global Networks* 9 (4): 441–61.
Loken, M., M. Lake, and K. Cronin-Furman. 2018. "Deploying Justice: Strategic Accountability for Wartime Sexual Violence." *International Studies Quarterly* 62 (4): 751–64.
Meger, S. 2016. "The Fetishization of Sexual Violence in International Security." *International Studies Quarterly* 60 (1): 149–59.
Merry, S. E. 2006. "Transnational Human Rights and Local Activism: Mapping the Middle." *American Anthropologist* 108 (1): 38–51.
———. 2009. *Human Rights and Gender Violence: Translating International Law into Local Justice*. Chicago: University of Chicago Press.
Mertens, C., and M. Pardy. 2017. "'Sexurity' and Its Effects in Eastern Democratic Republic of Congo." *Third World Quarterly* 38 (4): 956–79.
Pascucci, E. 2019. "The Local Labour Building the International Community: Precarious Work within Humanitarian Spaces." *Environment and Planning A: Economy and Space* 51 (3): 743–60.
Schulz, P. 2018. "The 'Ethical Loneliness' of Male Sexual Violence Survivors in Northern Uganda: Gendered Reflections on Silencing." *International Feminist Journal of Politics* 20 (4): 583–601.
———. 2019. "'To Me, Justice Means to Be in a Group': Survivors' Groups as a Pathway to Justice in Northern Uganda." *Journal of Human Rights Practice* 11 (1): 171–89.
Sesay, M. 2019. "Hijacking the Rule of Law in Postconflict Environments." *European Journal of International Security* 4 (1): 41–60.
Shepherd, L. J. 2016. "Making War Safe for Women? National Action Plans and the Militarisation of the Women, Peace and Security Agenda." *International Political Science Review* 37 (3): 324–35.
Shuayb, M. 2022. "Localisation Only Pays Lip Service to Fixing Aid's Colonial Legacy." *New Humanitarian*, February 8. https://www.thenewhumanitarian.org/opinion/2022/2/8/Localisation-lip-service-fixing-aid-colonial-legacy.
St. Germain, T., and S. Dewey. 2013. "Justice on Whose Terms? A Critique of International Criminal Justice Responses to Conflict-Related Sexual Violence." *Women's Studies International Forum* 37: 36–45.
Taylor, D. 2018. "Humiliation as a Harm of Sexual Violence: Feminist versus Neoliberal Perspectives." *Hypatia* 33 (3): 434–50.
Taylor, W. K. 2018. "Ambivalent Legal Mobilization: Perceptions of Justice and the Use of the Tutela in Colombia." *Law & Society Review* 52 (2): 337–67.
Theidon, K. 2007. "Gender in Transition: Common Sense, Women, and War." *Journal of Human Rights* 6 (4): 453–78.
Tronc, E., R. Grace, and A. Nahikian. 2019. *Realities and Myths of the "Triple Nexus": Local Perspectives on Peacebuilding, Development, and Humanitarian Action in Mali*. Humanitarian Action at the Frontlines: Field Analysis Series. Cambridge, MA: Harvard Humanitarian Initiative's Advanced Training Program on Humanitarian Action.

True, J. 2015. "A Tale of Two Feminisms in International Relations? Feminist Political Economy and the Women, Peace and Security Agenda." *Politics & Gender* 11 (2): 419–24.

Tsing, A. L. 2004. *Friction*. Princeton, NJ: Princeton University Press.

UN Security Council. 2000. Resolution 1325, Women and Peace and Security, S/RES/1325, October 31, 2000.

———. 2009. Resolution 1888, Women and Peace and Security, S/RES/1888, September 30, 2009.

———. 2013a. Resolution 2106, Women and Peace and Security, S/RES/2106, June 24, 2013.

———. 2013b. Resolution 2122, Women and Peace and Security, S/RES/2122, October 18, 2013.

———. 2015. Resolution 2242, Women and Peace and Security, S/RES2242, October 13, 2015.

———. 2019. Resolution 2467, Women and Peace and Security, S/RES 2467, April 23, 2019.

Afterword

From Extraction to Equity? Pathways to Better Practice

ALLEN KICONCO, ANNIE BUNTING, AND JOEL QUIRK

This project has been kicking around in one form or another for over a decade. Its origins can be traced back at least as far as 2012, when an application was made to fund a new project specifically focusing on research methods, conflict, and gender-based violence in Africa. This initial application was not successful. Some of its core ideas were later repackaged and became the foundation for a conference in Johannesburg in 2018. That conference in turn paved the way for this collection. While 2012 really was not that long ago, the political and intellectual environment which we inhabit today looks quite different from that of the not-too-distant past in a number of key respects. In this afterword, we briefly reflect on how and why conversations about research methods, knowledge economies, and gender-based violence and conflict in Africa have changed over the last decade, and where things might go from here. Our main goal is to contribute to larger conversations regarding better practices when it comes to fieldwork and knowledge production.

One entry point for thinking about the scale and effects of recent changes is through social media hashtags. The past decade will be at least partly defined in terms of #BlackLivesMatter, #RhodesMustFall, #MeToo, and #Whiteness. These and other similar hashtags have drawn attention to (1) the intersecting and institutionalized effects of racism and sexism, and (2) the systemic abuses and legacies of European imperialism and colonialism. It has become increasingly clear, moreover, that the elevated profile of these foundational issues has also generated a far-reaching political backlash (#MakeAmericaGreatAgain, #NotAllMen, #CriticalRaceTheory, #AllLivesMatter) from a range of individuals and institutions seeking to defend the previous status quo. This ongoing contestation has brought further urgency and intensity to issues highlighted in this collection. Questions about how knowledge gets generated, validated, and disseminated become increasingly important when the basic building blocks of history and society are heavily contested.

Scholars and researchers working on the history and politics of the African continent have primarily encountered these topics through the rubric of decolonization, a concept that has come to be applied—both sincerely and opportunistically—to a range of projects. Decolonization is here understood as an umbrella term that aligns with (but is not necessarily synonymous with) related concepts such as decoloniality and abolition (see Kaba 2021; Ndlovu-Gatsheni 2015). From this vantage point, decolonization has provided a framework for, first, synthesizing and analyzing preexisting bodies of work and, second, helping to both inform and inspire more-recent and ongoing endeavors. Previous efforts to grapple with Eurocentric models have attracted much greater interest and investment over the course of the last decade, especially in relation to twentieth-century responses to colonization and racism (e.g., Wilder 2015; Morris 2015). Earlier works on anticolonial struggles have also reached new audiences owing to the proliferation of decolonial reading lists and other pedagogical initiatives (e.g., DIA 2022; connectedsociologies .org). As part of this process, Eurocentric lists of "great thinkers" have been contested, and alternative figures, such as Audre Lorde and Frantz Fanon, have been widely endorsed as foundational starting points. Once this longer intellectual pedigree is recognized, more-recent work on decolonization chiefly appears as an extension and refinement of already well-established themes, rather than an entirely new phenomenon.

Yet there is also a further case to be made that more-recent developments have altered the terms of engagement in important ways (Moosavi 2020). The issues involved may not be new, but their political profile and intellectual valence have substantially changed over the course of the last decade. Numerous aspects of academic and intellectual practice have been critically scrutinized as part of this now far-reaching transformation. Decolonial theories and approaches (e.g., Connell 2007; Lugones 2010) have been paired with more focused case studies of specific practices relating to disciplinary conventions and canons, teaching and pedagogy, hiring practices and hierarchies, publishing and gatekeeping, and institutional histories, complicities, and mythologies (e.g., Ahmed 2012; Bhambra, Gebrial, and Nişancioğlu 2018; Bendix, Müller, and Ziai 2020). Research and practice relating to gender-based violence and conflict is no exception to these larger trends, as the contributors to this volume have demonstrated.

Epistemic questions regarding knowledge production, silencing, and consumption have been central to larger conversations regarding decolonization.

Both research methods and fieldwork acquire new dimensions and importance when considered through this lens. When this project was first conceived, in 2012, research methods were widely—but by no means universally (see Smith 2012; Kara 2020)—viewed as a technical and procedural challenge. This approach can be at least partly traced back to positivist models of social science, which unsuccessfully aspire to avoid explicit normative commitments. It can also be attributed to less theoretically informed and nonreflexive understandings of methods and fieldwork as a series of usually well-trodden procedural formulas, such as securing approvals and permissions, creating the sampling frame, collating data, and so on. From this technical standpoint, research methods and fieldwork appear as topics that are clearly integral to the larger research process, but do not necessarily appear as all that interesting in their own right, especially for nonspecialist audiences. This approach is epitomized by the much maligned (yet still necessary) approach favored by institutional review boards, in which being "ethical" is chiefly understood in terms of securing approval and following agreed-upon rules and protocols based upon a "do no harm" standard. Once bureaucratic certification has been secured, the "real action" can begin, and ethical considerations fade into the background.

This technical understanding of research methods has been heavily scrutinized over the last decade, building in part on earlier Black feminist thought (e.g., hooks 1984, 1990) and critical race scholars (e.g., Crenshaw 1989; Delgado and Stefancic 2001). Taking steps to avoid harming research participants is undoubtedly an important goal, but there is now much greater recognition that it should be understood as a minimal threshold. Ethical reflection and conduct cannot be conflated with bureaucratic certification, especially when concerns about legal liability become the main arbiter for institutional approval. It is also clear that challenging questions relating to epistemology, pedagogy, and positionality have become much more prominent. Once these different considerations are put together, research methods and fieldwork appear inescapably political, since technical procedures and proficiencies cannot be detached from larger power relations and the effects of positionality. Thus, the current environment is one where research methods and fieldwork (1) have acquired much greater visibility, (2) are more closely scrutinized, and (3) are increasingly being held up against more demanding and holistic standards. Much more is expected—yet not necessarily required—of researchers doing fieldwork now than of those working in the not-too-distant past. These developments have been felt in many parts of the globe, but their effects have been especially pronounced for researchers who study different aspects of the African continent and its peoples. Researchers and activists in or from South Africa have played a particularly important role within this larger transformation (e.g., Mupotsa 2019; Nyamnjoh 2016), and there has been a broader groundswell among African scholars, students, and researchers attempting to hold their European counterparts much more accountable, despite frequently occupying comparatively junior and/or precarious positions. There is a strong case to be made that the primary impetus for change has actually come from student activism via disruptive confrontation, rather than from academics (Maldonado-Torres 2016).

Decolonization does not mean entirely dismissing or never engaging with European actors or knowledge economies, but it does mean that the terms of engagement have to change, with equity serving as a core benchmark. European epistemologies cannot be used as a compass to measure the value of indigenous forms of knowledge and the methods used to produce it. In this context, the case for decolonization can be roughly divided into two main dimensions. The first dimension takes the form of compelling critiques of Eurocentric narratives, assumptions, beneficiaries, and knowledge practices. These critiques have strong theoretical roots and feature sustained engagement with questions of gender and sexuality (e.g., Tamale 2020; Vergès 2021). While different theorists favor different approaches, they collectively point to a shared conclusion: our understanding of the world in which we live has been grossly distorted by Eurocentric models and interests. There is still more to be done to better understand these dynamics, but the broad contours of these decolonial critiques are both powerful and inescapable. The higher education sector has been similarly exposed when subject to scrutiny (e.g., Smith 2012; Tuck and Yang 2012; Madhok 2022). It should come as no surprise, therefore, that there have been continual calls for decolonizing academic practices in recent times (e.g., Branch 2018; O'Halloran 2016). Decolonial critiques now have numerous supporters and endorsers, although the depth of this support still remains an open question.

The harder and increasingly more urgent question is what needs to be done in response to decolonial critiques. This is the second dimension: What should decolonial alternatives look like, and what kinds of steps are required to bring about decolonization in practical terms? Numerous people who agree with the broad contours of the decolonial critique routinely find themselves in opposite corners when it comes to the question of decolonial alternatives. This conversation was never going to be straightforward, since the scale of the challenges are such that even people with the best intentions are going to disagree regarding the best available approaches (see, e.g., Táíwò, Against Decolonisation, 2022). However, it is also a conversation that is further complicated by questions of positionality and politics. The participation of White academics and researchers within decolonial projects is always going to be controversial and contested, for very good reason (wa Ngũgĩ 2021; Phadi and Pakade 2016), so conversations about decolonial alternatives are necessarily complicated by prior questions about identity, solidarity, and fragility/fear (e.g., Matthews 2021; Ahmed 2004). This challenge has been further exacerbated by growing anxieties regarding co-optation and dilution. For a growing number of critics the radical promise and potential of decolonization has already been "mainstreamed" and captured (e.g., Táíwò, Elite Capture, 2022; Doharty, Madriaga, and Joseph-Salisbury 2021; Persard 2021). Higher education institutions have been quick to embrace the language of decolonization, but it is not clear this rhetoric has done much in practice. There remains a fundamental disconnect between the cumulative harms associated with colonialism and the very qualified steps taken in support of decolonization.

Some of the key issues at stake here were usefully captured in a widely circulated tweet by Canadian writer Jes Battis (2022) in February 2022, which reads as follows:

> Academia: how do we decolonize?
> Everyone: give the land back
> Academia: *creates Dean of Decolonization*

This reference to land is crucial. It helps to underscore the material dimensions of the systems of theft and dispossession that were foundational to settler colonialism. Any remedy to a material loss on this scale will not prove effective without providing material restitution, yet the response of the academy—and of many other institutions—has been to shift the terrain toward the symbolic, individual, and intellectual. Decolonization without material and structural transformation will not be true decolonization, yet there remains a widespread tendency to shy away from this key point, and instead reposition decolonization on comparatively safer—yet still contested and controversial—symbolic and intellectual grounds.

The newly appointed Dean of Decolonization is the punchline to the tweet. In the place of a genuine commitment we instead find a superficial exercise in bandwagoning and branding. And with this bait and switch the radical potential of decolonization gets deflected and diluted. There is no doubt that versions of this scenario have played out on many occasions over the last decade. However, this critique does not (and should not be expected to) sufficiently capture the constraints involved. University administrators have a mandate to both create and support decolonization initiatives as part of the academic project. They do not have a mandate to return stolen land, especially when nearly all the stolen land is owned by other people. It would take an extraordinarily brave university administrator to propose returning the land upon which the university stands, and anyone making such a proposal would undoubtedly be fiercely resisted by peers, alumni, donors, and others. Not returning land is the deeply entrenched default.

All actually existing forms of decolonization fall radically short of what is required from an ethical standpoint. This frequently makes them hard to evaluate. Some people declare their support for decolonization and then undercut its implementation. Others support decolonization yet end up favoring reforms over revolution for strategic reasons, calculating that smaller yet more immediate gains are all that can be secured right now. There are going to be occasions when it is hard to distinguish between these two different scenarios. Measures that fall short of a radical and materially oriented transformation will always be insufficient, yet the vast majority of supporters of and sympathizers with decolonial alternatives continue to concentrate their energies upon much smaller and more focused goals, which are usually framed as contributions to the eventual advancement of a more ambitious and longer-term agenda.

The vast majority of academics and researchers are not high-level administrators. They do not have a significant voice in institutional policies, but instead have much more specific responsibilities and obligations relating to teaching, research, and administration. It is also important to recognize, moreover, that this group comprises a huge number of people who do not have full-time, continual work but are hired on temporary consultancies and precarious contracts. As A. Afonso (2013) has argued, academic job markets are "structured in many respects like a drug gang, with an expanding mass of outsiders and a shrinking core of insiders." The outsiders—the majority—are highly skilled yet remain precarious, and they "forgo wages and employment security" in the hope of eventually securing a coveted insider position (Afonso 2013).

This observation is unlikely to come as a revelation to anyone reading this book, but it is nonetheless worth emphasizing here because it plays a crucial role in defining the context within which individual researchers and academics encounter decolonial approaches. It may be hard for individuals to bring about macrolevel changes in institutional policies, but they can—and should—attempt to apply decolonial arguments and insights to their day-to-day responsibilities. There is no settled consensus regarding exactly what this should look like, but a number of pathways have been developed over many years. They include the following:

- Reading, integrating, and applying the now-substantial theoretical literature on decolonial approaches and other related literatures from different time periods (e.g., Wynter 2003; Quijano 2007; Mignolo 2011).

- Interrogating existing bodies of historical knowledge using decolonial approaches, such as reading against the grain for subaltern silencing, white supremacy, and patriarchal privilege. This includes critically interrogating Eurocentric discourses and representations (e.g., Said 1978; Mudimbe 1988; Dabashi 2015).
- Reversing long-standing tendencies to prioritize the histories and experiences of European peoples while neglecting peoples in or from Africa and other parts of the globe (e.g., Abu-Lughod 1989; Frank 1998; Obeng-Odoom 2019).
- Making explicit the effects of both individual and institutional positionality with a view to decenter Whiteness and elevate subaltern voices (e.g., Hernandez 2019; Keane, Khupe, and Muza 2016). This includes doing so for the history and self-presentation of higher education institutions (e.g., Tabensky and Mathews 2015; Jansen 2019).
- Redressing severe and long-standing imbalances within knowledge economics associated with academic publishing and appeals to authority (e.g., Noda 2020; Medie and Kang 2018). This includes the politics of citation (e.g., Ahmed 2017).
- Reconfiguring course curricula and teaching models to decenter Eurocentric voices, perspectives, and classifications, thereby creating and holding space for non-European alternatives (e.g., Peters 2015; Arday, Belluigi, and Thomas 2021). This means recognizing that both the terms "non-European" and "Global South" also come with problems of their own, since they can superficially aggregate diverse perspectives and local contexts (Collyer et al. 2019; Moosavi 2020).
- Disrupting established hierarchies within teaching and learning, recognizing that crucial expertise and experience reside outside formal authority structures (Freire 2000; Darder, Baltodano, and Torres 2009).
- Rethinking established models of instruction and assessment, recognizing that they tend to reinscribe Eurocentric and patriarchal narratives, conventions, and priorities (e.g., hooks 1994; Paraskeva 2016; Godsell 2021).
- Recognizing and resisting the still-hegemonic position of English and other European languages within the academy and other elite spaces, including strengthening pathways for publication and communication in languages favored by people with an immediate stake in the topics under deliberation (Thiong'o 1986; Macedo, Dendrinos, and Gounari 2003).

- Destabilizing the authoritative status that tends to be assigned to official documents and written sources, thereby creating greater space for other models of knowledge and experience, such as oral histories, storytelling, music, and other artistic projects (e.g., Chilisa 2012, 128–57; Nyamnjoh 2012).

- Making genuine efforts to diversify the academy, especially in relation to hiring, promotion, and retention (e.g., Stewart and Valian 2018; Laursen and Austin 2020). This includes recognizing and responding to different kinds of lived experience within the academy (e.g., Khunou et al. 2019).

- Working in solidarity to support—without appropriating—the concerns of other members of the university community, such as students, marginalized communities, and/or precarious workers.

This list is incomplete. There are many other points that could be added, especially once larger political struggles (see, e.g., Davis et al. 2022; Walia 2013) and further consultative/procedural challenges associated with how priorities and positions get determined (see, e.g., Zavala 2013) enter into the equation. Academics have long been criticized for standing too far apart from practical politics and struggles, and decolonization as an academic project is similarly vulnerable to this kind of critique. As R. N. Pailey (2019) argues: "The problem with this 21st-century 'scholarly decolonial turn' is that it remains largely detached from the day-to-day dilemmas of people in formerly colonised spaces and places. Many academics mistakenly maintain that by screaming 'decolonise X' or 'decolonise Y' ad nauseam, they will miraculously metamorphose into progressive agents of change." There is undoubtedly an argument to be made here, although it does not necessarily apply to all academic projects equally. Some engage more directly with political struggles than others.

Three core themes come into focus once all these proposals and pathways are placed alongside each other: (1) decolonial alternatives have now been developed with a high degree of granular detail on many different fronts within the academy, (2) this collectively amounts to a radical and holistic overhaul of academic practices and associated knowledge economies, and (3) decolonization within the academy could still be tied more directly to larger political struggles and agendas. These examples also confirm that there is much more going on than decolonial critique. Decolonial alternatives already exist for virtually every aspect of academic practice.

There is one further arena that also needs to be incorporated into this equation: decolonizing fieldwork (see also Marchais, Bazuzi, and Lameke 2020; Dunia et al. 2019; Brigden and Hallett 2021). On this front, the following pathways need to be added to the previous list:

- Materially/meaningfully compensating participants/communities who provide time, expertise, experience, and information via fieldwork (this ethical obligation may not extend to people on high salaries and private health plans).
- Paying a decent wage for the expertise of research brokers and other fieldwork assistants, rather than leveraging labor market dynamics to drive down their wages and conditions.
- Sufficiently recognizing and making visible the contribution and expertise of local research collaborators/partners within published outputs and at other activities.
- Trying to develop pathways that enable local research collaborators/partners to also advance their own careers over time, rather than remaining within the same kinds of positions.
- Ensuring that communities with a direct stake in the research being conducted have a clear voice in shaping the design and ultimate goals of the research and associated fieldwork, thereby trying to ensure that the research aligns with their interests, experiences, and perspectives. This includes (but is not necessarily limited to) models of participatory action research.
- Ensuring that communities with a direct stake in the fieldwork are properly updated on its outcomes and therefore have an opportunity to learn/benefit from its findings. This includes making a sustained effort to make academic knowledge more accessible.
- Deliberately deciding not to undertake fieldwork in contexts where asking highly sensitive questions is likely to (re)traumatize research participants while only really benefiting the professional careers of the researchers asking the questions. One common example of this dynamic involves conducting yet another interview with victims/survivors of extreme trauma who have already been interviewed countless times.
- Destabilizing long-standing hierarchies that enable Northern academics and theorists to maintain their control of the "big picture" while reducing locals to "data collectors."
- Recognizing and responding to the complexities associated with differential experiences of safety, access, and "risk" within insecure environments.
- Recognizing the challenges associated with "giving voice to the voiceless," and thereby too comfortably assuming the role of speaking for communities and individuals who are capable of speaking for themselves (if they were actually asked to do so).

- Working in solidarity to support—without appropriating—the concerns of individuals and communities that shared their experience and expertise through fieldwork.

These points can be applied to many forms of fieldwork, but further layers also come into focus once questions relating to gender-based violence take center stage. This starts with the now well-documented risks associated with the retraumatization of survivors, the political complications associated with simplistic and misleading representations of wartime sexual violence in Africa, and the silences surrounding certain forms of gender-based violence, such as sexual violence against men and violence perpetrated by state officials. Decolonizing fieldwork on gender-based violence in Africa requires all these points and more.

Many of the points that feature on this second list also need to be paired with other points from both lists, and thereby understood in holistic terms (see, e.g., Darder 2019). There are hazards associated with compartmentalization (Patel 2015, 68–71). Mixed methods and integrated approaches are required in numerous contexts (Botha 2011). It is clear, for example, that dynamics relating to both theory and positionality have major ramifications for the design and implementation of fieldwork. Educational systems and pedagogical models both constrain and enable future research. Decolonial theories and critiques have major ramifications for how research gets set up and the kinds of questions it seeks to answer. The forms of language used to communicate research findings are crucial to their accessibility.

These connections between different aspects of the larger whole present a number of challenges and conundrums. In this context, we briefly highlight two different kinds of response: (1) ethical reflexivity and (2) de facto decoupling. These are not discrete alternatives, but can sometimes be found together (i.e., reflexivity can be applied to selected aspects of the larger whole). Ethical reflexivity involves efforts to develop a core of principles and orientations that establish a foundation for integrated action across multiple domains. Recent examples of this approach include love and care (Krystalli and Schulz 2022), *ubuntu* (Seehawer 2018), solidarity (Gaztambide-Fernández 2012), and more-established work on feminist praxis and positionality (Makana 2018; Whittingdale 2021). These approaches are not the same, but they broadly share a common set of concerns around ethical reflexivity, responsibility, and the bonds of community.

Reflexivity demands the recognition and interrogation of the multiple ways in which individuals and communities are embedded within hierarchies, histories, and power relations. These hierarchies cannot be avoided or (at least currently) transcended, but they can and should be interrogated and mitigated. This means different things for different kinds of people. Reflexivity can be best understood as a first step. Decolonizing fieldwork requires a synthesis of both ethical reflexivity and ethical responsibility, with the former informing how the latter should be applied when it comes to research and fieldwork design, research respondents and their communities, research assistants/partners, outputs, and so on. Ethical responsibilities do not end with research, but extend to the practical application and dissemination of knowledge. As David Ngira (2022) of the Rift Valley Institute argues, "To advance humanity rather than just advance knowledge itself, the decolonization project needs to become expansive and transcend boundaries so that knowledge is more accessible and dynamic." Reflexivity is also a precondition of dynamism. Ideas about ethical responsibilities can become inflexible scripts as time passes. The pathways identified above are undoubtedly useful when it comes to mitigating extractive logics, but they do not represent the final word on any topic. There must always be space for further recalibration.

Reflexivity is also integral to interpersonal relationships and bonds of community. Ideas about care, solidarity, ubuntu, and sisterhood are all predicated upon the ethical value of community, which can in turn be tied to a framework of shared cause and common purpose that has the potential to at least partially bring people together. Many researchers position their work as contributing to the advancement of larger normative goals, such as gender justice, institutional change, and more effective remedies for harm, which are broadly held in common with many of their local interlocutors. These shared goals can help to foster bonds of community, solidarity, and common purpose (although this gets much more complicated for ethnographies of violent perpetrators, among other populations). Hierarchies will always exist within communities, so there will always be a risk that appeals to a common cause become a mask for power relations, but this does not negate their ethical and interpersonal importance.

There is no doubt that reflexivity can play an important role within decolonization. It is also important to recognize, however, that not all applications of reflexivity amount to decolonization. Many forms of intimate labor also require reflexivity, yet these labors tend to be more likely to reinforce hierarchies than to challenge them (Boris and Parreñas 2010). Much the same logic applies to efforts to make knowledge more accessible. Some efforts will contribute to decolonization. Others will not. It depends on the kind of knowledge that is involved. Not all efforts to improve academic practice amount to decolonization, yet it can still be tempting (and politically advantageous) to include many things under a decolonial rubric (Tuck and Yang 2012).

This discussion helps to bring into focus a further challenge. Decolonial alternatives have continued to expand and deepen, but the number of people actually committed to doing the practical work of decolonization has not necessarily kept up with the pace of change. This contributes to a mismatch between decolonial ambitions and available resources. As we have seen above, decolonial alternatives are now well developed when it comes to theory, history, geography, positionality, pedagogy, publications, diversity in the academy, curriculum, language, archives, fieldwork, and accessibility. Universities rely on committed individuals to drive this agenda forward, but they consistently fail to provide the resources and support required to take action on multiple fronts.

This lack of resources contributes to an environment where there is a strong tendency to informally pick and choose, which we here characterize as de facto decoupling. Not all aspects of decolonization have been taken up to the same extent or in the same ways. There has been a pronounced emphasis on theory, which has increasingly taken the form of a highly specialized literature that can be hard for nonexperts to engage with. The practical application of decolonial theories is a challenge that is more often alluded to than taken up with sustained intensity. Making knowledge accessible outside the academy is not always a priority. It is much easier to alter course reading lists than to radically overhaul pedagogical practices. Innovations regarding curriculum and pedagogy tend to be concentrated in advanced classes, which get selected as optional courses by already invested students, rather than in compulsory first-year survey courses (which established academics generally try their best to avoid). Some "radical" theorists can quickly become conservatives whenever their privileges are challenged, such as when their underpaid graduate assistants and adjuncts strike for better working conditions. Decolonial alternatives that look holistic and radical on paper routinely end up being unevenly and episodically implemented in practice. More energy has been channeled into some pathways than others.

It is important not to take this line of critique too far. The main problem is not that some decolonial alternatives have been taken up to a greater extent than others. It is instead the sheer volume of expectations and obligations academics are now expected to attend to. When you do not have sufficient time or resources to discharge your responsibilities it becomes necessary to pick and choose. As Leon Moosavi observes (2020, 343), "The neoliberalisation of academia makes intellectual decolonisation almost impossible within universities. In such corporatised climates, academics are overburdened with a heavy workload which demands efficiency, impact and productivity against a backdrop which is characterised by excessive competitiveness, individualism, metrics and precarity." This is probably the single most important variable when it comes to implementing decolonial alternatives within the academy in our current moment. Too many academics are already drowning under the weight of unreasonable expectations and labor market competition. This starts with "publish or perish," but also extends to endless administrative procedures and heightened expectations from students (who wonder what they are paying for). Survey data confirms academics consistently overwork in response to unmanageable workloads and therefore struggle with mental health, relationships, and parenting (Williams 2022). The labor market bifurcation of "insiders" and "outsiders" (Afonso's analogy with a "drug gang") is also hugely consequential here, because it ends up supercharging competition among academic peers, with nonpermanent or nontenured staff being compelled to make ever-increasing sacrifices in an effort to eventually secure a privileged position on the "inside."

It can be hard to build bonds of community and solidarity under these kinds of conditions, since academics routinely end up in fierce competition with each other, with individual "market worth" being calculated against technocratic criteria. Decolonial pathways are not built for speed or efficiency, but instead require forms of careful and time-consuming labor that can frequently appear as a poor return on investment. Efforts have been made to resist the "isolating psychic and physical toll" (Mountz et al. 2015, 1237) associated with these dynamics, such as the feminist project of "slow scholarship," yet these initiatives remain extraordinarily difficult to implement at scale. It is very hard to apply the principles of slow scholarship if you do not have a permanent academic position. Burdens get placed upon individual academics, rather than being held collectively and institutionally.

This is the context within which academics encounter decolonial alternatives: decolonization effectively becomes yet one more thing individual academics have to grapple with (although academics in the Global South tend to have taken up this challenge much earlier than most of their Northern counterparts). Some academics are eager to take up the challenge since it aligns with their lived experiences and political convictions. Many academics are hesitant to take the plunge, yet they nonetheless feel obliged to take at least some steps and adjustments. In both cases decolonization is typically positioned as an additional set of expectations that gets stacked on top of their existing obligations: the metaphorical icing on the cake that can be added (or not) at the end once the cake has been completed, rather than one of the core ingredients required to make a cake in the first place. It is clear, for example, that decolonizing pedagogy is unlikely to be viewed as an acceptable substitute for publications. The publications come first. Few adjustments have been made to accommodate new expectations regarding decolonization, resulting in a situation where academics are faced with a hugely ambitious and holistic agenda, yet they do not necessarily get any respite from their existing obligations to help with its practical implementation.

This is where the rubber hits the road when it comes to decolonial alternatives. The holistic version of decolonization requires a range of things of academics that they cannot realistically implement alongside their already existing obligations, so they instead end up picking and choosing—and thereby at least partially decoupling—selected aspects of the larger whole. This is one of the major reasons why so much energy has been concentrated upon theory. Academics are usually already comfortable and conversant with theory, so it can be more easily assimilated into their existing work without radically increasing their workloads. There are also further incentives associated with labor market dynamics that assign greater weight to theoretical labor relative to other kinds of labor.

Decolonizing fieldwork and its associated knowledge economies requires a different set of orientations and responsibilities that are more likely to take many academics out of their comfort zones. Decolonizing fieldwork means finding additional material resources to ensure that respondents and assistants are properly compensated for their time and expertise. It means having difficult conversations with local communities/individuals regarding the design and implementation of research projects. It means ensuring that collaborators are properly acknowledged and respected. It means allocating additional time and work to ensure that the knowledge which gets produced ends up being accessible and relevant to communities where the research was conducted. It may even mean deciding not to conduct fieldwork at all. These are not the kinds of responsibilities that can be easily discharged, but instead require a long-term commitment to a different model of fieldwork and knowledge production.

Responsibility can also be understood in a number of different ways. One of the most significant impediments to structural transformation has been the degree to which responsibility for decolonization has been passed down to self-selecting individuals, rather than being treated as a collective responsibility. To make sense of these dynamics, we briefly draw upon the work of Wendy Brown, who has argued that neoliberalism has been marked by a combination of devolution and "responsibilization." Devolution (discussed further below) involves large-scale problems being "sent down the pipeline to small and weak units unable to cope with them," while responsibilization involves the "moral burdening" of "the individual as the only relevant and wholly accountable actor" (Brown 2015, 238, 240). Brown's argument is chiefly concerned with market logics, but it can also be extended to challenges and dilemmas associated with the implementation of decolonial alternatives. It is here, we would argue, that the uptake of decolonial approaches has also been marked by the "moral burdening" of individual academics, wherein the relative success or failure of decolonial pathways ends up being tacitly regarded as a question of individual investment, individual commitment, and individual ethical responsibility. Primary responsibility for the practical implementation of decolonial pathways tends to be informally delegated to self-selecting individuals on a discretionary basis.

This model of individual responsibility comes with any number of problems. As Brown (2015, 243) observes, "Responsibilized individuals are required to provide for themselves in the context of powers and contingencies radically limiting their ability to do so." Some academics have been able to "provide for themselves" despite these constraints, but doing so tends to require extraordinary efforts that go above and beyond. It is still possible to make some progress under this model, but it is unlikely to result in deep and lasting change because too much of the responsibility for developing decolonial pathways falls upon self-selecting individuals who take up the cause of decolonization alongside all their other existing obligations. Framing decolonization as an individual responsibility can also have the further effect of rendering individuals morally culpable when progress ends up falling short of expectations. The tacit assumption is that progress—or the lack thereof—can be traced back to relative levels of commitment: limited progress becomes a symptom of a lack of individual investment, rather than an effect of underlying structures. This approach does not necessarily present a challenge to the logics and interests of the neoliberal university.

As we observed above, much more is being expected—*yet not necessarily required*—of researchers doing fieldwork now than those in the not-too-distant past. Expectation is not the same as binding obligation. Individuals who operate according to extractive logics when conducting fieldwork are still unlikely to be penalized for using established conventions to their advantage as long as they adhere to minimal standards for conduct (i.e., they secure ethics approval and follow procedures). Individuals who want to do more than the minimum make a conscious choice to hold themselves to higher standards, but they are not really compelled to do so. Academics usually retain a tremendous amount of discretion over how much and in what ways they engage with decolonial pathways, especially as far as fieldwork and its knowledge economies are concerned. Academics who default to extractive models may enjoy competitive advantages over their peers who aspire to more equitable approaches.

These underlying logics extend to partnerships and collaborations, which have also emerged as a major focal point for decolonial scrutiny in recent times. Partnerships have become increasingly important due to the emergence of substantial funding streams that prioritize multiyear collaborations between individuals and institutions from multiple countries and from multiple backgrounds. Other partnerships emerge more organically and idiosyncratically. The numerous problems associated with partnerships—paternalism, the power of the purse, top-down agenda setting, epistemic imperialism—have been cataloged at length, both within this collection and in many other recent publications (e.g., Kalinga 2019; Jayawardane 2019). The more relevant topic for our purposes is the recent proliferation of proposals designed to challenge extractive tendencies.

Numerous proposals, principles, and pathways have been developed over the last decade to the point that it has become necessary to "get beyond the partnership debate" (Shivakoti and Milner 2022). Only a brief snapshot can be offered here. For C. Vogel and J. Musamba (2022, 8), collaborative worldmaking implicates "all stages of knowledge production including planning, data collection, analysis, translation (both conceptually and in bare linguistic terms) and writing." Toby Green (2019, 280) argues that "European and British funding streams can become directed at ends which seem divergent from their original intentions . . . which can help take baby steps towards a rebalancing of the power dynamic between Northern and Southern institutions." The 2020 "Johannesburg Principles on Building Equitable and Effective Partnerships for Migration Research" (MLT) identifies ten distinct areas where action is required, including diversifying agenda setting, fostering multilingual approaches, offering transparency and clear communication, mitigating the effects of precarious work, challenging restrictive visa regimes, and ensuring that "the voices of migrants are central to all research activities." In 2022 researchers gathered in Cape Town for the Seventh World Conference on Research Integrity to finalize a draft statement on "the promotion of fairness, equity and diversity in research collaborations and contexts." This draft featured a series of ambitious aspirations relating to fair practice, inclusivity, mutual trust and respect, acknowledgment of power relations, and promotion of indigenous knowledge (Horn et al. 2022).

Two different approaches to less extractive partnerships and collaborations can be identified in these examples. The first two (collaborative worldmaking and funding streams) can be characterized as cases of small-scale subversion and innovation, where a concerted effort has been made to reconfigure specific knowledge economies along more equitable and collaborative lines. The last two cases (the "Johannesburg Principles" and World Conference on Research Integrity) feature a broad-based approach that seeks to establish principles that other researchers can then apply in their own work. Both approaches have undoubtedly helped to advance this conversation, but they are also symptomatic of the limitations of current alternatives.

This is where we return to Wendy Brown's analysis of devolution, which involves large-scale problems being "sent down the pipeline." Small-scale subversion involves close collaborators making a deliberate effort to try to do things very differently in specific contexts. This is typically a self-selecting endeavor, and it requires a sustained effort to rise above dominant logics and interests. There is no doubt that small-scale subversion is tremendously important, but it still represents the exception to the rule. The vast majority of collaborations continue to be far more extractive than equitable. Devolving responsibility for the development of decolonial pathways to "small-scale units" is not a recipe for lasting change. The broad-based approach to ethical principles has the advantage of operating on a much grander scale, but it once again has notable limitations when it comes to practical implementation. Principles help to create expectations, rather than obligations, and the challenge of actually applying these models once again ends up being devolved downwards to self-selecting volunteers who are already burdened by many obligations.

This overall analysis ultimately points toward the continued dominance of extractive knowledge economies. It takes tremendous effort to bring about even modest change, and it will always be tempting for individuals and institutions who occupy privileged positions within existing systems to fall back upon established ways of doing things simply because they require lower levels of commitment and investment. Extraction is easy. Equity is hard.

Knowledge economies and professional incentives create market dynamics that pull against the kinds of careful and time-consuming labor which decolonial alternatives require. It is also clear, moreover, that rhetorical commitments to equity and ethical values tend to fall away whenever dominant economic and political interests are directly challenged. The recent history of COVID-19 vaccines in Africa is sadly instructive in this regard. Despite the unprecedented scale of the COVID-19 pandemic, pharmaceutical companies were still able to successfully thwart efforts to make life-saving vaccines readily available to people on the African continent. In May 2022, Oxfam (2022) reported that only 11 percent of people in low-income countries had been vaccinated, while the equivalent figure for high-income countries was 73 percent. This stark disparity can be directly traced to a set of policy decisions that prioritized private profits over public health. There is no doubt that tremendously important work has been done to develop decolonial pathways in recent times, but there still remains a treacherous mountain to climb.

In this context, many efforts to develop decolonial pathways can be loosely analogized to "fair trade" schemes, which aspire to set up more equitable alternatives to dominant "free trade" models for commodities such as coffee and chocolate. Fair trade requires people to choose to support alternative models of production and consumption, but only a minority of people voluntarily respond to this call. Dominant economic models are not directly challenged by fair trade, and it is not clear that purchasing products is an especially effective vehicle for actually bringing about larger reforms (and at least some products claiming to be "fair" have proven to be anything but on closer inspection). "Fair" trade schemes have played an important role in helping to sharpen political critiques of economic models, but they also have not done much—if anything—to change how they function. Recent and ongoing efforts to develop decolonial pathways are frequently subject to the same kinds of structural limitations and political constraints. Self-selecting individuals and voluntary commitments will always be valuable but insufficient.

References

Abu-Lughod, J. L. 1989. *Before European Hegemony: The World System A.D. 1250–1350.* Oxford: Oxford University Press.

Afonso, A. 2013. "How Academia Resembles a Drug Gang." *Impact of Social Science* (blog), December 11. https://blogs.lse.ac.uk/impactofsocialsciences/2013/12/11/how-academia-resembles-a-drug-gang.

Ahmed, S. 2004. "Declarations of Whiteness: The Non-performativity of Anti-racism." *Borderlands* 3 (2). borderlands.net.

———. 2012. *On Being Included: Racism and Diversity in Institutional Life.* Durham, NC: Duke University Press.

———. 2017. *Living a Feminist Life.* Durham, NC: Duke University Press.

Arday, J., D. Z. Belluigi, and D. Thomas. 2021. "Attempting to Break the Chain: Reimaging Inclusive Pedagogy and Decolonising the Curriculum within the Academy." *Educational Philosophy and Theory* 53 (3): 298–313. https://doi.org/10.1080/00131857.2020.1773257.

Battis, Jes (@jesbattis). 2022. "Academia: How do we decolonize?" Twitter, February 16, 9:21 p.m. https://twitter.com/jesbattis/status/1494029064654311425.

Bendix, D., F. Müller, and A. Ziai, eds. 2020. *Beyond the Master's Tools: Decolonising Knowledge Orders, Research Methods and Teaching.* London: Rowman and Littlefield.

Bhambra, G. K., D. Gebrial, and K. Nişancioğlu, eds. 2018. *Decolonising the University.* London: Pluto Press.

Boris, E., and R. S. Parreñas, eds. 2010. *Intimate Labors: Cultures, Technologies, and the Politics of Care.* Stanford, CA: Stanford University Press.

Botha, L. 2011. "Mixing Methods as a Process towards Indigenous Methodologies." *International Journal of Social Research Methodology* 14 (4): 313–25. https://doi.org/10.1080/13645579.2010.516644.

Branch, A. 2018. "Decolonizing the African Studies Centre." *Cambridge Anthropology* 36 (2): 73–91.

Brigden, N., and M. Hallett. 2021. "Fieldwork as Social Transformation: Place, Time, and Power in a Violent Moment." *Geopolitics* 26 (1): 1–17. https://doi.org/10.1080/14650045.2020.1717068.

Brown, W. 2015. *Undoing the Demos: Neoliberalism's Stealth Revolution*. New York: Zone Books.

Chilisa, B. 2012. *Indigenous Research Methodologies*. London: SAGE.

Collyer, F., R. Connell, J. Maia, and R. Morrell. 2019. *Knowledge and Global Power: Making New Sciences in the South*. Johannesburg: Wits University Press.

Connell, R. 2007. *Southern Theory: The Global Dynamics of Knowledge in Social Science*. Cambridge: Polity.

Crenshaw, K. W. 1989. "Demarginalizing the Intersection of Race and Sex: A Black Feminist Critique of Antidiscrimination Doctrine, Feminist Theory and Antiracist Politics." *University of Chicago Legal Forum* 139 (1). https://scholarship.law.columbia.edu/faculty_scholarship/3007.

Dabashi, H. 2015. *Can Non-Europeans Think?* London: Zed Books.

Darder, A. 2019. "Decolonizing Interpretive Research." In *Decolonizing Interpretive Research: A Subaltern Methodology for Social Change*, edited by A. Darder, 3–36. London: Routledge.

Darder, A., M. P. Baltodano, and R. D. Torres. 2009. *The Critical Pedagogy Reader*. New York: Routledge.

Davis, A. Y., G. Dent, E. Meiners, and B. Richie. 2022. *Abolition. Feminism. Now.* London: Penguin Books.

Delgado, R., and J. Stefancic. 2001. *Critical Race Theory: An Introduction*. New York: New York University Press.

DIA (Democracy in Africa). 2022. "The Decolonizing the Academy Reading List (Updated)." Democracy in Africa, August 21. https://democracyinafrica.org/decolonizing_the_academy/.

Doharty, N., M. Madriaga, and R. Joseph-Salisbury. 2021. "The University Went to 'Decolonise' and All They Brought Back Was Lousy Diversity Double-Speak! Critical Race Counter-Stories from Faculty of Colour in 'Decolonial' Times." *Educational Philosophy and Theory* 53 (3): 233–44. https://doi.org/10.1080/00131857.2020.1769601.

Dunia, O. A., S. Bisimwa, E. Cirhuza, M. E. Baaz, J. Ferekani, P. Imili, E. Kambale et al. 2019. "Moving Out of the Backstage: How Can We Decolonize Research?" *Disorder of Things* (blog), October 22. https://thedisorderofthings.com/2019/10/22/moving-out-of-the-backstage-how-can-we-decolonize-research/.

Frank, A. G. 1998. *ReORIENT Global Economy in the Asian Age*. Berkeley: University of California Press.

Freire, P. 2000. *Pedagogy of the Oppressed*. London: Bloomsbury.

Gaztambide-Fernández, R. A. 2012. "Decolonization and the Pedagogy of Solidarity." *Decolonization: Indigeneity, Education & Society* 1 (1): 41–67.

Godsell, S. D. 2021. "Decolonisation of History Assessment: An Exploration." *South African Journal of Higher Education* 35 (6): 101–20. https://doi.org/10.20853/35-6-4339.

Green, T. 2019. "North-South Dynamics in Academia." *Journal of African Cultural Studies* 31 (3): 280–83. https://doi.org/10.1080/13696815.2019.1630263.

Hernandez, K. 2019. "Centering the Subaltern Voice." In *Decolonizing Interpretive Research: A Subaltern Methodology for Social Change*, edited by A. Darder, 39–50. London: Routledge.

hooks, b. 1984. *Feminist Theory: From Margin to Center*. Boston: South End Press.

——. 1990. *Ain't I a Woman*. Boston: South End Press.

——. 1994. *Teaching to Transgress: Education as the Practice of Freedom*. New York: Routledge.

Horn, L., S. Alba, F. Blom, M. Faure, E. Flack-Davison, G. Gopalakrishna, C. IJsselmuiden et al. 2022. "Fostering Research Integrity through the Promotion of Fairness, Equity and Diversity in Research Collaborations and Contexts: Towards a Cape Town Statement (Pre-conference Discussion Paper)." OSF Preprints, May 16. https://doi.org/10.31219/osf.io/bf286.

Jansen, J. 2019. *Decolonisation in Universities: The Politics of Knowledge*. Johannesburg: University of the Witwatersrand Press.

Jayawardane, M. N. 2019. "The Capacity-Building-Workshop-in-Africa Hokum." *Journal of African Cultural Studies* 31 (3): 276–80. https://doi.org/10.1080/13696815.2019.1630265.

Kaba, M. 2021. *We Do This 'Til We Free Us*. London: Haymarket.

Kalinga, C. 2019. "Caught between a Rock and a Hard Place: Navigating Global Research Partnerships in the Global South as an Indigenous Researcher." *Journal of African Cultural Studies* 31 (3): 270–72. https://doi.org/10.1080/13696815.2019.1630261.

Kara, H. 2020. "Decolonising Methods: A Reading List." HelenKara.com, July 19. https://helenkara.com/2020/07/29/decolonising-methods-a-reading-list/.

Keane, M., C. Khupe, and B. Muza. 2016. "It Matters Who You Are: Indigenous Knowledge Research and Researchers." *Education as Change* 20 (2): 145–62.

Khunou, G., E. Phaswana, K. Khoza-Shangase, and H. Canham, eds. 2019. *Black Academic Voices: The South African Experience*. Cape Town: HSRC Press.

Krystalli, R., and P. Schulz. 2022. "Taking Love and Care Seriously: An Emergent Research Agenda for Remaking Worlds in the Wake of Violence." *International Studies Review* 24 (1). https://doi.org/10.1093/isr/viac003.

Laursen, S., and A. E. Austin. 2020. *Building Gender Equity in the Academy: Institutional Strategies for Change*. Baltimore: Johns Hopkins University Press.

Lugones, M. 2010. "Toward a Decolonial Feminism." *Hypatia* 25 (4): 742–59. https://doi.org/10.1111/j.1527-2001.2010.01137.x.

Macedo, D. P., B. Dendrinos, and P. Gounari. 2003. *The Hegemony of English*. Boulder, CO: Paradigm Publishers.

Madhok, S. 2022. "Extractivism and the Coloniality of Knowledge Production." *Engenderings* (blog), February 21. https://blogs.lse.ac.uk/gender/2022/02/21/extractivism-and-the-coloniality-of-knowledge-production/.

Makana, S. 2018. "Contested Encounters: Toward a Twenty-First-Century African Feminist Ethnography." *Meridians* 17 (2): 361–75. https://doi.org/10.1215/15366936-7176516.

Maldonado-Torres, N. 2016. "Outline of Ten Theses on Coloniality and Decoloniality." Frantz Fanon Foundation. http://caribbeanstudiesassociation.org/docs/Maldonado-Torres_Outline_Ten_Theses-10.23.16.pdf.

Marchais, G., P. Bazuzi, and A. A. Lameke. 2020. "'The Data Is Gold, and We Are the Gold-Diggers': Whiteness, Race and Contemporary Academic Research in Eastern DRC." *Critical African Studies* 12 (3): 372–94. https://doi.org/10.1080/21681392.2020.1724806.

Matthews, S. 2021. "Decolonising While White: Confronting Race in a South African Classroom." *Teaching in Higher Education* 26 (7–8): 1113–21. https://doi.org/10.1080/13562517.2021.1914571.

Medie, P. A., and A. J. Kang. 2018. "Global South Scholars Are Missing from European and US Journals: What Can Be Done about It?" The Conversation, July 29. https://theconversation.com/global-south-scholars-are-missing-from-european-and-us-journals-what-can-be-done-about-it-99570.

Mignolo, W. 2011. *The Darker Side of Western Modernity: Global Futures, Decolonial Options*. Durham, NC: Duke University Press.

MLT (Migration Leadership Team). 2020. "Johannesburg Principles on Building Equitable and Effective Partnerships for Migration Research." London International Development Centre. http://www.migration.org.za/wp-content/uploads/2021/02/JHB-principles.pdf.

Moosavi, L. 2020. "The Decolonial Bandwagon and the Dangers of Intellectual Decolonization." *International Review of Sociology* 30 (2): 332–54. https://doi.org/10.1080/03906701.2020.1776919.

Morris, A. 2015. *The Scholar Denied: W. E. B. Du Bois and the Birth of Modern Sociology*. Berkeley: University of California Press.

Mountz, A., A. Bonds, B. Mansfield, J. Loyd, J. Hyndman, M. Walton-Roberts, R. Basu et al. 2015. "For Slow Scholarship: A Feminist Politics of Resistance through Collective Action in the Neoliberal University." *ACME: An International Journal for Critical Geographies* 14 (4): 1235–59. https://acme-journal.org/index.php/acme/article/view/1058.

Mudimbe, V. 1988. *The Invention of Africa: Gnosis, Philosophy, and the Order of Knowledge*. Bloomington: Indiana University Press.

Mupotsa, D. S. 2019. "Knowing from Loss." *Sociological Review* 68 (3): 524–39. https://doi.org/10.1177/0038026119892403.

Ndlovu-Gatsheni, S. J. 2015. "Decoloniality as the Future of Africa." *History Compass* 13:485–96. https://doi.org/10.1111/hic3.12264.

Ngira, D. O. 2022. "Decolonizing Knowledge in Africa: Reflections on the RVI Research Communities of Practice Project." Rift Valley Institute blog, February 3. https://riftvalley.net/news/decolonizing-knowledge-africa-reflections-rvi-research-communities-practice-project.

Noda, O. 2020. "Epistemic Hegemony: The Western Straitjacket and Post-colonial Scars in Academic Publishing." *Revista Brasileira de Política Internacional* 63 (1): 1–23. https://www.redalyc.org/journal/358/35862763010/html/.

Nyamnjoh, F. 2012. "'Potted Plants in Greenhouses': A Critical Reflection on the Resilience of Colonial Education in Africa." *Journal of Asian and African Studies* 47 (2): 129–54. https://doi.org/10.1177/0021909611417240.

———. 2016. *#RhodesMustFall: Nibbling at Resilient Colonialism in South Africa*. Bamenda: Langaa RPCIG. https://doi.org/10.2307/j.ctvmd84n8.

Obeng-Odoom, F. 2019. "The Intellectual Marginalisation of Africa." *African Identities* 17 (3–4): 211–24. https://doi.org/10.1080/14725843.2019.1667223.

O'Halloran, P. 2016. "The African University as a Site of Protest: Decolonisation, Praxis, and the Black Student Movement at the University Currently Known as Rhodes." *Interface* 8 (2): 184–210.

Oxfam. 2022. "Governments Falling Woefully Short on Goal to Vaccinate 70% in Each Country by September." Oxfam, May 12. https://www.oxfam.org/en/press-releases/governments-falling-woefully-short-goal-vaccinate-70-each-country-september.

Pailey, R. N. 2019. "How to Truly Decolonise the Study of Africa: 'Epistemic Decolonisation' Cannot Happen in a Political Vacuum, Separated from the African Streets." Al Jazeera, June 10. https://www.aljazeera.com/opinions/2019/6/10/how-to-truly-decolonise-the-study-of-africa.

Paraskeva, J. M. 2016. *Curriculum Epistemicide: Towards an Itinerant Curriculum Theory*. New York: Routledge.

Patel, L. 2015. *Decolonizing Educational Research: From Ownership to Answerability*. New York: Routledge.

Persard, S. C. 2021. "The Radical Limits of Decolonising Feminism." *Feminist Review* 128 (1): 13–27. https://doi.org/10.1177/01417789211015334.

Peters, M. A. 2015. "Why Is My Curriculum White?" *Educational Philosophy and Theory* 47 (7): 641–46. https://doi.org/10.1080/00131857.2015.1037227.

Phadi, M., and N. Pakade. 2016. "The Native Informant Speaks Back to the Offer of Friendship in White Academia." In *Ties That Bind: Race and the Politics of Friendship in South Africa*, edited by S. Walsh and J. Soske, 288–307. Johannesburg: Wits University Press.

Quijano, A. 2007. "Coloniality and Modernity/Rationality." *Cultural Studies* 21 (2–3): 168–78. https://doi.org/10.1080/09502380601164353.

Said, E. 1978. *Orientalism*. London: Penguin.

Seehawer, M. K. 2018. "Decolonising Research in a Sub-Saharan African Context: Exploring Ubuntu as a Foundation for Research Methodology, Ethics and Agenda." *International Journal of Social Research Methodology* 21 (4): 453–66. https://doi.org/10.1080/13645579.2018.1432404.

Shivakoti, R., and J. Milner. 2022. "Beyond the Partnership Debate: Localizing Knowledge Production in Refugee and Forced Migration Studies." *Journal of Refugee Studies* 35 (2): 805–26. https://doi.org/10.1093/jrs/feab083.

Smith, L. T. 2012. *Decolonizing Methodologies: Research and Indigenous Peoples*. London: Zed Books.

Stewart, A. J., and V. Valian. 2018. *An Inclusive Academy: Achieving Diversity and Excellence*. Boston: MIT Press.

Tabensky, P., and S. Mathews, ed. 2015. *Being At 'Home': Race, Institutional Culture and Transformation at South African Higher Education Institutions*. Durban: UKZN Press.

Táíwò, O. 2022. *Against Decolonisation: Taking African Agency Seriously*. London: Hurst.

Táíwò, O. 2022. *Elite Capture: How the Powerful Took Over Identity Politics (and Everything Else)*. London: Pluto Press.

Tamale, S. 2020. *Decolonization and Afro-Feminism*. Wakefield, QC: Daraja Press.

Thiong'o, N. 1986. *Decolonising the Mind: The Politics of Language in African Literature*. London: James Currey.

Tuck, E., and K. W. Yang. 2012. "Decolonization Is Not a Metaphor." *Decolonization: Indigeneity, Education & Society* 1 (1): 1–40.

Vergès, F. 2021. *A Decolonial Feminism*. Translated by Ashley J. Bohrer. London: Pluto Press.

Vogel, C., and J. Musamba. 2022. "Towards a Politics of Collaborative Worldmaking: Ethics, Epistemologies and Mutual Positionalities in Conflict Research." *Ethnography*. First published online, April 21. https://doi.org/10.1177/14661381221090895.

Walia, H. 2013. *Undoing Border Imperialism*. Oakland: AK Press / Institute for Anarchist Studies.

wa Ngũgĩ, M. 2021. "White Privilege in African Studies: When You Are Done, Please Call Us." Brittle Paper, January 28. https://brittlepaper.com/2021/01/white-privilege-in-african-studies-when-you-are-done-please-call-us/.

Whittingdale, E. 2021. "Becoming a Feminist Methodologist While Researching Sexual Violence Support Services." *Journal of Law and Society* 48 (S1): 10–27. https://doi.org/10.1111/jols.12335.

Wilder, G. 2015. *Freedom Time: Negritude, Decolonization, and the Future of the World*. Durham, NC: Duke University Press.

Williams, T. 2022. "THE Work-Life Balance Survey 2022." Times Higher Education, November 10. https://www.timeshighereducation.com/depth/work-life-balance-survey-2022.

Wynter, S. 2003. "Unsettling the Coloniality of Being/Power/Truth/Freedom: Towards the Human, after Man, Its Overrepresentation—an Argument." *CR: The New Centennial Review* 3 (3): 257–337.

Zavala, M. 2013. "What Do We Mean by Decolonizing Research Strategies? Lessons from Decolonizing, Indigenous Research Projects in New Zealand and Latin America." *Decolonization: Indigeneity, Education & Society* 2 (1): 55–71.

CONTRIBUTORS

ANNIE BUNTING is professor of law and society at York University in Toronto. Her research includes sociolegal studies of marriage and childhoods, feminist international law, and culture, religion, and law. Since 2010, she has directed an international research collaboration (Social Sciences and Humanities Research Council–funded partnership) called "Conjugal Slavery in War: Partnership for the Study of Enslavement, Marriage and Masculinities" with historians of slavery, community-based researchers, and women's human rights scholars. She is the coeditor of *Marriage by Force? Contestation over Consent and Coercion in Africa* (2016) with Benjamin Lawrance and Richard Roberts; and *Contemporary Slavery: Popular Rhetoric and Political Practice* (2017, 2018) with Joel Quirk. She coproduced the museum exhibit *Ododo Wa: Stories of Girls in War*.

ALLEN KICONCO holds a PhD in African studies from the University of Birmingham and was a postdoctoral fellow at the University of the Witwatersrand (2017–21). Allen works on the lived experiences of women and girls in both conflict and postconflict settings of Africa, including abduction, captivity, sexual slavery, forced marriage, and forced pregnancy. Her work includes extensive fieldwork with ex-combatants and sexual-violence survivors in Uganda and Sierra Leone. Allen is the author of *Gender, Conflict and Reintegration in Uganda: Abducted Girls, Returning Women* (2021).

JOEL QUIRK is professor of politics at the University of the Witwatersrand. His work focuses on enslavement and abolition, work and mobility, social movements, gender and violence, historical repair, and the history and politics of Africa. Joel is the author or coeditor of seven books, and has also coedited special issues of *Social & Legal Studies*, *Review of International Studies*, *The Anti-Trafficking Review*, and *Slavery & Abolition*. Joel is a founding editor of openDemocracy's Beyond Trafficking and Slavery.

TEDDY ATIM has extensive experience as a practitioner and researcher in conflict and postconflict settings. She holds an MA in humanitarian assistance from the Fletcher School of Law and Diplomacy and the Friedman School of Nutrition Science and Policy at Tufts University, and an interdisciplinary PhD in international development from Wageningen University, the Netherlands. Currently, she is a visiting fellow at the Feinstein International Center at Tufts University, and a Championing Emerging Black Scholars postdoctoral fellow at York University, Canada. Her work focuses on the gender impact of conflict, fragility, and other forms of vulnerability. She is interested in examining the experience of women, men, boys, and girls and what their lives teach us about the continuum of violence and structural inequality in their communities. She led research and is a coapplicant on a six-year collaborative research project, "Conjugal Slavery in War: Partnerships for the Study of Enslavement, Marriage, and Masculinities" (Social Sciences and Humanities Research Council funded, 2015–22). She has also authored and coauthored peer-reviewed articles and book chapters, as well as several international reports, including *The Dust Has Not Yet Settled: Victims' Views on Remedy and Reparation in the Greater North of Uganda.*

LAWAN BALAMI obtained his master's degree in public health from University Putra Malaysia in 2016. He coordinated research and field activities conducted by the dRPC under the international research collaboration (Social Sciences and Humanities Research Council–funded partnership) "Conjugal Slavery in War: Partnership for the Study of Enslavement, Marriage and Masculinities." He is currently a public health, epidemiology and biostatistics lecturer at the University of Maiduguri, Nigeria. He is the founder and executive director of a nonprofit and nongovernmental organization called Explore Humanitarian Aid Initiative, which focuses on research and evidence generation to inform humanitarian and development interventions.

SYLVIE BODINEAU is an independent researcher in anthropology. After twenty years of experience in humanitarian child protection intervention, she decided in 2009 to join the academic world to "think her profession" and strengthen collaboration between research and intervention. Her research broadly explores the different worlds of humanitarian intervention, human rights, and protection of children and youth, with a critical eye embracing the complexity of the circuits between policymaking and practice. She is currently developing, in collaboration with Appolinaire Lipandasi, a participatory action research project with a group of former child soldiers who wish to make their situation known fifteen years after their demobilization, and is part of a collaborative interdisciplinary project on youth, gender violence, and gender justice at York University, Toronto. Rewarded with several distinctions during her academic career, she is the author of the book entitled *Figures d'enfants soldats: Puissance et vulnérabilité* (2012) and several articles, in particular "Vulnerability and Agency: Figures of Child Soldiers within the Narratives of Child Protection Practitioners in the Democratic Republic of Congo" (2014).

LEEN DE NUTTE obtained her PhD in educational sciences from Ghent University in 2023. Her research explored the upbringing of children in the context of prolonged collective violence in Kitgum District, northern Uganda. Leen was actively involved in the work of the Centre for Children in Vulnerable Situations (CCVS)-Uganda, an international NGO aiming to enhance the psychosocial and mental health of individuals, families, and communities in postwar northern Uganda. At CCVS-Uganda, Leen took on the role of representative of the board (2015–17) and executive director (2018–21).

APPOLINAIRE LIPANDASI is a teacher at the Higher Pedagogical Institute of Gemena, in the Department of Commercial and Administrative Sciences, in Sud-Ubangi, Democratic Republic of Congo (DRC). He has been working since 2013 in close collaboration with Sylvie Bodineau in research within the city of Gemena: as assistant interpreter for her doctoral research, "Droits de l'enfant en praxis: La protection des enfants kadogos en République démocratique du Congo," and currently as research field coordinator in a participatory action research with a group of former child soldiers who wanted to make their situation known fifteen years after their demobilization. Passionate about humanitarian work, he was one of the executives of the DRC Red Cross in Sud-Ubangi and has followed several training courses that have strengthened his operational capacities, in particular on local development planning, project/program management, humanitarian diplomacy, community engagement and accountability, and so on. He is the author of *Impact socio-économique des activités des ONGD membres de Bucongd sur la population de Gemena, de 2002 a 2006* (2018).

SAMUEL OKYERE is a senior lecturer in sociology in the School of Sociology, Politics and International Studies at the University of Bristol and a founding member of the Beyond Trafficking and Slavery hub on openDemocracy. He specializes in critical reflections on the interplay between human rights, power, inequality, ethnicity, and class under conditions of globalization. Over the last decade he has carried out extensive field research on mobilities (migration, trafficking, and smuggling) and migrants lived experiences, childhood and child rights, and forced and precarious labor. He is presently a member of the five-year European Research Council–funded project "Modern Marronage: The Pursuit and Practice of Freedom in the Contemporary World," held at the University of Bristol.

OTIM PATRICK ONGWECH is a video advocacy manager at the Refugee Law Project in Uganda whose passion for digital/visual storytelling was influenced by his work with forced migrants since 1998. Having lived as a forced migrant from 1986 to 1998, he has been able to parlay this lived reality into storytelling—a passion he currently pursues as a trainer in instructing refugee and host youth. The video project *Bringing Up Our Enemies' Child* has inspired his latest drive to document stories of children (born) of war as a means for "social therapy" among those affected by armed conflicts across Africa. Patrick is also a social change activist and a member of the Video4Change Network.

PHILIPP SCHULZ is a postdoctoral researcher at the Institute of Intercultural and International Studies at the University of Bremen. His research focuses on the gender dynamics of armed conflicts and political violence and postconflict transitions, with a particular focus on masculinities and conflict-related sexual violence against men: more recently with attention to the roles of love and care in armed conflict. He is the principal investigator of a research project that examines the political agency of male sexual violence survivors, funded by the German Research Foundation. His book *Male Survivors of Wartime Sexual Violence: Perspectives from Northern Uganda* (2020) is available on open access.

ANA STEVENSON is a lecturer at the University of Southern Queensland, Australia, and a research associate of the International Studies Group at the University of the Free State, South Africa. Her first book was *The Woman as Slave in Nineteenth-Century American Social Movements* (2019). Ana's research about women and transnational social movements across the United States, Australia, and South Africa has also appeared in journals such as *Humanity: An International Journal of Human Rights, Humanitarianism, and Development*; *Safundi: The Journal of South African and American Studies*; and the *Women's History Review*.

BETH W. STEWART teaches history and social sciences at Kwantlen Polytechnic University and Fairleigh Dickinson University. Her research examines the politics of belonging of children born of war and participatory research with young people. In 2018, she received her doctorate from the Institute for Gender, Race, Sexuality and Social Justice at the University of British Columbia, where she was also a Liu Scholar at the Liu Institute for Global Issues. Beth is also an established abstract artist (www.artbybws.com), creating art that expresses critical perspectives on issues including race, power, and conflict. Exhibiting paintings created in collaboration with children born of war in northern Uganda, she has employed art to share their stories with international public audiences.

REBECCA SWARTZ is a senior lecturer in history at the University of the Free State, South Africa. Her research focuses on humanitarianism, education, race and childhood, and slavery in the British Empire in the nineteenth century. Her first monograph, *Education and Empire: Children, Race and Humanitarianism in the British Settler Colonies, 1833–1880*, was published in 2019. Her research has appeared in *History Workshop Journal, Slavery & Abolition*, and the *Journal of Imperial and Commonwealth History*, among others.

HEATHER TASKER is a PhD candidate in socio-legal studies at York University. Her research explores gendered conceptions of harm and justice in conflict-affected and postconflict contexts. Heather's dissertation focuses on community responses to sexual exploitation and abuse committed by MONUSCO peacekeepers in the Democratic Republic of the Congo. Through her work with the "Conjugal Slavery in War" partnership, Heather has conducted collaborative research on the rights and needs of children born of war, experiences of harm and access to justice for survivors of forced marriage in conflict, and the development of international criminal law around sexual and gender-based violence.

UMAR AHMAD UMAR obtained his master's degree in development studies from Bayero University, Kano-Nigeria, in 2013. He is currently finalizing his LLM program at the University of South Wales. As senior program associate of the development Research and Projects Center (dRPC), he cocoordinated the research and other activities conducted by the dRPC under the international research collaboration (Social Sciences and Humanities Research Council–funded partnership) "Conjugal Slavery in War: Partnership for the Study of Enslavement, Marriage and Masculinities." He authored a chapter on listening to the stories of Boko Haram's wives in *Research as More Than Extraction? Knowledge Production and Sexual Violence in Post Conflict African Societies* (2020).

JUDITH-ANN WALKER is a full-time project coordinator of all the programs run by the development Research and Projects Center (dRPC). She holds a master's and a PhD in development studies from the International Institute of Social Studies, University of Erasmus, Rotterdam, and specializes in development project management, monitoring, and evaluation. She has over twenty years of programming experience in project design, development management and evaluation, and in mainstreaming gender in development interventions in Nigeria.

INDEX

abduction, 21, 39, 136, 205, 218; by Boko Haram, 1–2, 4, 118–20, 205, 255; by the LRA, 2–3, 24, 42, 138
abolitionism, 160, 166, 274
abortion, 239
Abrahams, Yvette, 159, 161, 164, 166, 171
academic marketplace, 8, 278, 285, 289
accountability: criminal, 262; demands for, 259; of donors, 229; humanitarian, 227–29; individual, 254, 286; institutional, 215–16, 219, 223; lack of, 262–63; mechanisms for, 43, 245; national discussion of, 235; of perpetrators, 262; of researchers, 68, 86, 119, 225, 276
Active Learning Network for Accountability and Performance in Humanitarian Action (ALNAP), 221
Afonso, A., 278, 285
Africa: Europeans in, 12–13; as field site for research, 15–20; history and politics of, 12; postcolonial states in, 13. *See also individual African countries*
African National Congress (ANC), Women's League, 167
amnesty, 24, 262
Amnesty International, 264
anthropology, 15, 69, 70, 169
anticolonial struggles, 274. *See also* colonialism
apartheid, 157, 167
Asad, Talal, 11
autonomy, 117, 122, 126, 135, 137, 201, 220–21; of children, 208
Awad, Mohamed, 167

Baartman, Sara, 156–66; exhibition of, 159–61, 163; in Great Britain, 158–61; slave/free status of, 26, 159–61, 164; in South Africa, 157–58

Bach, Renee, 6
Baines, Erin, 91–92, 195
Balami, Lawan, 255
Banyamulenge ethnic group, 239, 241–42, 243, 245–46
Basini, H., 266
Battis, Jes, 277
Beach, Adam R., 166, 169
Bemba, Jean Pierre, 76
beneficence, 117, 125, 220, 222
Binka, F., 200
bioethics, 216
Björkdahl, A., 259
Black Lives Matter movement, 51, 169, 273
body maps, 108–9
Boko Haram: abductions by, 1–2, 4, 118–20, 205, 255; and the CHE in Northeast Nigeria, 217–30; displaced persons' camps motivated by, 26
Branch, Adam, 233, 246
#bringbackourgirls/boys, 1–2
Bringing Up Our Enemies' Child (documentary), 27, 237–40, 246
Brown, T. M., 105
Brown, Wendy, 286–87, 289
Bruno, W., 222
Bukavu Series (blog), 69, 88n2
Bunting, A., 183, 263
Burundi, 239

Cabo Delgado (Mozambique), 4
Caledon Code, 159
Cambodia, 188
Campbell, S. P., 19
CBOs. *See* community-based organizations
Central African Republic (CAR), 39
Centre for Children in Vulnerable Situations (CCVS), 137, 144–45

Index

Césaire, Aimé, 199
Cesars, Hendrik, 158
Cesars, Pieter, 158
Chad, 217
Cheeseman, N., 17
Chibok abductions, 1–2, 4, 218
child labor, 120
children: abduction of, 2–3, 24, 42, 136, 138; autonomy of, 208; born into the LRA, 26, 90–112, 112n1, 136, 137, 140; born of rape, 232, 237–38, 245, 246–47; born of war, 23, 41, 63, 90–112, 112n1, 238, 261; cultural differences in protection of, 207–9; depoliticization of, 112n4; everyday lives of, 94; fathered by Boko Haram members, 121; gender identity of, 239; in humanitarian crises, 129; as research subjects, 25–26, 203–4; rights of, 70; sexual abuse and exploitation of, 203, 215; social exclusion of, 91, 113n8; stigmatization of, 140; street, 42; support for, 91; as victims, 23; voices of, 91, 111, 112; war-affected, 42, 111
child soldiers, 25–26, 136; former, 134; humanitarian interventions for, 69–71, 83–84; recruitment of, 70
Chow, Rey, 94
Christensen, M. J., 264
civil society organizations, 18, 27, 189, 216
Clark, Chris, 109
Clark-Kazak, Christina, 95, 105, 106, 108, 111
climate change, 217
Cole, D. C., 222
colonialism, 5, 6, 12–13, 25, 26, 93, 167, 195, 199, 210, 273; scientific, 200; settler, 277
colonization, 202, 209, 274
community-based organizations (CBOs), 136, 251, 252, 257, 258–59; challenges of, 256, 260–61; justice needs and priorities of, 253–54, 255, 265, 267–68; partnerships with researchers, 253; perspective compared to the UN, 249; roles of, 264; security risks and danger to, 266; support for, 249; use of legal mechanisms by, 264
community bonds/values, 283, 285
complex humanitarian emergencies (CHEs), 216–17, 219–20, 228, 229
Concerned Parents Association Uganda, 42, 65n1
Concordia University, 234
confidentiality issues, 40, 72, 91, 92, 117, 121, 122, 127–28
conflict identities, 18–19
conflict-related gender violence, 250–54. See also gender-based violence (GBV)

conflict-related sexual and gender-based violence (CRSGBV): impacts of, 258–59; increased attention to, 267–68; knowledge production about, 254; life stories of survivors, 124; response to, 181; survivors of, 118, 119, 120, 122, 124–30. See also gender-based violence (GBV); sexual violence
conflict-related sexual violence (CRSV), 233, 235, 246–47; narratives surrounding, 238–39
Congolese national anger, 260
Conjugal Slavery in War (CSiW), 21–22, 46, 120, 248–49, 255, 260, 268n3, 268n5
Convention on the Rights of the Child, 94
corruption, 223, 252, 256, 263, 265, 267
countering violent extremism (CVE), 9
Country Development Cooperation Strategy (2015–20), 223, 227
Country Development Cooperation Strategy (2020–25), 223–24, 227, 228
Coverage, Operation, Reach, and Effectiveness (CORE) group, 218–19
COVID-19 pandemic, 289
Crais, Clifton, 158, 161, 163, 164
critical race scholarship, 24, 201, 275
Cronin-Furman, K., 15
CRSGBV. *See* conflict-related sexual and gender-based violence
CRSV. *See* conflict-related sexual violence
CSiW. *See* Conjugal Slavery in War
cultural competence, 19
cultural taboos, 45, 55, 58, 64, 182, 236
cultural translation, 11
customary law, 250–51
Cuvier, Georges, 161

Dapchi abductions, 218
data collection: challenges of, 16, 119, 251; collaboration in, 288; confidentiality in, 127; in Democratic Republic of Congo, 72–73, 76, 80, 83, 86–87, 96, 108; ethical, 5, 171; in Ghana, 204; in Nigeria, 224–27; participatory, 186, 195; transparency in, 136; in Uganda, 136, 138, 144–46, 149–50, 179, 180, 185–86, 188, 194, 195
De Casanova, E. M., 105
decoloniality, 274
decolonization: and devolution, 286, 289; of education, 200; and European epistemologies, 276; and "fair trade," 290; of fieldwork, 280–82, 283, 286–88; of institutional policies, 278, 280, 284–85; of knowledge, 171; of knowledge production, 186;

meanings of, 7, 274; pathways to, 278–80; of pedagogy, 285–86; practical application of, 276–77; and reflexivity, 282–83; of research, 28, 69, 85, 88, 200, 274–90; and restitution, 277–78; support for, 7, 277–78; of universities, 199, 277
Democratic Republic of Congo (DRC): Banyamulenge ethnic group in, 239, 245–46; CBOs in, 249, 250, 256; children conceived in, 232; child soldiers in, 25, 69–70; community-based justice workers in, 251; conflict in, 3, 21, 39, 76, 84, 233; "forced integration" in, 246; humanitarian aid in, 6; internally displaced persons in, 218; perception of White people in, 78–80; postcolonial, 69, 87; postconflict, 22; research in, 25, 68–88; SOFEPADI, 249; Western intervention in, 76, 78
Denzin, N., 202
development Research and Project Centre (dRPC), 118, 120, 121, 255
Devex, 215
DevTech, 220, 224–27
Dibwe dia Mwembu, Donatien, 76, 88n4
Dixon-Woods, M. E., 201
documentary films, 27–28; *Bringing Up Our Enemies' Child*, 237–40, 246; *Gender against Men*, 236; *They Slept with Me*, 236–37; *What about Us?*, 234–35. *See also* Refugee Law Project (RLP)
Dodsworth, S., 17
Dolan, Chris, 234, 235, 236
Douma, N., 250
dRPC (development Research and Project Centre), 118, 120, 121, 255
Dunlop, Alexander, 158
Dutch Cape Colony, 158–59, 161–62
Dutch East India Company, 158
DuVernay, Ava, 169

Economic and Social Research Council, 201
Elbourne, Elizabeth, 164
El Refaei, E. S., 200
Elzer, Jan Michiel, 158
End Rape Now, 250
#EndSARS, 2
Enlightenment thought, 155
Ennis, M., 208
enslavement, 24, 26, 120, 156, 164, 166, 169–70. *See also* slavery
ethics. *See* research ethics
ethics blindness, 227–30
ethics creep, 206
Ethiopia, 4

ethnography, 69, 94–95, 96
Eurocentrism, 276
European Union, 216
exploitation: in Africa, 6, 7; of children, 129, 203, 215; labor, 167, 169; of local researchers, 48–49; sexual, 156, 167, 215; and slavery, 155, 156, 160, 166, 167, 170; of women, 157
extraction, 5–6, 28, 60, 195, 267, 289
extremism, 2, 9, 258

fair trade, 290
Fanon, Frantz, 274
Fausto-Sterling, Anne, 161
Federation of South African Women (FEDSAW), 167
Feinstein International Center (Tufts University), 43
female genital cutting, 22
feminism and feminist scholarship, 24, 163; African, 7; Black, 275; and the history of slavery, 156; postmodern, 68; and sexual violence in conflict, 254
Ferme, M. C., 22
field based monitoring (FBM), 224–26, 227
field based monitors (FBMs), 220
Finnegan, Diarmid A., 159–60
forced labor, 78, 119, 164, 169
forced migration, 43, 233, 235
forced recruitment, 39, 84
Free Black people, 158–59
freedom, 155–57, 159
"Freedom" (song), 168–69
Fricker, M., 209
friction, 28, 249, 256, 259, 266

GBV. *See* gender-based violence
gender: inclusion in race- and class-based oppression, 163; patriarchal norms of, 21; shared identity of, 187–88. *See also* conflict-related sexual and gender-based violence (CRSGBV); gender-based violence (GBV); sexual and gender-based violence (SGBV)
Gender against Men (documentary), 235, 236
gender-based violence (GBV): in Africa, 21–22, 273; codifying and prosecution of, 3; conflict-related, 250–54; decolonization of fieldwork on, 282; ethical and safety concerns in research on, 117; experienced by refugees, 235; increase in, 119; information about, 4; nature and meaning of, 171; organizations addressing, 9; perpetrated by state officials, 282; perpetrators of, 125;

305

Index

gender-based violence (GBV) (*cont.*) research and practice relating to, 274; research on, 40, 122, 162; research terminology, 156, 157; as response to poverty and frustration, 260; in South Africa, 166; studies on, 129–30; survivors of, 117, 121, 126–30, 250, 255–56, 268; transitional justice measures, 182; victims of, 134; work to address, 256. *See also* conflict-related sexual and gender-based violence (CRSGBV); rape; sexual and gender-based violence (SGBV); sexual violence
gendered crime, 264
gender equality/inequality, 257, 258
gender justice, 28, 259. *See also* justice
gender mainstreaming, 249
Ghana, 27, 203–7
Ghent University, 69, 139
Global Affairs Canada, 216
Gordon-Chipembere, Natasha, 164, 166
Gqola, Pumla Dineo, 164, 166, 167
Green, Toby, 288
Grimm, K., 238
Griqua National Conference, 165
Gross, Ariela, 170
Gulu University, 61, 111
Guta, A., 204

Haar, R. J., 222
Haiti, 215, 229
Hall, Budd, 183
Hall, Catherine, 158
Hannah-Jones, Nikole, 169
Hart, Jason, 94, 111
Hedgecoe, A., 204
Henry, Marsha, 3
Heykoop, Cheryl, 95
Hilhorst, D., 250
Höglund, K., 259
Holy Spirit Movement, 42
home visits, 96–97
Houge, A. B., 262
humanitarian aid and interventions: accountability in, 227–30; in CHE settings, 219–30; to child soldiers, 69–71, 83–84; for conflict-affected populations, 39–40, 42; in eighteenth century, 166; ethical guidelines for, 215–16, 268n2; international, 249; localization in, 266; for research respondents, 59, 108
humanitarianism, 6, 21, 266
human rights, 43, 70, 250; abuses of, 215
Human Rights Watch, 264
Hunt, M., 128

hybridity, 259
hypermasculinity, 23

ICC (International Criminal Court), 24, 76, 182, 253, 264, 269n10
imperialism, 5, 11–12, 199, 202, 209, 210, 273; epistemic, 288; ethical, 205
implementing partners (IPs), 224–25
infection prevention and control (IPC) measures, 226
informant bias, 123
informed consent, 27–28, 40, 58–59, 74–76, 121, 123, 126–27, 243; of children, 129; and illiteracy, 40, 58
Institute for Development Studies, 187
institutional review boards (IRBs), 124, 128, 136, 150, 202
Integrated Country Strategy (2015–20), 223
internally displaced persons (IDP), 26, 119–20, 122, 128, 136–38, 218, 234–35. *See also* Kyaka II refugee settlement
International Committee of the Red Cross and the Red Crescent, 80, 268n2
International Court of Justice, 3
International Criminal Court (ICC), 24, 76, 182, 253, 264, 269n10
international criminal justice, 256
international criminal law, 264
international development agencies, 19
international nongovernmental organizations (INGOs), 253, 254, 255, 257, 264, 266, 268
International Protocol on the Documentation and Investigation of Sexual Violence in Conflict, 23
International Red Cross and Red Crescent Movement, 80, 268n2
interviews: avoiding retraumatization in, 64–65, 252, 282; with children, 97–98; choice of language in, 11, 74, 75, 93, 97, 121, 243; confidentiality in, 128; with ex–child soldiers, 72–73; filming, 243–44; need for sensitivity in, 55–56; with parents in captivity, 138; qualitative, 64; regarding sensitive/stigmatized topics, 57–58; requirement for parental consent, 207–9; with sexual violence survivors, 120–21; snowball sampling, 72; spaces chosen for, 40, 46, 74, 93, 97, 127, 142–43; trust building, 241, 243
Invisible Children, 2
IRBs (institutional review boards), 124, 128, 136, 150, 202
Islamic State of Iraq and Syria (ISIS), 218

Index

Jacobsen, K., 18
Jim Crow, 169, 170
"Johannesburg Principles on Building Equitable and Effective Partnerships for Migration Research," 288
Juba Peace Agreement, 182, 233
justice: advancement of, 268; alternative ways of conceptualizing and enacting, 259; barriers to, 260; and education, 249; formal mechanisms of, 263; gender, 28, 259; gendered, 257–67; for gendered violence, 248; international, 264, 265, 266; international criminal, 256; local, 264, 265; localized perceptions of, 264; meaning of, 183; multiple understandings of, 251, 252, 263–64; national, 266; and poverty, 249; and reparations, 249; reparations as, 261–62; in response to sexual violence against men, 184–85, 190–91; for SGBV, 266; for survivors of GBV, 256, 264; systemic and structural barriers to, 256; transitional, 43, 179, 181–82, 185, 191
Justice and Reconciliation Project (JRP), 92–93, 108–11
Justice Survey, 248–49, 251–52, 254, 256, 259, 260, 262, 265–66
justice workers, 248–49, 251–54, 256

Karamojong cattle rustling, 42
Katsina boys, 1–2
Khoekhoe people, 158–59, 161, 163–66, 171
knowledge: academic, 281; colonial, 8, 207; cultural, 44, 93; decolonization of, 171; global, 160; hierarchies of, 41, 94; indigenous, 93, 288; local, 44, 47, 50, 183, 266; ownership of, 183; public, 87; scientific, 159; situated, 68
knowledge economies, 5, 6, 25, 28, 273, 276, 279, 280, 286–89; decolonization of, 286; extractive, 289; hierarchical, 15
knowledge production: academic, 161; by Africans, 14–15; by children, 90, 100–104; collaborative, 68–69, 80, 112, 144; community-led, 233; about conflict-related sexual and gender-based violence, 254; contemporary, 160, 166; decolonization of, 186; economy of, 264; encouragement of, 91; epistemic questions regarding, 274–75; extraction of, 6; geared toward the terms of the researched, 180; global, 160; hierarchies of, 9–10; multiple means of, 112; paradigms of, 171; and participatory action research (PAR), 182–83; political economy of, 6, 8–15, 25, 260; politics of, 4, 13–14, 182, 248, 268; process of, 6–7; reflecting institutional racism, 199; scientific, 157, 162; situated, 68–69; about slavery, 162–66; structural violence in, 41; using a mix of methods, 93
Kobo Toolbox platform, 251
Kony, Joseph, 2, 4, 136, 181
Kovach, Margaret, 110
Kunz, R., 238
Kwoyelo, Thomas, 182
Kyagulanyi, Robert Ssentamu (Bobi Wine), 168–69
Kyaka II refugee settlement, 232–33, 239, 240, 245, 246

Lake, M., 15, 251
Lake Chad basin, 217
Lakwena, Alice, 42
Landau, Loren, 9, 18
Lawrence, A., 234
Learning Program (TLP), 224
Lewis, J., 205
Liberia, 21, 216–17, 250, 251
literacy, 40, 58, 122
localization, 266–67
local researchers: access to research participants, 55–58; challenges of, 43–46, 52–55, 87; ethics review and approvals, 61–62; funding challenges, 47; inequality and exploitation of, 48–49; in an international research environment, 47–48, 50–52; local knowledge of, 87; managing high expectations, 59–61; mutual learning and capacity building, 49–50; obtaining informed consent, 58–59; research targeting, 62–63; and the retraumatization of research participants, 64–65. *See also* researchers
Lohne, K., 262
Lorde, Audre, 274
Lord's Resistance Army (LRA): captives of, 137, 150; children abducted by, 2–3, 24, 42, 138; children born into, 26, 90–112, 112n1, 136, 137, 140; children with parents in, 98; conflict in DRC, 233; conflict in South Sudan, 233; conflict in Uganda, 39, 42, 90, 136, 181, 233, 234, 235; mothers returning from, 26, 63; system of forced marriage and parenthood, 136; use of sexual violence by, 3
Lundy, P., 183, 184, 185
Lwanga, Charles, 169

MacDougall, D., 234
Mackenzie, C., 19

307

Index

Macmillan, W. M., 163
Makerere University, 42, 233
Mali, 217
malpractice, 6
Mamdani, Mahmood, 12, 165
Mandela, Nelson, 165
marriage: arranged, 22; "by capture," 22; child, 22, 119; forced, 1, 3, 21–22, 23, 39, 63, 90, 119, 120, 136, 140, 147
masculinity/masculinities, 23
Mbeki, Thabo, 165–66
McClintock, Anne, 161
McDowell, C., 19
McGovern, M., 183, 184, 185
Médecins Sans Frontières (Doctors Without Borders), 6
Media for Social Change, 237
Megan, B., 238
men: and family life, 247; as fathers in captivity, 136, 137–38, 140, 147, 148, 150; humiliation of, 238–39; marginalization of, 184, 245; as perpetrators, 23; raising children born from rape, 232, 237–38, 246–47; and the rape of women, 238–39; as survivors of sexual violence, 27, 235–36, 240; as victims, 23; workshop discussions with, 190–93
men and boys, sexual violence against, 4, 21, 22–23, 181–82, 187, 188, 282
Men of Courage, 27, 179, 187, 188, 190, 192
Men of Hope, 187, 195n3
Men of Peace, 195n3
mental health and psychosocial support (MHPSS), 126, 128–29, 137, 138
Merry, S. E., 70
#MeToo campaign, 51, 250, 273
missionaries, 6, 15, 78
monitoring, evaluation, and learning (MEAL) missions, 220, 224, 226, 227–28
Monitoring, Evaluation, and Learning (MEL) Activity, 224–25
monitoring and evaluation (M&E), 224
Moosavi, Leon, 284–85
Morris, N., 202
Mouvement de Libération du Congo (MLC), 76, 84
Mozambique, 4
Muller, Cornelius, 158
Musamba, J., 288
Museveni, Yoweri Kaguta, 136, 168
Musila, Grace, 10
Muthaka, I., 251

National Action Plans, 257
National Resistance Army (Uganda), 181

Ndlovu, Siphiwe Gloria, 166, 171
Ngira, David, 283
Niger, 217
Nigeria: Boko Haram in, 2, 26, 118–19; community-based justice workers in, 251; as "dangerous country," 205–6; ethnic groups in, 118; humanitarian programs in, 217; insecurity and conflict in, 263; internally displaced persons in, 26; Official Development Cooperation, 229; religious and ethnic conflict in, 118; research in, 26, 27, 117–30, 203–7, 217–30; violent abduction and marriage in, 21
Nixon, S., 204
nongovernmental organizations (NGOs), 19, 42, 70, 80, 85, 91, 97, 108, 111, 136, 137, 138, 139, 144, 189, 219, 250; international, 253, 254, 255, 257, 264, 266, 268; as local partners, 266. See also Witness (NGO)
nonmaleficence, 117
Norman, J., 187

Obote, Milton, 168
One Nutrition in Complex Emergency, 46
Ongwen, Dominic, 24, 182
oppression, gender-based, 172n1
Oxfam, 215, 229, 289

Pailey, R. N., 280
participatory action research (PAR), 180, 182–86, 193–94
paternalism, 21, 135, 200
patriarchy, 238, 239
peacebuilding, 249, 251, 257–58, 259; localization in, 266. See also justice
Pittaway, E., 19
police brutality, 2
political advocacy, 24–25
Porter, E., 201
positionality, 5, 21, 42, 93, 137, 275; feminist praxis and, 282; gender, 188; of researchers, 148, 149, 186
postcolonial scholarship, 163
postmodernism, 171
power dynamics, 44, 77, 275; asymmetrical, 105, 180, 186, 195; colonial, 200; hybridity in, 259; and reflexivity, 282–83; between researcher and subjects, 110, 144, 183, 194
power hierarchy, 144
power relations, 5
power sharing, 24
Pringle, J. D., 222
privacy issues, 40, 117

Index

privilege, 5, 45; European, 15; of researchers, 144; White, 6, 25, 52, 201

Proscovia, Aloyo, 92–93, 95, 97, 105–8, 110–12

prostitution, 163, 207, 239. *See also* transactional sex

psycho-legal clinics, 232

psychosocial support, 121, 126, 145, 188–89, 196n5, 236, 237

Puri, J., 221

Quijano, A., 208

Qureshi, Sadiah, 159, 161, 164, 166

racial injustice, 202

racial terrorism, 169

racism, 169, 273, 274; in humanitarian efforts, 6; institutional, 5–6, 199; and slavery, 167

rape: in conflict, 250; male, 182, 235; male survivors of, 179–82, 185–95; targeted, 246; as violation of women's rights, 238; wartime, 40, 179–82, 185–95, 233; weaponized, 257–58, 259; as weapon of war, 3, 21, 233, 239, 253, 258. *See also* sexual violence

Reaux, S., 161

reciprocity, 109–11, 192–93

reconciliation rituals and ceremonies, 182

Red Crescent Movement, 80

Red Cross Movement, 80

Reed, Holly, 216

refugee advocacy, 233

Refugee Law Project (RLP), 27, 180, 185, 187, 188–92, 194, 240; advocacy mission of, 246; *Bringing Up Our Enemies' Child* (documentary), 237–40, 246; *Gender against Men* (documentary), 236; organization of, 235–36; path to video advocacy, 233–37; Research and Advocacy department, 234; *They Slept with Me* (documentary), 236–37; in Uganda, 24, 232–33; video team, 240; *What about Us?* (documentary), 234–35

refugee studies, 43

Refugee Welfare Committees (RWCs), 241

reintegration challenges, 54

religious leaders, 242, 255

reparations, 249, 260, 261–62, 269n9, 269n10; and justice, 264

Republic of Haiti, 215, 229

research: consequences of, 117; empirical, 216; ethical approval for, 200–203; evaluation, 217; informant bias in, 123; legacies of imperialism and racism in, 199–200; phasing out, 149; reciprocity in, 109–11, 180, 192–93; as social work, 106–9. *See also* research locations; research methods; research topics

research brokers, 18, 138–42, 150, 189

researchers: and access to research subjects, 55–58, 138–42; accountability of, 68, 86, 119, 225, 276; building the research relationship, 82–83, 93, 104–6, 142–43, 188; choices and decisions of, 149–51; collaboration between, 7, 8, 16–17, 18, 25–26, 41, 46–52, 68–88, 137, 149, 267–68, 288; and cooperation with nonprofit organizations, 188–89; cultural competence of, 15–16, 19; and ethical consideration, 4–5; goals of, 18; hierarchies and division of labor among, 9–10, 14–15, 41, 48–49; and institutional actors, 8–9, 27, 253; and native informants, 16; neutral approach of, 184; origins of, 11–12; performing member checking, 148; political motivations of, 25. *See also* local researchers; positionality; power

research ethics: challenges of, 121–22, 199–210; in complex humanitarian settings, 215–30; and concern for research respondents, 252–53; in conflict and postconflict settings, 53–65; decoupling, 282–84; in the design of USAID/Nigeria's evaluation, 224–27; in DevTech concept notes, 225–26; "do no harm," 19, 40, 55, 94, 134, 221, 224, 226, 227, 275; ethical reflexivity, 282–83; ethics review and approvals, 27, 61–62; forms of consent, 19–20; funding concerns, 5, 8–9, 47, 85–86, 216, 260; in gender-based violence research, 117–30; infection prevention and control (IPC) measures, 226; and legal liability, 19; for "local" researchers, 44; in monitoring and evaluating humanitarian and CHE settings, 219–22; negative example of, 157; and the perspectives and experiences of justice workers, 248, 268; program monitoring and evaluation, 224–27; and race, 5; recommendations for ethical standards, 124–30; and research design, 47–48; research "targeting," 62–63; risk of poor adherence to, 125, 128; safety plans, 226; self-reflection toward, 171; in USAID/Nigeria's policy on evaluation in northeast Nigeria, 222–24

research ethics committees (RECs), 200–209

309

Index

research locations: Democratic Republic of Congo, 25, 68–88; Kyaka II refugee settlement, 232–47; Nigeria, 26, 27, 117–30, 203–7, 217–30; South Africa, 157–66, 165, 275; South Sudan, 39, 233; Sudan, 218; Uganda, 25–26, 27, 39–65, 90–112, 134–51, 179–95

research methods: in Africa, 15–20; changes in the research environment, 51–52; child-centered, 93–100, 112; collaborative, 8, 180, 182, 194–95, 199, 267–68, 288; in conflict and postconflict settings, 40, 65; decolonization of, 274–90; design and framing, 53–54; drawing, 95, 98–100; empirical, 195; ethical, 254–56; ethnographic-inspired, 94–95; exploitative and extractive, 144–45, 186, 194, 268; and frontline workers, 28; group discussions, 96; home visits, 96–97; indigenous, 200, 202; journaling, 95, 100, 101–3, 110; and legitimacy, 40–41; mixed methods / integrated approaches, 282; need for sensitivity in, 91, 94, 193; participatory, 94–95, 96, 108, 109, 180–86, 260; play as, 96; preapproved, 128; qualitative, 60, 64, 119–22, 124, 129, 171, 203; quantitative, 171; for research on conflict-related sexual and gender-based violence, 119–23; surveys, 28, 171, 248–49, 251–52, 255–56, 259–60, 262–66, 268n3, 285; with survivors rather than on survivors, 179–80; target audience, 10–11; Western-centric, 200; workshop discussions, 190–93. *See also* data collection; interviews

research respondents: anonymity of, 121, 122, 191, 244; autonomy of, 117, 122, 126, 135, 137, 201, 208, 220–21; concern for, 4, 252–53; expectations of, 18–19, 26, 45, 59–61, 81, 93, 123–24, 145–48, 189–90; gaining and negotiating access with, 55–58, 138–42; gendered and sociocultural realities of, 252; identification of, 17; providing for basic needs of, 59, 106–9; reasons for participating, 81–83; relationship with researcher, 82–83, 93, 104–6, 142–43, 188; retraumatization of, 64–65, 252, 282; safety and protection of, 127

research topics: children born of war, 90–112; child soldiers, 69–88; conflict, 9–10; conflict-related gender violence, 41–65, 250–54; formerly abducted mothers and fathers, 134–51, 232–47; gender, 9, 18; health, 9; human rights, 18; male survivors of wartime rape, 179–95; migration, 10; refugee studies, 18; rehabilitation, 18; sciences, 10; sexual (and gender-based) violence, 4–5, 20–25, 117–30, 235; slavery, 155–72; Women, Peace and Security (WPS), 9, 23, 248–49, 257, 258, 259, 261, 262, 264

responsibilization, 286–87
Rességuier, A., 77
retraumatization, 64–65, 252, 282
revictimization, 125, 134
Review Ethics Committees (RECs), 61, 66n10
#RhodesMustFall, 199, 273
Ricoeur, P., 72
Ritchie, J., 205
Robins, S., 183, 184, 185
Rossi, Benedetta, 169–70
rule-of-law building, 250–51
Rwanda, 21, 24, 245, 251
Rwanda genocide, 245
RWCs (Refugee Welfare Committees), 241
Ryan, C., 259, 266

Sabati, S., 202
safety issues, 226, 240
Salafia movements, 218
San people, 165
Sardan, J.-P., 70, 75
Save the Children, 42
Scully, Pamela, 21, 158, 161, 163
Secure Livelihoods Research Consortium (SLRC), 46, 66n4
security risks, 266–67
Senghor, Léopold Sédar, 199
Sesay, M., 250
Seventh World Conference on Research Integrity, 288–89
sexism, 273
sexual abuse, 203
sexual and gender-based violence (SGBV): complicating factors, 239; frequent occurrence of, 256; global attention for, 266; justice for, 266; research on, 122, 235; survivors of, 251, 252; toward women and girls, 182; used by terrorist groups, 119, 258; and women's rights, 236. *See also* conflict-related sexual and gender-based violence (CRSGBV); gender-based violence (GBV); sexual violence
sexuality, patriarchal norms of, 21

310

Index

sexual slavery, 119, 120
sexual violence: against children, 1; during conflict, 3, 20–22, 54–55, 91, 118, 119, 181, 233, 238, 258, 262; difficulty of researching, 28; government and international policy responses to, 24; and the LRA, 39; marginalization of, 181; measures addressing, 262; against men and boys, 4, 21, 22–23, 181–82, 187, 188, 282; militarized, 249; policy and advocacy issues, 21; in postconflict contexts, 253; prevention and redress of, 128, 249; raising awareness about, 250; research methods and ethics, 4–5, 20–25; response to, 247; root causes of, 261; sexual assault, 109; and slavery, 156; survivors and victims of, 18, 45, 134, 253; tactical, 260; and terrorism, 257–58; and the Ugandan military, 3; UN approach to, 259; against women and girls, 3–4. *See also* conflict-related sexual and gender-based violence (CRSGBV); gender-based violence (GBV); marriage, forced; rape; sexual and gender-based violence (SGBV)
sharia law, 118
Shekau, Abubakar, 1
Shuayb, Maha, 267
Sierra Leone, 18, 21, 22, 24, 250, 251
(Silent) Voices from the Field workshop, 69
sisterhood, 283
situated knowledge, 68–69
Sivasundaram, Sujit, 161
1619 Project, 169
slavery, 155–72; Atlantic, 169; classificatory, 170; definitions of, 169–71; and enslaved labor, 157; extraverted, 170; history of, 155–57; knowledge production about, 162–66; metaphorical, 170; modern, 156, 162; in Northern Uganda, 39; sexual, 119, 120; in the United States, 169. *See also* enslavement
SLRC (Secure Livelihoods Research Consortium), 46, 66n4
Smith, Linda Tuhiwai, 93
social justice, 183, 210
social media hashtags, 273
Social Sciences and Humanities Research Council of Canada (SSHRC), 15, 120, 260
social therapy, 233, 237, 240
SOFEPADI, 249
South Africa, 157–66, 165, 275
South Sudan, 39, 233. *See also* Sudan

Special Court of Sierra Leone, 22
Sphere Project, 268n2
spying, 120
SSHRC (Social Sciences and Humanities Research Council of Canada), 15, 120, 260
state crime, 3
Stewart, Beth, 183
St. Mary's College, 3
storytelling, 72–73, 96, 100–104, 112
Strijdom, J. G., 167
Sudan, 218. *See also* South Sudan
Sud-Ubangi Red Cross, 71
suicide, 236
suicide bombings, 119, 120
Sultana, Farhana, 107
Supplementary Convention on the Abolition of Slavery, the Slave Trade, and Institutions and Practices Similar to Slavery, 166–67
survivor support groups, 179, 253
Swaminathan, Srividhya, 166, 169

taboos, 45, 55, 58, 64, 182, 236
Taylor, Charles, 24
Taylor, Whitney, 264
"teaching to goal," 127
tek-gungu, 181, 236
terrorism, 257–58; in Nigeria, 205–6; racial, 169; response to, 2, 9; and sexual violence, 257–58
They Slept with Me (documentary), 236–37
Third World Approaches to International Law (TWAIL), 24
13th (documentary), 169
Tigray (Ethiopia), 4
torture, 39, 84, 232
traditional leaders, 228, 255
Trafficking Victims Protection Reauthorization Act, 228
transactional sex, 41, 57, 207. *See also* prostitution
transitional justice, 43, 179, 181–82, 185, 191
translation and transcription, 73, 75, 85–86, 97, 141–42, 196n7; cultural translation, 11
transparency, 26, 53, 68, 69, 136, 151, 288
travel restrictions, 11, 15
tribunals, 262, 264
True, J., 261
Tuck, E., 7
Tufts University, 43
TWAIL (Third World Approaches to International Law), 24

311

Index

ubuntu, 282, 283
Uganda: Banyamulenge ethnic group in, 239, 241–42, 243, 245–46; children born of war in, 91; community-based justice workers in, 251; Congolese youth in, 106; Constitution of, 168; instability in, 42; male-directed sexual violence in, 181; military, 3, 42; missing and disappeared persons in, 41, 54, 63; Office of the Prime Minister (OPM), 240; postconflict, 179; Refugee Law Project, 24, 27; research in, 25–26, 27, 39–65, 90–112, 134–51, 179–95, 232–47; response to sexual violence against men in, 182; slavery in, 157, 168–69; survivors in, 54; violent abduction and marriage in, 21, 25; war against the LRA, 39, 42, 90, 136, 181, 233, 234, 235
Uganda Communication Commission, 240
Uganda National Council of Science and Technology (UNCST), 61–62, 139, 151n2, 240
Ugandan Bush War, 168
Uganda Police Force, 240
Umar, Umar Ahmad, 255
UN Development Programme, 218
United Nations, 166, 167, 253; approaches to weaponized rape, 259; on gender and war, 264. *See also* Women, Peace and Security (WPS)
United Nations High Commissioner for Refugees, 119, 240
United Nations Security Council, 215, 248; Resolution 1325, 257, 261, 262; Resolution 1888, 261; Resolution 2106, 261; Resolution 2122, 261; Resolution 2467, 23, 261, 262
universities, ethics approval processes, 27
University of Cape Town, 199
University of Lubumbashi, 76
University of Maiduguri, 120
USAID, 27, 46
USAID/Nigeria, 217, 219, 227–28, 229; policy on evaluation in northeast Nigeria, 222–27; RFP stipulations, 224–25, 228–29
Utas, Mats, 108

vaccinations, 289
Van Den Berg, Sayra, 18, 144
vernacularization, 70, 266, 269n11
"victimcy," 108
video advocacy, 233–47; clearance/access requirements, 240–41; and community ownership, 244–45; dissemination, 244–45; filming, 243–44; security issues, 244; trust building, 241–43; validation, 244
Video Advocacy Institute (Concordia University), 234
video documentation, 233–47
violence: collective, 134, 136, 137, 143; conflict-related, 252; factors enabling, 262; gendered, 249; intimate partner, 260; localized perceptions of, 264; political, 2; sexual, 1; structural, 41; wartime, 21; against women, 117, 257. *See also* gender-based violence (GBV); sexual violence
virtue and communitarian ethics, 201
Vogel, C., 288

Wainaina, Binyavanga, 94, 111
Walker, G., 251
war crimes, 39
Warom Child and Youth in Development, 113n8
Watchlist on Children and Armed Conflict, 215
What about Us? (documentary), 234–35
White, Hayden, 171
#Whiteness, 273
White privilege, 6, 25, 52, 201
white supremacy, 199
WHO. *See* World Health Organization
Wilson, E., 183, 184
Wilson Michael, G., 204
Wine, Bobi (Robert Ssentamu Kyagulanyi), 168–69
Witness (NGO), 234
Women, Peace and Security (WPS), 9, 23, 248–49, 257, 258, 259, 261, 262, 264
women and girls: abduction of, 1–2, 4, 118–19, 120, 205, 218, 255; affirmation of the role of, 257–58; in CHE settings, 229; in conflict and postconflict settings, 40, 42, 257–58; enslaved, 161–62; and family life, 247; formerly abducted, 255; humanitarian-assistance programs engaging, 219–20; marginalization of, 207; as mothers, 105–6; as mothers in captivity, 136–38, 140, 148, 150; as mothers of children born into the LRA, 92, 97, 121; nonliterate, 122; oppression of, 171; as peacebuilders, 257–58; sexual violence against, 3–4; as sex workers, 207; in South Africa, 166; in stories of war and conflict, 254; as survivors, 54–55; in Ugandan culture, 238, 241; as victims, 23, 63, 250, 258. *See also* marriage

Women in Chains (pamphlet), 167
Women's League (ANC), 167
Women's March on Pretoria, 167
Worden, Nigel, 164
workshop discussions, 190–93
World Health Organization (WHO), 117, 121, 125, 127, 128, 188; guidelines for ethics in research, 216, 220–21; Multi-Country Study on Women's Health and Domestic Violence against Women, 117–18
WPS. *See* Women, Peace and Security
Wright, Jonathan Jeffrey, 159–60

Yang, K. W., 7

Zarma, Rahina, 255
Zawadi, Mambo, 249